D0782477

# Economics of
# State and Local
# Government

# ECONOMICS OF STATE AND LOCAL GOVERNMENT

## HENRY J. RAIMONDO

PRAEGER

New York
Westport, Connecticut
London

**Library of Congress Cataloging-in-Publication Data**

Raimondo, Henry John.
    Economics of state and local government / Henry J. Raimondo.
      p.  cm.
    Includes bibliographical references and index.
    ISBN 0–275–93122–6 (alk. paper) —  ISBN 0–275–93937–5 (pbk : alk. paper)
    1. Local finance—United States.  2. Finance, Public—United
States—States.  I. Title.
HJ9145.R35    1992
336.73—dc20      91–7783

British Library Cataloguing in Publication Data is available.

Library of Congress Catalog Card Number: 91–7783
ISBN: 0–275–93122–6 (hb.)
      0–275–93937–5 (pbk.)

First published in 1992

Praeger Publishers, One Madison Avenue, New York, NY 10010
An imprint of Greenwood Publishing Group, Inc.

Printed in the United States of America

∞™

The paper used in this book complies with the
Permanent Paper Standard issued by the National
Information Standards Organization (Z39.48–1984).

10 9 8 7 6 5 4 3 2 1

*To*
*Florence, Henry, and Dolores*

# Contents

# Tables and Figures

**TABLES**

## FIGURES

# *Acknowledgments*

My understanding of state and local governments comes from many places. It began with my graduate studies at the University of Wisconsin in Madison and developed a practical edge when I joined the Bureau of Local Fiscal Information and Policy Analysis in the Wisconsin Department of Revenue. The trip from the university to the statehouse was a real education in state and local public finance. The Advisory Commission on Intergovernmental Relations (ACIR) in Washington, DC made the next contribution with its brand of applied public policy research and exposure to researchers and practitioners from across the nation.

At this point, it was my turn to pass on whatever I had learned from these experiences. My thanks to the undergraduate students at Douglass College and the University of Massachusetts/Boston and my graduate students at the Eagleton Institute of Politics at Rutgers University, New Jersey and at the McCormack Institute of Public Affairs at University of Massachusetts at Boston. I always tried to convey my interest and enthusiasm for this subject.

Of course, there are people to thank along the way: Gordon Folkman, Michael Harder, Robert Lampman, Alan Rosenthal, Mark Saltzman, Joseph J. Seneca, John Shannon, Carl Van Horn, and David Walker. I also appreciate the work of James Dunton, executive editor at Praeger, and the reviewers who offered constructive comments on an earlier version of this manuscript. My thanks to Stephen Hatem, production editor at Praeger, and Lisa MacLeman for copy editing the manuscript. Holly Lee of Lee Graphics in Brookline, Massachusetts prepared the diagrams throughout the text.

My wife, Beverly, and my son, Benjamin, encouraged me to complete this project. Given the costs, I am not sure why. I will always count on them.

# CHAPTER 1

## Introduction

### ROLE OF STATE AND LOCAL GOVERNMENTS

In the United States, the sheer number of state and local governments makes them difficult to ignore. While there is one national government, there are fifty state governments and tens of thousands of local governments. Local governments serve counties, municipalities, townships, school districts, and special districts. Almost every one of us—voters, lobbyists, the mass media, politicians, and economists—pay attention to the news out of the nation's capital. After all, parents tell their children to grow up to be president, not governor, county executive, or mayor. While most of the attention is focused on the federal government, state and local governments deserve some also.

The federal government is suffering from policy paralysis trying to reconcile a reluctance to increase taxes, deficits, and the tension between the Democrat Congress and the Republican presidency. State and local governments, in turn, are generally collecting taxes and providing education, protecting the environment, caring for AIDS patients, financing affordable housing, and putting police and firefighters on the street.

Voters have generally shown high regard for state and local governments in part because they have some control over their policy decisions. That control comes about because state and local governments are close to the people. (Of course, sometimes familiarity breeds contempt.) They are responsive to changing public concerns, flexible enough to adjust their priorities, and occasionally innovative in managing their programs. These features have earned state and local

**Table 1–1**

**Receipts, Outlays, Surplus/Deficit for State and Local Governments by Decade (in billions of 1982 dollars)**

| Years | Receipts | Outlays | Surplus/Deficit | Surplus/Deficit As a % of Receipts |
|-------|----------|---------|-----------------|------------------------------------|
| 1950-9 | $1,166.1 | $1,199.2 | - $ 33.1 | - 2.8% |
| 1960-9 | 2,245.4 | 2,238.1 | + 7.3 | + .3 |
| 1970-9 | 3,993.5 | 3,764.2 | + 229.3 | + 5.7 |
| 1980-6 | 3,452.1 | 3,136.3 | + 315.8 | + 9.1 |

*Source*: National Income and Product Accounts, *Survey of Current Business*, various years.

governments the title of "laboratories of democracy." Public policies introduced at the subnational level often find their way onto the national public policy agenda.

The economics of state and local governments has at least one feature in common with baseball. The subject abounds with statistics. For example, what is the size of the state-local public sector? In 1986, state and local governments spent $453.9 billion, an amount equivalent to 10.8 percent of the gross national product. By way of contrast, the federal spent $1,030.2 billion, an amount equivalent to 24.5 percent of the gross national product. As the primary public service provider, state and local governments employ many more workers than the federal government (state-local: 475.5 full-time equivalent employees per 10,000 population versus federal: 120.5 full-time equivalent civilian employees per 10,000 population). The statistics on size tell us that 11 cents of every dollar generated in the United States economy goes to state and local governments. That 11 cents is the outcome of a very complex set of fiscal arrangements. The next pair of questions deals with what state and local governments spend on and how they raise revenues.

## FISCAL PROFILE OF STATE AND LOCAL GOVERNMENTS

The economics of state and local governments revolves around expenditure and tax policies. A look at the National Income and Product Accounts (NIPA) summarized in Table 1–1 reveals the changing financial fortunes of state and local governments. All fiscal data are presented in constant 1982 dollars. State and local government receipts (tax, nontax, and intergovernmental revenues) are summed up over each decade. For example, from 1950 to 1959, state and local governments collected almost $1,166.1 billion (constant 1982 dollars), they spent $1,199.2 billion (constant 1982 dollars), and they ran a deficit of $33.1 billion (constant 1982 dollars) which is equal to 2.8 percent of their receipts. While state and local governments' receipts and outlays have grown over the years, receipts have grown faster. During the period 1980 to 1986, state and local

**Table 1–2**
**State and Local Governments' Expenditure by Selected Type and by Decade (in billions of 1982 dollars)**

| Years | Operations | Capital | Interest | Total | In 1982 Dollars |
|---|---|---|---|---|---|
| | -----------Percentage Spent on----------- | | | | |
| 1950–9 | | | | | |
| State | 59.7 | 38.0 | 2.4 | 100.0 | $ 356.6 |
| Local | 71.1 | 25.5 | 3.4 | 100.0 | $ 804.0 |
| 1960–9 | | | | | |
| State | 60.8 | 35.9 | 3.2 | 100.0 | $ 672.8 |
| Local | 74.7 | 21.2 | 4.1 | 100.0 | $1,377.6 |
| 1970–9 | | | | | |
| State | 74.2 | 21.4 | 4.3 | 100.0 | $1,330.1 |
| Local | 79.0 | 16.7 | 4.3 | 100.0 | $2,524.3 |
| 1980–6 | | | | | |
| State | 79.2 | 14.4 | 6.4 | 100.0 | $1,252.4 |
| Local | 80.3 | 14.2 | 5.5 | 100.0 | $2,204.8 |

*Source*: U.S. Bureau of Census, *Census of Governments*, various years.

governments have run up a surplus of $315.8 billion (constant 1982 dollars) which is equal to 9.1 percent of receipts. In general, the state and local government sector is faring well and far better than its deficit-ridden federal government partner. This conclusion does not mean that all state and local governments are doing well. That will become clear as you read on (if you have not already experienced the effects of regional economic disparities).

If state and local governments are doing relatively well financially, it would be heartwarming to know if they are servicing the public well. The fiscal profile cannot tell us that, but it can generally say what state and local governments have been and are doing with their financial resources. Table 1–2 divides state and local government outlays into spending on current operations (i.e., the costs of everyday public services), capital investment (e.g. roads, bridges, sewer systems, public school buildings, recreational facilities, and the like), and interest on their debt. Again, the figures are presented in constant 1982 dollars and summed up over each decade.

During the 1950–59 decade, state government spent almost 60 cents of each dollar on current operations, 38 cents on public capital investment (i.e., public infrastructure), and a little over 2 cents on interest on debt. The comparable numbers for local governments are 71 cents of each dollar on operations, 25 cents on capital investment, and a little over 3 cents on interest on debt. Over the years, what trends are noteworthy?

Current operations are claiming an ever-increasing share of state and local governments' resources. During this period, current operations at the state level

**Table 1–3**

**State Government Tax Revenues by Selected Taxes and by Decade (in billions of 1982 dollars)**

| Years | ---------Percentage Raised from Taxes on---------- | | | | | Percentage & Total In 1982 Dollars |
|---|---|---|---|---|---|---|
| | Personal Income | Corporate Income | General Sales | Selective Sales | Other | |
| 1950–9 | 9.9 | 7.0 | 22.8 | 35.8 | 24.4 | 100.0% $   52,131.6 |
| 1960–9 | 14.8 | 7.0 | 26.5 | 31.4 | 20.4 | 100.0% 777,928.0 |
| 1970–9 | 23.3 | 8.3 | 30.4 | 23.4 | 14.5 | 100.0% 1,376,572.9 |
| 1980–6 | 28.7 | 8.5 | 31.7 | 17.2 | 13.9 | 100.0% 1,223,136.3 |

*Source*: U.S. Bureau of Census, *Census of Governments*, various years.

have grown from 60 cents out of each dollar to almost 80 cents—mostly on education, public welfare, highways, and health and hospitals; at the local level the increase has been from 71 cents to 80 cents—mostly on education, health care, police and fire protection, and sanitation.

Spending on public capital is down, if not out. Over the years, expenditures on capital at the state level have fallen from 38 cents out of each dollar to 14 cents; at the local level the decrease has been from 26 cents to 14 cents. The share of state and local government resources allocated to debt service has grown. Interest payments at the state level have gone from 2 cents out of each dollar to 6 cents; at the local level the increase has been from 3 cents to 5 cents. While the state and local government sector is faring well overall, current operations have grown substantially, investment has declined, and debt service has modestly picked up.

Taxes are the principal source of revenues to finance state and local government programs. Table 1–3 illustrates tax changes for state governments. In the 1950s, personal income taxes contributed 10 cents of every dollar collected through taxes. In the 1980s, that amount had grown to almost 29 cents. The parallel comparison for corporate income taxes shows a modest increase from 7 cents of every dollar collected to 8.5 cents. State governments are reluctant to tax business income. They fear the taxman will frighten the businessman away. Sales taxes are the linchpin of the state tax system. Combined general and selective sales taxes account for almost 59 cents of every dollar collected in the 1950s and 49 cents in the 1980s. That overall figure conceals a shift away from selective sales taxes toward general sales taxes.

Table 1–4 displays the trends in taxation for local governments. In the 1950s, property taxes contributed 87 cents of every dollar collected through taxes. In the 1980s, that amount had dropped to 75 cents. That decline is the product of

**Table 1–4**
**Local Government Tax Revenues by Selected Taxes and by Decade (in billions of 1982 dollars)**

| Years | -----Percentage Raised from Taxes on----- | | | | Percentage & Total In 1982 Dollars |
| | Property | Sales | Personal Income | Other | |
| --- | --- | --- | --- | --- | --- |
| 1950–9 | 87.2 | 6.7 | 1.1 | 4.9 | 100.0%<br>$ 432,061.7 |
| 1960–9 | 86.9 | 7.2 | 2.2 | 3.7 | 100.0%<br>730,476.4 |
| 1970–9 | 81.8 | 10.1 | 4.6 | 3.5 | 100.0%<br>1,044,508.0 |
| 1980–6 | 75.3 | 14.7 | 5.8 | 4.2 | 100.0%<br>776,750.5 |

*Source*: U.S. Bureau of Census, *Census of Governments*, various years.

the tax revolt of the 1970s and surge in state government aid to local governments. Sales taxes show an increase from almost 7 cents of every dollar collected to almost 15 cents. Income taxes, both personal and business, also have grown from 1 cent of every dollar collected in the 1950s and 6 cents in the 1980s. These are signs of local revenue diversification.

The profile is complete. The behavior of state to local governments that these tables hint at is the substance of the economics of state and local governments.

## ORGANIZATION OF THE BOOK

The relationship between regional economic performance and state-local government finance begins the discussion of the economics of state and local governments. The regional economy dictates the flow of tax revenues to state and local governments, as well as the potential demand for public services. Chapter 2 offers a theory of regional economic performance and a description of the economic geography of the United States.

The organization of the public sector is next. Chapter 3 develops the political dimension of the federal system: how did it come about; what contemporary political theories explain how it works; and what are the trends as federalism heads into the twenty-first century. Chapter 4 sets out the economic dimension of federalism. The economic dimension proceeds from the market failure associated with public goods and externalities. Market failure helps define the three broad functions of the public sector. These three functions must be assigned to national or subnational governments. In some cases, a function may be shared.

Chapter 5 continues this discussion with a set of guidelines for delegating services to different levels of government. Once it is determined who should do what, state and local government spending decisions can be examined. That examination raises several questions. Should differences in spending levels among the states be a matter for national concern or the anticipated outcome of a federal system? What factors affect state-local spending levels? What role does the political system play in this process? Although final answers to these questions are not always apparent, economic principles establish an approach to developing answers.

Spending on elementary and secondary education is looked at more closely. Education brings together the performance of the regional economy, market failure, local autonomy in a federal system, and the law. Chapter 6 describes several methods to finance elementary and secondary education that adjust for regional economic differences, correct for market failure, balance local autonomy against national interests, and satisfy the law. This last aspect is significant since a wave of court challenges to state-local educational finance systems has recently surfaced in the United States.

Chapter 7 moves the analysis to the other side of the fiscal ledger; namely taxation in a federal system. While all state-local government taxes should conform to basic economic principles, additional aspects of taxation in a federal system are explained; for example, taxes and regional economic performance, federal deductibility of state-local taxes, and the criteria to judge a good tax.

Chapters 8 through 10 examine three major state-local taxes: property taxes, sales taxes, and personal income taxes. Each chapter follows the same progression: assess the economic justification of the tax, explain how the tax works, identify base and rate issues, determine who pays the tax, and apply the criteria for a good tax. The property tax presents unusual issues regarding assessment and administration, state-imposed fiscal limit laws, and who pays it. The sales tax highlights the effect that mobility of people has on tax policy, the border problem. A dramatic example is cigarette smuggling across state lines. Beyond the border problem, the equity of the sales tax is important. Personal income taxes are next. Inflation, work disincentives, and federal deductibility head the list of topics concerning this form of taxation.

Chapter 11 introduces two increasingly popular forms of nontax revenue: user charges and gambling revenues. User charges which can efficiently allocate public goods/services under the right circumstances allow state and local government officials to separate out specific goods/services from the public budget process. These goods/services can then be administered through special service districts. Gambling revenues, especially lottery revenues, fill the role of a ''painless'' tax. Although they have been a modest source of revenues, their appeal is growing.

Chapter 12 takes a different angle on fiscal policy. It pulls together evidence on the distribution of taxes, expenditures, and net benefits associated with state and local government fiscal policy. This material answers the question of who actually benefits from state and local governments.

The final chapter deals with the grants-in-aid system. A grants-in-aid system takes into account the regional economy, and the spending needs and the tax capacity of a jurisdiction. Intergovernmental transfers have had a rich history over the past thirty years. After we establish where the grants-in-aid system has been, Chapter 13 looks at what effect different types of grants have on the spending decisions of grant-receiving governments.

# CHAPTER 2

---

# The Regional Economies of the United States

## PREVIEW

The regional economies of the United States provide an important backdrop for a system of government that stresses decentralized public decision making. These decentralized governments rely upon the level of regional economic activity to meet their public service obligations. Trends in population, employment, income, and construction describe regional economic activity. The performance of regional economies differs. Various models explain why regional economic performance varies from coast to coast. A look at what regional economic differences mean for the operation of state and local governments concludes this chapter.

## INTRODUCTION

Just as the performance of the national economy often points the way for federal government taxing and spending policies, the performance of the regional economy normally defines the fiscal limits that confront state and local governments. The condition of the regional, state, or local private economy determines revenue-raising capacity and indicates spending priorities. In turn, these fiscal policies may affect the operation of the regional, state, or local private economy.

For example, prolonged unemployment in a region means a higher demand for public services as people turn to the government for assistance. At the same time, tax collections fall because of the chronic unemployment. On the other side, a booming regional economy places a strain on so-called public infrastructure (e.g., highways, mass transit, water and sewer systems). If this strain is not addressed, the regional economy will eventually stagnate. So any discussion of the economics of state and local governments starts with a description of regional economic activity across the United States.

## PEOPLE, JOBS, INCOME, AND CONSTRUCTION TRENDS

A review of the literature on the regional economies of the United States show that this topic has been cast in such terms as the Megastates (Peirce, 1972), the Frostbelt vs. the Sunbelt (Sale, 1975; Havemann and Stanfield, 1977), the nine nations of North America (Garreau, 1981), and the bicoastal economy ("Living on a Coast Pays Off," 1988). Each of these titles pinpoints the ebb and flow of economic activity in the United States over some period of time. By its very nature, any description of the dynamic regional economies of the United States cannot be accurate for long. Yet the description which follows identifies the results of long-term trends at work in the United States for the period 1982–87. (For descriptions of regional economic change prior to this period see: Sternlieb and Hughes, 1977a; ACIR, 1980a; Weinstein, Gross, and Rees, 1985.)

These trends deal with the spatial location and the growth in the number of people and jobs, and the amount of personal income and construction spending. They measure the economic well-being of regional economies. What are the trends in regional economies across the United States? A map and a series of tables can capture these trends. Figure 2–1 is the standard U.S. Bureau of Census map of the United States. It divides the country into regions and then further divides the regions into divisions. The census regions and divisions are: Northeast (Middle Atlantic and New England); North Central (East North Central and West North Central); South (South Atlantic, East South Central, and West South Central); and West (Mountain and Pacific). Figure 2–1 also shows the specific states in each region. How well are these regional economies performing? The analysis begins, as it should, with people.

### People

Table 2–1 locates the population of the regions and divisions in 1982 and 1987. It also calculates the percentage growth in population over this period and then distributes the share of the growth across the map. Where were the 243 million Americans in 1987? By sheer population size, they lived in the following divisions with the largest states in parentheses: East North Central (Illinois and Ohio), South Atlantic (Florida), Middle Atlantic (New York and Pennsylvania), Pacific (California), and West South Central (Texas).

The nationwide population growth rate was 5.2 percent during this period. What were the population changes across these regions from 1982 to 1987? The highest growth rate was in the West (9.9 percent) followed by the South (7.7 percent), the Northeast (2.0 percent), and the North Central (1.0 percent). On

**Figure 2–1**
**Census Regions and Geographic Divisions of the United States**

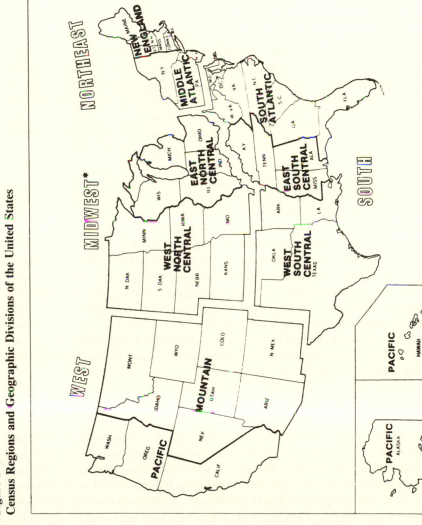

U.S. DEPARTMENT OF COMMERCE
Bureau of the Census

* The Midwest Region was designated as the North Central Region until June 1984

**Table 2–1**
**Level and Change in Population by Region, 1982–87 (population in thousands)**

| Region & Division | Population 1982 | Population 1987 | Change Number | Change Percent | Share of-the Change |
|---|---|---|---|---|---|
| UNITED STATES | 231372 | 243400 | 12028 | 5.20% | 100.00% |
| NORTHEAST | 49309 | 50277 | 968 | 1.96 | 8.05 |
| Middle Atlantic | 36878 | 37433 | 555 | 1.50 | 4.61 |
| New England | 12431 | 12844 | 413 | 3.32 | 3.43 |
| NORTH CENTRAL | 58958 | 59538 | 580 | 0.98 | 4.82 |
| East North Central | 41607 | 41904 | 297 | 0.71 | 2.47 |
| West North Central | 17351 | 17634 | 283 | 1.63 | 2.35 |
| SOUTH | 77861 | 83884 | 6023 | 7.74 | 50.07 |
| South Atlantic | 37689 | 41684 | 3995 | 10.60 | 33.21 |
| East South Central | 14872 | 15290 | 418 | 2.81 | 3.48 |
| West South Central | 25300 | 26910 | 1610 | 6.36 | 13.39 |
| WEST | 45244 | 49700 | 4456 | 9.85 | 37.05 |
| Mountain | 12069 | 13167 | 1098 | 9.10 | 9.13 |
| Pacific | 33175 | 36533 | 3358 | 10.12 | 27.92 |

*Source*: Calculated from U.S. Bureau of Census data.

the high growth side, the individual states that deserve mention are: Arizona (17.4 percent), Florida (14.8 percent), Nevada (14.8 percent), California (11.6 percent), Georgia (8.0 percent), and New Mexico (9.6 percent). On the low growth side, many states in the Northeast and North Central regions experienced a slight population increase while Wyoming (−3.9 percent), West Virginia (−3.3 percent), and Iowa (−2.5 percent) actually experienced a population decline.

Of the almost 12 million additional people in the United States over this period, the South accounted for 50 percent (led by the South Atlantic division, especially Texas and Florida) and the West accounted for 37 percent (led by the Pacific division, especially California). As the Census data have indicated for many years, the U.S. population is fanning out from the Northeast and North Central regions to the South and West regions.

The Bureau of Economic Analysis (BEA) has published population projections that cover the period 1988 to 2000 (Johnson, Kort, and Friedenberg, 1990). The allure of the west apparently continues to the end of the twentieth century. The average annual population growth rate from 1988 to 2000 by region is: Northeast .47 percent (New England .68 percent with New Hampshire at 1.12 percent and Middle Atlantic .40 percent), South .72 percent (South Atlantic .99 percent with Florida at 1.40 percent, East South Central .44 percent, and West South Central .44 percent), North Central .45 percent (both East North Central and West North Central .44 percent), and West 1.23 percent (Mountain 1.20 percent with Nevada at 2.20 percent and Pacific 1.24 percent with California at 1.33 percent). The population wrap-up is surely summed up with a booming, "Westward ho!"

**Table 2–2**
**Level and Change in Employment by Region, 1982–87 (employment in thousands)**

| Region & Division | --Employment-- 1982 | 1987 | -----Change ---- Number | Percent | -Share of- the Change |
|---|---|---|---|---|---|
| UNITED STATES | 99277 | 112440 | 13163 | 13.26% | 100.00% |
| | | | | | |
| NORTHEAST | 21398 | 23805 | 2407 | 11.25 | 18.29 |
| Middle Atlantic | 15521 | 17204 | 1683 | 10.84 | 12.79 |
| New England | 5877 | 6601 | 724 | 5.50 | 5.50 |
| | | | | | |
| NORTH CENTRAL | 25371 | 27840 | 2469 | 9.73 | 18.76 |
| East North Central | 17523 | 19279 | 1756 | 10.02 | 13.34 |
| West North Central | 7848 | 8561 | 713 | 9.09 | 5.42 |
| | | | | | |
| SOUTH | 32754 | 37819 | 5065 | 15.46 | 38.48 |
| South Atlantic | 16156 | 19578 | 3422 | 21.18 | 26.00 |
| East South Central | 5783 | 6500 | 717 | 12.40 | 5.45 |
| West South Central | 10815 | 11741 | 926 | 8.56 | 7.03 |
| | | | | | |
| WEST | 19754 | 23018 | 3264 | 16.52 | 24.80 |
| Mountain | 5229 | 5960 | 731 | 13.98 | 5.55 |
| Pacific | 14525 | 17058 | 2533 | 17.44 | 19.24 |

*Source*: Calculated from U.S. Bureau of Labor Statistics data.

## Jobs

Table 2–2 captures the employment story from 1982 to 1987. There were 112 million people employed in 1987. The level of employment is highest in the South (South Atlantic division, especially Florida and Texas); followed by the North Central region (East North Central division); the Northeast region (Middle Atlantic division, especially New York); and the West region (Pacific division, especially California).

Nationwide employment growth was 13.3 percent from 1982 to 1987. Employment growth during this period shows a different regional ranking. The West region (led by California and Washington) had employment growth of 16.5 percent; the South region (led by Alabama, Florida, Maryland, North Carolina, and Virginia) grew by 15.5 percent; the Northeast (led by Middle Atlantic division) tallied 11.3 percent; and the North Central region grew by 9.7 percent. Of the 13 million newly employed people, the South and the West regions accounted for almost 63 percent of the added employment. In this regard, Florida with 29.0 percent and California with 18.7 percent are particularly high employment growth states.

The BEA study mentioned earlier also projects employment trends from 1988 to 2000. The average annual growth in employment looks similar to the population growth rates; namely, the Northeast .84 percent (New England at .88 percent led by New Hampshire's 1.21 percent and Middle Atlantic at .82 percent led by New Jersey's 1.07 percent), South 1.12 percent (South Atlantic at 1.29 percent led by Florida's 1.71 percent, East South Central at .95 percent led by Tennessee's 1.04 percent, and West South Central at .93 percent led by Texas's

Table 2–3
**Level and Change in Manufacturing Employment by Region, 1982–87
(employment in thousands)**

| Region & Division | Manufacturing Employment 1982 | Manufacturing Employment 1987 | Change Number | Change Percent | Share of the Change |
|---|---|---|---|---|---|
| UNITED STATES | 18798 | 19065 | 267 | 1.42% | 100.00% |
| NORTHEAST | 4695 | 4309 | -386 | - 8.22 | -144.56 |
| Middle Atlantic | 3257 | 2940 | -317 | - 9.73 | -118.73 |
| New England | 1438 | 1369 | - 69 | - 4.80 | - 25.84 |
| NORTH CENTRAL | 5331 | 5451 | 120 | 2.25 | 44.94 |
| East North Central | 4077 | 4135 | 58 | 1.42 | 21.72 |
| West North Central | 1254 | 1316 | 62 | 4.94 | 23.22 |
| SOUTH | 5783 | 5953 | 170 | 2.94 | 63.67 |
| South Atlantic | 2881 | 3136 | 255 | 8.85 | 95.51 |
| East South Central | 1256 | 1351 | 95 | 7.56 | 35.58 |
| West South Central | 1646 | 1466 | -180 | -10.94 | - 67.42 |
| WEST | 2989 | 3270 | 281 | 9.40 | 105.24 |
| Mountain | 551 | 608 | 57 | 10.34 | 21.35 |
| Pacific | 2438 | 2662 | 224 | 9.19 | 83.90 |

*Source*: Calculated from U.S. Bureau of Labor Statistics data.

1.04 percent), North Central 1.04 percent (East North Central at 1.10 percent led by Illinois's and Indiana's 1.00 percent, West North Central at .93 percent led by Minnesota's 1.09 percent), and West 1.54 percent (Mountain at 1.53 percent led by Nevada's 2.31 percent and Pacific at 1.54 percent led by California's 1.63 percent). Whether jobs draw people or people draw jobs, people and work are heading South and West.

The employment story is not finished until manufacturing employment is described. The figures in Table 2–3 reveal that manufacturing employment accounts for 19 million jobs. In 1987, regional manufacturing employment placed the South region first (led by the South Atlantic division, especially North Carolina and Texas); the North Central region (led by the East North Central division, especially Illinois, Michigan, and Ohio); the Northeast region (led by the Middle Atlantic division, especially New York and Pennsylvania); and the West region (led once again by the Pacific division, especially California).

There are two stories in the manufacturing employment growth figures. The first is the decline in manufacturing employment in the Northeast region, 386,000 manufacturing jobs were lost in this four-year period. Especially hard hit were Connecticut, Massachusetts, New Jersey, New York, and Pennsylvania. This follows the decade of the 1970s when these same states experienced an economic collapse in the manufacturing sector (Sternlieb and Hughes, 1977b). The BEA projections indicate that the Northeast will continue to lose manufacturing employment at an average annual rate of .33 percent from 1988 to 2000.

The most often-voiced concern is that a prolonged loss of manufacturing employment will undermine all sectors of the regional economy. This economic

Table 2–4
**Level and Change in Real Personal Income by Region, 1982–87 (in 1982 dollars; total in billions)**

| Region & Division | Real Personal Income 1982 | Real Personal Income 1987 | Change Number | Change Percent | Share of the Change |
|---|---|---|---|---|---|
| UNITED STATES | 2561.5 | 3153.2 | 591.7 | 23.10% | 100.00% |
| NORTHEAST | 593.8 | 750.9 | 157.1 | 26.46 | 26.55 |
| Middle Atlantic | 444.9 | 551.2 | 106.3 | 23.89 | 17.97 |
| New England | 148.9 | 199.7 | 50.8 | 34.12 | 8.59 |
| NORTH CENTRAL | 646.6 | 751.7 | 105.1 | 16.25 | 17.76 |
| East North Central | 459.6 | 533.4 | 73.8 | 16.06 | 12.47 |
| West North Central | 187.0 | 218.3 | 31.3 | 16.74 | 5.29 |
| SOUTH | 789.1 | 972.9 | 183.8 | 23.29 | 31.06 |
| South Atlantic | 386.4 | 524.6 | 138.2 | 35.77 | 23.36 |
| East South Central | 128.1 | 153.3 | 25.2 | 19.67 | 4.26 |
| West South Central | 274.6 | 295.0 | 20.4 | 7.43 | 3.45 |
| WEST | 532.0 | 677.7 | 145.7 | 27.39 | 24.62 |
| Mountain | 126.1 | 151.7 | 25.6 | 20.30 | 4.33 |
| Pacific | 405.9 | 526.0 | 120.1 | 29.59 | 20.30 |

*Source*: Calculated from U.S. Bureau of Census data.

relationship is called *direct linkage* (Cohen and Zysman, 1987). The assertion is that high paid service jobs will not replace manufacturing jobs. Rather, service jobs complement manufacturing jobs. If manufacturing declines, service jobs will dwindle. The question is whether manufacturing job losses in the Northeast will limit regional economic growth in the years to come. Stay tuned.

The second story is the growth in manufacturing employment fueled by a rise in exports in the North Central region, the South region, and most noteworthy, in the West region. The North Central region with states like Iowa, Kansas, Minnesota, Nebraska, North Dakota, South Dakota, and Wisconsin has added manufacturing jobs because of the rise in exports (Robbins, 1988). The South Atlantic division increased manufacturing employment by 255,000 and the West, especially the Pacific division increased manufacturing employment by 281,000. From 1988 to 2000, BEA projections show an average annual growth rate in manufacturing employment by region as follows: North Central .19 percent, South .45 percent, and West .71 percent. The conclusion is that manufacturing employment is virtually at a standstill in the United States, but some regions mentioned above, are going against the tide and adding manufacturing employment.

## Income

People at work translates into personal income for private and public uses. Table 2–4 follows the income trail. During the period 1982 to 1987, the level of real total personal income amounted to $3.2 trillion (in 1982 dollars) and was highest in the South region (led by South Atlantic division, especially Florida and Texas); North Central (led by East North Central division, especially Illinois and Ohio); Northeast (led by Middle Atlantic region); and the West (led by Pacific division, especially California).

Real income growth was 23.1 percent nationwide during this period. The South Atlantic division (35.8 percent) with Florida, Georgia, Maryland, and Virginia; New England division (with 34.1 percent) with Connecticut, Massachusetts, and New Hampshire; Pacific division (29.6 percent) with California; and Middle Atlantic division (23.9) with New Jersey and New York surpassed the nationwide growth figure.

Of the $591.7 billion dollars in real income added to the national total, the South and the West regions accounted for 55 percent of the gains. California, Florida, Massachusetts, and New York claimed significantly large shares of the new income growth. These real income figures also show the vulnerability of regional economies. Falling energy prices, among other factors, caused income declines in the West South Central division, especially in Louisiana and Oklahoma, while the drought of 1988 slowed income growth in the West North Central division.

Projections on personal income growth are the result of growth trends in population, employment, and hourly earnings. The BEA study finds that average annual growth in real personal income (expressed in 1982 dollars) from 1988 to 2000 will be greatest in the West 2.38 percent (Mountain at 2.52 percent and Pacific at 2.33 percent), South 2.07 percent (South Atlantic at 2.24 percent, East South Central at 1.87 percent, and West South Central at 1.87 percent), North Central 1.71 percent (East North Central 1.66 percent and West North Central at 1.85 percent), and Northeast 1.59 percent (New England at 1.63 percent and Middle Atlantic at 1.57 percent).

## Construction

Investment in new construction also provides a measure of the performance of a regional economy. The construction trends can be broken down into residential and nonresidential investment. Table 2–5 looks at the real 1982 dollar value of new structures and additions to existing structures for 1982 and 1987. In 1987 the nationwide value of new residential construction was $103.0 billion. The level of new residential construction was greatest in the South region (led by the South Atlantic division, especially Florida, Georgia, and Virginia); followed by the West region (led by the Pacific division, especially California); the Northeast region (led by the Middle Atlantic division, especially New York and New Jersey); and the North Central region (led by the East North Central division, especially Illinois).

The nationwide growth rate of the value of residential construction was 77.6 percent from 1982 to 1987. The growth rate shows the following regional ranking order: the Northeast region (led by New England division, especially Rhode Island, New Hampshire, and Massachusetts); the North Central region (led by

**Table 2-5**

**Level and Change in Residential Construction by Region, 1982-87 (in 1982 dollars; total in millions)**

| Region & Division | Value of Residential Construction 1982 | 1987 | Change Number | Percent | Share of the Change |
|---|---|---|---|---|---|
| UNITED STATES | 57999 | 102944 | 44995 | 77.58% | 100.00% |
| NORTHEAST | 7229 | 19227 | 11998 | 165.97 | 26.67 |
| Middle Atlantic | 4844 | 11923 | 7079 | 146.15 | 15.73 |
| New England | 2385 | 7304 | 4919 | 206.24 | 10.93 |
| NORTH CENTRAL | 8820 | 19126 | 10306 | 116.84 | 22.90 |
| East North Central | 5157 | 13330 | 8173 | 158.49 | 18.17 |
| West North Central | 3663 | 5795 | 2132 | 58.21 | 4.74 |
| SOUTH | 28330 | 37565 | 9235 | 32.60 | 20.52 |
| South Atlantic | 13179 | 25986 | 12807 | 97.18 | 28.46 |
| East South Central | 3371 | 4925 | 1554 | 46.10 | 3.45 |
| West South Central | 11780 | 6653 | - 5127 | - 43.52 | -11.39 |
| WEST | 13620 | 27077 | 13457 | 98.80 | 29.91 |
| Mountain | 5268 | 6356 | 1088 | 20.66 | 2.42 |
| Pacific | 8352 | 20720 | 12368 | 148.09 | 27.49 |

*Source*: Calculated from U.S. Bureau of Census data.

the East North Central division, especially Michigan); the West region (led by the Pacific division, especially California); and the South region (led by the South Atlantic, especially Virginia and Maryland). The West South division actually experienced a decline in the value of residential construction in Arkansas, Louisiana, Oklahoma, and Texas.

Of the additional $45.0 billion in 1982 real dollars invested in residential construction from 1982 to 1987, the West and the Northeast regions accounted for approximately 56 percent. The West region (led by the Pacific division, especially California) added $13.5 billion in real 1982 dollars; the Northeast region (led by the Middle Atlantic region, especially New York) added $12.0 billion; the North Central region (led by the East North Central division, especially Illinois) added $10.3 billion; and the South region (led by the South Atlantic division, especially Florida) added $9.2 billion.

The details on the real value of nonresidential construction mirrors those on residential construction. Table 2-6 sets out the story with the real 1982 dollar value of new structures and additions to existing structures for 1982 and 1987. In 1987 the nationwide value of new nonresidential construction was $88.5 billion. The level of nonresidential construction was greatest in the South region (led by the South Atlantic division, especially Virginia, Florida, and Georgia); followed by the West region (led by the Pacific division, especially California); the North Central region (led by the East North Central division, especially Michigan); and the Northeast region (led by the Middle Atlantic division, especially New Jersey and New York).

The nationwide growth rate of the value of residential construction was 56.1 percent from 1982 to 1987. The growth rate shows the following regional ranking

Table 2–6
**Level and Change in Nonresidential Construction by Region, 1982–87 (in 1982 dollars; total in millions)**

| Region & Division | ---Value of--- Non-Residential Construction 1982 | 1987 | Change Number | Percent | –Share of- the Change |
|---|---|---|---|---|---|
| UNITED STATES | 56718 | 88530 | 31812 | 56.09% | 100.00% |
| NORTHEAST | 8586 | 18453 | 9867 | 114.92 | 31.02 |
| Middle Atlantic | 6059 | 13297 | 7238 | 119.46 | 22.75 |
| New England | 2527 | 5156 | 2629 | 104.05 | 8.27 |
| NORTH CENTRAL | 10684 | 19467 | 8783 | 82.21 | 27.61 |
| East North Central | 7213 | 14489 | 7276 | 100.87 | 22.87 |
| West North Central | 3471 | 4978 | -1507 | 43.42 | 4.74 |
| SOUTH | 23177 | 30172 | 6995 | 30.18 | 21.99 |
| South Atlantic | 9631 | 18124 | 8493 | 88.18 | 26.70 |
| East South Central | 2473 | 4843 | 2370 | 95.82 | 7.45 |
| West South Central | 11073 | 7206 | -3867 | -34.92 | -12.16 |
| WEST | 14271 | 20438 | 6167 | 43.21 | 19.38 |
| Mountain | 4332 | 4958 | 626 | 14.44 | 1.97 |
| Pacific | 9939 | 15480 | 5541 | 55.75 | 17.42 |

*Source*: Calculated from U.S. Bureau of Census data.

order: the Northeast region (led by Middle Atlantic division, especially New York); the North Central region (led by the East North Central division, especially Michigan); the West region (led by the Pacific division, especially California); and the South region (led by the South Atlantic, especially Georgia and Virginia). The West South Central division actually experienced a decline in the value of nonresidential construction in Louisiana, Oklahoma, and Texas.

Of the additional $31.8 billion in 1982 real dollars invested in nonresidential construction from 1982 to 1987, the Northeast and the North Central regions accounted for more than half. The Northeast region (led by the Middle Atlantic division, especially New Jersey and New York) added $9.9 billion; and the North Central region (led by the East North Central division, especially Michigan) added $8.8 billion; the South region (led by the South Atlantic region, especially Virginia, Florida, and Georgia) added $7.0 billion; and the West region (led by the Pacific division, especially California) added $6.2 billion in real 1982 dollars.

Pulling together the data on population, employment, manufacturing employment, income, and construction investment, the notion of Gross State Product (GSP) reveals regional economic trends. Table 2–7 displays real per capita GSP for 1986 and real growth rate in per capita GSP during the period 1982 to 1986. The Pacific division (per capita GSP: $16,963), the New England division ($16,917), and the Middle Atlantic division ($16,482) boast the highest per capita GSP. These divisions along with the South Atlantic division also lead in real GSP growth rate. The more vulnerable economic divisions are: East South Central ($12,234) with three of the poorest states (Kentucky, Alabama, and Mississippi), and the South Atlantic ($13,983) with two of the poorest states

**Table 2–7**
**Gross State Product: Per Capita (1986), Rank (1986), and Growth Rate (1982–86)**
**(1982 dollars)**

| Region & State | Per Capita | Rank | Growth Rate | Region & State | Per Capita | Rank | Growth Rate |
|---|---|---|---|---|---|---|---|
| USA | $15239 | | 13.9% | | | | |
| N.E. | 16917 | | 27.8 | E.S.C. | $12234 | | 13.6% |
| ME | 12945 | 41 | 21.9 | KY | 12488 | 43 | 9.1 |
| NH | 15803 | 14 | 29.1 | TN | 13198 | 39 | 18.5 |
| VT | 13990 | 28 | 23.9 | AL | 11898 | 45 | 16.4 |
| MA | 17361 | 7 | 29.2 | MS | 10627 | 50 | 6.8 |
| RI | 13668 | 32 | 23.0 | | | | |
| CT | 19414 | 3 | 28.5 | W.S.C. | 14987 | | - 5.8 |
| M.A. | 16482 | | 20.7 | AR | 11688 | 46 | 15.0 |
| | | | | LA | 14492 | 23 | -16.1 |
| NY | 17888 | 4 | 22.9 | OK | 13210 | 38 | -12.3 |
| NJ | 17803 | 5 | 23.9 | TX | 15943 | 11 | - 3.7 |
| PA | 13533 | 33 | 13.8 | | | | |
| | | | | Mt. | 14570 | | 6.5 |
| E.N.C. | 14717 | | 16.4 | | | | |
| | | | | MT | 13016 | 40 | - 4.8 |
| OH | 14355 | 25 | 15.3 | ID | 11519 | 48 | 8.0 |
| IN | 13522 | 34 | 15.8 | WY | 20179 | 2 | -21.2 |
| IL | 15907 | 12 | 14.3 | CO | 15875 | 13 | 7.8 |
| MI | 14686 | 21 | 23.3 | NM | 13987 | 29 | - 4.4 |
| WI | 14089 | 26 | 12.3 | AZ | 14062 | 27 | 21.3 |
| | | | | UT | 12637 | 42 | 10.1 |
| W.N.C. | 14587 | | 11.3 | NV | 17680 | 6 | 12.5 |
| MN | 15729 | 16 | 16.3 | Pac. | 16963 | | 13.8 |
| IA | 13476 | 35 | 4.1 | | | | |
| MO | 14451 | 24 | 16.7 | WA | 15258 | 17 | 15.1 |
| ND | 13854 | 31 | - 9.6 | OR | 13409 | 36 | 14.9 |
| SD | 12134 | 44 | 7.6 | CA | 17340 | 8 | 15.4 |
| NE | 14545 | 22 | 8.9 | AK | 32127 | 1 | -27.1 |
| KS | 15131 | 18 | 9.6 | HI | 15944 | 10 | 11.6 |
| S.A. | 13983 | | 20.1 | | | | |
| DE | 16208 | 9 | 15.3 | | | | |
| MD | 15024 | 19 | 22.1 | | | | |
| VA | 15774 | 15 | 23.1 | | | | |
| WV | 11011 | 49 | 1.1 | | | | |
| NC | 13972 | 30 | 21.7 | | | | |
| SC | 11608 | 47 | 17.0 | | | | |

*Source*: Calculated from data in Johnson, Kort, and Friedenberg, 1990.

(South Carolina and West Virginia) followed by Mountain, West North Central, East North Central, and West South Central.

While there will be exceptions, even major exceptions, to any characterization of the performance of the regional economies of the United States, the lasting impressions from the data in Tables 2–1 through 2–6 are that people, jobs, personal income, and construction are moving south and west (manufacturing jobs are moving out of the United States); leaving the United States during the 1982 to 1986 period with a dynamic bicoastal—Northeast and West regions— economy. The South and North Central regions are currently in a slump although individual states like Florida, Georgia, Illinois, Maryland, Michigan, and Virginia are faring quite well. As the U.S. economy sluggishly moves into the 1990s, even this description of regional economic performance is changing. The Northeast region, especially the New England region, is slumping, while the South Atlantic and West regions are booming (Butterfield, 1990; Levine, 1990). There is another way to summarize the performance of the regional economies of the United States—playing the ratings game.

## RANKING THE STATES: THE RATINGS GAME

There are many ways to rate state economic performance. The debate goes on about which approach produces the most accurate measures to be used by business people, public managers, and researchers (Carlson, 1988). Table 2–8 offers a sample of three surveys of state economic performance: the first two are composite measures, one by *INC.* magazine and the other by the Corporation for Enterprise Development (CED), and the third is simply a per capita personal income measure. Other well-known rankings are published by Grant Thorton (1986) and ACIR (1986a). The methodology of the two composite measures are somewhat involved, so they will only be summarized here. Consult the references for a detailed explanation of the rating.

The first column of Table 2–8 lists the states ranked by their INC score. That score tries to measure "how a state is doing in stimulating entrepreneurial activity and economic expansion" (*INC.*, 1989). The score is calculated over a four-year period, in this case 1984–88. It combines three areas: *job generation* (the absolute change in total employment from 1984–1988), *new businesses* (new companies founded in 1984 or later that had employed at least ten employees by 1988), and *young company growth* (companies founded in 1980 or later that had registered a *growth index* of at least 20 between 1984 and 1988; a growth index is simply absolute growth in employment multiplied by percentage growth in employment). A score of 100 is the highest tally a state can receive.

The INC measure supports the notion of a dynamic bicoastal economy led by Nevada and California in the West region; New Hampshire in the Northeast region; and Virginia, Maryland, Georgia, Florida, Delaware, and North Carolina in the South region. Many of the states in the South region and especially in the North Central region rank relatively low on the INC measure.

The CED grading of the states is more thorough; that is, if the number of factors is at all related to thoroughness. Again, this summary cannot do justice to the CED methodology. In brief, CED looks at performance, business vitality, capacity, and policies.

*Performance* includes employment, income, job quality (i.e., health coverage, hourly earnings, working poor), equity (i.e., income distribution and black-white income differentials), and quality of life (i.e., crime rate, infant mortality, life expectancy). The Northeast region fares very well on this measure. Joining the Northeastern states are states from the North Central region, especially Minnesota and Wisconsin, but also Michigan, Illinois, Ohio, and Indiana. States in the South region fared the worst.

*Business vitality* includes competitiveness (i.e., exports, manufacturing investment, the presence of Fortune 1000 companies) and entrepreneurial energy (i.e., business formation rates, self-employment, minority and women business ownership). States from the West region, for example, Alaska, Arizona, California, and Colorado are joined by Texas and Florida from the South region and many states from the Northeast region in leading this category. Again, the bulk of the states from the South region fall low on the business vitality component.

*Capacity* measures the state's activity in the areas of human resources (i.e., labor force skills, educational quality, technological innovation), finance capacity (i.e., capital resources, capital utilization), infrastructure (i.e., transportation systems, sewerage treatment, airport capacity), and amenities (i.e., the number of doctors, the level of arts funding). The Northeast region dominates the top rankings joined by Maryland, Virginia, Colorado, and California. For the third time, the South region fills the bottom slots.

The *policies* component takes account of state regulation, tax code, public works, and aid to distressed communities. The Northeast and North Central regions are among the leaders in this last category. More thinly populated West and South region states rank among the lowest states.

The CED findings do not easily fit the bicoastal tag. Certainly, states along the eastern and western coasts rank high in the CED analysis. However, several states in the North Central region—Minnesota, Wisconsin, Illinois, and to a lesser extent Michigan and Ohio—match their coastal counterparts. What comes through very clear is that many states in the South region are not prospering as much as their coastal and midwestern neighbors.

The third and last measure is a simple ranking of the states by their projected 2000 per capita personal income (adjusted to 1982 real dollars). The national average is $15,345. Sixteen states are above this figure. The Northeast with six states and the West with four dominate that group of sixteen states.

The performance of the regional economies of the United States has been viewed from several angles: individual factors, such as population, employment, income, and construction; and a sample of state-ranking schemes. From all of this, a picture of the location of economic activity in the United States should have emerged. The picture shows a vibrant bicoastal economy joined by several states from the North Central and the South regions. Overall, the vast majority of states in the South region do not share in the economic vitality of the bicoastal economy regardless of how economic performance is measured. The next task is to explain why these regional differences occur and change over time.

Table 2–8

Ranking the States' Economic Performance: Three Alternative Methods

| RANK | States | INC Score 1/ 1989 | Ranking the States in 1987 on CED Measures of ... 2/ Performance | Business Vitality | Capacity | Policies | Per Capita Personal Income 2000 3/ (1982 Dollars) | RANK |
|---|---|---|---|---|---|---|---|---|
| 1 | Nevada | 87.02 | Massachusetts | Alaska | Massachusetts | Michigan | Connecticut $20503 | 1 |
| 2 | New Hampshire | 81.15 | Connecticut | Arizona | Connecticut | Ohio | New Jersey 19932 | 2 |
| 3 | Virginia | 79.84 | New Hampshire | California | California | Minnesota | Massachusetts 18694 | 3 |
| 4 | Maryland | 75.75 | Minnesota | Texas | Colorado | NEW YORK | New York 17852 | 4 |
| 5 | Georgia | 74.39 | Maine | Colorado | New York | PENNSYLVANIA | Maryland 17665 | 5 |
| 6 | Florida | 73.56 | Wisconsin | Vermont | Minnesota | Massachusetts | New Hampshire 17363 | 6 |
| 7 | Delaware | 72.59 | Rhode Island | WASHINGTON | Rhode Island | New Jersey | California 17113 | 7 |
| 8 | North Carolina | 67.78 | Vermont | Florida | Delaware | California | Alaska 16765 | 8 |
| 9 | Tennessee | 66.93 | California | Utah | Arizona | WISCONSIN | Virginia 16345 | 9 |
| 10 | California | 66.69 | Hawaii | Massachusetts | Vermont | Maine | Illinois 16131 | 10 |
| 11 | Arizona | 65.38 | New Jersey | Minnesota | New Jersey | MARYLAND | Nevada 15855 | 11 |
| 12 | Hawaii | 64.61 | New York | NEW HAMPSHIRE | Pennsylvania | Connecticut | Delaware 15747 | 12 |
| 13 | South Carolina | 64.33 | Nebraska | Connecticut | Maryland | Florida | Rhode Island 15555 | 13 |
| 14 | Vermont | 59.96 | Washington | NEW MEXICO | Illinois | VERMONT | Minnesota 15508 | 14 |
| 15 | New Jersey | 57.69 | Kansas | Idaho | Hawaii | Illinois | Florida 15496 | 15 |
| 16 | Maine | 57.22 | Delaware | New York | Alaska | IOWA | Michigan 15361 | 16 |
| 17 | Massachusetts | 54.90 | Virginia | Maryland | Oregon | KENTUCKY | Washington 15316 | 17 |
| 18 | Connecticut | 53.96 | Maryland | Oklahoma | Texas | MISSOURI | Colorado 15311 | 18 |
| 19 | Washington | 52.92 | Pennsylvania | Kansas | Washington | OREGON | Hawaii 15219 | 19 |
| 20 | Alabama | 52.21 | Colorado | LOUISIANA | Wisconsin | SOUTH CAROLINA | Pennsylvania 15173 | 20 |
| 21 | Indiana | 52.12 | Utah | OREGON | Kansas | WASHINGTON | Kansas 14986 | 21 |
| 22 | Utah | 51.05 | Indiana | Delaware | New Mexico | WEST VIRGINIA | Missouri 14592 | 22 |
| 23 | Oregon | 50.86 | Alaska | MICHIGAN | Virginia | Hawaii | Wisconsin 14575 | 23 |

22

| Rank | State | Value | | | | | State | Value[3] | Rank |
|---|---|---|---|---|---|---|---|---|---|
| 24 | Pennsylvania | 50.46 | Nevada | Virginia | Montana | Arizona | Ohio | 14531 | 24 |
| 25 | Kentucky | 50.08 | Michigan | Indiana | Iowa | INDIANA | Nebraska | 14322 | 25 |
| 26 | Ohio | 49.30 | North Dakota | New Jersey | Utah | RHODE ISLAND | Georgia | 14297 | 26 |
| 27 | Michigan | 48.59 | SOUTH DAKOTA | Maine | North Dakota | New Mexico | Vermont | 14193 | 27 |
| 28 | New York | 48.22 | Missouri | MISSOURI | Ohio | TEXAS | Indiana | 14031 | 28 |
| 29 | Wisconsin | 45.06 | Iowa | OHIO | Missouri | VIRGINIA | Maine | 14014 | 29 |
| 30 | Minnesota | 44.97 | Ohio | WYOMING | New Hampshire | Arkansas | Arizona | 13926 | 30 |
| 31 | Texas | 44.87 | OREGON | Nebraska | Oklahoma | COLORADO | Oregon | 13908 | 31 |
| 32 | Rhode Island | 44.82 | Arizona | Hawaii | Florida | DELAWARE | Texas | 13851 | 32 |
| 33 | Illinois | 43.13 | IDAHO | West Virginia | Wyoming | GEORGIA | Iowa | 13849 | 33 |
| 34 | Mississippi | 41.52 | Illinois | Nevada | Nebraska | KANSAS | North Carolina | 13481 | 34 |
| 35 | Missouri | 40.95 | Wyoming | Georgia | Michigan | LOUISIANA | Tennessee | 13192 | 35 |
| 36 | Kansas | 39.30 | Montana | RHODE ISLAND | Idaho | MISSISSIPPI | Oklahoma | 12937 | 36 |
| 37 | Colorado | 39.14 | Florida | Montana | Georgia | MONTANA | Wyoming | 12898 | 37 |
| 38 | West Virginia | 38.07 | North Carolina | Illinois | North Carolina | NEBRASKA | Montana | 12474 | 38 |
| 39 | New Mexico | 38.82 | Georgia | KENTUCKY | Louisiana | NORTH CAROLINA | North Dakota | 12461 | 39 |
| 40 | Arkansas | 36.37 | Texas | NORTH DAKOTA | Indiana | OKLAHOMA | South Dakota | 12330 | 40 |
| 41 | Iowa | 34.03 | Oklahoma | Arkansas | South Dakota | UTAH | South Carolina | 12304 | 41 |
| 42 | Nebraska | 33.04 | West Virginia | IOWA | Nevada | New Hampshire | Alabama | 12247 | 42 |
| 43 | Idaho | 27.39 | Arkansas | TENNESSEE | Tennessee | South Dakota | Idaho | 12181 | 43 |
| 44 | Louisiana | 26.95 | NEW MEXICO | South Carolina | Maine | Alabama | Kentucky | 12178 | 44 |
| 45 | South Dakota | 22.98 | TENNESSEE | Wisconsin | Kentucky | IDAHO | New Mexico | 11949 | 45 |
| 46 | Oklahoma | 22.25 | Kentucky | South Dakota | Alabama | NEVADA | Louisiana | 11680 | 46 |
| 47 | North Dakota | 18.52 | South Carolina | North Carolina | South Carolina | North Dakota | Utah | 11605 | 47 |
| 48 | Montana | 17.24 | Alabama | Pennsylvania | Arkansas | WYOMING | Arkansas | 11594 | 48 |
| 49 | Alaska | 14.67 | Mississippi | Alabama | West Virginia | Alaska | West Virginia | 10921 | 49 |
| 50 | Wyoming | 3.00 | Louisiana | Mississippi | Mississippi | TENNESSEE | Mississippi | 10631 | 50 |
| | | | | | | | USA Average | 15345 | |

*Note:* A state in capital letters is tied with the state immediately preceding it in the rankings.

[1] "INC's Annual Report on the States," INC., October 1989.

[2] CED, *Making the Grade*, 1987.

[3] Real 1982 dollars, Bureau of Economics Analysis, 1990.

## THEORIES OF REGIONAL ECONOMIC DEVELOPMENT

There are many theories about why regions grow (Nourse, 1968; Doeringer et al., 1987, 1990; Terkla et al., 1991). To give a sense of the various theories, this section describes two that highlight the role of exports—the *export base theory* and the *product cycle theory*.

### Export Base Theory

A sophisticated measure of regional economic activity is gross state product (GSP) (listed in Table 2–7). GSP is the sum of consumer goods demanded and produced locally; investment goods demanded and produced locally; government goods demanded and produced locally; and the sales of goods produced locally, but sold outside the region, namely exports. (Some may be familiar with these concepts from the Keynesian income determination model. For a review of that model, see Ruffin and Gregory, 1986 or Lipsey, Steiner, and Purvus, 1987.)

In the regional economy, the level of economic activity determines the level of consumer goods, investment goods, and government goods. For example, increases in the level of government goods and services do not spur on the economy. State and local governments cannot issue money or ordinarily operate at a deficit. Rather, a growing economy enables the government to expand. Even local consumption cannot by itself lead the drive for economic growth. The adage in regional economics is that a regional economy cannot grow "by taking in its own laundry." (If each household washes its neighbor's clothes, does the laundry swap generate additional income or jobs?) So the burden for economic growth rests with exports (Oakland, 1979).

Exports are central to the growth of the regional economy because they mean additional income *to* consumers and producers in the region *from* consumers and producers outside the region; the inflow of income from exports leads to the growth of nonexport-producing industries; and the outflow of products from the region's export activities allows for the shifting of regional taxes outside the regional boundaries.

Analysts point to the changing fortunes of the energy-producing states of the South region, especially the West South Central division that consists of Louisiana, Oklahoma, and Texas as an example of the export base theory at work. When energy exports flourished, so did these states' economies. When the oil glut materialized and energy prices tumbled, these states' economies followed suit, as Tables 2–1 through 2–7 showed.

The Northeast region, especially New Hampshire, Massachusetts, and New Jersey is another example of the export base theory at work. The market for hi-tech products and services has boomed and these states were ready to ride the crest of the new product development in this area (Moscovitch, 1986; Knight and Barff, 1987/88; Bradbury and Browne, 1988). Simply, these states had the skills, products, and services that the national and international economy sought.

The result has been a rapidly expanding Northeast regional economy driven by a growing export sector. Again, the information in Tables 2–1 through 2–7 support this analysis.

### Product Cycle Theory

This theory is a variation on the export base theory. Again, exports play a significant role in the rise and the decline of a region's economic fortunes. The product cycle theory traces the exported product through three stages of its development: the new product stage, the maturing product stage, and the standardization stage (Vernon, 1966). Each of these stages has a different meaning for the region's economic well-being.

The *new product stage* takes up the product at the point of its introduction into the market. Labor intensive production techniques (relatively high reliance on labor relative to capital), old or outmoded production technology, and relatively small output levels are the features of the production process at this point. These characteristics are present because this stage represents the transition between an old production technology and a yet-to-emerge new production technology for this product. The new product does find a market outside the regional borders so demand for exportation increases over time. The exportation of the product means regional growth just as the export base theory would predict.

The *maturing product stage* describes the next phase of product development. Demand for the product grows outside the region. Producers respond by introducing new standardized production technology, shifting away from labor intensive production to capital intensive production (relatively high reliance on capital relative to labor), capturing economies of scale (falling per unit costs as output increases), and increasing the amount produced. Also, new producers enter the market to compete for the regional market and the export market. The demand for the product continues to expand as does the regional economy. In the next stage, the regional economy takes a turn for the worse.

The *standardization stage* describes that phase of production where the production technology has become standardized and often copied within and outside the region that witnessed the product's initial development. The growth in the number of producers means that competition to sell the product has become very price sensitive. Any element of the production process that significantly affects costs—land, labor, capital, and shipping costs, and government policies—will tip the competition to producers within the region or outside the region. If producers outside the region can undercut their competitors within the region by enough of a margin, then the improbable will have occurred; that is, the region which developed the product will actually be buying it from producers located outside the region.

The deindustrialization of the Northeast and North Central regions as shown by the loss of manufacturing employment in Table 2–4 and the growth in manufacturing employment in the South region, South Atlantic division and the West region, Pacific division serve as examples of the product cycle theory. Manufacturing has long been at the core of the regional economies of the Northeast and the North Central rgions, but those regions act as if they have entered the standardization stage of the product cycle theory where the regional economy loses its product market to competing producers located elsewhere, in this case the South and the West regions and outside the United States.

## SUMMARY

1. The performance of the regional economy dictates the public service demands and the tax resources available to operate state and local governments. Unequal regional growth can lead to unequal public service and/or tax levels.

2. U.S. Bureau of Census data and various state-ranking schemes show that regional economies of the United States have been changing throughout the 1980s. In terms of population, employment, income, and construction, the Northeast and West regions have prospered. The results have been mixed for the North Central and South regions. The Northeast and North Central regions have lost and are losing manufacturing jobs to other regions and other countries.

3. Two theories that explain differences in regional economic performance are the export base theory that stresses regional economic growth driven by the exportation of products outside the regional borders, and the product cycle theory that ties a region's economic fate to various stages of a product's market life.

# CHAPTER 3

## The Federal System in the United States

**PREVIEW**

The trip from the American Revolutionary War to a federal system of government was a chance excursion. This chapter places federalism into a political context: it begins with a definition of federalism; summarizes aspects of the colonial experience which led to a reorganization of the American system of government; describes a set of political theories that explain how the federal system works; and sets out the dominant features of a federal system. Finally, the chapter leaves the reader with several trails to follow in order to anticipate the future developments in American federalism.

**INTRODUCTION**

The quarrelsome politics leading up to 1786 gave the United States a federal system of government. From that day to this, the federal system has been at the center of some noteworthy political quarrels. The United States is not the only country to adopt such a troublesome, yet serviceable, system. There are many countries with similar governmental organizations. Three that researchers have studied are: Australia, Canada, and West Germany (ACIR, 1981a, 1981b, 1981c). While this chapter looks at the political and historical evolution of federalism, Chapter 4 develops an economic theory of federalism. These two chapters set the stage for an examination of the spending and taxing policies of state and local governments.

## FEDERALISM DEFINED

A federal system is a compromise between a unitary government and a confederation. On one extreme is a unitary government which stresses a strong national government. It has the unilateral power to grant authority to or withdraw authority from regional and local governments. On the other extreme is a confederation which stresses powerful state governments. They can delegate authority to and limit the authority of any national government.

In the true spirit of compromise, a federal system draws upon the strengths of each system to address the public interest needs of the nation and the states. A political definition of *federalism* states that, ''it is a system of government that includes a national government and at least one level of subnational governments (states, provinces, local governments) and that enables each level to make some significant decisions independently of the other(s)'' (Nice, 1987, p. 2).

This definition means that within a federal system there exists a constitutional division of governmental functions between/among the levels of government. Within its assigned functions, each level is supreme. No one level can change the division of functions unilaterally. Last, there must be adequate resources to support a central and subnational governments. If not, discretionary authority over a governmental function has little meaning (Peltason, 1979; Reagan and Sanzone, 1981). Of course, there is a simple way to look at the American federal system. It is the arrangement which keeps over 83,000 units of government—national, states (50), counties (3,042), municipalities (19,200), towns (16,691), school districts (14,721), and special districts (29,532)—working together to serve the public interest.

The love-hate relationship with the national government that characterizes federalism in general and American federalism in particular is a unique outcome of American history. Aspects from the colonial experience, especially the relationship between the colonies and Great Britain and that among the colonies, provide the historical backdrop for the beginning of American federalism.

## OUT OF CONFEDERATION INTO FEDERALISM

In 1777, the Continental Congress approved the Articles of Confederation to conduct the war and unite the states after the British were defeated. Since the colonists viewed government power as a threat to individual freedom, the Articles provided for little centralized governmental authority. There was no congressional power over commerce; no congressional power to tax; no federal court system; and no congressional power to coerce state action. The states were and remained supreme. In short order, the Articles were beset by problems. The Confederation could not pay its debts; nor manage day-to-day governmental operations; nor establish a uniform commercial code; nor negotiate foreign treaties unless the states agreed to cooperate. Pressure grew for a change in the Articles. The states, in response, agreed to convene a Constitutional Convention.

At the time of the convention two opposing forces were at work on the new country. One pushed for the decentralization of authority; in the extreme, keep the states independent of one another. Several aspects of colonial life contributed to this position—state patriotism, vested state political and economic interests, religion, the state culture, and the poor transportation and communication network in the new country. Another force pressed for the centralization of authority; in the extreme, bring the states together to form one unified country. There were aspects of colonial life that fostered this position—common language, shared legal system, interstate trade interests, the goodwill among the states which had developed in the fight for independence, and the need for a common defense in the future (Leach, 1970). These forces were to play themselves out during and after the Constitutional Convention.

Many historians and political scientists have pointed out that few Americans expected the participants at the Constitutional Convention to abandon the Articles of Confederation. The participants were to patch up that plan. Meeting in secret, the state representatives prepared a constitution which called for a federal system of government. That system seemed to balance the two opposing forces mentioned above. Unlike the Articles, the Constitution specified the powers of the national government: levy taxes, borrow money, regulate domestic and foreign commerce, conduct foreign relations, and maintain an army and navy. Further, the national government had direct contact with the people, not just through the states (Mitchell and Mitchell, 1975; Wills, 1981).

While the convention was quite specific about the operation of some aspects of the new national government, the working relationship between the national government and the state governments—the heart of the federal system—was left unexplained. In hindsight, that omission was probably for the better. The Constitution of the United States offers some guidelines on federal-state and interstate relations in Article IV: States' Relations; however, little which explains the grand sweep of intergovernmental relations. In Article VI, section 2, the so-called *supremacy clause*, the Constitution states an important principle of federalism:

This Constitution, and the Laws of the United States which shall be made in Pursuance thereof; and all Treaties made, or which shall be made, under the author of the United States, shall be the supreme Law of the Land, and the Judges in every State shall be bound thereby, any Thing in the Constitution or Laws of any State to the Contrary notwithstanding.

This article establishes that the powers of the national government may be limited, but within the defined powers, they are supreme. In prescribed areas, the states must take a backseat to the national government (Peltason, 1979). Even *The Federalist Papers*, especially Numbers 9, 16, 39, and 40 do not go much beyond this level of generality. As a result, political theories that claim to solve the riddle and describe the operation of the federal system have evolved.

## POLITICAL THEORIES OF FEDERALISM

The lack of detail about intergovernmental relations in the Constitution created a conceptual vacuum that a group of political theories has rushed to fill. These theories usually fall into two broad categories: *competitive theories* and *interdependent theories* of federalism. Neither of these categories discusses the role of local governments in federalism. Rather they refer to the two levels of government—national and states—recognized in the Constitution.

Not surprisingly, the first theories of federalism see the system in competitive terms. The country was just beginning, every individual, farmer, merchant, and politician was marking his territory. As the society matured and its problems became more intractable, cooperation became more appealing.

### Competitive Theories

A competitive theory of federalism traces the superiority of one level of government over another based on the Constitution or other evidence, such as a series of Supreme Court cases or *The Federalist Papers*. The notion is that the framers of the Constitution reflected the people's wish that one level of government be dominant over the other.

Dominance is important because the one common assumption of any competitive theory of federalism is that there is a fixed amount of governmental power for which the national and the state governments are vying. One level's gain is the other level's loss. That assumption adds some significance to the outcome of the competition. So which level was meant to be dominant? Which subservient? The evidence is unclear. So the theories cover all possibilities. There are three competitive theories of federalism: *nation-centered federalism, state-centered federalism*, and *dual federalism*.

*Nation-centered Federalism.* The theory proceeds along these lines. The Constitution emanates from the American people. Therefore, any national government that the Constitution creates is the focus of political power and should meet the needs of the American people. Some trace this theory back to Alexander Hamilton's contributions in *The Federalist Papers* and the (Chief Justice John) Marshall Supreme Court decision (1819) in *McCullock v. Maryland*. In that case, Maryland had levied a tax on the Baltimore branch of the Bank of the United States. McCulloch, the cashier of the bank, refused to pay. He argued that Maryland had no power to tax an "instrumentality of the federal government" under Article I, section 8 of the Constitution. The Marshall Court supported this position and provided added justification for this theory (Peltason, 1979; Goldman, 1987).

Proponents of this theory believe that the national government is in a better position than the states to serve the public interest. The national government has a broader view of the issues at hand, access to more highly skilled personnel, and will act on the problem. Their view of the states is just the opposite: provincial interests dominate state government; states do not have the know-how to deal with complex problems; and states delay then scurry off in many, often conflicting directions, to address the identical problem.

While everyday governmental actions cannot easily be assigned to one theory or another, the government's actions in the civil rights area clearly fits this theory. The Fourteenth Amendment which deals with "citizenship, privileges and immunities of United States citizenship, due process, and equal protection of the laws" places the national interest over the states' (ACIR, 1981d). At one time or another, Abraham Lincoln, Theodore Roosevelt, and Franklin Roosevelt showed their support for this theory. With few exceptions, the U.S. Supreme Court supports this theory (Nice, 1987; Leach, 1970).

*State-centered Federalism.* This theory asserts that the state government called the Constitutional Convention to draft a document that would limit the power of the national government. Further, the existence of a national government does not restrict the powers of the states, but the powers of the states do restrict those of the national government. The states are meant to be the dominant force in the federal system.

Proponents of this interpretation of federalism often point to Article I, Section 8 which in their minds restricts national government taxing power: "The Congress shall have Power to lay and Collect Taxes, Duties, Imposts and Excises to pay the Debts and provide for the common Defence and general Welfare of the United States." There is no mention made of the general power to legislate for the general welfare, although advocates of state-centered federalism have lost that battle long ago. In addition, the gospel for every supporter of this theory is the Tenth Amendment which reads, "The powers not delegated to the United States by the Constitution, nor prohibited by it to the States, are reserved to the States respectively, or to the people." However, the modern view is that this amendment does not limit the national government in exercising the powers that the Constitution grants it.

The traditional arguments for this theory are that the division of government power prevents its concentration at the national level and, therefore, protects individual freedom; the states are closer to the people and can better represent their various interests and address their varied needs; and independent states can experiment in the public policy arena rather than follow some uniform policy.

Thomas Jefferson and later John C. Calhoun were early, noteworthy, sometime supporters of this position. In more recent times, this strict interpretation of the role of the states in the federal system, while implemented with the Articles of Confederation, has few prominent supporters.

*Dual Federalism.* The third competitive theory takes some of the edge off the previous two by proposing that a balance exists between the national government and the state governments. There is no need for one level to dominate the other because the Constitution has created "collateral spheres of power." This phrase means that each level of government is sovereign within its own domain. We are all kings/queens of our castle. Luckily, there are enough castles to go around so that we do not have to confront one another. The same principle holds for dual federalism.

A baking analogy (for some reason, researchers have used baking analogies to describe various theories of federalism) offers another view of dual federalism. Dual federalism and its spheres of independent power have come to be known as *layer cake* federalism. The chocolate and vanilla are unchallenged in their own layers!

Advocates of this theory argue that nation-centered federalism can be too rigid and state-centered federalism too parochial. What is needed is a clear division of governmental responsibilities using the guidelines stated in the Constitution. If such a division can take place, then each level of government will be supreme in its designated areas.

The national government will manage its public policy areas, the state governments theirs with little need for competition between the two levels of government. It sounds quite simple. All that is needed is for the levels of government to agree upon the sorting out of responsibilities into national versus state categories. Of course, this is a task which has gone over 200 years without a completely acceptable sort. Despite this fact, academic researchers and government practitioners often referred to the theory of dual federalism to explain American federalism in this century until 1960 (Elazar, 1962).

The dual theory also overlooks the possibility that cooperation between the levels of government might best serve the public interests. If economic growth and job creation are primary responsibilities of the national government and if education is the primary responsibility of the state governments, then how does the dual theory of federalism cope with poorly educated young men and women who are ill-prepared to take positions in a high technology-based economy? The answer may be in cooperation between the levels of government so that educational preparation and job placement are connected.

Recall that the entire set of competitive theories assumes that power in a federal system is constant. In fact, intergovernmental cooperation may actually expand governmental power. The expansion of governmental power to serve the public interest which cooperation offers is what supports an alternative set of theories about how the federal system works.

### Interdependent Theories

The interdependent theories of federalism rely not so much on the interpretations of passages in the Constitution or Supreme Court cases, but on a willingness and determination to address a problem. The problems with which the public sector deals are not usually tidy. So it should come as no surprise that the intergovernmental relations which this set of theories of federalism supports are, to be polite, flexible. Do not expect any neatly drawn lines of authority, any well-defined functional responsibilities, or any layer cakes. There are three interdependent theories of federalism: *cooperative federalism, creative federalism,* and *new federalism.*

*Cooperative Federalism.* This view of federalism was first spelled out in the 1950s. It holds that the different levels of government should assist one another in serving the public interest because the public sector is, in fact, a single mechanism with many centers of power. Federal, state, and local governments, when appropriate, should share functional responsibilities and work together; not quarrel over who is responsible for what. Gone is the neatness of the layer cake. In its place appears the swirls of *marble cake federalism* (Grodzins, 1965).

Public services like transportation, law enforcement, conservation, and job training illustrate the point of cooperative federalism. Each of these services has an implication for each level of government. An effective transportation system is equally important to the cities and suburbs, as it is to the region, the state, and the nation. All can contribute financial resources, technical know-how, and political cooperation to design, build, operate, and maintain a transportation system.

While new labels (like *rowboat* federalism and *bamboo fence* federalism) have popped up on the federalism scene to describe contemporary intergovernmental relations, the spirit of cooperative federalism often guides federal, state, and local governments' working relationships as they cope with shelters for homeless people, treatment for AIDS patients, violators of drug laws, and the migration of undocumented aliens.

*Creative Federalism.* Creative federalism is an extension of cooperative federalism. Why the extension? A crisis of the times can force the federal system to adapt. That is what happened in the 1960s.

The problems of poverty and urban decline required the federal system to change. Both President Lyndon Johnson (1964) and New York Governor Nelson Rockefeller (1962) advocated a work plan for federalism that went beyond the cooperative theory. They advocated a working partnership that emphasized a direct federal-local government association (bypassing the states) and agreements between government and nongovernment organizations to solve social problems. Creative federalism was the watchword for the Great Society.

Theories of federalism born out of crisis may come and go as the crisis subsides. However, the legacy of the creative federalism is local government access to the federal government which it did not always have and numerous contract services (e.g., refuse collection, engineering services, solid waste disposal, hospitals, nursing services, assessing, and even prisons) between government and nongovernment vendors which have expanded over the years. In fact, some on the public policy scene have taken the contract services portion of the theory of creative federalism and argued for reduced government involvement in public service provision and more private provision (''privatization'') of public services (Savas, 1982).

*New Federalism.* This interdependent theory of federalism is closely related to the competitive theories of state-centered and dual federalism. New federalism has become a shorthand label which calls for a cut in the federal bureaucracy, streamlining federal regulations on state and local governments, the decentralization of public sector activities, and the granting of broad local discretion in the public service area. Its exact meaning is still evolving. Since 1972, the United States has had two versions of new federalism.

Under President Richard Nixon's (and later Gerald Ford's) version, state and local governments received increased funds from the federal government coupled with fewer federal regulations on how that money should be spent. The cornerstone financial assistance program that accompanied Nixon's new federalism was commonly known as General Revenue Sharing. (It has since been eliminated.)

Under President Ronald Reagan's version, there was an attempt to reduce the federal government's role in domestic policy by shifting a group of public service responsibilities from the federal government to the state governments without an actual increase in federal assistance for these programs. The National Association of State Governors turned down this offer. The Reagan version of new federalism resulted in fewer federal grants.

President George Bush has endorsed this notion of new federalism. His proposed highway legislation calls for limiting federal spending to major national arteries and delegating costly, new responsibilities for construction and upkeep of local roads to the states. The states, in turn, would be expected to increase state and local fuel taxes and tolls (Cushman, March 7, 1990). The Bush administration highway initiative is but the latest in a decade-long shift of responsibilities away from the federal government to state and local governments without any financial support (Tolchin, 1990a).

With few specifics offered in the Constitution, generations of political leaders and academics have produced a variety of theories on the operation of the federal system. Regardless of the theory that Americans find most convincing, this process shows that federalism is an extremely flexible (some would say chaotic) system of government. It is a system that can bend to the needs of the times.

At present, interdependent theories of federalism guide the workings of American federalism. A concoction of cooperation between/among levels ("cooperative federalism"), the involvement of nongovernmental organizations in government activities ("creative federalism"), and the perceived movement toward greater decentralization ("new federalism") produce the brew that is contemporary federalism. Although the federal government has the authority, record level deficits and conservative political ideology dictate its passive role. State and local governments have been left to grapple with society's problems. Some can take on their public problems because they possess the will, the know-how, and the resources. Many cannot take on their public problems because they lack the resources.

## FEATURES OF AMERICAN FEDERALISM

In a sense, the Constitution sets out the federal system as a riddle that each successive generation of Americans tries to solve. At different times and in different policy areas, the solution has been to strengthen the states; have a dominant federal government; or have the federal, state, and local governments work together. Whatever the form of the solution, there are several features of the federal system which stand out.

## Tension Between Diversity and Uniformity

The decentralization of authority in a federal system permits governments across the United States to adopt their own approach to identifying and solving problems. The United States prides itself on the regional diversity that exists from New England to the Southwest. Of course, not only do problems vary region by region, but so does people's willingness to turn to the government to address those problems. The adage is that the level of government closest to the people knows and can deal with their problems best. This diversity has a bright and dark side. The bright side is that diversity can and does lead to public policy innovation. The dark side is that diversity can and does lead to interjurisdictional competition for people, jobs, and investment. This competition may not always be in the interest of the macroeconomy.

Federalism discourages any attempt at uniformity in public policy because uniformity ultimately means too much government for some people and too little for others. Uniformity in public policy, however, is not a dead issue. As people move from one region of the United States to another, the pressure for uniformity appears to grow. The security which uniformity across the country provides can be seen in the private sector with the growth of fastfood chains, hotels, radio stations, and the like. Why else would there be a New York deli industry in Boulder, Colorado?

The public sector has its parallel. For example, highways across the country must meet certain standards; elementary and secondary education services must be competitive anywhere in the country; even refuse removal is conforming to a standard. So within the federal system the pressure for uniformity exists. The more public problems teach people that they are connected with one another, the more the pressure for a uniform solution. This tension between the appeal of diversity and, in some cases, the real need for a uniform solution is a tension in the federal system that regularly appears in public policy debates.

## Fragmentation of Authority

The alternative theories on the workings of federalism should bring home the point that federalism is a system built on opposing forces. One set of opposing forces concerns public sector power. One group that supports a federal system distrusts power and sees the system as a means to scatter it among the levels of government thereby rendering it less dangerous to individual freedoms. Another group that also supports a federal system sees power as a means to accomplish public goals. By spreading power among the levels of government, this group believes that the opportunities to serve the public interest will multiply.

The distribution of power in a federal system does create problems. Once a problem is recognized, which level of government initiates action to address it? Which level will pay for the solution? Because of each level's own interests and limited resources, the approach to a problem is fractionalized. Each level of government deals with a part of the problem and accepts a part of the program cost. And the sum of the parts never quite equals the whole.

For example, the growing number of undocumented aliens who are crossing the border to work in the Southwestern part of the United States is putting pressure on the social service systems of many municipalities. As demand for health care, housing, schooling, and food programs increases, which level of government is responsible for these services? The municipalities try to meet the increased demand, but the federal government must devise a policy to regulate traffic across the country's borders. Each level struggles with a piece of the problem because of the fragmentation of authority in a federal system.

### Need for Coordination

The allure of diversity and the fact of shared power over numerous units of government mean that the federal system requires intergovernmental coordination. Governments act independently. There is no simple, low-cost mechanism to coordinate their actions. The result can lead to duplication of effort, conflicting program goals, and an avalanche of paperwork and regulations. Intergovernmental coordination is necessary for the efficient administration of a federal system.

### Fiscal Imbalances

Autonomy and diversity for state and local governments require an adequate source of revenue. To go it alone and be different to boot costs money. Certainly, the state and local resource base depends upon the performance of the regional economy. Slow growth or a downright decline can only result in budget problems. However, a prosperous regional economy translates into tax revenues to finance the desired level of public services.

A federal system assumes a distribution of resources which gives meaning to autonomy and diversity in public policy. There are two consequences to this assumption. Fiscal pressure creates a climate for tax competition between and among state and local governments. The need to attract people, jobs, and investment can force state and local government to negotiate with the private sector while looking over their shoulders at their neighboring jurisdictions. Also, the federal system has a built-in fiscal mismatch. The distribution of revenue-raising devices in American federalism is such that often state and local revenue systems cannot expand fast enough to keep pace with the growing costs and added responsibilities associated with state and local public services.

Regardless of the developments in American federalism, as long as it remains the organizational structure of the public sector, the federal system will be tormented by the tension between diversity and uniformity, the fragmentation of authority, the need for coordination, and fiscal imbalances across the country and levels of government. Each of these features or any combination of them makes it more difficult for the public sector to serve the public interest. So the organization of the public sector can inhibit its performance. In a sense, these four features are constant through time. This chapter concludes with another perspective; namely, what are some developments in American federalism that merit watching over time.

## TRENDS IN THE AMERICAN FEDERAL SYSTEM

Trends in three areas could indicate the direction which the American federal system will take over the next decade. The three areas are: Supreme Court decisions, revenue-raising patterns, and experiments in state and local government organization.

Since the 1930s, the Supreme Court has shown a tendency to favor the federal government in cases where state and local actions clash with federal authority. This is especially so in the area of commerce, but also extends to the areas of civil liberties and equal protection under the law. Recent cases illustrate exactly how vulnerable state and local governments are at the hands of the Court. (Much of the following interpretation of the Court's recent decisions relies on Goldman, 1987.)

For example, the Court has generally sided with Congress in any test of its commerce powers versus the powers reserved to the states under the Tenth Amendment. Over the years this result has come to mean that federal regulations can be extended to govern state decisions in many areas formerly thought of as state functions. The notion of state sovereignty is immediately jeopardized. If the state government cannot determine how it will carry out its own responsibilities, what does federalism mean? (Hint: not much!)

In 1976, the Court took one step back from this established position in *National League of Cities v. Usery*. The Court stated that a provision of the Fair Labor Standards Act which affects wages and overtime practices did not apply to state employees working on "traditional" state functions. This 5–4 Court decision surprised most observers at the time. The case marked the first time in many years that the Court recognized a limit on the legislative branch's commerce powers versus state sovereignty.

The victory was short-lived. In 1985 by another 5–4 vote (the same Justice was the swing vote in each decision), the Court overturned *Usery* and reaffirmed its previous position. In the case of *Garcia v. San Antonio Metropolitan Transit Authority*, the Court held that federal overtime standards must be followed by states even when the employees are performing essentially state functions. As far as the Court is concerned, there are virtually no limits on the commerce powers of the U.S. Congress, least of all any limit established by some unspecified notion of state sovereignty.

The Court struck again on the state sovereignty issue in 1988. In *South Carolina v. Baker*, the Court voted 7–1 that the federal personal income tax could be levied against the interest paid on certain forms of state and local bonds without violating the Tenth Amendment or the intergovernmental tax immunity doctrine which confers tax exempt status on state and local bonds. In the lone dissent, Justice Sandra Day O'Connor wrote that the decision threatened the sovereign states by "depriving them of this tax immunity, which would increase their dependence on the National Government." With a touch of melodrama, the *Wall Street Journal* in an editorial proclaimed that "the Supreme Court finally has completed its long march toward gutting the Constitution's 10th Amendment of all meaning" ("Federalism's Funeral," 1988).

But wait. There is more nation-centered federalism to come. In the 1990 Kansas City, Missouri school segregation case, the Supreme Court ruled in a 5–4 decision that federal judges may order local governments to increase taxes to remedy "constitutional violations." Some Court observers claim that the decision set a precedent. Federal judges have the power to take an active role in the management of activities traditionally delegated to state and local governments (Greenhouse, 1990; Lewis, 1990).

No wonder a group of state and local officials from fifteen states are calling for a constitutional amendment that will restore what they preceive to be lost authority. One proposed change would modify Article 5 to enable states to initiate constitutional amendments. A second change would alter the Tenth Amendment so that the courts must decide which powers are reserved to the states (Tolchin, 1990b). While the odds do not favor these changes, stay tuned!

While in these cases the specific issues were fair labor standards, tax immunity, and the power to tax, the trend appears clear and has been for some time. The Supreme Court places federal authority ahead of state sovereignty. American federalism is not a state-centered system. State sovereignty, in fact, has no absolute meaning in terms of implied authority. As defined by the Supreme Court, state sovereignty runs second to federal authority in a two-person race. That is not likely to change. The legal trend favors growing federal authority.

"Follow the money" was the suggestion that the informant called "Deep Throat" offered the two *Washington Post* reporters working on the Watergate scandal. That same advice reveals another trend in American federalism. Table 3–1 presents the federal government share of public sector general revenues (measured in comparison to state and local government revenues and as a percent of the total public sector revenues) over six time periods, ranging from 1930 to 1986. All dollar figures have been converted into constant 1982 dollars.

Aside from the absolute growth in the total public sector to which Americans have become accustomed, the table shows the ebb and flow of federal dominance

**Table 3–1**
**Federal Share of Public Sector Total General Revenues for Selected Time Periods (in millions of 1982 dollars) (1)**

| Time Periods | Total Public Sector General Revenue (2) | Ratio of Federal to State & Local | Federal as a Percent of Total |
|---|---|---|---|
| 1930-9 | $1,248.1 | .46 | 31% |
| 1940-9 | 3,100.1 | 2.39 | 70 |
| 1950-9 | 4,643.6 | 2.60 | 72 |
| 1960-9 | 6,053.5 | 1.82 | 65 |
| 1970-9 | 6,923.0 | 1.19 | 54 |
| 1980-6 (3) | 5,378.4 | 1.20 | 54 |

(1) Using appropriate GNP deflators
(2) General revenues include taxes and miscellaneous revenues.
(3) This time period contains only 7 years versus 10 years in the other periods.

*Sources*: *Historical Statistics of the United States: Colonial Times to 1970*, Part 2, and Bureau of Economic Analysis, *The National Income and Product Accounts* (statistical tables for various years).

in the revenue-raising field. For example, in the 1930–39 period, state and local governments raised the bulk of public dollars. The federal government accounted for 31 percent of total general revenues. Another perspective is that for every $1.00 state and local governments raised, the federal government collected 46 cents. All that changes in the succeeding decades.

Beginning in 1940, the federal government surpasses the state and local governments as a revenue collector. World War II forces the federal government to collect 70 percent of total public sector revenues and $2.39 for every one $1.00 the subnational governments collected. The superior revenue-raising position of the federal government has remained, but the gap between the levels has decreased. In the 1980–86 period, the federal government collects 54 percent and $1.20 for every $1.00 raised at the state and local government levels. Some have argued that the fiscal clout of the federal government is even greater than it seems because the federal government has used its money advantage to regulate the actions of state and local government (Kettl, 1983).

The federal government possesses the superior revenue-raising instruments as later chapters will demonstrate. In the past several years, the federal government has borrowed rather than raise taxes and has been a passive partner on the domestic scene. While the trend shows that state and local governments have had to rely more on their own revenue capacity, the federal government has the ability to assert its dominance whenever it reacquires the national will to do so. But for now, the state and local governments have grabbed the fiscal initiative and generally acted in a responsible manner. The trend shows an increased fiscal self-sufficiency on the part of state and local governments which the federal government has forced upon them. That is not necessarily an improvement and not necessarily a permanent situation. But with the president and the Congress standing in the shadow of the budget deficit, the trend may be correct in calling for a period of fiscal self-reliance of "go-it-alone" federalism for the state and local governments.

The final area is the state and local experimentation with governmental organization. Not only does this show the adaptability of the federal system, but also the determination of local governments to provide public services in an efficient manner. The Advisory Commission on Intergovernmental Relations (ACIR, 1974a, 1974b) and Hallman (1977) have followed these experiments. The evidence shows the development of many different forms of governmental organization: special districts, intergovernmental service agreements, transfer of public services, confederation, unification, and federation; and public-private organization: privatization. These forms will be described here with some prominent examples of their implementation.

*Special districts* are defined as limited purpose governmental units that exist as corporate entities and which have substantial fiscal and administrative independence from general purpose local government. There were 29,532 special districts in 1987, an increase of 3.3 percent over 1982. This growth rate compares with an overall increase in governmental units of 1.1 percent within the same period. They may exist within a community or across communities. A sample of the services most often provided is: utilities (e.g., water, transit, electric, and gas), natural resources (e.g., drainage, soil conservation, flood control, and irrigation), sewerage, housing and urban renewal, and parks and recreation.

*Intergovernmental service agreements* are agreements between/among cities, towns, and counties to help each other on special occasions, for one jurisdiction to provide services on a regular basis to another unit, or to work together to provide services. The package of services that jurisdictions have covered with these agreements includes: police and fire protection, prisons, recreation services, and road maintenance.

Another adjustment that the federal system can undertake is the *transfer of functions*. Simply, one jurisdiction transfers services to another jurisdiction usually from a municipality to a county or special district. Transferred services often are transportation systems, hospitals, and planning activities.

*Confederation* is an organization under which governments unite to accomplish a common goal, but keep their independence. Governments usually come together in a confederated system when a public problem and the required response exceeds their resources or political boundary. Some notable examples are Association of Bay Area Governments (ABAG) in and around the San Francisco Bay Area, California; the Metropolitan Atlanta Council of Local Governments, Georgia; and the Mid-American Regional Council of Kansas City, Missouri. These confederated systems deal with issues of metropolitan planning, health care, transportation, the environment, and affordable housing.

For those who still are not convinced of the usefulness of confederated systems

at the national or subnational level, there is another form of government called
*unification*. This form calls for a single government that is responsible for a
metropolitan area and its developing fringe area. There are a few examples of
unification government: Anchorage, Alaska; Baton Rouge, Louisiana; Colum-
bus, Ohio; Indianapolis, Indiana; Jacksonville, Florida; Lexington, Kentucky;
and Nashville, Tennessee.

Last comes a familiar governmental organization, federation at the substate
level. *Federation* establishes a local and metropolitan level of government to
serve the public service needs of the people. Minneapolis-St. Paul, Minnesota; Nassau County, New York; and Dade County, Florida have been the
most successful versions of substate federated systems in the United States. In
all three cases, the metropolitan level government tends to planning, the court
system, crime detection, transportation issues, the library system, public welfare,
and the like. The appeal of these experimental forms is uneven and their implementation is slow. But their long history shows that the local governments
can adapt to the problems that they face. This trend supports the vitality of local
governments.

*Privatization* represents a public-private arrangement designed to provide public goods/services at the lowest cost per unit. Since it is a popular public-private
enterprise surrounded in some controversy, this discussion will try to sort out
what we know about privatization. Critics of government spending have always
railed against waste in government. Government waste, however, is an elusive
concept. It is often better captured with a humorous anecdote than a specific
dollar amount. In part, this is so because public goods/services are different than
private goods/services. Public goods/services are sometimes more difficult to
produce and distribute than private goods/services. (They may involve nonrival
consumption, free riders, redistribution, and Baumol's disease as the next two
chapters will show.) On top of all this, public goods/services are dependent on
the vagaries of the political process.

When all is said and done, organizing the delivery of public goods/services
in order to minimize the waste of public resources requires responsible public
management that links together finances and delivery. In the public realm, the
traditional linkage is public funding usually through taxes and public delivery
usually through government agencies. In the 1980s, the perception of government
waste created such public skepticism regarding government that new (or at least
what seemed to be new) linkages between service funding and service delivery
received public attention. The "new" linkage called for public funding and
private delivery of public goods/services. Its name (which was yet another blow
to the elegance of the English language) is privatization, or the shift of productive
activity from the public sector to the private sector. (The following discussion
draws on Donahue, 1989.)

By shifting good/service delivery away from public sector bureaucrats, privatization promises the efficient provision of public goods/services (Linowes,
1988). That promise rings true if the shift satisfies a simple "rule for privati-

zation.'' The rule has five elements. First, the good/service must be precisely defined. Second, there must be a truly competitive process by which the public sector selects a private vendor. Third, the performance of the private contractors must be evaluated. Fourth, the public sector must be able to replace inept private contractors. Fifth, the government must be concerned about the end result, not the means by which the public good/service is provided.

These elements of the rule create incentives for efficient good/service production. The government knows what it wants done (first element); a bidding process identifies the lowest cost vendor who can do the job (second element); the public sector reviews the work of the vendor and dismisses him/her if the work is substandard (third and fourth elements); and the government allows the vendor to work out how the good/service should be provided (fifth element). Taken together, the elements of the rule for privatization simulate the conditions of a perfectly competitive market that lead to low cost provision of a good/ service.

State and local governments in the United States have long experimented with privatization in government contracting for a variety of services; for example, car towing, legal services, tree trimming, ambulance service, garbage collection, firefighter, utilities, transportation, prison operation, and job training (Valente and Manchester, 1984; Savas, 1982). The research evidence on the efficiency gains associated with privatization is rich enough to please proponents and opponents alike! For example, it is cheaper to have private vendors collect garbage than public agencies (Savas, 1977; Bennett and Johnson, 1979). There is apparently no cost advantage associated with private vendors in water utility operation (e.g., Byrners, Grosskopf, and Hayes, 1986) or electric utility operation (e.g., Atkinson and Halvoren, 1986). (For an international perspective on privatization, see: Borcherding, Pommerehne, and Schneider, 1982.) However, one study (Stevens, 1984) that is often sighted in the public policy debate on privatization deserves some discussion.

The study is significant not only because it offers a strong endorsement of privatization, but also because it reveals the limits of shifting responsibilities for public goods/services from the public to the private sector. This study looked at twenty cities in the Los Angeles metropolitan area that contracted out eight different services: asphalt overlay construction, janitorial service, traffic signal maintenance, street cleaning, trash collection, turf maintenance, tree maintenance, and payroll preparation. With the exception of payroll preparation, the study found large cost savings associated with the privatization of these services. What makes this finding even more impressive is that private vendors accomplished it without any discernible reduction in the quality of the service.

Three factors seem to contribute to the ''same quality-lower cost'' feature of privatization of these services. Private vendors exhibit more flexibility in managing their ventures. They have more up-to-date production technology. Last, they bear lower labor costs. Labor appears to receive less when private vendors provide the service than when public agencies do. Depending on one's point of view, either the public sector overpays its employees or private contractors underpay theirs. There is little in the published research that will settle this issue.

Privatization should not be dismissed as an antigovernment ideologue's fantasy nor should it be embraced as the antidote to a bloated, bumbling government bureaucracy. It is, however, a good/service delivery arrangement that will be part of the government in the 1990s. There are efficiency gains to be had in the privatization of public good/service provision if the good/service fits the "rule for privatization." Of course, even if the good/service satisfies the rule, beware of the economic loss to labor. It may not always represent an efficiency gain, but rather a cut in wages and benefits for workers.

The three trends—legal, financial, and organizational—send a mixed message. The federal government retains the legal authority and financial might to dominate the federal system, but it is the local governments that experiment with organizations to deliver public services. Expect interdependent theories of federalism to guide the American system in the coming decade and the federal government to reassert itself in the revenue-raising area.

## SUMMARY

1. Federalism is a system of government that includes a national government and at least one level of subnational government and that enables each level to make some significant decisions independently of the other(s).

2. The Constitution and other documents associated with the Constitutional Convention give few details and conflicting directions concerning the operation of the federal system.

3. As a result, political theories have developed to explain the federal system. These theories fall into two broad categories: competitive (e.g., nation-centered, state-centered, and dual federalism) and interdependent (e.g., cooperative, creative, and new federalism).

4. Regardless of the theory of federalism, the American federal system possesses four major features that affect its ability to serve the public interest: tension between diversity and uniformity, fragmentation of authority, need for coordination, and fiscal imbalances.

5. There are three trends which indicate the direction American federalism might take in the coming decade: Supreme Court decisions that favor the federal government, revenue-raising patterns that show the federal government with the capability to raise revenues, but forcing the state and local governments to be more self-reliant, and government organization with some experimentation at the substate level.

# CHAPTER 4

## The Journey from Private Markets to Fiscal Federalism

### PREVIEW

An efficient private market system leaves few tasks for the public sector. When the private market fails, the public sector's role expands. Private market failure defines the functions of the public sector. This chapter works through this argument by describing the features of the private market, listing the conditions under which the private market works and fails, and developing the functions of the public sector. Next it delegates these functions to different levels of the public sector. The resulting organization is called *fiscal federalism*. The allocation function under fiscal federalism is then discussed.

### INTRODUCTION

In a free market economy, the operation of the private market defines the role of the public sector. If the private market works, then the public sector, like the Maytag repairman in the long-running television commercial, has little to do. In order to identify the functions of the public sector in general and those of state and local governments in particular, the process begins with the workings of the private market. What makes it work? What makes it fail? What does market failure have to do with the activities of the public sector?

## CASE FOR THE PRIVATE MARKET

In an idealized world, a working private market allocates society's resources *efficiently* (no reorganization of production or consumption decisions could make anyone better off without hurting someone else). A working private market has many attractive features in addition to efficiency: it decentralizes economic power and reduces the need to coerce individuals; it encourages risk taking which can lead to innovation and economic growth; and it drives prices toward average total costs. A centralized planning board would find it difficult to reproduce these features. For an introduction to the operation of the market system, see Lipsey, Steiner, and Purvis (1987) and Ruffin and Gregory (1986).

Such a commendable economic performance should not be taken lightly nor does it come easily. The everyday marketplace must satisfy four conditions to match the idealized marketplace described above.


*Perfect Competition*—Each market must be perfectly competitive. A perfectly competitive market means producers have no power in setting the price. They accept the price as given and sell as much as they can at that price. Economists describe the producer in this situation as a "price taker." This lack of market power leads to efficient, minimum per unit cost production.

*Information*—A major cost of any transaction between buyer and seller, often overlooked or underestimated, is the cost of "shopping around" prior to the purchase. Shopping around includes checking product quality, comparing product prices, and learning about the seller's reputation. Low cost information must be readily available to facilitate a market transaction, assure the buyer that he/she is getting his/her money's worth, and force the seller to respond to competition.

*Complete Markets*—A market must exist for each good for which the cost of production is less than the amount that buyers are willing to pay.

*Exclusion and Rival Consumption*—The private market requires that the exclusion principle hold and that consumption be rival in nature. The *exclusion principle* means that a person must pay the price to consume the product. Nonpayment means no consumption. *Rival consumption* means that one person's consumption of a particular unit of a product prevents another person from consuming *that* particular unit. Most products that people consume meet these two conditions so that people take them for granted.


The case for the private market system rests upon the economic performance that the market promises. That promise fades when any or all of the four conditions—perfect competition, information, complete markets, and exclusion and rival consumption—are not met. At the same time the promise of the private market fades, the role of the public sector becomes more discernible.

## CASE FOR PUBLIC SECTOR INTERVENTION IN THE MARKET

The case for public sector intervention in the market starts out as merely the opposite of the case developed above, but then adds to it. The reason is that the four conditions assure efficiency in the marketplace. Obviously, if they are not satisfied, then the public sector acts to restore market efficiency. Efficiency considerations aside, the public sector also changes market results even if they are arrived at efficiently out of a concern for equity; and maintains the stability of the macroeconomy. The case for the public sector begins with efficiency. (For more detail on the question of public intervention in the market, there are several excellent public finances texts available, Hyman, 1983; Musgrave and Musgrave, 1984; Rosen, 1988; and Stiglitz, 1988.)

### Market Failure

When any or all of the four conditions for the operation of the private market are not satisfied, economists refer to this outcome as market failure. *Market failure* means that the private market economy is no longer efficient. Analysts can trace market failure to a breakdown in each of the four conditions.

*Failure of Competition.* If a seller has the power to influence the market price of a good/service (a *price-setter*), then the market will not be efficient. Competition forces a seller to produce the good at its lowest possible unit cost. A price-setter will select a price that is greater than minimum per unit cost because this price would increase his/her profits. It also leads to market inefficiency. Buyers pay more than they would have for a product. As a result, they have less income remaining to purchase other products. Failure of competition can take several forms; the most extreme one is called a monopoly.

*Costly/Misleading Information.* The private market assumes that buyers and sellers have access to the information that they require to make efficient consumption and production decisions. Often this is not the case. Information like any other good/service may be costly or misleading. Buyers and sellers working with incomplete information will make inefficient allocation decisions. A buyer of an auto, a stereo, or a kitchen appliance requires information to choose the product which meets his/her needs. The less complete the information, the more likely the buyer will make the incorrect selection. That unintentional error in judgment can lead to an inefficient pattern of resource use.

*Incomplete/Nonexistent Markets.* Unlikely as it may seem, there is not always a market for each good/service where the costs of production are less than the amount that people are willing to pay for the good/service. This situation occurs most often in the case of insurance and loans. One example of incomplete markets for loans may be close to home. Prior to 1965, potential students found it difficult to finance their college educations by borrowing the money. Private lending institutions were not active in the education loan market. Incomplete markets force buyers and sellers to restrict their actions and reallocate their resources in a less efficient manner.

*Nonrival Consumption.* The principle of exclusion and rival consumption are necessary conditions for the market to operate efficiently. Not all goods/services satisfy this condition. Any good/service in which one person's consumption of a particular unit does not diminish another person's consumption of that particular unit is called a *public good.* Nonrival consumption characterizes a public good. *Nonrival consumption* means that once the good is provided additional people may consume the public good with no additional cost of providing it. National defense, broadcast radio and TV, street lights, and street musicians are examples of public goods (and nonrival consumption). The images shown on the large TV screen in the local tavern are available to all. One person's TV watching does not interfere with another person's (unless the second person wants to watch another channel, but that is another story whose outcome may depend on the size of the two people).

Public goods represent a problem with which the private market cannot deal. For example, take the street musician. Once she begins to play, anyone who wants to hear her performance can. Some listeners will drop a donation in her music case as a token of their appreciation. Others (like me and you?) listen and leave. The noncontributors recognize that the music is free because the entertainment is nonrival consumption in nature. These people are called *free riders.* They enjoy without paying. This cannot happen with a private good/service where nonpayment means no consumption. Of course, the danger is that too many free riders could mean the end to the street musician's career. One day she does not show up on the corner. Free riders cause the market to misallocate resources for the provision of public goods. Public goods are an important element in the economics of state and local governments. So they will be discussed in more detail later in this chapter.

### Change Market Results

To this point, the case for public sector intervention in the private market has been made on efficiency grounds. There is another reason which justifies public sector action in the marketplace; that is, even though the market is working efficiently, society does not favor the results. Voters use the political process to reach a consensus on what is a fair and equitable distribution of income and goods/services. Some would broaden the meaning of market failure to include the market's inability to meet social goals, as well as the efficiency goal.

Whether the question deals with the distribution of income, or the distribution of goods/services (for example, adequate supply of affordable housing, minimum diet, or equal access to education), society may evaluate the market allocation as inequitable according to an agreed-upon normative (value-based) standard. In this case, society will charge the public sector with altering the market outcome to conform with the normative standard.

**Maintain the Macroeconomy**

Another role for the public sector in the private market is to facilitate trade between consumers and producers, insure full employment of human and physical resources, guard against inflation, and stimulate economic growth. No one buyer or seller, no group of buyers or sellers can guarantee these outcomes. In fact, the behavior of groups of buyers and sellers can work against ease of trade, full employment, price stability, and economic growth.

## ACTIVITIES OF THE PUBLIC SECTOR

The case for the public sector rests on three areas in which market's performance can come up short. Market deficiencies, in turn, define the role of the public sector. The public sector acts to restore efficiency, change market outcomes, and/or maintain the macroeconomy. There are widely accepted names and descriptions for the public sector activities associated with each of these areas.

The *allocation function* covers all public policies that restore an efficient allocation of resource use in the market; such as policies to monitor and maintain competition in the marketplace, assist in the provision of information that consumers and producers require, encourage the creation of markets that the private sector fails to establish, and insure the provision of public goods. Under the allocation function, the public sector usually acquires factor inputs (e.g., labor, land, and capital) to use in the production of public services like police and fire protection, education, highway construction and maintenance, and protection of the environment. The public sector purchases these inputs outright, contracts for them, or in unusual circumstances uses its police power to seize them.

The *redistribution function* includes public policies that make the actual distribution of income and goods/services fair and equitable. These policies usually range from cash transfers from rich to poor, food stamps, farm price supports, and subsidies for rent, mass transportation, elementary and secondary education, and the like. The public sector uses its taxing and spending powers to shift resources from one group or community to another as in the case of state aid to local communities and school aid to local school districts.

The *stabilization function* refers to public policies that are designed to maintain full employment, stabilize prices, achieve a favorable balance of trade, and assure economic growth. Public sector tax and expenditure decisions which influence all these areas are called *fiscal policy*. In general, economists talk about increasing spending and cutting taxes during economic downturns to increase demand for goods/services and cutting spending and raising taxes during economic upswings to decrease demand for goods/services.

Table 4–1 summarizes the presentation to this point. The table starts with the assumptions of the idealized private market, the sources of market failure (broadly

**Table 4-1**
**Market Operations, Market Failures, and Public Sector Intervention**

| Idealized Private Market | Forms of Market Failure | Public Sector Function and Sample Responses |
|---|---|---|
| **Efficiency based on:** ⟹ | **Market Inefficiency Caused by:** ⟹ | **ALLOCATION FUNCTION** |
| Perfect Competition | Failure of Competition | Legal Action Against Firms |
| Information | Costly or Misleading Information | Truth in Advertising |
| Complete Markets | Incomplete or Non-existence of Markets | Subsidized Loans |
| Exclusion Principle & Rival Consumption | Public Goods and Spillovers | Public Provision/Subsidy of Good/Service |
| **Distribution based on:** ⟹ | **Unacceptable Market Results:** ⟹ | **REDISTRIBUTION FUNCTION** |
| Each individual's contribution to the production process. | To conform to an agreed upon fair or equitable distribution of goods/services or income | Food Stamps<br>Subsidize Rents<br>Subsidize Medical Care |
| **Stabilization based on:** ⟹ | **Instability in the Macroeconomy:** ⟹ | **STABILIZATION FUNCTION** |
| Efficient markets always adjust to avoid inflation and recession. | Using tax and expenditure policies to maintain full employment, stabilize prices, achieve a favorable balance of trade, and assure economic growth. | Change Taxes and Expenditure Levels (e.g., cut personal income taxes) |

*Source:* Musgrave and Musgrave, 1989.

defined), to the functions of the public sector justified by these failures combined with general samples of public sector responses.

## DELEGATION OF PUBLIC SECTOR ACTIVITIES

The activities of the public sector have been described. To accomplish the policy goals in each of these areas, public managers must decide what organizational structure is compatible with each of these functions. The structure can run the gamut from centralized decision making to decentralized decision making and any structure in between. The task is to determine whether the functions themselves offer a clue to the appropriate structure. Earlier Oates (1972) and more recently King (1984) have set out a theory of public sector structure organized around the three functions—allocation, redistribution, and stabilization.

### Providing Public Goods/Services

The allocation function plays no favorites when it comes to levels of government. Both the centralized government and the decentralized governments can provide public goods/services. What determines which level? The answer lies with the specific public good in question.

Recall that a public good is nonrival in nature. Nonrival consumption defines a pure public good. While this pure public good is conceptually correct, it is not likely to describe many real world goods/services. Distance, congestion, or traffic could compromise the pure public good.

For example, suppose fire protection is considered a public good. The quality of fire protection services may vary by how far from the firehouse a person lives. In this case, distance affects the quality of the public good. A public beach in New Jersey is also a public good. If you are the solitary figure on the beach, the quality of the public good is certainly different than if you are one of the multitude at the Jersey shore on a summer weekend. In this case, congestion affects the quality of the public good. To capture public goods in the real world, the notion of *impure public goods* is useful. An impure public good reminds the economist that the quality of a public good does not remain constant, but varies with the circumstances which surround the provision of the good.

What does an impure public good have to do with the delegation of the allocation function between/among centralized and decentralized governments? As in the case of fire protection services, every impure public good has a *benefit area*. The benefit area is nothing more than the geographical area over which the impure public good's quality remains unchanged. For some of these goods, the benefit area is small or local; for example, fire protection, recreational services, refuse removal, etc. For some of these goods, the benefit area is larger, or regional; for example, airport services, environmental safeguards, mass transit, etc. And for some of these goods, the benefit area is larger still, or nationwide;

for example, national defense, perhaps elementary and secondary education services.

The point is that these different benefit areas guide the delegation of the allocation function. National benefit areas warrant the attention of the central government; subnational benefit areas call for the attention of the assortment of decentralized governments. This approach explains why the section began by saying that both the centralized government and the decentralized governments can provide public goods/services. The allocation function is shared depending upon the size of the benefit area.

### Establishing Redistribution Policy

Although decentralized governments engage in redistribution, a centralized government performs this function more effectively than decentralized governments. The division of responsibility works itself out like this. The central government announces the overall redistribution policy goals; goals that were reached through the political process. For example, if the public sector redistributes income from rich to poor, then the central government would define the degree of that income redistribution and the method used to accomplish the task.

If the tasks of defining policy goals and establishing the method were left to decentralized governments, then people would have an incentive to move either to avoid a severe redistribution tax burden or to benefit from a more generous transfer payment. That movement would then undermine the redistribution goals. In simple terms the assertion is that if City A plans an income tax on rich people to finance higher welfare payments for poor people, then the rich may move to City B or more poor people may come to City A. For example, New York City in the late 1960s and early 1970s engaged in substantial local redistribution. The fallout was the flight of many businesses and upper and middle income people to the Connecticut and New Jersey suburbs (Morris, 1980).

Decentralized governments can contribute to the redistribution function (Pauly, 1973). In some redistributive programs, the central government sets the broad policy objective, and the decentralized governments design a system of achieving that objective in the local economy. They administer the national program. In the end, the primary responsibility for the redistribution function must reside with the central government.

### Stabilizing the National Economy

Although decentralized governments contribute to and share in the consequences of any stabilization policy measures, the central government is primarily responsible for the stabilization function. The reasons are straightforward enough. In terms of fiscal policy, decentralized governments will have little influence on the macroeconomic goals of a full employment, price stability, a favorable

**Table 4–2**
**Responsibility for Public Sector Activities**

| Public Sector Activity | Level of Government Centralized | Decentralized |
|---|---|---|
| Allocation | --------------Shared-------------- | |
| Redistribution | Primary | Administrative Assistance |
| Stabilization | Primary | None |

*Source*: Musgrave and Musgrave, 1989; Oates, 1972.

balance of trade, and economic growth. Chapter 2 illustrated this point by showing that the performance of the regional economy varies from state to state.

A decentralized government has little control over its own jurisdiction's economic performance because it is often an *open economy*. An open economy means that income is not retained in the jurisdiction because goods/services which people buy are produced in other jurisdictions. If a decentralized government implemented a fiscal policy to increase demand by cutting its taxes, then the bulk of any increased spending associated with that tax cut would occur outside the jurisdiction. So much for using local fiscal policy to expand the local economy.

Another feature of fiscal policy is deficit financing, simply, spending money you do not have. Deficit financing also would not work very well for a decentralized government. A decentralized government would routinely face a consequence of deficit financing which the U.S. economy has only recently encountered. For the decentralized government, the debt would very likely be external debt. External debt is money owed outside of the jurisdiction. In the short term, the jurisdiction would enjoy the spending that the debt finances. In the long term, future residents of the jurisdiction could experience a cut in actual public services quality as more and more of their taxes go to pay interest on the external debt. In fact, most decentralized governments have limits on their debt levels, like the often discussed constitutional amendment that requires a balanced budget.

Monetary policy also does not support a decentralized stabilization policy. If each and every decentralized government controlled its own currency, then the temptation would be to print money to purchase goods/services rather than tax residents; tempting for a local economy, inflationary for a national economy. In short, the primary responsibility for stabilization policy must reside with the centralized government. As a result, the delegation of the public sector's activities follows the pattern in Table 4–2. Few studies have separated the combined federal, state, and local budget into the functional areas which this section describes. Netzer's (1974) study for the 1965–66 fiscal year has carried out the

**Table 4–3**

**Percentage Distribution of Direct Civilian Public Expenditure by Public Sector Activity and Level of Government, 1965–66**

| Public Sector Activity | Expenditure by Level of Government | | | |
|---|---|---|---|---|
| | Federal | State | Local | All Levels |
| Total | 33% | 23% | 44% | 100% |
| Allocation | 26 | 33 | 41 | 100 |
| Redistribution | 61 | 18 | 21 | 100 |
| Stabilization | 64 | 36 | 0 | 100 |

*Source*: Netzer, 1974.

exercise. While there is no claim that current data mirror these results, the results generally support the conclusions of this section. Table 4–3 sums up the study's conclusion.

The delegation of responsibility for public sector activities follows the pattern outlined in the section above. Allocation is shared (F: 26 percent, S: 33 percent, and L: 41 percent); redistribution is primarily federal government work (F: 61 percent); as is stabilization policy (F: 72 percent). While Chapter 3 described the historical and political reasons for the federal system, this division of activities offers an economic theory that justifies the federal system. The section concludes with an economic definition of *fiscal federalism*: "A public sector with both centralized and decentralized levels of decision-making in which choices made at each level concerning the provision of public services are determined largely by the demands for these services of residents . . . in the respective jurisdiction" (Oates, 1972, p. 17).

## ALLOCATION ACTIVITY UNDER FISCAL FEDERALISM

Under fiscal federalism, the different levels of the public sector share the allocation function. Specific public goods/services are assigned according to their benefit areas. This process can achieve an efficient spatial allocation of resources by eliminating free riders, or people who consume the public good/service, but understate the benefit which they derive from it.

To develop this point further, this section will develop the conditions under which resources are allocated efficiently for public goods/services production; look at three possible spatial resource allocation situations (only one of which is efficient) which could arise in a federal system; and make the case for why the federal system will work its way to the efficient spatial allocation solution.

### Step 1: The Rule for the Optimal Provision of Public Goods

Assume for the moment that free riders are not an obstacle to allocating resources efficiently for public goods/service production. People, in effect, reveal

**Figure 4–1**
**Illustration of the Principle of Fiscal Equivalency**

```
BBBBBBBBBBBBBBBBBBBB        PPPPPPPPPPPPPPPPPPPPP       ▪ ▪ ▪ ▪ ▪ ▪ ▪ ▪ ▪ ▪ ▪ ▪ ▪ ▪ ▪ ▪ ▪ ▪
B                  B        P                   P       ▪                      ▪
B     PPPPPPPPP    B        P                   P       ▪                      ▪
B     P       P    B        P      BBBBBBBBBB ▪         ▪                      ▪
B     P       P    B        P      B         ▪         ▪                      ▪
B     PPPPPPPPP    B        P      B         ▪         ▪                      ▪
B                  B        P      B         ▪         ▪                      ▪
BBBBBBBBBBBBBBBBBBBB        PPPPPPPPP ▪ ▪ ▪ ▪ ▪ ▪ ▪ ▪ ▪  ▪ ▪ ▪ ▪ ▪ ▪ ▪ ▪ ▪ ▪ ▪ ▪ ▪ ▪ ▪ ▪ ▪ ▪

        CASE I                      CASE II                     CASE III
```

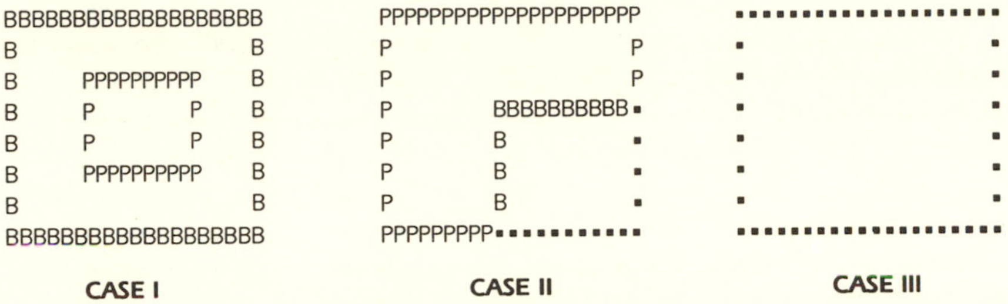

**B**: Benefit Area　　　**P**: Political Jurisdiction　　　▪: Overlap of Benefit Area with Political Jurisdiction

their preferences for the specific amount of a public good/service. People are willing to state what that specific amount of the public good/service is worth to them; what benefit it provides for them. No lying, no underestimating the value, just a straightforward calculation of what the specific amount of a public good/ service is worth to them. They write out a check for that dollar value.

Efficient allocation of resources requires that the total dollar value on the checks collected from all people equals the cost of providing the specific amount of the public good/service. Economists, of course, have a formula for that: the sum of the marginal benefits (the check amounts) equals the marginal cost of production (Samuelson, 1954, 1955). Any deviation from this optimal provision of public goods rule relating the value of benefits and the cost of production is not efficient: either too much is paid for the amount that is provided leading to unused resources or too little is paid to cover the cost for the amount provided leading to losses and a stop in production.

## Step 2: The Principle of Fiscal Equivalency

The next step in this progression is to reintroduce free riders into the process. In addition, the problem of efficient spatial resource allocation for public goods/ services brings together benefit areas and political boundaries. Olson (1969) has examined this problem using three cases shown in Figure 4–1 below.

Case I shows that the benefit area (B) for the public good exceeds the political boundaries (P) of the jurisdiction. The jurisdiction provides a public service whose benefits go beyond the political jurisdiction; for example, a local park used by children from the neighboring towns. Free riders outside of the political jurisdiction can benefit from the provision of the public good/service without paying what it is worth to them; in fact, they might pay nothing at all. In Case I, the sum of the marginal benefits (if they were revealed) is greater than the cost of production. Case I fails the rule for the optimal provision of a public goods/service. If everyone paid the value of his/her marginal benefit, then the public good, the local park, could be expanded or improved. As it is, the park is just congested.

This case provides an example of an economic *spillover*. Spillovers occur in the situation when a third party (someone beyond the immediate buyer or seller) receives the benefit or cost of a consumption or production decision. The exclusion principle is, therefore, violated. In an increasingly complex and congested society, spillovers are commonplace; for example, landscaping your front yard benefits your neighbors, music on a subway may benefit you or annoy you (depending on your musical tastes), and water pollution exacts a cost on anyone who uses water for consumption, business, or recreation.

Case II displays a situation where the benefit area (B) is smaller than the political boundary (P). So all residents are paying for a public good/service, but only some of the people are receiving it; for example, special street lighting in a designated section of town. In Case II, the sum of the marginal benefits (if they were revealed) is less than the cost of production. Case II fails the rule for the optimal provision of a public goods/service.

Case III has the benefit area (B) coinciding with the political boundaries (P). The square box indicates overlapping boundaries. All pay for the public good/service and all receive it. In Case III, the sum of the marginal benefits (assuming that they were revealed) is equal to the cost of production; for example, snow removal. Everyone pays the value of his/her marginal benefit, everyone has his/her street cleared in the winter. Case III satisfies the rule for the optimal provision of a public good/service. When the rule is satisfied because the benefit area and the political boundary coincide, it is called the *principle of fiscal equivalency*. Can political jurisdictions be efficient in the provision of public goods? In other words, can they attain the principal of fiscal equivalency in public service provision? They can come close. Step 3 explains how.

## Step 3: Achieving the Principle of Fiscal Equivalency

Recall the reason why the principle of fiscal equivalency was developed. Centralized and decentralized governments are sharing the allocation function under a federal system. Whatever the level of government, it must perform the allocation function efficiently. Case III above described a situation where the benefit area of the public good/service coincides with the political boundary of the jurisdiction. The result is an absence of free riders. What process would lead to a Case III solution? A Case III solution can be achieved when a community forms, through the movement of people, or the adaptability of the state and local governments.

*Community Formation: The Theory of Clubs.* One opportunity to satisfy the principle of fiscal equivalency occurs at the formation stage of a community. Think of a community as if it were a *club*. A club usually means a voluntary association of people who band together for a particular service or benefit. In this instance, like-minded people are banding together to guarantee that they receive a particular level and quality of public goods/services for an acceptable tax-price. All who receive the public goods/services will pay for them. So at the outset, Case III is satisfied, as is the principle of fiscal equivalency.

How does the process of community formation work? How does the process of community formation depend upon the type of public good/service demanded? How does the process account for crowding effects in the use of the public good/service? What role do the costs of public good/service provision play in this process? Buchanan (1965) developed the *theory of clubs* to answer these questions. This section summarizes his work. (See also, Sandler and Tschirhart, 1980.)

The theory of clubs begins with some simplifying assumptions: the community is formed around one specific public good/service; people are alike in terms of what gives them satisfaction (they have the same utility functions); and they share the costs of the public good/service and its use equally. At the formation stage, the community or club must decide what the level of public good/service will be and how many members will be associated with the community or club.

The answer to these questions starts with the relationship between total cost per member and the number of members for any given level of public good/service. The more members that the community or club accepts, the lower the total cost per member. Some frugal (if not downright cheap) member will suggest that the community or club admit an unlimited number of new members to lower the total cost per member to almost zero. Is that a wise suggestion? Be careful of free services!

Each new member generates congestion costs. In some sense, each new member detracts from the quality of the public good/service that the community or club offers. Think about the consequences of too many people at the municipal pool, or strolling through the park, or using the public campsite. So the rule for the admission of new members should be that the reduction in total cost per member associated with each new member should be greater than or equal to the increase in the congestion cost associated with each new member. (In economic jargon, the marginal decrease in membership fees should at least equal the marginal increase in congestion costs.) This rule holds for any given amount of public good/service. For service level S', this rule must be satisfied. There is some optimum membership size M' associated with S' that meets the rule. If the community or club expands the level of public good/service from S' to S'', then the rule will dictate a change in the optimum number of community or club members from M' to M''. Figure 4–2a shows this outcome.

Since the total cost of public good/service level S'' is greater than S', the savings associated with each new member is greater. For the same reason, the congestion costs associated with each new member will be smaller. So a public good/service level increase leads to an increase in the number of members in

**Figure 4–2**
**Illustration of the Theory of Clubs**

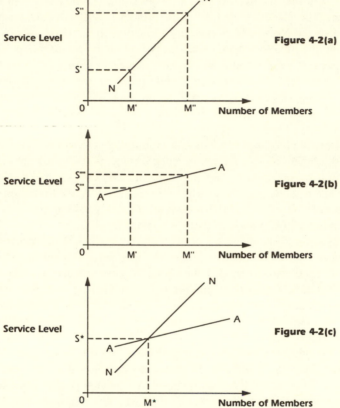

Figure 4-2(a)

Figure 4-2(b)

Figure 4-2(c)

*Source*: James W. Buchanan, "An Economic Theory of Clubs," *Economica* 32 (February 1965), pp. 1–14. Reprinted by permission of *Economica*.

the community or club. In fact, the line NN shows a range of public good/service level-number of members combinations of which (M', S') and (M'', S'') are two examples.

The line NN shows the optimum number of members a community/club should have for each level of the public good/service. It does not indicate what the level of the public good/service should be. Determining the optimum level of the public good/service is the immediate task at hand. Another rule will be established. For any given number of members of the community or club, the additional benefit associated with increasing the level of the public good/service must be greater than or equal to the additional cost of increasing the level of the public good/service. (In economic jargon, the marginal benefit must be greater than or equal to the marginal cost of increasing the level of the public good/

service). Figure 4–2b illustrates this procedure. For M' members of the community or club, the weighting of additional benefits and additional costs leads to an optimal level of service of S'' '.

What if the number of members of the community or club increases from M' to M''? More people means crowding conditions in gaining access to the public good/service. Therefore, the additional benefit to each member of the community or club associated with an increase in the level of the public good/service should increase. The increase relieves the crowding conditions to some degree. On the cost side, more members also means more people are sharing the additional cost of an increase in the level of the public good/service to the community or club. Lower costs and higher benefits translate into a higher level of the public good/service from S'' ' to S'' ''. So the level of public good/service associated with M' members is S'' ''. If this logic were repeated for each new membership level, the line AA would be traced out in Figure 4–2b.

The answer to the question (that began all of this) what the level of public good/service will be and how many members will be associated with the community or club, is close at hand. Line AA is imposed on line NN. This is done in Figure 4–2c. The optimum level of the public good/service and the associated optimum number of members of the community or club occurs at the intersection of NN and AA, or M* and S*. This point represents the optimum public good/service level for a given number of members and the optimum number of members given a level of public good/service. The community or club satisfies Case III and, therefore, the principle of fiscal equivalency.

*Movement of People: Tiebout Model.* Tiebout (1956) constructed a model (commonly referred to as the *Tiebout model*) based on the premise that in general "like people tend to congregate." Not exactly a very startling proposition. Look around your own neighborhood. People in these neighborhoods may have much in common. This assumption is more easily accepted than those of many other economic models.

In fact, if people find themselves in neighborhoods where they feel "out of place," often they move away. Tiebout stresses the mobility of people, a very common American phenomenon. The term that is often applied to this assumption is that people "vote with their feet." If someone does not like what they experience, they can go elsewhere. While this assumption is useful, appealing, and may even describe individual behavior, it can be pushed too far and lose its usefulness. There are many limits to mobility; for example, insufficient funds, racial discrimination, and family and social networks.

For Tiebout, the term "like people" did not have any racial or ethnic connotation. He was, in fact, classifying people by their willingness and ability to pay taxes and their demand for public goods/services. Some people choose high tax, high public service communities; others choose low tax, low public service places. Everyone thinks that they have chosen high tax, low public service communities; hence, the chronic question: What am I getting for my taxes?

The Tiebout model sets up a marketplace for selecting a local community.

People sort themselves based on their tax and spend preferences (Buchanan and Goetz, 1972; Reschovsky, 1979). In this way, the benefit area coincides with the political boundary of a jurisdiction (Case III above). Fiscal equivalency is achieved and this process eliminates free riders. There is a list of assumptions which make the Tiebout model work.

Research since the publication of the Tiebout model has suggested changes in some of these assumptions (Hamilton 1975a, 1975b; Bewley, 1981). Whether the model is appealing or simplistic, the assumptions are worth noting. They are:

1. Individuals (called consumer/voters) are fully mobile. The cost of moving is not a consideration. Think of mobility as a costless activity.
2. Individuals possess complete information about the tax and spend policies in each community. (See your local real estate agent.)
3. There are a large number of communities from which to choose. Each individual can find one which suits his/her tax and spend preferences.
4. Employment is not a restriction to moving. Jobs are available.
5. Public services show no external (dis)economies between communities.
6. There is an optimal (ideal) community size based on the cost of providing public services to various numbers of people.
7. Communities encourage individuals to settle if the communities are too small (less than their optimal size and experiencing overcapacity in their public service system). Communities also discourage individuals from settling if the communities are too big (larger than their optimal size and experiencing undercapacity in their public service system).

Some of these original assumptions may make you shake your head, raise your eyebrows, or whatever other physical gesture you use to express disagreement. A sample of reservations about the Tiebout assumption would include: individuals are not fully mobile; they often possess incomplete tax and spend information about communities; and employment is a restriction in moving from place to place. However, do not dismiss the Tiebout model as out of hand. There is some evidence that supports its usefulness.

Since 1956 when the Tiebout article appeared, researchers have tested it again and again (Zodrow, 1983). The tests take the form of capitalization studies. The capitalization studies are based on the notion that if individuals move around to find their preferred tax and spend combination, then the different combinations should reveal themselves in community property values. For example, holding all other features of the community constant, communities with higher quality public services should also possess higher property values; those with lower quality public services lower property values. The evidence is unsettled. Oates (1969) presented evidence for capitalization in a sample of 53 communities in northern New Jersey; Edel and Sclar (1974) disputed the evidence outright by denying that capitalization takes place in a perfectly operating Tiebout-like world; and Meadows (1976) finds a much lower level of capitalization present than

Oates did by redoing the analysis using a different analytical technique. What do all these mean? The capitalization argument alone is not going to settle the argument about whether the Tiebout model accurately describes everyday location decisions.

Although the evidence is ambiguous about the Tiebout model, the model serves as a useful device to argue that decentralized governments can efficiently perform the allocation function. There are enough examples of families who chose their communities based on the quality of the school system, retirees who congregate in "retirement" communities, and communities that flaunt their relative tax position to attract residents to support the Tiebout model as an insightful analytical tool.

*Adaptability of State and Local Governments.* The last approach looks at adaptability of government organizations. Individuals need not move around to reach a Case III solution. They can stay in their communities and pressure the government to respond to their tax and spend preferences by changing how government is organized to deliver services. The Advisory Commission on Intergovernmental Relations (ACIR) over the years (1973 and 1974a) and Hallman (1977) have documented adaptability of the federal system to provide public goods/services efficiently. The evidence shows the development of many different forms of governmental organizations which could be interpreted as an attempt to satisfy the principle of fiscal equivalency (in effect, to move from a Case I or Case II situation to a Case III situation); thereby achieving allocative efficiency. Chapter 3 already reviewed these structural changes when it discussed special districts, intergovernmental service agreements, transfer of functions, confederation, unification, and federation.

## SUMMARY

1. The case for the private market rests upon four conditions: perfect competition, information, complete markets, and exclusion and rival consumption.

2. Private market failure justifies the intervention of the public sector. Market failure that leads to inefficiency can be attributed to a violation of one of the four conditions stated above, especially the presence of the public goods and free riders. Other forms of market failure are associated with an unfair distribution of resources and instability in the macroeconomy.

3. The public sector has three broad functions: allocation, redistribution, and stabilization. These three define the nature of public sector actions in the private market economy.

4. These three functions lend themselves to a federal system of government in which the centralized and the decentralized government share the allocation function; the centralized government has primary responsibility for redistribution and stabilization activities.

5. The principle of fiscal equivalency and the processes by which it is achieved, namely, the theory of clubs, the Tiebout model, and the adaptability of governments, set out the general guidelines for sharing the allocation function in a federal system.

# CHAPTER 5

## State and Local Government Public Service Responsibilities and Expenditures

**PREVIEW**

This chapter draws on the political history and economic theory just completed to develop guidelines for the delegation of service responsibilities in a federal system. The organization of service delivery required by the guidelines is matched against the actual organization of service delivery. With a sense of "who does what," the next task is to prepare a profile of the current level of state-local public service spending. A conceptual model is presented to explain state-local spending differences. This is followed by a survey of empirical research on state-local expenditure decisions. The chapter concludes with a discussion of selected, contemporary state-local expenditure issues.

**INTRODUCTION**

The political history and the economic theory developed earlier, although general in nature, serve a very specific purpose. The material provided the conceptual foundation for assigning service responsibilities in a federal system. In this chapter, we begin the descent from the nation's founding documents and economists' abstract concepts to practical guidelines for the delegation of service responsibilities in a federal system. These guidelines answer the "who does what" question.

## GUIDELINES FOR THE DELEGATION OF SERVICE RESPONSIBILITIES

Three central government activities spring from the nation's founding documents. They are constitutional in nature (Durenberger, 1982). First, the central government should secure individual rights and liberties that the Constitution guarantees to all Americans; for example, voting rights, equal employment opportunities, and legal services. Second, the central government should defend U.S. interests and conduct foreign relations in the world community. Third, the central government should promote economic growth and regulate interstate commerce, the stabilization function. Most observers would agree that the central government should engage in these activities. Many other governmental activities are subnational in nature. Therefore, they must be assigned to a state and/or local government.

In the case of the allocation of public goods/services, the size of the benefit area of the public good/service is very influential in determining whether the central or decentralized level of government is responsible for the particular service. (Refer to Tables 4–2 and 4–3 and Figure 4–1.) However, the size of the benefit area is not the only consideration in determining the delegation of service responsibility. The choice of a political jurisdiction that will be responsible for the provision of a public service should be based on the following guidelines: economies of scale, fiscal equivalency, fiscal adequacy, political accountability, and administrative effectiveness (Hirsch, 1965; Hallman, 1973; ACIR 1974b, 1974c; Breton and Scott, 1978; Break, 1980). Let's describe each element.

*Economies of scale* in this context means that the responsible political jurisdiction should be large enough to take advantage of falling average unit costs in service provision. For example, as the number of people served increases, the per person cost of serving them falls, holding service quality constant. Of course, total costs are increasing. Conversely, a political jurisdiction should not be so small that it experiences diseconomies of scale (increasing average unit costs) in service provision.

*Fiscal equivalency* refers to the principle of fiscal equivalency. The benefit area of the public good/service must coincide with the political boundary. This equivalency assures that the sum of marginal benefits of the service to the people is equal to the marginal cost of the service to the people. There are no free riders. No one outside the political jurisdiction receives the benefit of the service.

*Fiscal adequacy* requires that the political jurisdiction which is responsible for a specific service must have the fiscal resources to pay for the provision of that service.

*Political accountability* means that government officials who are responsible for the provision of public services are accountable to the residents of the jurisdiction. People know who is in charge; they have access to that individual; they can hold that individual responsible for the quality of the delivered service.

*Administrative effectiveness* includes the management know-how and the legal authority to discharge any obligations in delivering the public service.

Table 5–1 applies these guidelines to 11 state-local service categories. State and local government officials take into account these criteria in delegating service responsibilities. These criteria are not the stuff of abstract discussions, but useful public management considerations. The extreme left column in Table 5–1 contains the general service category (e.g., Education, Fire, etc.) and a brief description of specific services in that category (e.g., elementary and secondary education, fire companies, etc.) The middle five columns list the elements of the criteria for the delegation of service responsibilities. The Yes-No format in Table 5–1 answers a series of four questions which you should keep in mind as you read Table 5–1.

1. Does the nature of the public service lead public officials to expect significant economies of scale in the provision of the service? (Yes, if economies of scale are expected. No, if they are not expected.)
2. Is the public service likely to satisfy the principle of fiscal equivalency; that is, Case III in Figure 4–1 and no free riders?
3. Should financial resources be redistributed (from "rich" to "poor" jurisdictions) so that resource-poor jurisdictions can provide an efficient amount of the public service?
4. Is political accountability essential for the efficient provision of the public service?

The last question, not in the Yes-No format, is:

5. Based on management techniques and legal authority, what is the appropriate size for the public service area—local or areawide?

The extreme right column indicates which subnational government unit—state, county, municipality/township, school district, or special district—was the dominant service provider in 1985–86 and in how many states. Dominant service provider is defined as the level of government that pays for at least 55 percent of the total direct state-local expenditure.

Two services illustrate what Table 5–1 tells us about the delegation of state-local public services. Elementary and secondary education is not likely to generate economies of scale (Hirsch, 1960; Riew, 1966; Kiesling, 1967). (The answer is No to the first question.) Educational services are likely to produce benefits which exceed the political jurisdiction. A specific level of educational services benefits the individual pupils and members of the local jurisdiction, perhaps, the state, the region, and the nation. That is why the answer is No to the second question. State governments redistribute resources to fund education in poor jurisdictions so the answer is Yes to the third question. Many citizens consider local political control of school operations essential to the effective provision of this service; therefore, the answer is Yes to the fourth question. Last, the administrative unit that possesses the legal authority and managerial know-how to operate an education program is judged to be "local" in geographic size. As the last column reports, forty states place the responsibility for the

## Table 5–1
### Delegation of Service Responsibilities: Theory versus Practice

| State-Local Service Description | Guidelines for Delegation of Service Responsibilities | | | | | Dominant Service Provider, 1985-6 (Number of States in parentheses) |
|---|---|---|---|---|---|---|
| | Economies of Scale | Fiscal Equivalency | Fiscal Adequacy | Political Accountability | Administrative Effectiveness | |
| Education<br>Elementary & secondary | No | No | Yes | Yes | Local | School Districts (40)<br>Counties (4) |
| Fire<br>Fire Companies | No | Yes | No | Yes | Local | Municipalities (49)<br>County (1) |
| Health<br>Hospitals | Yes | No | Yes | No | Areawide | Shared: States, Counties, and Municipalities (23)<br>State (21) |
| Housing<br>Public housing management & construction | No | No | Yes | Yes | Local | Shared: States, Municipalities, and Special Districts (20)<br>Special Districts (15) |
| Libraries | No | Yes | No | Yes | Local | Municipalities (24)<br>Shared: Counties and Municipalities (12) |
| Parks and Recreation<br>Playgrounds, local parks, skating rinks & swimming pools | No | Yes | No | Yes | Local | Municipalities (28)<br>Shared: States, Counties, and Municipalities (16) |
| Police<br>Patrol, Traffic Control Routine Investigation | No | Yes | No | Yes | Local | Municipalities (37)<br>Shared: Counties and & Municipalities (12) |
| Refuse<br>Collection | No | Yes | No | No | Local | Municipalities (44)<br>County (4) |
| Streets & Highways<br>Local streets & sidewalks, repairs, cleaning, snow removal, & lighting | No | No | No | No | Local | Counties (23)<br>Municipalities (21) |
| Transportation<br>Mass transit, airport, & port facilities | Yes | No | No | Yes | Areawide | Municipalities (22)<br>State (9) |
| Water and Sewer<br>Local mains | Yes | No | No | No | Areawide | Municipalities (34)<br>Shared: Special Districts and Municipalities (14) |

*Sources*: Hirsch, 1965; ACIR, 1974b, 1974c.

provision of elementary and secondary education services predominantly in the hands of school districts; four states assign this service to the counties. The actual delegation of responsibility is consistent with the elements of the criteria.

Police activities are the second service. These are not likely to generate significant economies of scale (Schmandt and Ross, 1960). (The answer is No to the first question.) This fact argues for smaller versus larger service areas. Police services are not likely to produce benefits which exceed the political jurisdiction (Pack and Pack, 1978; Gonzalez and Mehay, 1985). That is why the answer is Yes to the second question. Police services are funded out of local resources. There is no redistribution of resources to fund police in poor jurisdictions so the answer is No to the third question. Many citizens consider local political control of the police department operations essential to the provision of this service; therefore, the answer is Yes to the fourth question. Last, the administrative unit that possesses the legal authority and managerial know-how to operate a police force to provide the services listed is judged to be "local" in geographic size. As the last column reports, in 37 states police services are delegated to the municipalities while in 12 states these services are shared by counties and municipalities. Given the answer to the five questions, this actual delegation is generally expected. With these two illustrations, the rest of Table 5–1 can be understood for the remaining 9 public services.

Of course, individual states' characteristics influence the outcome of the actual service assignment decision. The state-by-state variation can be seen by reading down the extreme right column. Even with this variation, state and local officials have evolved a system of service responsibilities that is generally consistent with the guidelines. The guidelines add to the explanation of how and why jurisdictions act in accordance with the theory of clubs and the Tiebout model and why jurisdictions use the different governmental organizations. Why might subnational governments enter into local service agreements to provide parks and recreation services? Such an agreement might achieve fiscal equivalency. Why might health services be transferred from municipalities to counties? Such a transfer might take advantage of economies of scale and administrative effectiveness.

Our discussion of government organization has covered the distance from political history and economic theory to a specific set of practical guidelines to determine "who does what" in a federal system. This subject probably generates little attention among citizens. However, the next topic has always generated controversy among citizens, their elected public servants, politicians, and the members of the bureaucracy. That subject is state-local government expenditure levels.

## STATE-LOCAL GOVERNMENT EXPENDITURES: AN OVERVIEW

A look at state-local government expenditures offers another perspective on what these levels of government do; it reveals what their priorities are; and it

**Table 5–2**
**Profile of Selected State-Local Expenditure Items, 1986–87 (per capita)**

| Selected Expenditure Items (1) & (2) | United States Average | Range (3) | Ratio of High to Low States (All States) (4) | Ratio of High to Low States (Excl. Highest 5 & Lowest 5) (5) |
|---|---|---|---|---|
| Current Expenditure | $2355 | $1629 - 8167 | 5.01 | 1.52 |
| Elementary & Secondary Education | 644 | 421 - 1828 | 4.34 | 1.51 |
| Public Welfare | 339 | 157 - 658 | 4.19 | 2.65 |
| Hospitals | 165 | 40 - 380 | 9.50 | 3.62 |
| Health | 69 | 27 - 151 | 5.59 | 1.98 |
| Highways | 215 | 134 - 1112 | 8.30 | 2.04 |
| Police | 101 | 43 - 211 | 4.91 | 2.12 |
| Fire | 45 | 16 - 97 | 6.06 | 2.82 |
| Corrections | 68 | 21 - 174 | 8.29 | 2.88 |
| Parks & Recreation | 45 | 15 - 98 | 6.53 | 3.10 |
| Sewerage | 61 | 7 - 176 | 25.14 | 2.44 |
| Interest on Debt | 172 | 77 - 1802 | 23.40 | 2.46 |

Notes:  (1) Current expenditures excludes capital outlay.
(2) The sum of the itemized expenditures does not equal the total. This itemized list is only a partial list.
(3) Range is simply the spread between the lowest spending state and the highest spending state.
(4) The ratio of high to low spending state is the high spending state divided by the low spending state.
(5) The right most column is the high spending state divided by the low spending state after excluding the top 5 and bottom 5 states.

*Source*: U.S. Bureau of Census, *Census of Governments*,1988.

highlights variations in spending. This look is comparable to sneaking a peek at someone's checkbook.

Table 5–2 gets the examination underway. This table provides a profile of selected state-local government expenditure items for 1986–87. The expenditures are for current operations (capital outlay is excluded) and presented in per capita terms (spending per person). The revenues that finance these expenditures come from all sources: taxes, charges, and intergovernmental grants. The data are taken from the U.S. Bureau of Census, *Government Finances*. The average per capita spending in the United States by state-local governments in 1986–87 was $2,355. Although eleven expenditure items are listed, ranging from education to interest on debt, five items (elementary and secondary education, public welfare, hospitals, highways, and interest on debt) represent approximately two-thirds of the $2,355 figure. If state and local governments were looked at separately, then the priorities for state governments would be education, public welfare, and aid to local governments. The comparable list for local governments would be education, police, and sanitation.

Table 5–2 also offers several glimpses at spending variations in the U.S. federal system. For example, while the overall average per capita spending is $2,355, it may vary from a high of $8,167 (Alaska) to a low of $1,629 (Arkansas). The ratio of the highest spending state to the lowest spending state is 5.01; that is, Alaska spends $5.01 for every $1.00 Arkansas spends. Since Alaska's figure is something of an anomaly, another view is needed. An alternative view that is less influenced by the behavior of the high and low spending states is to drop off the five highest spending states and the five lowest spending states and recalculate the ratio. This gives a ratio of the sixth-ranked state (Massachusetts $2,720) to the forty-fifth ranked state (Kentucky $1,794). That ratio is 1.52; that is, Massachusetts spends $1.52 for every $1.00 Kentucky spends.

Comparable figures are calculated for each of the expenditure categories. The variation in per capita current expenditure across these items is the natural outcome of a decentralized governmental system. Using the conservatively estimated ratio in the extreme right column, spending on hospitals (3.62) appears to have the largest gap from top to bottom state, followed by parks and recreation (3.10) and corrections (2.88). Spending on education (1.51), highways (2.04), sewerage (2.44), and health (1.98) show smaller gaps.

What is the tie-in between spending variation and the delegation of service responsibilities? As long as the responsibility for the provision of the service is delegated in a fashion that satisfies the theory of clubs, the Tiebout model, and the guidelines presented in Table 5–1, the variation may be efficient, as well as the desired outcome within a federal system. The fact that per capita fire expenditures vary from $16 to $97, a ratio of 6.06 (or more conservatively 2.82) need not trouble citizens, politicians, or analysts because the actual responsibility for fire services appears to satisfy the theory of clubs, the Tiebout model, and the guidelines in Table 5–1. Some people prefer the $16 level of service; while others demand the $97 level of service. People find their way to the appropriate local jurisdiction. And all is well in the federal system.

Does the conclusion change in the case of education, health and hospitals, and public welfare? Should society tolerate spending differences in these services? Does it matter that these services appear to violate the principle of fiscal equivalency; that is, the benefit area may exceed the political boundary (Case I)? Think about these questions as we take another look at the spending data.

Table 5–3 also displays per capita state-local expenditures for 1986–87. This table divides the spending between state and local governments and shows the state government percentage share of the combined state-local spending. These data tell us, in effect, who is doing the spending regardless of who is raising

**Table 5–3**

**State and Local Government Spending by Level of Government, 1986–87 (per capita)**

| Region & State | Spending by Level of Government State | Local | %State | Region & State | Spending by Level of Government State | Local | %State |
|---|---|---|---|---|---|---|---|
| USA | $ 934 | $1410 | 39.8% | | | | |
| N.E. | | | | E.S.C. | | | |
| ME | 1207 | 991 | 54.9 | KY | $ 956 | $ 838 | 53.3% |
| NH | 918 | 1031 | 47.1 | TN | 800 | 984 | 44.8 |
| VT | 1474 | 1018 | 59.1 | AL | 896 | 932 | 49.0 |
| MA | 1405 | 1296 | 52.0 | MS | 730 | 1059 | 40.8 |
| RI | 1511 | 1066 | 58.6 | | | | |
| CT | 1294 | 1274 | 50.4 | W.S.C. | | | |
| M.A. | | | | AR | 802 | 827 | 49.2 |
| | | | | LA | 1026 | 1101 | 48.2 |
| NY | 1199 | 2299 | 34.3 | OK | 879 | 1025 | 46.2 |
| NJ | 1081 | 1187 | 46.9 | TX | 637 | 1266 | 33.5 |
| PA | 882 | 1244 | 41.5 | | | | |
| | | | | Mt. | | | |
| E.N.C. | | | | MT | 1080 | 1331 | 44.8 |
| OH | 856 | 1307 | 39.6 | ID | 760 | 1001 | 43.2 |
| IN | 796 | 1123 | 41.5 | WY | 1392 | 2231 | 38.4 |
| IL | 895 | 1294 | 40.9 | CO | 840 | 1534 | 35.4 |
| MI | 1135 | 1525 | 42.7 | NM | 1048 | 1187 | 46.9 |
| WI | 1000 | 1557 | 39.1 | AZ | 763 | 1420 | 35.0 |
| | | | | UT | 1070 | 1084 | 49.7 |
| W.N.C. | | | | NV | 813 | 1489 | 35.3 |
| MN | 1023 | 1809 | 36.1 | Pac. | | | |
| IA | 928 | 1255 | 42.5 | | | | |
| MO | 738 | 1032 | 41.7 | WA | 1015 | 1302 | 43.8 |
| ND | 1427 | 1086 | 56.8 | OR | 1036 | 1454 | 41.6 |
| SD | 1014 | 952 | 51.6 | CA | 911 | 1858 | 32.9 |
| NE | 885 | 1268 | 41.1 | AK | 5211 | 2938 | 63.9 |
| KS | 775 | 1376 | 36.0 | HI | 1815 | 505 | 78.2 |
| S.A. | | | | | | | |
| DE | 1579 | 1086 | 59.2 | | | | |
| MD | 1045 | 1272 | 45.1 | | | | |
| VA | 892 | 1172 | 43.2 | | | | |
| WV | 1047 | 936 | 52.8 | | | | |
| NC | 764 | 1046 | 42.2 | | | | |
| SC | 911 | 932 | 49.4 | | | | |
| GA | 737 | 1297 | 36.2 | | | | |
| FL | 602 | 1325 | 31.2 | | | | |

*Source*: U.S. Bureau of Census, *Government Finances*, 1988.

the revenue. On average across the nation, state governments spend $934 versus local governments $1,410, or 39.8 percent of the total state-local spending. State governments dominate in Hawaii (78.2 percent), Alaska (63.9 percent), Delaware (59.2 percent), Vermont (59.1 percent), and Rhode Island (58.6 percent). Local governments dominate in Florida, California, Texas, New York, Arizona, and Nevada. This division reflects individual residents' preferences concerning the delegation of function responsibilities and the fiscal capacity of the state versus the local governments.

Table 5–4 takes the last look at per capita state-local expenditures; this time

Table 5–4
Comparison of Level and Growth of Current Per Capita State-Local
Expenditures

```
-----------------------------------------------------------------
              Average Level in 1986-87:      $2355
      Average Real Growth from 1982-83 to 1986-87:   13.56%
-----------------------------------------------------------------
```

| High and Falling (8) | | High and Rising (9) | |
|---|---|---|---|
| Alaska | 347/52 | Wyoming | 154/101 |
| Michigan | 113/72 | New York | 149/126 |
| Rhode Island | 110/61 | California | 120/134 |
| Wisconsin | 109/90 | Minnesota | 120/102 |
| North Dakota | 107/85 | Massachusetts | 115/140 |
| Oregon | 106/31 | New Jersey | 114/149 |
| Vermont | 106/97 | Delaware | 113/157 |
| Montana | 102/88 | Connecticut | 109/138 |
| | | Colorado | 101/105 |

| Low and Falling (22) | | Low and Rising (11) | |
|---|---|---|---|
| Hawaii | 99/-27 | Maine | 94/124 |
| Washington | 99/80 | Arizona | 93/125 |
| Maryland | 98/16 | Ohio | 92/107 |
| Nevada | 98/12 | Pennsylvania | 91/104 |
| New Mexico | 95/ 5 | Utah | 91/117 |
| Illinois | 93/74 | Virginia | 88/114 |
| Iowa | 93/39 | Florida | 82/128 |
| Kansas | 91/47 | Indiana | 82/107 |
| Nebraska | 91/77 | South Carolina | 78/141 |
| Louisiana | 90/15 | Tennessee | 76/113 |
| Georgia | 86/88 | Missouri | 75/105 |
| West Virginia | 84/99 | | |
| New Hampshire | 83/58 | | |
| South Dakota | 83/64 | | |
| Oklahoma | 81/60 | | |
| Texas | 81/85 | | |
| Alabama | 78/62 | | |
| North Carolina | 77/91 | | |
| Kentucky | 76/96 | | |
| Mississippi | 76/75 | | |
| Idaho | 75/87 | | |
| Arkansas | 69/81 | | |

*Source*: Calculated from U.S. Bureau of Census, *Government Finances*, 1982–83 and 1986–87.

on a state-by-state basis. The presentation of the data takes into account the relative level of state-local spending in 1986–87 and the relative real growth rate in spending from 1982–83 to 1986–87. Thus, two dimensions of state-local spending behavior is captured: level and growth. Based on these two dimensions, the fifty states are divided into four groups.

The method used to calculate relative level and growth and then divide the states is as follows. (A similar method has been used by ACIR, 1977a.) The procedure begins with the level of spending in 1986–87. The average per capita spending level for the United States is $2,355, as shown in Table 5–2. To estimate each state's relative spending level, the individual state's spending is divided by the national average. The result is multiplied by 100. For example, New Jersey spends $2,692 per person. If that figure is divided by the national average and multiplied by 100, the rounded-off result is 114. In other words, New Jersey spent approximately 14 percent more than the national average on per capita state-local public services. Generally, any state whose level number (the first number listed next to the state's name) is greater than 100 spends *more* than the national average. These states are placed in the High category, that is, higher than the national spending average. There are seventeen of these states.

If the same method is used on Louisiana which spent $2,127, the result would be 90, or 90 percent the national average. (Remember to round-off to a whole number.) Again, any state whose level number is less than 100 spends less than the national average. These states are placed in the Low category, that is, lower than the national spending average. There are thirty-three of these states.

The procedure continues with the real growth in state-local government expenditures. The same method is used to calculate relative growth. The average real growth rate in per capita spending for the United States during this specific period is 13.56 percent. To estimate each state's relative real growth rate, the individual state's real growth rate is divided by the national average. The result is multiplied by 100. Again, let's use New Jersey as an example. New Jersey's actual real growth over these three years is 20.20 percent. If that figure is divided by the national average and multiplied by 100, the rounded-off result is 149. In other words, New Jersey's spending grew by approximately 49 percent more than the national average. Generally, any state whose growth number (the second number listed next to the state's name) is greater than 100 grew more than the national average. These states are placed in the Rising category, that is, rising faster than the national growth average. There are twenty of these states.

If the same method is used on Louisiana whose expenditures grew by 2.03 percent in the period, the result would be 15, or 15 percent the national average growth rate. (Remember to round-off to a whole number.) Again, any state whose level number is less than 100 grew by less than the national average. These states are placed in the Falling category, that is, they are falling relative to the national growth average. There are thirty of these states. This procedure produces four categories: High and Rising, High and Falling, Low and Rising, and Low and Falling with respect to the national level of spending and the national growth rate in spending. It is a procedure that dramatically illustrates the relative standing of each state on these two dimensions.

Table 5–4 lists the states by name and the total in each category. States that are traditionally associated with high spending—New York, Minnesota, California, Michigan, New Jersey, Massachusetts, and Wisconsin—live up to their reputations. While the southern tier of the country from the East Coast (Virginia, North Carolina, South Carolina, Georgia and Florida) to the energy states and the sun-parched states (Louisiana, Texas, and Arizona) joins with many of the plains states (Kansas, North Dakota, South Dakota, and Nebraska) to dominate the low spending categories. In many instances, a state's position in Table 5–4 is directly related to the performance of its regional economy. As far as the four categories, Table 5–4 shows nine states in the High and Rising group, eight states in the High and Falling group, eleven states in the Low and Rising group, and twenty-two states in the Low and Falling group.

Tables 5–2 through 5–4 certainly illustrate the variation in per capita state-local government expenditures. The next section describes a conceptual model that explains what characteristics are associated with these variations. That information can predict future variations, and help to counter them, if need be.

## A MODEL OF STATE-LOCAL GOVERNMENT EXPENDITURE DECISIONS

The spending decision on state-local public goods/services is similar to the one that everyone faces as they walk through the "mom and pop" corner store or the sprawling shopping mall. What do I want to buy? Is it available? What is the item's price? Can I afford it? Any model of state-local government spending decisions begins with these questions because they embody the elements of supply and demand.

Just like the individual consumer, the spending decision on a state-local public good/service must bring together the demand for the public good/service, how the public good/service is made (production), and the cost of this production. Any model of state-local expenditure decision process will explain how these elements come together. Siegel (1966) has set out the framework of such a model. As with many models, it simplifies reality, but tries to retain the essential relationships. Siegel's model illustrates how "population, production conditions, factor costs, income, outside finance, and conditions of private supply" influence state-local spending on a given public good/service. Figure 5–1 captures the essential features of the model.

There are four quadrants. Quadrant I is a modified demand schedule. It shows the relationship between the jurisdiction's population and the quantity demanded of a specific public good/service. Quadrant I assumes that there is a direct (positive) relationship (up to some point) between the population and the level of the public good/service. Quadrant II captures production conditions; what economists call the production function. It shows the relationship between factor inputs (e.g., land, labor, and capital) into the production process and quantity of public good/service output obtained. It assumes a direct relationship between inputs and output; that is, all factors increase at a proportionate rate and result in increasing output, first at increasing rates, then decreasing rates. Quadrant III represents factor costs. This quadrant translates physical amounts of the factor inputs into dollars. What does it cost to purchase these inputs? Again, a positive relationship exists between inputs and costs; as inputs increase, costs increase. Last, Quadrant IV shows the relationship between population and dollars; spe-

**Figure 5–1**
**Framework for State-Local Government Expenditure Decisions**

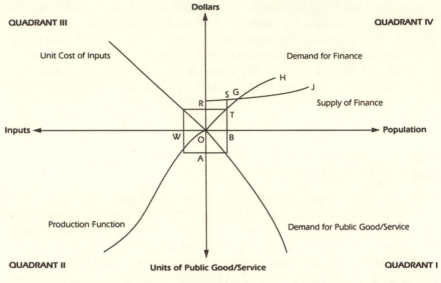

*Source*:  Barry Siegel, "On the Positive Theory of State and Local Expenditures," in *Public Finance and Welfare*, ed. Paul Kleinsorge (Eugene: University of Oregon Books, 1966). Reprinted by permission of University of Oregon Books.

cifically, the demand for finance and supply of finance. *Demand for finance* is derived from Quadrants I through III in a manner explained below. *Supply of finance* is the amount of revenue raised from the jurisdiction's revenue system, as the population changes, while holding the tax and nontax revenue structure fixed. In other words, tax rates are fixed, but population changes affect revenue collections. Both schedules assume a direct relationship between population and demand for and supply of finance.

With the descriptions behind us, let us work through Figure 5–1. For a given jurisdiction population, OB, the quantity demanded of a specific public service will be OA (Quadrant I). To produce OA the jurisdiction requires OW factor inputs (Quadrant II). OW factor inputs cost OR dollars (Quadrant III). Quadrant IV and the finance issue is next.

The demand for finance schedule, OH, is derived from and takes its shape from the information in Quadrants I through III; in the same manner that the population-level of public good/service and inputs-cost relationship were traced out above. Thus, the demand for finance schedule is highly sensitive to changes in any of the schedules in Quadrants I through III. If people demand a level of public good/service (like OB), then it is likely that they will demand the dollars (like OR) to finance that public good/service.

The supply of finance is another matter. This schedule, OJ, shows how levels of jurisdiction income (from tax, nontax, or external sources) and wealth affect service provision. As stated above, it is constructed by assuming that the structure of the revenue system is left unchanged, but the population changes. For example, if people move into a jurisdiction, then property values might increase. With tax rates fixed, the increase in the value of property will increase the tax revenues from the property tax.

In the example above with population OB, the supply of financing exceeded the demand for financing by ST. This outcome means that the jurisdiction could afford the level of OA of public good/service. That does not always happen! In fact, if population growth and the corresponding demand for public good/service increased, a jurisdiction's demand for financing could exceed its supply of financing (the difference between GH and GJ). That fiscal gap is comparable to what many large cities in the United States face on an annual basis.

What is the reward for working through Figure 5–1? It tells us that elements of demand, production considerations, costs restrictions, and finance issues all affect the level of state-local government expenditures. As these components change from jurisdiction to jurisdiction and from state to state, the level of state-local government expenditures will change. The result is the variations that were observed in Tables 5–2 through 5–4.

The model in Figure 5–1 also allows the analyst to anticipate future changes in any of these factors by shifting the appropriate schedule. Typical changes might be:

- A given population wants computer literacy courses or sex education courses added to the school curriculum. The demand schedule in Quadrant I would rotate down or in a clockwise direction (for nondigital clock people), changing the entire diagram. This change affects the demand for finance schedule.

- Technology improves in the delivery of a public good/service (e.g., sanitation trucks are introduced that require only one person to drive and pick up trash). The production function in Quadrant II would rotate downward in a counterclockwise direction. This change affects the demand for finance schedule.

- Costs of providing a public good/service increase as a result of a recently negotiated public employee union contract. The cost schedule in Quadrant III rotates upward in a clockwise direction. This change affects the demand for finance schedule.

- The city council raises tax rates. The supply of finance schedule in Quadrant IV rotates upward in a counterclockwise direction.

Figure 5–1 also warns about the fiscal gap that can occur because the demand for public goods/services can exceed the supply of financing. This fiscal gap occurs because jurisdictions' service responsibilities may exceed their revenue-raising authority. In other words, there is a mismatch between the spending obligations and the available revenue-raising devices at the state-local levels.

## THE POLITICAL PROCESS AND THE STATE-LOCAL EXPENDITURE DECISION

This discussion of a model of state-local government expenditure decisions began with a comparison of state and local governments to the individual consumer. That comparison holds in many respects. One important respect in which it does not hold is that the state-local government expenditure decision is collective in nature. Unlike the individual consumer, state and local government expenditure decisions must work their way through a political process: a vote of the people, school board, city council, or legislature.

This study of the political process and its impact on public decision making is the field of *public choice theory*. This field touches upon far more than can be reviewed in this section. (For a survey of public choice theory, see Buchanan, 1975; Mueller, 1979.) Several public choice concepts are especially useful in explaining variations in state-local expenditures (Bish, 1971). These public choice considerations take their place alongside demand, production, costs, and finance in determining state-local expenditure levels.

### Voting Rules

In any government decision, the ideal is for everyone to agree on a course of action. In that way no one is forced to do what they do not want to. A *rule of unanimity* requires that all voters consent to a specific action. Unanimity is difficult to disagree with. Groups of people, especially large groups, rarely achieve it. Part of the reason that unanimity is often beyond a voting group's reach is that the cost of complete agreement on any action, in terms of time, information, and organizational resources can be prohibitive. So unanimity is not the usual voting rule that governing bodies or popular elections follow.

When unanimous agreement is put aside, what takes its place? The most popular voting rule is majority rule. *Majority rule* means that a government action is consented to if more than 50 percent of the voters approve. Figure 5–2 illustrates the majority rule. Five people called A, B, C, E, F (to protect their identities) in a hypothetical town are voting to determine how many additional streetlights should be installed in the town. The largest number that the majority of voters agree to will be installed. Each voter has a demand curve for streetlights (DA, DB, DC, DE, and DF); each voter pays a fixed amount for this installation (the tax price); and very significantly, each voter will not support more streetlights than his/her preferred amount, but will support less.

With the above assumptions, the vote would be 5–0 for three streetlights (unanimity rule); 4–1 for four streetlights; 3–2 for five streetlights; 2–3 for six streetlights; and 1–4 for seven streetlights (someone is afraid of the dark). The largest number of streetlights that the majority of voters agree to is five (3–2 vote). Something besides light comes out of this vote. When the majority rule is in effect as described above, the outcome can be predicted by the median

**Figure 5–2**
**Majority Rule and the Median Voter Hypothesis**

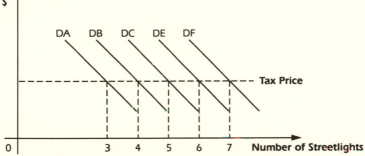

voter. This is called the *median voter hypothesis*. For these purposes, the median voter hypothesis states that a vote on any level of government expenditure will be the amount preferred by the median voter. The median voter wants more spent than half the remaining voters (the median voter is excluded from the total) and less spent than the other half of the remaining voters. In the example above, person C in Figure 5–2 is the median voter and the outcome is five streetlights, the amount person C preferred.

Many, but not all, empirical studies have found evidence that is consistent with the median voter hypothesis. Usually these studies conclude that median income is associated with a given level of a public good (Barr and Davis, 1966; Davis and Haines, 1966; Inman, 1978; Pommerehne, 1978). Other studies have looked at the distribution of voters in referenda results and found that the referenda results were in line with median voters' preferences (Holcombe, 1980; Munley, 1984; McEachern, 1978).

In addition to the median voter hypothesis, another important conclusion emerges from this simple example. The outcome of a collective choice does not have to satisfy each individual's preference. While a majority were willing to support five streetlights, that number matched only one person's desired amount. Two people actually opposed the choice, but had to go along with it.

**Voting Problems**

This last point concerning the lack of correspondence between a collective outcome and individual preferences raises the issue of problems with voting in general and the majority rule in specific. Voting usually does not capture the depth of a voter's feeling about an issue (called *intensity*); does not guarantee an efficient allocation of collective resources; and does not always produce consistent outcomes. Tables 5–5 and 5–6 illustrates these three points.

Table 5–5 shows the majority rule in operation in a five-person jurisdiction attempting to decide on a specified amount of a public good/service. To simplify

**Table 5–5**
**Hypothetical Distribution of Benefits and Costs of a Public Good/Service for a**
**Five-Person Jurisdiction**

--------------------------------------------------------------------------------

Part (a)

| Individuals | Dollar Value of Benefits | Tax Levied on Each Person | Net Benefit or Net Cost | Vote |
|---|---|---|---|---|
| A | $ 400 | $ 200 | +$200 | Yea |
| B | 300 | 200 | + 100 | Yea |
| C | 250 | 200 | + 50 | Yea |
| D | 100 | 200 | - 100 | Nay |
| E | 50 | 200 | - 150 | Nay |
| Total | $1100 | $1000 | +$100 | Yea |

Part (b)

| Individuals | Dollar Value of Benefits | Tax Levied on Each Person | Net Benefit or Net Cost | Vote |
|---|---|---|---|---|
| A | $ 280 | $ 200 | +$ 80 | Yea |
| B | 260 | 200 | + 60 | Yea |
| C | 220 | 200 | + 20 | Yea |
| D | 100 | 200 | - 100 | Nay |
| E | 0 | 200 | - 200 | Nay |
| Total | $ 860 | $1000 | -$140 | Yea |

the example, several assumptions are made. Voters determine their position on the public good/service based on the net benefits they receive (the difference between how they value the public good/service and the taxes paid). The tax levied on each of the five people is fixed at $200. If a person's net benefit is positive, then he/she votes for (yea) the public good/service. If it is negative, then he/she votes against (nay) the public good/service.

Part a of Table 5–5 shows the case where the majority rule produces an efficient decision, but intensity of feeling does not matter. Three individuals have net benefits greater than zero (i.e., A, B, and C) and two do not (i.e., D and E). The proposition to provide the public good/service carries 3–2. Fortunately, the production of the public good/service is efficient; that is, the total dollar value of benefits exceeds the total taxes levied ($1,100 vs. $1,000). Of course, each person has one vote. For person A that vote spells $200 in net benefits, for person E it spells − $150 in net benefits. Under the "one person, one vote" scheme, there is no way to differentiate these differences in net benefits or intensity. The inability to do exactly that can lead to inefficient outcomes.

Part b of Table 5–5 shows how the majority rule coupled with a "one person, one vote" scheme that does not capture intensity of voters' feelings can lead to an inefficient outcome. Back in the five-person jurisdiction, individual voters still make decisions based on net benefits. Again, three voters have net benefits greater than zero (i.e., A, B, and C); and two do not (i.e., D and E). However, since the magnitude of the gain or the cost to the individual voter is not accounted for, an inefficient decision results. The public good/service is supported even though total benefits are less than total costs ($860 vs. $1,000). The government undertakes a project which loses $140 for the five-person jurisdiction.

Inconsistency is the next gremlin for the majority rule. Under the majority rule, rational voters can make inconsistent choices. This result is often called the *paradox of voting*. Table 5–6 gives a display of the paradox of voting in action. The five-person jurisdiction now has three public goods/services to vote up or down—sanitation, police, and education. If the public goods/services are taken separately, then each would be passed even though each is inefficient based on the comparison of total benefits to total costs. It is the problem of intensity again. To be consistent the five voters who supported each service separately would be expected to support a budget consisting of the three identical services. They do not! They vote it down by a margin of 3–2. All the decisions are very logical based on the distribution of net benefits, but they lead to very inconsistent results.

So voting under the majority rule fails to match individual preferences with collectively arrived at choices; capture intensity of voters' feelings; and produce consistent results. These are some of the problems in relying on the majority rule to determine levels of state-local expenditures. Differences in levels of state-local government expenditures can be traced, in part, to these foibles of the voting process.

## Political Players

The majority voting rule and the median voter certainly help to determine the levels of state-local government expenditures and state-local spending variations. While the Tiebout model creates competition among subnational governments within and across state lines so that they are efficient, some economists have argued that the nature of the political process generates pressure for increased state and local spending (Bartlett, 1973; Gwartney and Wagner, 1988). In simple terms, here is how the public choice economists see the budget process.

Consumer/voters will support public action that they believe is in their interest. All too often, however, consumer/voters do not realize what action benefits them most, if at all. There is a reason. Most consumer/voters have fragmentary information concerning public issues. Learning the issues is a costly, time-consuming task. We trust our officials, the thirty-minute TV news report, or the weekly national news magazines to keep us informed. But that's simply not enough. We are not very well informed. This dereliction of duty is called the ''rational ignorance effect.'' Lobbyists, politicians, and bureaucrats exploit our rational ignorance for their advantage.

Politicians are elected government officials. Their motivation is simple: get reelected. Public choice economists contend that politicians are determined to maximize their popular votes on election day, although vote maximization is

**Table 5–6**
**Hypothetical Distribution of Benefits and Costs of Three Services for a Five-Person Jurisdiction**

| INDIVIDUALS | SANITATION | | | POLICE | | | EDUCATION | | | TOTAL | | |
|---|---|---|---|---|---|---|---|---|---|---|---|---|
| | Benefits | Cost | Vote | Benefits | Cost | Vote | Benefits | Cost | Vote | Benefits | Cost | Vote |
| A | $ 240 | $ 200 | Yea | $ 500 | $ 400 | Yea | $ 100 | $ 800 | Nay | $ 840 | $1400 | Nay |
| B | 240 | 200 | Yea | 100 | 400 | Nay | 100 | 800 | Nay | 440 | 1400 | Nay |
| C | 240 | 200 | Yea | 500 | 400 | Yea | 1000 | 800 | Yea | 1740 | 1400 | Yea |
| D | 100 | 200 | Nay | 100 | 400 | Nay | 1000 | 800 | Yea | 1200 | 1400 | Nay |
| E | 100 | 200 | Nay | 500 | 400 | Yea | 1000 | 800 | Yea | 1600 | 1400 | Yea |
| TOTAL | $ 920 | $1000 | YEA | $1700 | $2000 | YEA | $3200 | $4000 | YEA | $5820 | $7000 | NAY |

not necessary to get reelected. Governors, state legislators, mayors, members of the city council, and members of the school board will strive to appeal to the uninformed positions of the median voter in their jurisdiction and the requests of the special interest lobbying groups, since that is where the votes are. If a politician refuses to support popular and/or lobbyists' causes, then a political competitor could well replace him/her.

There is a private market analogy. If a producer neglects to maximize his/her profits, then he/she runs the risk of failure. If a politician neglects to maximize votes, then he/she runs the risk of political defeat. This process of searching for the median voter and catering to the lobbyists increases state-local expenditures.

Bureaucrats are the next culprits in this process. They are nonelected state-local government officials who manage government programs. Their motivation is job security. Job security comes with control over public resources, the budget. The sequence works like this: the larger the slice of the budget, the greater the control, and the greater the job security (Niskanen, 1975).

Bureaucrats have several distinct advantages in the political process: they often control the information about state-local programs; they rarely must respond directly to the voting public; they can act as if they were monopoly suppliers since the state-local government is often the exclusive supplier of a public good/ service; and there is no bottom line in the public domain to which the bureaucrat can be held. These advantages serve the bureaucrats' motivation to increase their job security because they allow the bureaucrats to push for increases in the state-local budget unchecked by the voter and encouraged by the politician.

The result is that the political process introduces a dynamic into the budgeting process that may not automatically combat inefficiency and may encourage growth in state-local expenditures. Suppose a local government introduces a program that will generate benefits for a minority of residents in the jurisdiction, but will be paid for by all the residents in the jurisdiction. The cost per taxpayer is small. The benefits to the select few is significant. The political imperative for the select few is to organize and lobby the consumer/voters and the politicians.

Following the principle of rational ignorance, the consumer/voters have little incentive to understand the issues surrounding the program since the tax cost to the individual taxpayer is small relative to the cost of understanding the consequences of implementing the program. The select few will lobby the politician with promises/threats concerning his/her reelection. So the politician will have every incentive to support the program and convince the electorate to do the same. The bureaucracy welcomes this expansion of the local government, so there will be no opposition from them. The politician supports the program publicly; bureaucrats endorse it; and consumer/voters approve it (without knowing why). Local government expands its services and its taxes.

In this way, state-local expenditure decisions are part of a push-pull process. The Tiebout model of community choice, production, costs, and finance considerations outlined in Figure 5–1 create incentives to push the process toward an efficient spending decision. The voting rules, voting problems, and political players create incentives to pull the process toward an inefficient, expanding state-local budget.

## EMPIRICAL ESTIMATES OF THE DETERMINANTS OF STATE-LOCAL EXPENDITURES

For almost forty years, economists have tried to estimate the determinants of state-local expenditures, in many cases without the benefits of the Siegel model or public choice theory. The empirical studies were undertaken to improve the general understanding of the expenditure decision process at the state and local levels and to explain spending variations among the fifty state-local fiscal systems.

Fabricant (1952) completed one of earliest of these "determinant studies," as they came to be known. He found that the following were closely associated with state-local spending levels in the then forty-eight states: (1) personal income—a measure of public service demand; (2) population density (i.e., people per square mile)—a measure of economies of scale; and (3) urbanization (i.e., percent of the population living in urban areas)—a measure of congestion costs. Publication of this study unleashed a good deal of research energy in this area. For example, Hirsch (1960), Fisher (1961), Kurnow (1963), Miner (1963), Sacks and Harris (1964), Bahl and Saunders (1965), Osman (1966), and Denzau (1975) all contributed to the determinants of state-local spending literature. Generally, their results reaffirmed, refined, and added to Fabricant's findings that:

• Personal income is positively associated with the following state-local expenditure categories: general, education, police, fire, and highways. The only exception is sanitation.

• Density is negatively associated with general, sanitation, and highways; and positively associated with education, police, and fire.

• Urbanization is positively associated with general, education, police, fire, and sanitation. The only exception is highways.

• Federal and state aid is positively associated with general, education, police, fire, sanitation, and highways.

Dissatisfaction with this literature began to appear as fast as the next determinants study. While there were several major objections to the studies, they gravitated around the charge that even though there may be some logical explanations for the empirical results, the studies did not satisfy the economic theory presented in Figure 5–1 and the discussion of public choice theory. The studies mixed cost and quality issues; they ignored production considerations, like economies of scale; and they mishandled the analysis of federal and state aid. The studies reported that the above determinants were associated with state-local spending decisions, but no study explained how or why (Siegel, 1966; Bahl, 1969).

More recent research has tried to deal with these deficiencies. Davis and Haines (1966) incorporated public choice theory into the analysis and documented a role for the median voter in state-local spending decisions. Three pairs of authors based their research on a model of supply and demand and public choice theory (Bergstrom and Goodman, 1973; Borcherding and Deacon, 1972; Ohls and Wales, 1972). Borcherding and Deacon built a model that took into account production, costs, the median voter, and demand factors. Ohls and Wales set up a demand and supply relationship where demand was based on per capita personal income, per capita federal grants, and tax price and supply was based on public employees' wage levels, density, change in population, and the percent of the population in nonmetropolitan areas.

In addition to the more comprehensive approach to the question of state-local spending decisions, these recent studies are important because they provide estimates of price and income elasticities. Price elasticity indicates how sensitive or responsive demand is to "tax price" changes. Generally, price elasticity for state-local public goods/services has been found to be inelastic; that is, the quantity demanded is not very sensitive to tax price changes. A percentage change in the tax price does not attract people to or draw people away from the public good/service in any relatively large numbers. Of course, a tax price increase will lead to a decrease in quantity demanded, ceteris paribus (that is, all things being equal), but the percentage change in quantity demanded is less than the percentage change in tax price. One implication is that subsidizing the tax price of a service will not lead the jurisdiction to increase substantially its level of the public service.

Income elasticity is also an important characteristic of a public good/service. This concept indicates how sensitive quantity demanded for a public good/service is relative to income—in other words, the percentage change in quantity demanded divided by the percentage change in income. Income elasticity is useful in predicting how a jurisdiction's demand for a public good/service will respond to changes in income—growth or decline.

Table 5–7 reports the income elasticity estimates which Borcherding and Deacon calculated for a variety of state-local public goods/services. With the exception of Parks and Recreation, most state-local expenditure items are less than 1.0. This fact means that a one percentage point change in income will lead to a less than one percentage point change in the public good/service. Spending on public goods/services responds to changes in personal income, but it is not overly sensitive to these changes. A relatively large change in personal income leads to a relatively small change in public goods/services.

## ISSUES IN STATE-LOCAL GOVERNMENT EXPENDITURE DECISIONS

With the economic and public choice theories of state-local expenditure decision making set out and with the review of empirical studies complete, three

**Table 5–7**
**Income Elasticity Estimates for State-Local Public Goods/Services**

| Public Good/Service Category | Income Elasticity Estimate | Comments |
|---|---|---|
| General | .64 | Estimates vary from .34 to .89. |
| Local Education | .94 | Other estimates are lower, see Denzau (1975). |
| Higher Education | .69 | |
| Highways | .10 | Other estimates have gone as high as .90. |
| Health & Hospitals | .16 | Other studies have gone as high as .51. |
| Police | .82 | Police and Fire estimates have |
| Fire | .88 | gone as low as .52. |
| Sewer & Sanitation | .04 | |
| Parks & Recreation | 2.74 | Income elasticity estimates tend to be at or near 1.00. |

*Source*: Borcherding and Deacon, 1972; and "Comments" drawn from Inman, 1979.

contemporary issues in state-local spending remain. They are the cost of public goods/services, state imposed mandates, and across state spending differences.

## Cost of Public Services

The cost of providing public services certainly influences state-local government spending decisions. Costs can affect the mix of public expenditures, the expenditure level, and the quality of the services. Since most, if not all, state-local public goods/services rely on labor more than machinery (e.g., those people you see in the AFSCME commercials: the teacher, the sanitation worker, the police, the firefighter, and the hospital staff worker), there are not many opportunities to increase productivity using capital—not because public employees refuse to work harder, but because of the nature of the production process for state-local public goods/services. A machine alone cannot teach elementary school children, pick up trash, or provide general public safety.

There appear to be more opportunities for the use of productivity-increasing technology in the private sector. Wages in the private sector increase as private sector employees' productivity increases. Yet wages to public employees must keep pace with their private sector counterparts in order to attract competent people. So wages for the public sector employees increase, not necessarily because of productivity increases, but to stay competitive with the private sector. That production-cost fact about state-local public goods/services is important because the cost of providing the public good/service at the same quality level will tend to increase over time. State-local governments will pay ever increasing amounts for the same quality good/service. This upward trend is not likely to stop as long as the service is provided. This outcome has a name, *Baumol's disease*, after the economist who first advanced this argument (Baumol, 1967). State-local spending increases over time, but public good/service quality may stagnate or even decline.

An example of Baumol's disease is found in a study of New York City spending patterns between 1965 and 1972 (Greytak, Gustely, and Dinkelmeyer, 1974). Of the total increase in spending, 43 percent was attributed to inflation. Samples by department were police (39 percent), fire (44 percent), and schools (53 percent). Increases in labor costs drove the inflation growth. Costs obviously play an influential role in spending levels within a state-local government system and contribute to spending differences that exist across the fifty state-local government systems in the United States.

## State-Imposed Mandates

A growing phenomenon in the area of state-local expenditures is state imposed mandates. Mandates include any constitutional, statutory, or administrative action that limits or places requirements on local governments (Minge, 1977; ACIR, 1978). They can change procedural operations within a jurisdiction; create new programs or improve the quality of existing programs; guide interjurisdictional relations; exempt property from the tax base; and establish standards for employees' salary, working conditions, and benefit packages. In a period of tight resources, mandates allow the state government to deliver benefits to their constituents by ordering local governments to make the delivery. This imposed service delivery certainly affects local spending decisions.

Mandates are most often used in the following service areas: local employees' retirement and working conditions, police, fire, education, environmental protection, and social services. Table 5–8 summarizes the results of survey of state imposed mandates by geographic area. In 1976, the maximum number of mandates that the survey identified was 77. The region with the fewest average mandates was the Southeast (average of 27); the region with the highest number was the Far West (average of 46). The comparable information for the states is Alabama with the fewest (11) and California with the highest (52) (ACIR, 1978).

The delegation of responsibilities within a federal system and the distribution of financial burdens fuel the controversy over state imposed mandates. Proponents of mandates argue that local governments may be administratively responsible for services that have statewide benefit areas. Because the criteria in Table 5–1 have not been followed in delegating these services, local governments left to pursue their own interests will not provide an efficient amount of the service. Therefore, the state government must dictate the service level throughout the benefit area. An offshoot of this argument is that state courts may order uniform service levels in accordance with the state constitution or state statutes.

**Table 5–8**
**State Imposed Mandates by Geographic Region, 1976 (Average Number in Region)**

| Region | Mandates in Selected Program Areas | | | | Total Number |
| | Employment | Police | Fire | Education | All Areas |
| --- | --- | --- | --- | --- | --- |
| United States | 7 | 7 | 6 | 7 | 35 |
| New England | 8 | 7 | 7 | 8 | 35 |
| Middle Atlantic | 6 | 7 | 6 | 10 | 37 |
| East North Central | 5 | 5 | 7 | 7 | 37 |
| West North Central | 8 | 8 | 6 | 7 | 38 |
| East South Central | 5 | 5 | 4 | 6 | 27 |
| West South Central | 7 | 7 | 6 | 9 | 33 |
| Mountain | 9 | 7 | 6 | 5 | 37 |
| Pacific | 6 | 5 | 9 | 8 | 46 |

*Source*: ACIR, 1978.

Opponents of the state imposed mandates see them as violation of the theory of clubs and the Tiebout model that leads to a loss of local autonomy. Local choice in spending and taxing is the single-most important reason why people select the jurisdiction in which they live. Now the state government blurs the distinctions among jurisdictions by mandating service levels across jurisdictions. On top of this loss of local autonomy, the state insists that local jurisdictions must pay the costs associated with the mandate. The allegation is that the state is frequently unaware of the full cost of the mandate.

The local cry that you hear is for state reimbursement for state imposed mandates. If the state imposes a mandate because of a statewide benefit area, then local government officials argue that the total benefits of the service should be divided into state interests and local interests. State reimbursement to local governments would then be based upon the relative proportion of state interests in any mandated program. That is a neat argument, but a difficult administrative task. Some proponents of state imposed mandates simply expect local governments to reorder their local priorities and make do without state reimbursement for the mandated program. They argue that local governments are often already recipients of state aid and that assistance is adequate. This issue in state-local spending is obviously not settled.

## State-Local Spending Differences

Differences exist in state-local spending levels. That observation should come as no surprise unless you are reading this chapter from the back to the front. Tables 5–2 through 5–4 documented these differences across service categories and across the fifty state-local government systems. You have all the reasons for these differences: production, cost, demand, finance, and public choice considerations outlined in Figure 5–1 and estimated in the reported determinant studies. Are these differences nothing more than the principle feature of a federal system; namely, diversity? Or do they represent a significant public problem that requires federal government involvement in state-local government spending decisions? The answer lies with the principle of fiscal equivalency and the notion of fiscal adequacy.

Using the principle of fiscal equivalency, differences in state-local government spending levels are a public problem if the benefit area of a specific public good/service exceeds the political borders, a Case I situation. Again, this is an instance where the service has been delegated to an incorrect level of government. The consequence is that an inefficient level of the public good/service is being provided. A higher level of government must intercede to restore efficiency by delegating the public good/service correctly (perhaps, using one of the organizations described in Chapter 3) or by assisting the level of government that is providing the public good/service with additional funding.

Using the notion of fiscal adequacy, differences in state-local government spending levels are a public problem if a political jurisdiction has inadequate fiscal resources to provide even a minimum level of the specific public good/service. Of course, there are two difficulties with this rule. What constitutes inadequate resources? What level of a public good/service represents a minimum level?

The discussion of the political theory of federalism already warned us that fiscal imbalances and uniformity (even at a minimum level) in the provision of public good/service are not issues with which a federal system deals easily. In addition, the fiscal adequacy approach to the problem of spending differences assumes that the federal system is based upon one of the three theories of interdependent federalism described in Chapter 3. If state-local spending differences are due to inadequate resources, then the federal government should assure adequate resources.

## SUMMARY

1. Guidelines exist for the delegation of responsibility for public goods/services. These guidelines include: economies of scale, fiscal equivalency, fiscal adequacy, political accountability, and administrative effectiveness. Actual service delivery appears generally to conform to these guidelines.

2. There are variations in per capita state-local government expenditure levels and growth rates across the fifty state-local systems. These variations also exist across service categories. Such variation is the natural consequence of a federal system of government.

3. A model of state-local spending decisions would take into account production, costs, demand, and finance considerations. Differences in these elements would explain state-local spending variations.

4. Public choice theory also contributes to the explanation of state-local spending decisions and variations. Voting rules, the role of the median voter, voting problems with intensity of preferences and inconsistency of choices, and the motivations of politicians and bureaucrats influence state-local government spending levels.

5. Empirical studies have tried to measure the influence of the above elements on state-local spending decisions. Earlier "determinant studies" were incomplete. More recent studies have captured the economic and political factors in the state-local spending decision. These studies have also produced price and income elasticity estimates for state-local pubic goods/services.

6. Three contemporary problems affect state-local spending and require some intergovernmental cooperation: cost of public goods/services that tend to increase because of few opportunities for labor productivity gains; state imposed mandates which shift the fiscal burden from state government to local governments; and spending differences associated with a violation of the principle of fiscal equivalency and/or the notion of fiscal adequacy.

# CHAPTER 6

---

# Financing Public Elementary
# and Secondary Education

## PREVIEW

Public elementary and secondary education usually commands the largest share of the budgets of state and local governments. This chapter draws upon the economic theory developed earlier to reveal the nature of this public service, why state and local governments provide this service, and how it is funded in a federal system. By insisting on equality of educational opportunity, the courts have often defined the method of financing public education. Funding methods that the courts have accepted will be reviewed.

## INTRODUCTION

Over the years in the United States, state governments have set aside approximately one-third of their budgets for public education. Local governments put aside even more, approximately 45 percent. No other single state-local public service commands this level of budgetary support. An examination of education services offers an opportunity to bring to bear the economic theory developed in previous chapters on a single state and local public finance issue. Education brings together issues on market failure, the principle of fiscal equivalency, the delegation of functional responsibilities, and the clash between allocation and redistribution goals. In addition, education illustrates the role of court decisions in the provision of a public service.

## EDUCATION, MARKET FAILURE, AND FEDERALISM

For the economist, education is a service that possesses some unusual properties. In one sense, it is certainly a private good that satisfies the exclusion principle; that is, the individual alone who is acquiring an education receives the benefits (financial and nonfinancial). In another sense, it also possesses public good qualities; that is, the benefits of education go beyond the individual who acquires the education. Education—especially elementary and secondary education—generates spillover effects. A *spillover* affects someone beyond the immediate buyer or seller, in this case someone beyond the individual who is acquiring the education.

Society shares in the benefits that education generates or the costs in which an inadequate education results. As Friedman (1962) stated years ago, a democratic society depends upon its people's literacy, knowledge, and shared values. This dependency extends beyond a person's locality across the entire nation. Poorly educated people not only limit their own horizons, but also limit their locality's development opportunities and through migration and voting limit society's possibilities. The conclusion that education possesses spillover effects means that the private market cannot provide an efficient level of educational services. Spillovers are a form of market failure that prevent the market from allocating resources efficiently. This type of market failure justifies the public sector's intervention in the market for educational services.

While the issue of public sector intervention is straightforward enough, spillover effects associated with education present additional problems to a public sector organized around the principles of federalism. Case I in Figure 4–1 showed how spillover effects can lead to a violation of the principle of fiscal equivalency. The benefit area exceeds the boundaries of the political jurisdiction. Certainly, if the spillover effects of elementary and secondary education extend nationwide, but the administrative authority rests in the hands of the state legislature, or more likely the local school board, then there is a Case I situation and a violation of fiscal equivalency (Barlow, 1970).

The mismatch between benefit area and political boundaries also shows up in the delegation of functional responsibilities for education. Table 5–1 sets out the criteria for the delegation of function responsibilities in a federal system. In the discussion summarized in Table 5–1, the conclusion was reached that education failed to satisfy the principle of fiscal equivalency. (Recall the No answer to the second question.) Despite this outcome, the local governmental unit was the administrative unit. Forty states left the elementary and secondary education function in the local school district's hands. Under these circumstances, there is no certainty that government intervention will provide elementary and secondary education services in an efficient method. This analysis raises the question that the provision of elementary and secondary education has nationwide implications that may be too significant to be left to local school boards. Yet until recently, there has been no call for national standards for or national takeover of public elementary and secondary education. We are left with a case for government intervention based on spillover effects. We are also faced with a violation of the principle of fiscal equivalency. In a federal system, that violation implies a less than efficient allocation of resources for education.

## DETERMINANTS OF SPENDING ON ELEMENTARY AND SECONDARY EDUCATION

Putting aside the question of level of responsibility for education, this section identifies the factors that influence education spending levels. In turn, these factors determine whether there is equality of educational opportunity within a single and across the fifty states of the United States. A series of empirical studies have identified, affirmed, and reaffirmed elements that have a direct (or positive) relationship or an inverse (or negative) relationship with per pupil educational spending levels (Hirsch, 1960; Denzau, 1975). Many factors that would seem to influence per pupil education spending levels apparently do not; for example, education level of the adult population, the percent of the population that is nonwhite, district size, state aid levels, and percent of the dwelling units that are owner-occupied. There are, however, several distinguishable positive and negative determinants.

### Positive Determinants

To say that a factor has a direct or positive relationship with the level of per pupil education spending means that the value of the factor and the level of per pupil education spending vary in the same direction. As the factor increases in value, the spending level increases in value. The reverse also holds. Some of the positive factors that have proven statistically significant over a series of empirical studies are: median family income, federal aid, equalized assessed property value per pupil, population density, and the percent of secondary school students. The first three of these factors capture the ability to finance spending on education. The next two factors measure cost considerations. (Population density is often associated with economies of scale, and secondary school programs are often more costly than their elementary school counterparts.)

What this information means is that the level of per pupil educational spending varies with the level of per pupil assessed property valuation. As per pupil assessed valuation increases (all else equal), the level of per pupil educational spending increases. Again, the opposite also holds. Later in the chapter, this particular relationship is going to take on added importance in the legal debate on education financing policies.

### Negative Determinants

To say that a factor has an inverse or negative relationship with the level of per pupil education spending means that the value of the factor and the level of per pupil education spending vary in the opposite direction. As the factor increases in value, the spending level decreases in value. The reverse also holds. Some of the negative factors that have proven statistically significant over a series of empirical studies are: tax price per pupil and the percent of the population living in urban areas. The first of these factors stands for the price of the service. Demand theory predicts that the relationship should be negative. The second factor points out a difference between per pupil spending levels in urban schools and nonurban schools.

### Price and Income Elasticity

Empirical studies have also estimated price and income elasticities for education services (Inman, 1979). The price of education services is usually measured as percent of each education dollar paid by the local taxpayer after adjusting for matching aid (if matching aid covers 25 percent or .25, the price of each education dollar to the local taxpayer is 75 cents, or .75) or the local taxpayer's per capita taxes after adjusting for intergovernmental aid and federal deductions of state and local taxes. The general result regardless of how price is measured is that the price elasticity for elementary and secondary education services is inelastic.

Recall what this means. Price elasticity answers the question, "How will the quantity demanded by taxpayers respond to a change in the price which they must pay for the service?" Of course, as the price increases, their quantity demanded will fall and as the price decreases, their quantity demanded will rise. What will be the magnitude of the rise or fall? That is where price elasticity comes into play. Taxpayers are not very sensitive to price changes when it comes to educational services. The percentage change in the quantity of educational services will be less than the percentage change in the tax price. Specifically, a 1 percent change in the price of educational services will lead to a less than 1 percent change in the level of educational services. Estimates vary from .07 percent to .94 percent. Neither tax price hikes nor declines will have much effect (in relative percent terms) on the quantity of educational services. Education is not a price sensitive service. This conclusion holds for almost all goods/services that are considered "necessities."

Income elasticity measures percentage changes in the level of educational services relative to percentage changes in income levels. Again, what does this mean? Income elasticity answers the question, "How will a change in taxpayers' income affect the quantity of education which they demand?" In the case of education, an increase in taxpayers' income will lead to an increase in quantity demanded of the service. But how much of an increase?

Taxpayers are moderately sensitive to changes in income when it comes to purchasing educational services. The percentage change in the quantity of educational services will be less than the percentage change in taxpayers' income. Specifically, a 1 percent change in taxpayers' income will lead to a .46 to .65 percent change in the level of educational services. For education services, income elasticity tends to fall in the range from .46 to .65, though some studies show higher estimates. Education is moderately sensitive to income changes.

These results are more than mind-numbing economic concepts. They hint at policy directions if the state government seeks to encourage local school districts to change their level of educational spending. Price elasticity shows the effect of aiming state policies at the local tax price for education, while income elasticity shows the effect of concentrating state policies at the overall income (or resource) base of the local school districts.

## EDUCATIONAL SPENDING PATTERNS IN THE UNITED STATES

There are several policy issues that have gained attention in the area of elementary and secondary education. They include: desegregation, measuring student performance, improving the productivity of teachers, and general school financing. (For an overview on several of these issues, see Coleman and Kelly, 1976, and Murnane, 1985.) This section concentrates on general school financing. We begin with a look at the spending data across the fifty states.

Table 6–1 offers several perspectives on educational spending in the United States for the 1985–86 fiscal year. The states are ranked in descending order by their per pupil current expenditure levels. Alaska leads the nation with per pupil spending of $8,044; Utah pulls up the rear with $2,297. The national average is $3,677. Twenty states spend above the national average. The ratio of the highest spending state to the lowest spending state for the fifty states is 3.50. This means that Alaska is spending $3.50 per pupil for every $1.00 per pupil Utah spends. If the top five states and the bottom five states are excluded from the range, then the ratio of high (Rhode Island: $4,669) to low (Arkansas: $2,642) for the forty states is 1.77. Rhode Island spends $1.77 per pupil for every $1.00 per pupil Arkansas spends.

Another perspective on educational spending is per capita spending levels. The range goes from a high of $1,548 (Alaska) to a low of $405 (Mississippi). That range produces a ratio of high to low of 3.82. Alaska spends $3.82 per capita for education for every $1.00 Mississippi spends. If the top five states and the bottom five states are excluded, then the range for the forty states becomes $742 (New Mexico) to $483 (New Hampshire). The ratio of high to low is now 1.53. Again, the meaning is that New Mexico spends $1.53 per person for every $1.00 New Hampshire spends.

The third perspective that Table 6–1 offers is a sample of the per pupil spending differences within state that exist in 1985–86. A sample of school districts with an enrollment of at least 15,000 pupils was surveyed. The extreme right column of Table 6–1 displays the number of these districts in each state. A blank space means that there are none in the state. For example, Alaska has none; New York has six. The ratio of high to low per pupil spending districts within a state was calculated. Those ratios show that per pupil spending differences exist not only

**Table 6–1**

**Perspectives on 1985–86 Educational Spending: Per Pupil, Per Capita, and Sample Differences (ranked in descending order by per pupil spending)**

| State | Educational Spending Per Pupil | Per Capita | Ratio of High to Low Spending Districts (Enrollment > 15,000) | Number of Districts |
|-------|------|------|------|------|
| Alaska | $8044 | $1548 | | |
| New York | 5616 | 782 | 1.26 | 6 |
| New Jersey | 5544 | 787 | 1.31 | 6 |
| Wyoming | 5479 | 1336 | | |
| Connecticut | 4888 | 731 | 1.27 | 3 |
| Rhode Island | 4669 | 600 | | |
| Delaware | 4517 | 669 | | |
| Maryland | 4349 | 644 | 1.65 | 11 |
| Montana | 4337 | 809 | | |
| Massachusetts | 4255 | 605 | 1.83 | 5 |
| Pennsylvania | 4235 | 610 | | |
| Wisconsin | 4168 | 656 | 1.18 | 4 |
| Oregon | 4123 | 670 | 1.11 | 4 |
| Kansas | 3914 | 666 | 1.05 | 3 |
| Minnesota | 3864 | 671 | 1.44 | 3 |
| Michigan | 3789 | 682 | 1.40 | 12 |
| Hawaii | 3766 | 581 | | |
| Colorado | 3740 | 642 | 1.25 | 11 |
| Florida | 3731 | 516 | 1.42 | 26 |
| Washington | 3705 | 708 | 1.43 | 10 |
| UNITED STATES | 3677 | 619 | | |
| Illinois | 3621 | 532 | 1.26 | 5 |
| California | 3573 | 620 | 1.51 | 53 |
| Iowa | 3568 | 606 | 1.08 | 3 |
| Vermont | 3554 | 587 | | |
| Ohio | 3547 | 593 | 1.32 | 8 |
| Texas | 3384 | 730 | 1.60 | 58 |
| New Mexico | 3374 | 742 | | |
| North Carolina | 3366 | 553 | 1.37 | 12 |
| Maine | 3346 | 603 | | |
| Nebraska | 3285 | 547 | | |
| Virginia | 3210 | 565 | 1.88 | 11 |
| Missouri | 3155 | 492 | 1.75 | 6 |
| Nevada | 3142 | 526 | | |
| New Hampshire | 3115 | 483 | | |
| North Dakota | 3059 | 553 | | |
| Louisiana | 3046 | 550 | 1.51 | 16 |
| Georgia | 2980 | 551 | 1.65 | 11 |
| Indiana | 2973 | 550 | 1.34 | 6 |
| South Dakota | 2967 | 549 | | |
| South Carolina | 2912 | 566 | 1.15 | 6 |
| Oklahoma | 2867 | 553 | 1.24 | 6 |
| Kentucky | 2853 | 480 | 1.42 | 3 |
| Arizona | 2829 | 499 | 1.45 | 9 |
| West Virginia | 2821 | 541 | 1.16 | 4 |
| Arkansas | 2642 | 481 | | |
| Tennessee | 2533 | 457 | 1.84 | 10 |
| Alabama | 2508 | 472 | 1.30 | 6 |
| Idaho | 2390 | 516 | | |
| Mississippi | 2305 | 405 | | |
| Utah | 2297 | 664 | 1.53 | 6 |

*Source*: Calculated from U.S. Bureau of Census, *Government Finances* data.

across states, but also within a single state. For example, Virginia's school spending patterns generated a ratio of 1.88 for 11 districts; Massachusetts's 1.83 for five districts; Arizona's 1.45 for nine districts.

Why the emphasis on these differences? In a federal system that champions decentralization, local decision making, and community formation based on the theory of clubs and the Tiebout model, these differences are to be expected. Indeed, they are to be celebrated. But wait! Hold the celebration. These spending differences may be far more than the result of decision making in a federal system. They may indicate inefficiencies in service provision. They may indicate inequities within a single state and across the fifty states. Over the recent past, legal challenges to educational financing have treated these spending differences as inequities; specifically, a denial of equality of opportunity in the provision of educational services.

## EQUALITY OF EDUCATIONAL OPPORTUNITY

### Alternative Definitions

Equality of educational opportunity is one of those social goals that is hard to resist, especially when it can mean so many different things to different people. Over the years, experts in education have identified an assortment of definitions of equality of educational opportunity to suit the tastes (Coleman, 1966; Arrow, 1971; Wise, 1972). Some examples would be: *full opportunity* (each person should be permitted to attain their "maximum" development); *foundation* (each person should receive a satisfactory minimum program offering); *minimum attainment* (each person should reach a specified level of attainment); *leveling* (resources should be allocated inverse to a person's talents so each one has an equal chance of success); *competition* (resources should be allocated in direct proportion to each person's ability so that society gets the most for its money); and *equal dollars per pupil* (a fixed level of spending per pupil regardless of educational "needs"). At different periods of time, different definitions are in the ascent or on the decline.

The debate surrounding the exact meaning of equality of educational opportunity has propelled another definition to the forefront, a definition that turns on dollars. Children in less wealthy school districts are receiving fewer dollars for their schooling than children in wealthier school districts. Specifically, spending on education cannot be related to the wealth of the school district. The educational financing system should blur the wealth distinctions which exist across districts within a state. In that way, educational spending decisions are not limited by the wealth of the local school district and equality of education opportunity is served in rich and poor districts alike.

**Table 6–2**
**An Illustration of the Revenue Formula Applied to Educational Financing**
**(amount to be raised per pupil listed in the table)**

| District (V/P) | Tax Rates | | | | | | | |
|---|---|---|---|---|---|---|---|---|
| | .025 | .029 | .034 | .038 | .039 | .044 | .045 | .049 |
| #1 -- $102,000 | $2550 | $3000 | $3468 | $3925 | $3975 | $4488 | $4553 | $4998 |
| #2 -- $157,000 | 3925 | 4553 | 5338 | 5966 | 6123 | 6908 | 7065 | 7693 |

### Educational Financing in Brief

Educational spending (excluding spending on capital outlay) is the sum of contributions from the local, the state, and the federal governments. The federal share is relatively minor, less than 10 percent of the total. Often it is dedicated to special or innovative programs (ACIR, 1981e). For these reasons, we will put the federal share aside. The state share is usually dependent upon the local contribution to education. So we begin by focusing on the local share.

The local school board budgets an amount for the elementary and secondary school system. This amount is raised by levying a tax on local property. In 1985–86, property taxes accounted for 97.4 percent of all school districts' tax revenues and 80.7 percent of their general revenues from own sources. The property tax dominates educational financing decisions. (The property tax is examined in Chapter 8.) The property tax for education operates on a simple revenue formula.

$$E = t \text{ times } V \tag{6–1}$$

The amount to be raised for education (E) equals the rate (t) times the property base (V). The property base (V) consists of the full market value of the taxable real estate and personal property.

This formula can also be expressed in per pupil terms by dividing both sides of the equation by the number of pupils (P).

$$E/P = t \text{ times } V/P \tag{6–2}$$

The resulting formula is the amount to be raised per pupil (E/P) equals the rate (t) times the per pupil base (V/P).

This simple formula (in per pupil terms) is illustrated in Table 6–2. The table shows the amount to be raised per pupil (E/P) and the tax rate (t) for two school districts. The districts have different per pupil property bases (V/P). District 1 has 15,000 pupils and $1.530 billion in property value, or $102,000 per pupil property base ($1.530 billion divided by 15,000). District 2 has 15,000 pupils

**Figure 6–1**
**Illustration of Spending and Tax Advantages**

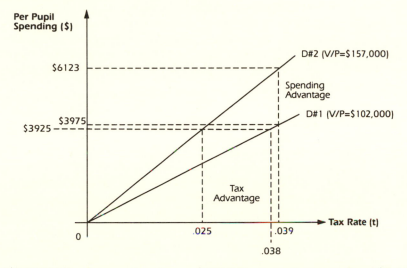

and $2.355 billion in property value, or $157,000 per pupil property base ($2.355 billion divided by 15,000). The amount to be raised per pupil is calculated by multiplying the tax rate (t) times the per pupil property base (V/P). For example, in District 1 the tax rate (.025) times the per pupil property valuation ($102,000) equals the amount to be raised per pupil ($2,550). Holding the per pupil property base constant, the general rule is that as the tax rate increases, the amount to be raised per pupil also increases. To illustrate this point, if the tax rate increases from .025 to .049 in District 1, the amount to be raised per pupil increases from $2,550 to $4,998. The same calculations can be carried out for District 2. The results are also shown in Table 6–2.

Next compare the results across the two districts. A tax rate of .039 nets an amount to be raised per pupil of $3,975 in District 1 and $6,123 in District 2. The difference in per pupil amounts is due to the difference in per pupil property base in the two districts. The difference in the amount to be raised per pupil that comes about as a result of holding the tax rate constant and varying the per pupil property base is called a *spending advantage*. Another comparison would take an amount to be raised per pupil of $3,925. This amount means a tax rate of .038 in District 1 and .025 in District 2. The difference in tax rates that comes about holding the amount to be raised per pupil constant and varying per pupil property base is called a *tax advantage*.

Figure 6–1 displays the general tax rate and amount to be raised per pupil relationship, as well as the spending and tax advantages. The x-axis shows the tax rate (t). The y-axis is the amount to be raised per pupil (E/P). The per pupil property base is held constant within a district. As the tax rate increases, the amount to be raised per pupil increases (holding the per pupil property base constant) for District 1 just as Table 6–2 indicated. The same relationship between tax rate and the amount to be raised per pupil can be drawn for District 2. Notice that if the per pupil property base increases, the line in Figure 6–1 is steeper than it was at the lower per pupil property base. The tax and spending advantages can also be illustrated using the same examples cited above from Table 6–2. Given a tax rate of .039, the spending advantage is illustrated by a per pupil spending level of $3,975 in District 1 and $6,123 in District 2. Given a spending level of $3,925, the tax advantage is illustrated by a tax rate of .038 in District 1 and .025 in District 2.

### The Legal Challenge

Two celebrated cases sum up the legal challenge to educational financing that swept across the United States in the 1970s: *Serrano v. Priest* (1971) in California and *Rodriguez v. San Antonio School Board* (1971) in Texas. While these two cases are mentioned, almost two-thirds of the states experienced court challenges to their school finance plans during this time (Reischauer and Hartman, 1973). These legal appeals are not confined to the past. Recent legal challenges modeled after these two cases have appeared in the late 1980s and into 1990 in Kentucky, Montana, New Jersey, Texas, and West Virginia ("Boost for School Financing Parity," 1988; Suro, 1989; Fiske, 1989). As these five states illustrate, legal challenges are not limited to the poorest states or the weakest state school systems. A recent study published by the American Association of Parents and Children grouped states according to six broad areas: parental involvement, Head Start participation, student-teacher ratios, per student spending, graduation rates, and standardized test scores. Of the five states that face a court challenge to their school financing system: New Jersey and Montana were "graded" in the B Group (the groups ranged from A, B, C, D, and F), West Virginia was in the C Group, Kentucky in the D Group, and Texas in the F Group (Ramstad, 1990).

The Kentucky and New Jersey cases in particular led to major reforms in their state school aid formulas. These two states will be watched during the 1990s to judge the success of the next wave of school finance legal challenges (Fiske, 1990; Sullivan, 1990). These legal challenges show no sign of abating. In fact, they may be the beginning of a nationwide reexamination of how equitably we finance public elementary and secondary education in the United States. A court case is not always necessary. The governor and legislature in Mississippi have initiated school funding changes without the threat of a court case, although there is some doubt about the rapid implementation of these changes (Celis, 1990a).

The spending and the tax advantages illustrated in Table 6–2 and Figure 6–1 form the basis for the legal challenge brought against the school financing systems in *Serrano* and *Rodriguez*. The assertion is that even with the addition of the state government contribution to educational spending the per pupil spending varies directly with per pupil property base. The higher the per pupil property base is, the higher the per pupil spending will be. In other words, the state contribution does little to offset the spending and the tax advantages within a state. It may even reenforce these advantages. If this direct spending-property base relationship holds within a state, then elementary and secondary school children living in property poor districts are being denied the same educational resources that their counterparts receive in property rich districts.

In legal terms, the schoolchildren are not receiving equal protection under the law, a guarantee of the Fourteenth Amendment of the United States Constitution and a provision of many state constitutions (Coons, Clune, and Sugarman, 1970). The children's treatment under the law varies with the wealth of the school district in which they live. In the case of *Serrano* the California State Supreme Court employed a *negative definition* of equality of educational opportunity, as did a three-judge federal panel in the case of *Rodriguez*. The courts did not pick among the many and varied definitions of equality of educational opportunity described above. They stated what they did not want to happen (the term "negative" definition). The courts did not want a school financing plan in which the spending advantage and, therefore, the tax advantage were present (Schoettle, 1972).

The California Supreme Court did not say that the property tax is necessarily an illegal means of raising revenues for education, nor did it say that equal dollar expenditures per pupil are required in all schools or districts. Simply, the ruling said that the quality of a pupil's education cannot be a function of the relative wealth of the district or the state in which the child resides. The three-judge federal panel in Texas issued the same warning. It is the responsibility of the state to ensure that communities that paid the same tax rates or extended equivalent efforts in behalf of education received services of an equal quality. The U.S. Supreme Court rejected *Rodriguez* by a 5–4 vote. Thus, the Serrano principle embodied in *Rodriguez* is not the law of the land. However, a series of state supreme court cases have kept this issue alive and forced state governments to respond to the spending-property base relationship. The nature of the response is the next subject.

## STATE-LOCAL EDUCATIONAL FINANCE OPTIONS

State-local financing schemes for elementary and secondary education divide into three broad categories: one that emphasizes the local school district originally called *district power equalizing*, one that emphasizes the state government called *full state assumption*, and one that emphasizes the individual called an *education voucher*. What follows is a description of each scheme and an assessment based on three questions: (1) Does the scheme satisfy the negative definition of equality of educational opportunity set out by the courts? (2) Who is central to the educational finance decision? and (3) What other factors beyond financial considerations, if any, are involved in the educational finance decision?

### District Power Equalizing

*Description.* Coons, Clune, and Sugarman (1970) advanced the notion of a school financing scheme that was built around the fiscal authority of the local school district, but still satisfied the Serrano principle set down by the California State Supreme Court. That scheme is called district power equalizing, or DPE. More recently, a DPE plan has come to be known as a *guaranteed tax base* plan, or GTB. In its pure form, this proposal equalizes the per pupil wealth (property) base among local school districts within a state. School districts that make similar tax efforts (as measured by the tax rate, t, in the simple revenue formula described above) will have identical per pupil spending regardless of their actual per pupil property valuation. This plan does not mean all districts have the same tax rate and/or per pupil spending level. It does mean that the greater the effort, the higher the per pupil spending. A simple DPE system is:

$$SA = E/P \text{ times } (1 \text{ minus the ratio of V/P to GV}) \qquad (6\text{--}3)$$

$$E/P = (t \text{ times V/P}) \text{ plus } SA \qquad (6\text{--}4)$$

We have already seen E/P (per pupil spending), t (tax rate), and V/P (per pupil property base). What is new in these two formulas is SA, per pupil state aid, and GV, per pupil state guaranteed property base. GV is the amount of per pupil property base that the state government places at the disposal of each local school district to finance education regardless of what the actual local school district per pupil property base is.

The example below illustrates (6–3) and (6–4). Suppose that the DPE scheme is applied to the two school districts in Table 6–2. In that example, District 1 had a per pupil property base (V/P) of $102,000 and District 2 a V/P of $157,000. We assume that each district spends $3,925 per pupil (E/P) and that the state government guarantees each of these districts a per pupil property base (GV) of the average of the two actual figures (one half of the sum of $102,000 plus $157,000), or $129,500. In that case, the DPE calculations are:

*District 1*

$$SA = E/P \text{ times } (1 \text{ minus the ratio of V/P to GV}) \qquad (6\text{--}3')$$

$$SA = \$3925 \text{ times } (1 \text{ minus } (\$102,000/129,500))$$

$$= \$3925 \text{ times } (1 \text{ minus } .788)$$

$$= \$832 \text{ (rounded off)}$$

$$E/P = (t \text{ times V/P}) \text{ plus } SA \qquad (6\text{--}4')$$

$$\$3925 = (t \text{ times } \$102,000) \text{ plus } \$832$$

$$t = .030$$

**Figure 6–2**
**Illustration of District Power Equalizing System Using Equations 6–3 and 6–4**

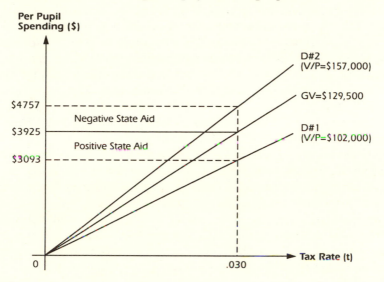

*District 2*

$$SA = E/P \text{ times } (1 \text{ minus the ratio of V/P to GV}) \tag{6-3''}$$
$$SA = \$3925 \text{ times } (1 \text{ minus } (\$157{,}000/129{,}500))$$
$$= \$3925 \text{ times } (1 \text{ minus } 1.212)$$
$$= -\$832 \text{ (rounded off)}$$
$$E/P = (t \text{ times } V/P) \text{ plus } SA \tag{6-4''}$$
$$\$3925 = (t \text{ times } \$157{,}000) \text{ plus } (-\$832)$$
$$t = .030$$

Despite its having an actual per pupil property base advantage, District 2 spends the same amount as District 1 ($3,925) for the same tax effort (.030). The reason is that since it possesses a higher per pupil property base, District 2 is forced to turn over the additional amount that it raises ($832) to the state government in the form of a ''negative aid'' payment. This arrangement assures that the same tax effort nets the same per pupil spending regardless of the actual per pupil property base in a district. Each and every district is tied to the state guaranteed per pupil property base. Of course, if the voters of District 2 decided to spend more than $3,925, say $5,338, they could do so. Then the tax rate would jump to .041 and the negative aid payment would increase to $1,132. Figure 6–2 illustrates the DPE calculations discussed above.

If both districts spend $3,925 per pupil, then the tax rate will be .030. District 1 raises $3,093 on its own per pupil property base of $102,000 and receives

$832 per pupil in state aid. District 2 raises $4,757 on its own per pupil property base of $157,000 and surrenders $832 in a negative aid payment. If District 2 decides to raise its per pupil spending level to $5,338, then its tax rate increases to .041 and its negative aid payment increases to $1,132 per pupil.

*Assessment.* A brief assessment of DPE begins with the court ordered negative definition of equality of educational opportunity. The DPE system described above satisfies this definition. The spending and tax advantages that led to cases like *Serrano* and *Rodriguez* have been eliminated. Every student regardless of the actual per pupil property valuation (V/P) of his/her district has a state guaranteed property base (GV) amount from which the district can draw (Treacy and French, 1974; Feldstein, 1975; Ladd, 1975).

DPE supports the libertarian view that local school districts should control local spending and taxing decisions. Control of the educational finance decision is in the hands of the local school district. Through a voting process with all the strengths and weaknesses reviewed in Chapter 5, the local school district selects the per pupil spending level (E/P) and tax rate (t). Because the local school district retains controls over the educational finance decision, we can expect variations in per pupil spending levels across districts within a state. These variations cannot be attributable to differences in per pupil property base (V/P) since DPE has neutralized these, but per pupil spending differences will remain.

They remain because other factors besides per pupil property base influence per pupil spending. Under the theory of clubs and the Tiebout model, these "other" factors led to the formation of the district in the first place. They are generally referred to as the tastes and preferences people have for public goods/ services. Efficiency requires that the budgetary process should reflect the local school district's tastes, perceived needs, and income (Brazer, 1971). Specifically, they have already been identified in the discussion on determinants of educational spending. Recall that median family income, population density, federal aid, percent secondary students, and percent of population living in urban areas all affect per pupil spending. DPE neutralizes per pupil property base differences and shifts the emphasis to differences in these other factors.

### Full State Assumption

*Description.* A plan that eliminates locally raised revenues for financing public elementary and secondary education and that authorizes the state government to distribute school aid in a uniform manner so that any students with similar educational characteristics receive similar support, regardless of their place of residence, is called *Full State Assumption*, or FSA. Nowadays, FSA has been called a Foundation plan. FSA has been on the educational finance scene for some time (Morrison, 1930, and more recently Cooper, 1971).

In its pure form, the following set of equations captures the most important features of FSA:

SE = E* times SP  (6–5)

SE is statewide spending for education. It equals a statewide per pupil spending level (E*) times the number of pupils in the state (SP). E* can vary by category of student. For example, categories can include: grade level, geographic location, learning disability, and so on.

St = SE divided by SV  (6–6)

St is the statewide property tax rate. It equals statewide spending for education (SE) divided by the statewide property base (SV).

LR = St times LV  (6–7)

LR is the amount of property taxes raised within a local jurisdiction. It equals the statewide tax rate (St) times the local property base (LV).

LE = E* times LP  (6–8)

LE is the amount of spending for education within a local jurisdiction. It equals the statewide per pupil spending level (E*) times the number of pupils in the local jurisdiction.

SA = LE minus LR  (6–9)

SA is the amount of state aid (positive or negative—by now you should be used to the notion of negative state aid) for a local jurisdiction. It equals the amount of spending within a local jurisdiction (LE) minus the amount of property taxes raised within a local jurisdiction (LR).

The example below illustrates equations (6–5) through (6–9) for the two districts introduced in Table 6–2. Remember that District 1 has a per pupil property base of $102,000 and District 2 a per pupil property base of $157,000. Each district has a total enrollment of 15,000. Total state enrollment is 30,000. The statewide spending for education (E*) is $4,500.

SE = $4500 times 30,000 = $135,000,000  (6–5′)

St = 135,000,000 divided by $3,885,000,000  (6–6′)

($3,885,000,000 is the state property base. It is the sum of 15,000 times $102,000 *plus* 15,000 times $157,000.)

St = .034749

*District 1*

LR = .034749 times $1,530,000,000 = $53,166,023  (6–7′)
LE = $4500 times 15,000 = $67,500,000  (6–8′)
SA = $67,500,000 minus $53,166,023 = + $14,333,977  (6–9′)

*District 2*

LR = .034749 times $2,355,000,000 = $81,833,977            (6–7″)

LE = $4500 times 15,000 = $67,500,000            (6–8′)

SA = $67,500,000 minus $81,833,977 = − $14,333,977            (6–9′)

In the simple example above, the FSA scheme transfers resources from the "rich" District 2 to the "poor" District 1. In this way, the same statewide tax rate (.034749) results in the same statewide spending per pupil ($4,500).

*Assessment.* An FSA scheme, like the one just described, certainly satisfies the negative definition of equality of educational opportunity. FSA assumes an egalitarian approach in the distribution of school aid monies since it allocates aid in some uniform manner. Regardless of the actual local per pupil property base, per pupil spending is established statewide without exception. In this way, there will be no violation of the principles embodied in the *Serrano* and the *Rodriguez* decisions. FSA should reduce inequalities in educational opportunities since it rules out per pupil spending disparities. Moreover, some taxpayers will benefit by a shift to a statewide property tax that removes interjurisdictional tax inequities.

The control of the education finance decision is in the hands of the state government. FSA eliminates the local control that DPE stresses in the name of equality. Modifications of this tight state control can come in two forms: a spending classification system that allows for spending variations based on students' needs and a "local add-on" that allows local jurisdictions to add to the statewide E* (Rossmiller, 1972).

The centralization of the education finance decision under FSA means that other socio-economic factors that can play havoc with the equity of the DPE system are swept aside. Variations in family income, the grade composition of the school enrollment, the degree of urbanization of the population by local jurisdiction do not enter into the FSA decision process. Unlike the DPE system, local differences do not lead to local disparities in per pupil spending for education. The price? Centralization of the education finance decision. Is that too high a price? It is left up to the voters and the reader. In almost all the states, the answer is that the price is, indeed, too high.

## Education Voucher

*Description.* Friedman (1962) proposed education vouchers over two decades ago. Twenty-five years later they are part of the conservative school reform chic. Education vouchers work like this. The state government takes on the primary responsibility of financing public elementary and secondary education. The family of each school-age child receives a voucher (a ticket) worth a specified amount to be spent on an elementary or secondary education; for example, the voucher might be worth $4,000. The child may enroll in any public (in some proposals public or private) school. The school accepts the voucher as payment of tuition. In turn, the school redeems the voucher for a cash payment from the state government. These funds are used to operate the school.

There are two principal modifications to this plan that advocates often mention. First, the price of the voucher may be contingent upon the income of the family and family size. Some families may receive the voucher "free"; and others might pay $3,500 for it. Second, the families may be permitted to *add* on to the amount of the voucher. For example, a family may take the voucher with a face value of $4,000 and add $2,000 to meet a $6,000 tuition bill.

Still another variation on the general voucher notion is "choose-a-school" or "open enrollment" programs. Students may select any public school within the state system. Their state aid support follows them to their new school. If that school is outside the district in which they reside, then the local district loses that state aid. Again, if the amount of state aid is $4,000, each student could shop around for a school. The school of choice receives the $4,000 from the state, while the local district loses $4,000 if the school is outside its boundaries. At this time, open enrollment programs are being tried and talked about in many states; for example, Massachusetts, Washington, and Wisconsin. However, the model program has been operating with some success in Minnesota since 1985 (Putka, 1988; Loth, 1988; and Wells, 1990a, 1990b). Using a slightly different approach, the voters of Oregon have approved the granting of tax credits to cover tuition for private school or expenses for educating a child at home (Celis, 1990b).

The emphasis on forcing the schools to compete for students is designed to impose market discipline on the public education system. Competition for students among the schools, the argument goes, will improve the quality of the education program. Administrators, teachers, and staff must stay on their toes and off their laurels in order to remain competitive. As a result, proponents of these schemes assert that the students can only gain.

*Assessment.* Although educational vouchers and choose-a-school programs stress marketplace competition rather than equality of educational opportunity, these educational finance options would appear to satisfy the negative definition of equality of education opportunity. Afterall, the local per pupil property base does not determine the per pupil educational spending. In fact, a student can take his/her voucher and spend it in the school of his/her choice regardless of the student's place of residence or the school's location.

These options mix public financing with private choice. The state pays for the student's education. However, the individual student or his/her family chooses the school in which to enroll. Unlike DPE or FSA, these options emphasize individual choice; an emphasis that is very much in the Tiebout model tradition. Let the individual seek out the level of desired public education rather than having the state or locality impose the level of a public good/service.

Three fears, in particular, dampen many people's enthusiasm for the education voucher or the choose-a-school program. These fears may be more imaginary than real. However, if they turn out to be real, then they pose serious problems for the advancement of these proposals.

Racial segregation of the schools is often the first criticism of these plans. An education voucher or a choose-a-school program is viewed as a means of allowing white schoolchildren to escape inner-city public schools. If that proves to be true, then racial segregation in the public schools will be more real than ever. These plans must overcome the charge that they will, in effect, undo the integration/desegregation efforts through which many inner city residents have often painfully lived.

A spin-off of the racial segregation allegation is that these plans will skim off the best students from the inner city schools. Suburban schools will actively recruit students just the way American colleges and universities do. The question is whether student recruitment should be a factor at the elementary and secondary level. In addition, can inner city schools compete for these students under these plans while they also try to satisfy their mission of educating all inner city children, including those least fortunate?

Last, disparities in family wealth could reenter the education financing decision. If the education voucher allows an individual family to add-on to the base that the voucher establishes, then education spending per pupil will vary directly with family wealth. That could easily be interpreted as a violation of the negative definition of equality of educational opportunity. The voucher would then advance marketplace competition, but sacrifice equality of educational opportunity.

Where does the description and assessment of these three educational finance options—DPE, FSA, and vouchers—leave the issue? Under certain conditions, all three could meet the modest standard set by the negative definition. Favoring one plan over another will determine your position on who should be central to the education finance decision: The local school district? The state government? The individual family? Or it may come down to the other factors involved in the education finance decision. In the case of DPE, how do socio-economic class distinctions within a local school district influence per pupil spending decisions? In the case of FSA, can people tolerate the degree of centralization required to mute these socio-economic class distinctions? In the case of the voucher, is the fear of racial segregation, the pressures of and the potential abuses inherent in student recruitment, and disparities in family wealth enough to frighten you concerning the voucher notion?

## SUMMARY

1. Education is a public service that mixes aspects of a private good with those of a public good. In short, it possesses spillover effects that lead to market failure. The geographic distribution of these spillover effects raises questions concerning the delegation of the responsibility for this public service to the local school district.

2. Determinant studies have revealed factors that influence per pupil education spending

levels. On the positive side, specific variables are median family income, federal aid, per pupil property base, population density, and proportion of secondary school students. On the negative side, specific variables are tax price and percent of population living in urban areas. These determinant studies also show education to have a price elasticity less than 1.0 and an income elasticity less than 1.0.

3. Per pupil educational spending levels vary across the United States. Variations have attracted the state courts' attention. These courts' have evolved a negative definition of equality of educational opportunity that states that the quality of a pupil's education cannot be a function of the relative wealth of the district of the state in which the child resides.

4. In accordance with the negative definition, three types of educational financing options have been discussed and implemented across the United States. One stresses the local district, district power equalizing; another stresses the state government, full state assumption; and the third stresses the individual family, the education voucher or choose-a-school program. Personal preferences on who should be central to the education financing decision and the role of socio-economic distinctions determine support for one of these three options.

# CHAPTER 7

---

## *State and Local Taxation in a Federal System*

## PREVIEW

State and local governments generally raise almost 45 percent of the revenues that the United States public sector collects. This chapter serves as an overview of the state-local government tax system. It reviews two economic principles of taxation; looks at current state-local tax practices; and then discusses the implications of setting tax policy in a federal system. That discussion leads to the development of a criteria for a "good" tax system.

## INTRODUCTION

The debate over state-local tax practices has raged for decades and is still ongoing. Governors battle with members of the legislature, mayors fight with members of the city council, and school superintendents bargain with members of the school board. Often the taxpayers feel that they are onlookers at their own fiscal trial. There is, however, more to establishing tax policy than political wangling. Economists have developed two long-standing principles of taxation. The justification of any tax should start with one of these two principles.

## PRINCIPLES OF TAXATION

Two competing economic principles come into play whenever economists seek to justify a tax. The two principles are the *benefit principle* and the *ability to pay principle*. The first principle stresses efficiency; the second principle stresses equity. This rush to justify does not mean that every tax completely satisfies one of the two principles. However, they do serve as a means to classify state-local taxes (Musgrave and Musgrave, 1989).

### Benefit Principle

Copying the private market, the benefit principle states that the tax payment for a public good/service should equal the value of the benefit received by an individual who consumes the public good/service. This relationship defines more than a tax principle. It offers a tax-expenditure formula because the benefit principle links together tax and expenditure policies. An individual pays, exactly pays, for any benefits received as a result of the provision of a public good/ service. This relationship not only rules out public sector redistribution activity, but also is very consistent with the theory of clubs and the Tiebout model.

Implementation of the benefit principle is difficult. In addition to the chronic problem of free riders, the benefit principle requires a precise knowledge of the distribution of public good/service benefits across all individuals. While that precise knowledge is not likely, there have been taxes imposed that are justified on benefit principle grounds; for example, license fees, turnpike tolls, and hotel room taxes. Other examples include special property tax assessments for street repair, curbing and the like; and gasoline taxes dedicated to highway maintenance. None of these examples, though, completely satisfies the benefit principle.

The last tax mentioned above—the dedicated gasoline tax—is an example of *earmarking*. Earmarking means that the government has stated the specific use for tax revenues. Earmarking introduces rigidities into the budget process and reduces the discretionary authority of public managers. However, voting on the earmarked taxing-spending proposal forces people to reveal their preferences for public goods/services (Buchanan, 1963).

### Ability to Pay Principle

Putting aside the private market, the ability to pay principle states that an individual's tax payment has little to do with the value of public good/service benefits received, but everything to do with an individual's economic well-being. The ability to pay principle states that individuals with equal economic well-being will pay the same taxes and individuals with greater economic well-being will pay higher taxes. In short, the amount an individual pays varies directly with his/her economic well-being. The first part of this statement (''equal treatment of equals'') refers to a rule for treating individuals of equal economic well-being, or *horizontal equity*. The second part of the statement refers to a rule for treating individuals of unequal economic well-being, or *vertical equity*. Unlike the benefit principle, the ability to pay principle breaks the link between taxes and spending. Taxes are considered in isolation. Spending on public goods/ services is a related, but separate decision. The ability to pay principle paves the way for financing public sector redistribution activities.

Implementation of the ability to pay principle also encounters two general controversies. The first deals with the tax base. How should the public sector measure an individual's economic well-being? The question is central to the ability to pay principle, but the answer is not obvious. Some economists argue that economic well-being requires a comprehensive measure of income, or accretion (addition) to an individual's wealth over a period of time. Other economists argue that economic well-being requires a comprehensive measure of consumption over a period of time. Income based taxes may well offer a superior measure of ability to pay, but they also may affect willingness to work and save. (The empirical evidence is far from conclusive.) Consumption based taxes may well encourage savings and accelerated economic growth. (Again, the empirical evidence is far from conclusive, but a switch from income to consumption based taxes could lead to administrative problems and tax inequities.) Needless to say, the answer in theory to the preferable tax base question is unresolved. The answer in fact, at least in the United States, is resolved. Some form of the income based measure is used to capture ability to pay (Davies, 1986; Pechman, 1983).

The second controversy surrounding the ability to pay principle deals with the tax rate. If an income based measure is assumed, then how should vertical equity be achieved? In other words, as an individual's income increases, how should the tax burden increase? The choices are a system of taxes based on *progressive rates* (as income increases, the taxes paid as a percentage of income increase), *proportional rates* (as income increases, the taxes paid as a percentage of income remain constant), or *regressive rates* (as income increases, the taxes paid as a percentage of income decrease). Under different circumstances, each of these tax structures may satisfy the standard of vertical equity that calls for increased tax payments as an individual's income increases (Blum and Kalven, 1953). The politically accepted definition of vertical equity in the United States is that at the federal government level some degree of progressive tax rates is apparent, at the state government level proportional tax rates, and at the local government level regressive tax rates (Phares, 1980; Pechman, 1985).

## TAXATION IN A FEDERAL SYSTEM

Americans enjoy a hair-raising ride, especially if it takes some unexpected twists. Apparently that trait goes back to the founding fathers because the federal system they created gives the state and local tax decision enough twists to compare favorably with a Six Flags roller-coaster ride. The federal system invites state and local governments to fashion their own distinctive tax policy. They pick the level and the form of their tax systems. Now the twist! These tax decisions are not carried out in a vacuum. Residents, businesses, and other state and local governments react to them. There is an incentive in the federal system for one state to exploit the tax decisions of its neighbor for its own advantage. Why? What is at stake?

### Taxes and the Regional Economy

State and local governments compete for business retention and expansion (Testa and Allardice, 1988). While private market forces (e.g., a skilled workforce, low interest financing, available land, a modern transportation system, sufficient energy supplies, affordable housing, and so on) do in fact dominate the business investment process, the system of federalism distorts this process so that state and local governments act as if their tax policies dictate business investment decisions.

The Federal Reserve Bank of Chicago has estimated that in the 1980s, thirty-eight states have offered construction loans and forty states have offered some form of tax break to businesses to entice them to locate within the state's borders. Some experts claim that the price tag for state and local government incentives to sway businesses to come around runs as high as $30 billion a year. Not the magnitude of the savings and loan bail-out, but not small potatoes! During the 1980s, some examples of business location and expansion incentives are: Illinois offered Sears $178 million to stay in state; again Illinois offered Chrysler-Mitsubishi $183 million; Michigan offered Mazda $120 million; and New York comes in with $235 million for Chase Manhattan Bank, $98 million for NBC, and $97 million for Citicorp. One frustrating part of the state and local governments business incentive programs is that it is never clear that the incentive produces more resources for the public sector and increased social welfare for the community than it costs (Guskind, 1990).

Taxes in general and state taxes in particular suffer from the "funhouse mirror" effect. We have all stood before a funhouse mirror and laughed at the distorted image of ourselves—our large features vanish and our small features dominate. The funhouse mirror effect distorts the role of state and local taxes. Many times their role in economic performance is marginal, but suddenly appears dominant. The role of state and local governments moves from backdrop to centerstage while private market forces and the federal government's policies disappear into the chorus. This outcome is generally contrary to both the theory and the practices of business retention and expansion.

In this upside-down world, the *paradox of competition* manifests itself; that is, interstate competition for business investment may ultimately be harmful to the state's well-being. The perception that this competition determines business retention and expansion decisions puts pressure on state and local governments to participate in a high cost, uncertain bidding process. State and local governments may grant excessive tax breaks to attract business investment. The tax break may be excessive in one of two ways. The state and local governments may misjudge the revenue benefits to the jurisdictions relative to other investment projects over the long run and simply "give more back" than the jurisdiction receives in new revenues. In addition, state and local governments may grant tax breaks to businesses that would have located in the state without the tax incentive. Because businesses can play one state against another, this paradox of competition can be bias toward excessive tax breaks. The result of this competition is that the original taxpayers, residential and commercial-industrial, must pay for the excessive tax break. Alternatively, they can resist any tax increases and jeopardize existing public service levels.

The paradox of competition can be illustrated with a card-playing analogy. Suppose a casino sponsored a poker game. A player has no chance of winning except by playing. For its part the casino receives a share of the pot regardless of which player wins or loses. The casino always wins. Interstate competition for economic development bears a painful resemblance to the casino poker game. Business assumes the role of the casino. The states become the poker players. Each player's (state's) bid forces the other players (states) to respond with higher bids or drop out. As the pot grows, there is one sure winner, the casino (the business). A state's overall well-being may be the loser because the resources for the bid comes from foregone tax revenues. As the bid increases, potential taxes decrease. With their drop, the quality of state supported public goods/ services could also decline. This decline in state well-being is possible because of the *principle of the inverse bid*. In this poker game, the player with the weakest hand may raise the stakes in order to win the hand. The consequence is that even though the weak player will usually lose, he/she has raised the bets placed by other (stronger) players and increased the casino's share.

In this way, federalism creates a pitfall for state economic development strategy. Often states are set against one another, the states with the weakest economic prospects may offer overly generous enticements to a particular firm. The firm, in turn, uses these bids as leverage against other states' offers. In the end, the firm may well choose the state in which it had planned to locate all along. Now the firm has received greater tax inducements than it would have without the interstate competition. The increased inducements come at the expense of state well-being. How does the poker game analogy translate into an economic model?

## Impact of Tax Policy on Mobile Factors

Along with "things that bump in the night," we are told that people (and the businesses that they run) are afraid of taxes. In a federal system, this fear, if it exists, is exploited. One state's tax hike is another state's economic bonanza. For example, in 1990 Governor Jim Florio of New Jersey proposed and signed into law the state's largest, single tax hike, almost $3 billion. Before the ink was dry on the bill, the state's newspapers carried stories of businesses moving across the border to Pennsylvania (Schwab, 1990; Schwaneberg, 1990). Again, in 1990 Governor Michael Dukakis of Massachusetts signed into law the commonwealth's largest, single tax hike, almost $2 billion. Governor Judd Gregg of New Hampshire responded by sending letters to 2,700 Massachusetts businesses singing the praises of the business climate in his state (Allvin, 1990). Before we all accept this argument, let's examine the conceptual model that generates this conclusion.

The economic model begins with a federal system based on the Tiebout assumptions. People are mobile and the local jurisdictions are the same in every way. People, jobs, and capital will move from one jurisdiction to another to avoid an unfavorable change in their tax position. For the sake of simplicity, the model consists of two adjacent jurisdictions: Westown and Eastown. The results, of course, can be extended to a larger number of jurisdictions. Both towns raise revenues using a head tax (or a fixed per capita tax (Oates, 1972)).

The people of Eastown decide to experiment with the town's tax system. A property tax (for these purposes, a tax on the value of real estate) replaces the head tax in Eastown. The only difference between Westown and Eastown is the head tax versus the property tax. (This is the ceteris paribus assumption.) In a Tiebout environment where people (all factors) have full mobility, what are the consequences of this difference?

The switch to a property tax could drive up land rents and housing costs in Eastman relative to Westown. On the supply side, the imposition of a property tax in Eastown raises land and housing costs by increasing factor prices. On the demand side, people will move to Eastown since they no longer have to pay the head tax there in order to receive public goods/services. The tax switch lowers the perceived price of public goods/services.

The property tax could also discourage new construction and maintenance of existing structures in Eastown relative to Westown. Economists hold that people budget an amount for their housing costs (including mortgage payments, property taxes, repair costs, etc.) and transportation. If property taxes increase as they would in Eastown, then funds from the household budget would be pulled away from repair and maintenance to cover the tax increases.

Enough with the property tax! The people of Eastown abandon the property tax and switch to a general sales tax (for these purposes, a tax on the value of all consumption expenditures). Now the only difference between Westown and Eastown is the head tax versus the sales tax. In a Tiebout environment where people (all factors) have full mobility, what are the consequences of this difference?

Under the right circumstances, mobile high spenders in Eastown would be tempted to move to Westown since they would fare better (pay lower taxes) with the head tax than the general sales tax. The same could be said for low spenders in Westown. They might well move to Eastown since the head tax would be a greater tax burden for them than the general sales tax.

While this Eastown-Westown migration might prove less likely, a more likely consequence would require shoppers in Eastown traveling to the stores in Westown to do their shopping and avoid the general sales tax. (Without getting too melodramatic, there is also an incentive to smuggle goods from Westown and sell them illegally in Eastown.) This footloose shopper personifies the *border problem* where shoppers cross political borders to avoid sales taxes. Storeowners in New York City claim they are victims of the border problem as they watch potential clients travel to New Jersey malls. Storeowners in Massachusetts can sympathize with their New York City counterparts as Massachusetts shoppers travel to New Hampshire to spend their money. Incidentally, *blue laws*, or laws that require store closings on Sunday, may also add to a border problem.

Eastowners now turn away from the sales tax to a personal income tax (for these purposes, a proportional tax on all income regardless of source). Now the only difference between Westown and Eastown is the head tax versus the personal income tax. In a Tiebout environment where people (all factors) have full mobility, what are the consequences of this difference?

Economists have long discussed the impact of taxing personal income on the "work, not work" decision, called the *work-leisure trade-off*. In short, the more that the public sector taxes personal income and reduces take-home pay, the more people will pick leisure over work (people will work less). Of course, the degree to which people can afford to choose to work or not tempers this general conclusion. (The elasticity of the labor supply curve addresses this issue.)

While the work-leisure trade-off is a general problem of personal income taxation, another implication of Eastown's personal income tax versus Westown's head tax arises because of the federal system. It deals with the selection of an individual's community of residence. The argument goes like this. People compare their tax burden in Eastown with theirs in Westown. High income people face a greater dollar tax burden in Eastown so they move their residence to Westown. Low income people face a greater dollar tax burden in Westown so they move their residence to Eastown. Aside from the costs of migration between communities, the result is that the personal income tax base in Eastown is gradually eroding. To maintain a specified level of public goods/services would require Eastown to raise its personal income tax rates which would accelerate the inflow/outflow of people. And the cycle goes round and round.

Having faced an increase in land rents and housing costs, a loss of consumer spending, and an out-migration of high income people, Eastowners switch from a personal income tax to a corporate income tax (for these purposes, a tax on net corporate income). Now the only difference between Westown and Eastown is the head tax versus the corporate income tax. In a Tiebout environment where people (all factors) have full mobility, what are the consequences of this difference?

The initial impact of the corporate income tax makes production more expensive in Eastown relative to Westown. These production cost differentials, ceteris paribus, encourage business expansion to and relocation in Westown over Eastown. This conclusion produces the enduring notion that relatively high taxes discourages economic development. (Remember the distortions of the funhouse mirror.)

According to this model which relies upon mobility and the ceteris paribus assumption, tax differentials have some powerful effects: high land rents and housing costs, lost consumption spending, the flight of high income people, and the exodus of business investment. If these are the symptoms of the disease, then there must be an antidote.

The antidote is *tax harmony* or *tax harmonization*. Tax harmony requires that jurisdictions cooperate with one another to design and implement a tax system. That system should reduce the incentive for people, jobs, and capital to move from one jurisdiction to another exclusively for tax advantages. This cooperation does not imply uniform tax policy across all jurisdictions. It does mean that if people, jobs, and capital are highly mobile, jurisdictions should agree to tax these elements in a similar fashion. It does mean that a system of taxes should rely on taxing immobile economic factors, if possible. It does mean that tax systems should be similar across equivalent levels of government, but vary to a greater degree across different levels of governments (Oates, 1972; Break, 1980).

### Impact of Tax Policy on Tax Exportation

The federal system offers yet another joyride with unexpected twists for state and local government tax officials. These officials can set tax policy in such a way that some portion of the tax burden is shifted to taxpayers outside the jurisdiction. This practice is called *tax exportation* or *tax exporting* (McClure, 1967; Hogan and Shelton, 1973; Phares, 1980). Tax exporting means that non-residents are subsidizing a jurisdiction's public goods/services for residents. Nice if you can get it!

Many taxes can be designed to shift tax burdens outside the taxing jurisdiction: general and selective sales taxes, licenses, corporate income taxes, property taxes, and severance taxes on minerals and timber (Shelton and Vogt, 1982). Tax shifting may occur through higher prices for goods and services produced within the jurisdiction, but sold outside the jurisdiction. Texas oil and gas, Wyoming coal, Washington timber, Louisiana tourism, Nevada gambling, Maine potatoes, and Massachusetts hi-tech services are examples.

Of course, one jurisdiction's tax exporting is another jurisdiction's tax importing. If a resident of New York buys a Washington state apple, the tax embedded in the price of that apple is exported by Washington and imported by New York. *Tax importation* or *tax importing* is the tax levied by one jurisdiction and paid by a nonresident (the resident of another jurisdiction). Tax importing is usually associated with taxes on gasoline, tobacco, alcohol, recreation, and general consumption expenditures. The federal system creates an incentive to establish tax policy that maximizes tax exporting and minimizes tax importing.

Not every state can succeed at both. A study of tax exporting and importing for 1975–76 shows that the biggest net winners (over $100 million) were California, Louisiana, New York and Texas. The biggest net losers (over $100 million) were Indiana, Missouri, New Jersey, Ohio, and Pennsylvania (Phares, 1980). Much has changed since then, but regions that have built their economy

**Table 7-1**
**Profile of Selected State-Local Revenue Items, 1986–87 (per capita)**

| Selected Revenue Items | United States Average | Range (1) | Ratio of High to Low States (All States) (2) | Ratio of High to Low States (Excl. Highest 5 & Lowest 5) |
|---|---|---|---|---|
| Current Own Source Revenue | $2347 | $1499 – 9414 | 6.28 | 1.62 |
| Total Taxes | 1665 | 990 – 3162 | 3.19 | 1.76 |
| Income Taxes | 437 | 0 – 1043 | NA | 12.88 |
| Sales Tax | 593 | 143 – 1068 | 7.47 | 1.85 |
| Property Tax | 498 | 124 – 1187 | 9.57 | 3.75 |
| Charges & Misc. Rev. | 573 | 362 – 6114 | 16.89 | 1.86 |

Notes: (1) Range is simply the spread between the lowest revenue state and the highest revenue state.

(2) The ratio of high to low revenue state is the high revenue state divided by the low revenue state.

*Source*: U.S. Bureau of Census, *Census of Governments*, 1988.

around the export base theory stand a good chance of playing and prospering at the tax exportation game.

## STATE-LOCAL GOVERNMENT REVENUES: AN OVERVIEW

Table 7-1 provides a profile of specific state-local government revenues for 1986–87. (Also, see Carnevale, 1988.) The revenues are called *own source revenues* (OSR) because they are raised from taxes and charges. OSR is presented in per capita terms (OSR per person). The data are taken from the U.S. Bureau of Census, *Government Finances*. The average per capita OSR in the United States for state-local governments in 1986–87 was $2,347. Taxes represent almost 71 percent of OSR. If state and local governments were looked at separately, then the primary revenue source for state governments was sales taxes and for local governments property taxes.

Table 7-1 also displays revenue variations in the U.S. federal system. For example, while the overall average per capita OSR is $2,347, it may vary from a high of $9,414 (Alaska) to a low of $1,499 (Arkansas). The ratio of the highest OSR state to the lowest OSR state is 6.28; that is, Alaska raises over $6.00 for every $1.00 Arkansas raises. Since Alaska's figure is something of an anomaly, another comparison is needed. An alternative view that is less influenced by the behavior of the high and the low OSR states is to drop off the five highest OSR states and the five lowest OSR states and recalculate the ratio. This gives a ratio of the sixth-ranked state (Delaware $2,797) to the forty-fifth-ranked state (Missouri $1,727). That ratio is 1.62; that is, Delaware raises $1.62 for every $1.00 Missouri raises.

Comparable figures are calculated for each of the revenue items. The variation in per capita OSR across these items is the natural outcome of a system of decentralized government. Using the conservatively estimated ratio in the extreme right column, revenues raised by income taxes (13.17) appear to have the largest gap from top to bottom state, followed by property taxes (3.60), sales taxes (1.85), and charges (1.80).

Table 7–2 offers another perspective on state-local government tax policy. The states are listed by Census region. Not only is per capita OSR shown, but also the level of OSR raised for every $1,000 of personal income. (We will discuss the State Share column shortly.) On average in the United States, the per capita OSR is $2,347 and for every $1,000 of personal income state and local governments collected $162 in OSR. This ratio of OSR to personal income in thousands becomes a measure of tax effort across the country.

The groupings support a tendency in tax policy formulation discussed under the heading of taxation in a federal system; that is, while state and local governments can independently establish tax policy, they are very much aware of their neighbors' tax policy. Neighboring states might well set similar levels of taxation to avoid the paradox of competition. For example, Michigan, Minnesota, and Wisconsin; California, Colorado, and Oregon; and Connecticut, Massachusetts, New Jersey, and New York have above average per capita OSR levels. In the same vein, Maine, New Hampshire, and Vermont; and the southern region exhibit below average per capita OSR levels. Within these clusters, there may be little opportunity for tax competition, but across clusters there is ample opportunity. For example, the New England region is divided evenly between above average and below average per capita OSR states. This fact virtually guarantees that the Massachusetts-New Hampshire border war will continue. (For a recent exchange, see Gold, 1989.)

Table 7–2 also raises the issue of equity in the federal system in the form of spending and/or tax advantages that income rich states possess relative to their income poor neighbors. (Chapter 6 introduced these concepts in the analysis of education financing.) A review of Table 7–2 shows that for most states there is a direct association between the ratio of OSR to personal income and the per capita OSR. As the ratio increases, the per capita OSR increases and vice versa. However, for some states the ratio of OSR to personal income is below the national average of $162, but the per capita OSR is above the national average of $2,347. Examples with the ratio of OSR to personal income and per capita OSR in parentheses are: Connecticut ($143, $2,787), Maryland ($152, $2803), and New Jersey ($152, $2,530). These states are income rich states that can raise relatively more per capita OSR with less effort than the average state in the United States. Examples of income poor states that show a higher than average

**Table 7-2**
**State-Local Per Capita Own Source Revenue (OSR), the Relation of OSR to**
**$1,000 Personal Income (PY), and the State Government Share of OSR, 1986-87**

| Region & State | Per Capita OSR | Relation of OSR to $1000 PY | State Share | Region & State | Per Capita OSR | Relation of OSR to $1000 PY | State Share |
|---|---|---|---|---|---|---|---|
| USA | $2347 | $162 | 55.5% | | | | |
| **N.E.** | | | | **E.S.C.** | | | |
| ME | 2092 | 165 | 67.1 | KY | $1713 | $153 | 69.5% |
| NH | 1965 | 127 | 49.2 | TN | 1684 | 142 | 54.1 |
| VT | 2251 | 171 | 65.9 | AL | 1757 | 156 | 61.9 |
| MA | 2676 | 152 | 67.1 | MS | 1649 | 170 | 56.6 |
| RI | 2404 | 167 | 68.8 | | | | |
| CT | 2787 | 143 | 63.2 | **W.S.C.** | | | |
| **M.A.** | | | | AR | 1499 | 136 | 64.5 |
| | | | | LA | 2016 | 178 | 58.3 |
| NY | 3542 | 208 | 47.4 | OK | 1874 | 151 | 59.5 |
| NJ | 2803 | 152 | 60.1 | TX | 2024 | 151 | 44.4 |
| PA | 2118 | 149 | 56.0 | **Mt.** | | | |
| **E.N.C.** | | | | MT | 2161 | 180 | 53.4 |
| OH | 2096 | 151 | 56.7 | ID | 1702 | 151 | 61.7 |
| IN | 1883 | 144 | 60.3 | WY | 4067 | 307 | 55.1 |
| IL | 2169 | 140 | 52.4 | CO | 2471 | 164 | 45.2 |
| MI | 2482 | 169 | 56.7 | NM | 2449 | 217 | 72.6 |
| WI | 2398 | 173 | 60.8 | AZ | 2293 | 174 | 54.3 |
| | | | | UT | 2066 | 190 | 57.7 |
| **W.N.C.** | | | | NV | 2397 | 162 | 56.1 |
| MN | 2910 | 195 | 55.4 | **Pac.** | | | |
| IA | 2228 | 166 | 56.1 | | | | |
| MO | 1727 | 126 | 55.8 | WA | 2355 | 160 | 62.5 |
| ND | 2211 | 175 | 65.3 | OR | 2410 | 183 | 52.1 |
| SD | 1801 | 153 | 54.4 | CA | 2697 | 164 | 57.9 |
| NE | 2220 | 161 | 48.0 | AK | 9414 | 521 | 76.0 |
| KS | 2372 | 163 | 44.5 | HI | 2536 | 174 | 80.4 |
| **S.A.** | | | | | | | |
| DE | 2797 | 190 | 78.8 | | | | |
| MD | 2530 | 152 | 58.1 | | | | |
| VA | 2064 | 137 | 58.1 | | | | |
| WV | 1740 | 165 | 69.2 | | | | |
| NC | 1860 | 151 | 63.5 | | | | |
| SC | 1820 | 163 | 64.8 | | | | |
| GA | 2078 | 158 | 48.6 | | | | |
| FL | 2072 | 146 | 46.3 | | | | |

*Source:* U.S. Bureau of Census, *Government Finances,* 1988.

ratio of OSR to personal income and a lower than average per capita OSR are: Iowa ($166, $2,228), Louisiana ($178, $2,016), Mississippi ($170, $1649), and Utah ($190, $2,066).

The discussion of tax policy in a federal system coupled with the overview of the current state-local government fiscal data points out some unresolved public policy disputes. One such disagreement deals with the degree of centralization in a federal system and its effect on the growth of the public sector called the *Leviathan hypothesis*. Two economists (Brennan and Buchanan, 1980) have argued that as individual voters turn over control of public spending to higher levels of government, the preferences of the politicians, bureaucrats, and special-interest lobbyists at these higher levels replace the preferences of the voters for the amount of spending and taxing. The switch from decentralized to centralized decision making leads to an inevitable expansion of the public sector. In short, the greater the degree of decentralization of fiscal decision making, the lesser will be the share of private income claimed by the public sector.

Proponents of the Leviathan hypothesis would favor the delegation of functional responsibilities to local governments over state governments and, most certainly, over the federal government. These individuals would find several examples from Table 7–2 to illustrate their point. For example, if you compare per capita OSR, the effort measure, and the state share of state-local government OSR (the column labeled State Share), then three states appear to demonstrate the effects of centralization which the Leviathan hypothesis predicts; namely, high per capita OSR and high tax effort: Alaska ($9,414, $521), Hawaii $2,536, $174), and Delaware ($2,797, $190). On the other hand, three states demonstrate the effects of decentralization; namely, low per capita OSR and low tax effort: New Hampshire ($1,965, $127), Florida ($2,072, $146), and Texas ($2,024, $151). Of course, Table 7–2 also lists several inconsistencies. Among them, New York ($3,542, $208) shows a decentralized state-local public sector and high per capita OSR and tax effort and Indiana ($1,883, $144) and Kentucky ($1,713, $153), plus many of the states in the East and West South Central divisions show a centralized state-local public sector and low per capita OSR and tax effort.

As you might expect by now, more rigorous empirical economic study of the Leviathan hypothesis has produced contradictory results. One study (Oates, 1985) has concluded that there is no strong relationship between the size of government and the degree of centralization. Another (Raimondo, 1989) shows that the Leviathan hypothesis may manifest itself on a service-by-service level. Total general expenditures and public welfare seem to claim a greater share of private income as the degree of centralization increases. On the opposite side, education expenditures seem to claim a smaller share of private income as the degree of centralization increases. The result is more ambiguous for other expenditure categories. The last word is that there is no consensus among economists on whether the Leviathan hypothesis holds. Through the years, politicians (like Presidents Johnson, Nixon, and Reagan) have tinkered with the federal system as if the Leviathan hypothesis was a fact. President Johnson centralized functions to expand the size of the public sector, while Presidents Nixon and Reagan decentralized functions to shrink the size of the public sector.

The overview of the current state-local government fiscal data also allows for further elaboration on the earlier question of the impact of tax policy on the performance of the regional economy. The economic model makes the case that tax differences lead to some significant economic development/growth effects. Some recent studies support this proposition (summarized in Newman and Sullivan, 1988). However, the vast bulk of empirical evidence on intraregional and interstate business investment decisions has not supported that conclusion (Due, 1961; Oakland, 1978).

Two recent studies deserve mention. The first study measured state-local business tax collections as a percentage of the level of net business income across the fifty states (Wheaton, 1983). This study uses 1977 Bureau of Census data. As the competitive game of state-local tax determination would predict, there are variations in these percentage among the states. The New England region ranked the highest (10.2 percent of net business income went to pay state-local business taxes), while the East South Central region ranked the lowest (5.6 percent).

The Wheaton study shows that the highest business tax percentages are in the states with the highest income and the highest level of business activity. Table 7–3 is a simple demonstration of Wheaton's point. It divides the 50 state-local systems into those whose per capita OSR is above the national average (called High) and those below the national average (called Low). Next, the fifty states are arranged by per capita gross state product (GSP) first introduced in Chapter 2. States whose per capita GSP was above the national average are placed in a group labeled High and those below the national average are in a group labeled Low. The number in the parentheses is the ratio of OSR to GSP which indicates the percent of the GSP claimed by the state-local public sector.

Of the 20 states which have a High per capita own source revenue, 13 also have a High per capita gross state product. Of the 30 states which have a Low per capita own source revenue, twenty-six also have a Low per capita gross state product. These results do not support and, in fact, are contrary to the notion that high taxes choke off economic activity. Thirteen states do have high taxes and generate among the highest gross state products. On the opposite side, 26 states have low taxes and are saddled with the lowest per capita gross state products. The percent of gross state product claimed by the state-local public sector (the number in the parentheses) bears little on this question. In light of this conclusion, do business taxes discourage business activity? Acting as if the answer is yes is far from correct.

The second study measures the effect of state-local taxes on business profitability (Papke and Papke, 1984). A "representative" firm (with specified characteristics) was moved from state to state. The profitability of that firm was calculated in each state. This technique isolated the impact of state-local taxes on the profitability of the representative firm. There are variations in profitability associated with state-local tax differences. Since state-local business taxes are such a small share of business costs, it would require a relatively large change in these taxes to cause a small change in business profitability. Changes of this magnitude are not common.

While the tax-economic performance issue is hotly debated, most economists have argued that when adjustments are made to the state and local tax burden on businesses, state and local taxes are an insignificant element in the business

**Table 7–3**

**Gross State Product versus Own Source Revenues, 1986–87 (GSP and OSR in per capita terms)**

| Per Capita State Product | Per Capita Own Source Revenues | |
|---|---|---|
| | HIGH | LOW |
| HIGH | Alaska (.257) a/<br>Wyoming (.177)<br>Connecticut (.126)<br>New York (.174)<br>New Jersey (.138)<br>Nevada (.119)<br>Massachusetts (.135)<br>California (.136)<br>Delaware (.151)<br>Hawaii (.139)<br>Colorado (.136)<br>Minnesota (.162)<br>Washington (.135) | Texas (.111)<br>Illinois (.120)<br>New Hampshire (.109)<br>Virginia (.115) |
| LOW | Kansas (.137)<br>Maryland (.148)<br>Michigan (.148)<br>Wisconsin (.149)<br>New Mexico (.153)<br>Rhode Island (.154)<br>Oregon (.158) | Georgia (.123)<br>Nebraska (.134)<br>Louisiana (.122)<br>Missouri (.105)<br>Ohio (.128)<br>Arizona (.143)<br>Vermont (.141)<br>North Carolina (.117)<br>North Dakota (.140)<br>Pennsylvania (.137)<br>Indiana (.122)<br>Iowa (.145)<br>Florida (.136)<br>Oklahoma (.124)<br>Tennessee (.112)<br>Montana (.146)<br>Maine (.142)<br>Utah (.143)<br>Kentucky (.120)<br>South Dakota (.130)<br>Alabama (.129)<br>Arkansas (.112)<br>South Carolina (.137)<br>Idaho (.129)<br>West Virginia (.139)<br>Mississippi (.136) |

a/ The figure in parentheses is the ratio of OSR to SDP, or the percent of SDP claimed by the state-local public sector.

*Source*: Calculations based on data in Tables 2–7 and 7–2.

expansion/relocation decision. These adjustments lower the eventual tax bill that businesses pay. Examples of these adjustments are the federal deductibility of state and local taxes, the link between taxes and public goods/services and infrastructure which business demands (the benefit principle at work), and shifting the tax burden to consumers or workers (ACIR, 1980b; Reschovsky et al., 1983).

The *federal deductibility* of state and local taxes is a unique feature of tax policy in a federal system. Prior to the Tax Reform Act of 1986, the federal government allowed taxpayers who itemized their deductions to subtract from

**Table 7-4**
**Tax Savings Associated with Federal Deductibility of State-Local Income, Sales, and Property Taxes, 1982 (per capita tax savings and tax savings as a percent of taxes)**

| Region & State | Per Capita Tax Savings | Tax Savings as a % of Taxes | Region & State | Per Capita Tax Savings | Tax Savings as a % of Taxes |
|---|---|---|---|---|---|
| USA | $ 106 | 8.72% | | | |
| N.E. | | | E.S.C. | | |
| ME | 70 | 6.47 | KY | $ 65 | 7.32 |
| NH | 68 | 7.15 | TN | 33 | 4.10 |
| VT | 75 | 6.59 | AL | 49 | 6.08 |
| MA | 155 | 10.88 | MS | 39 | 5.07 |
| RI | 116 | 8.96 | | | |
| CT | 135 | 9.41 | W.S.C. | | |
| M.A. | | | AR | 49 | 6.36 |
| | | | LA | 31 | 2.95 |
| NY | 233 | 12.33 | OK | 89 | 7.93 |
| NJ | 167 | 11.46 | TX | 43 | 4.16 |
| PA | 83 | 7.10 | Mt. | | |
| E.N.C. | | | MT | 41 | 3.48 |
| OH | 82 | 7.45 | ID | 64 | 7.31 |
| IN | 51 | 5.64 | WY | 33 | 1.35 |
| IL | 101 | 8.05 | CO | 110 | 9.43 |
| MI | 144 | 10.51 | NM | 38 | 3.65 |
| WI | 137 | 9.61 | AZ | 76 | 7.14 |
| | | | UT | 91 | 9.45 |
| W.N.C. | | | NV | 57 | 4.70 |
| MN | 150 | 10.18 | Pac. | | |
| IA | 75 | 6.40 | | | |
| MO | 70 | 7.52 | WA | 63 | 4.82 |
| ND | 42 | 3.82 | OR | 117 | 9.52 |
| SD | 20 | 2.19 | CA | 155 | 11.59 |
| NE | 87 | 7.59 | AK | 45 | .92 |
| KS | 80 | 7.09 | HI | 116 | 7.96 |
| S.A. | | | | | |
| DE | 162 | 12.73 | | | |
| MD | 185 | 13.70 | | | |
| VA | 113 | 10.33 | | | |
| WV | 34 | 3.50 | | | |
| NC | 77 | 8.45 | | | |
| SC | 73 | 8.31 | | | |
| GA | 87 | 8.94 | | | |
| FL | 50 | 5.17 | | | |

*Source*: U.S. Bureau of Census, *Government Finances*, and *President's Tax Proposal*, 1985.

their taxable personal income payments made to state and local governments for income, sales, and property taxes. Table 7-4 shows the per capita tax savings associated with the deduction provision and the tax savings as a percentage of the per capita taxes on a state-by-state basis. Across the nation, the per capita tax savings was $106 in 1982. This amount represented 8.72 percent of per capita taxes. In other words, an average taxpayer saved almost 9 cents on every one dollar paid in state and local taxes. This savings varies by state. Maryland taxpayers saved almost 14 cents for each one dollar paid, while Tennessee taxpayers saved only 4 cents.

By allowing taxpayers to deduct some portion of their state and local taxes, the federal government reduces the tax difference between the high and the low tax state. (For a general discussion of deductibility, see: Oakland, 1985; Raimondo, 1985; and Bridges, 1966.) For example, if you and I have identical economic circumstances, but you live in a low tax state and I live in a high tax state, then I can deduct a greater amount from my federal personal income taxes than you. I receive a greater tax savings.

Again, Table 7–4 uses 1982 data to illustrate the argument. In New England, the per capita state-local tax differences between New Hampshire and Massachusetts was $474 (Massachusetts $1,425 versus New Hampshire $951). Massachusetts taxpayers on average received $87 more than their New Hampshire counterparts in tax savings associated with the deduction (a difference in tax savings of $155 for Massachusetts minus $68 for New Hampshire, or $87). That additional $87 tax savings for Massachusetts taxpayers closes New Hampshire's tax advantage from $474 to $387 ($474 minus $87).

Perhaps, another example will help understanding of the effect of federal deductibility. In the Middle Atlantic division, the per capita state-local tax differences between New Jersey and Pennsylvania was $288 (New Jersey $1,457 versus Pennsylvania $1,169). New Jersey taxpayers on average received $84 more than their Pennsylvania counterparts in tax savings associated with the deduction (a difference in tax savings of $167 for New Jersey minus $83 for Pennsylvania, or $84). That additional $84 tax savings for New Jersey taxpayers closes Pennsylvania's tax advantage from $288 to $204 ($288 minus $84).

The deduction has reduced, although not eliminated, the tax advantage. Even though the deduction can lessen the tax threat posed by low tax states to high tax states, state and local government officials in high tax states have not exploited the deduction to their advantage. This deductibility provision in the federal personal income tax is still in the Federal Tax Code. However, the Tax Reform Act of 1986 has decreased the savings by removing state-local sales taxes from the deduction. At this time, the federal deduction applies only to state-local income and property taxes. This tax arrangement is still under scrutiny. There is talk in Washington (what else?) that the Bush administration favors capping the federal deduction for state personal income taxes as part of a national deficit reduction plan (Rosenbaum, 1990; Kolbert, 1990b).

The discussion of the impact of tax differences on the regional economy should conclude with a broader perspective than the tax issue affords. A recent examination of economic growth initiatives which state governments (especially Massachusetts, Michigan, and Pennsylvania) have successfully undertaken stresses the state government's role in stimulating technological innovation (e.g., Ben Franklin Partnership in Pennsylvania), filling gaps in the capital market (e.g., market rate loans to small businesses, businesses without collateral, or minority-owned businesses), promoting small business (e.g., incubators and small business development centers), encouraging exports (e.g., New York-New Jersey XPORT program), improving labor-management relations (e.g., MIL-RITE Council in Pennsylvania and CRIL in Massachusetts), and sponsoring education and training programs (e.g., Industrial Services Program in Massachusetts) (Osborne, 1987, 1988). Maybe taxes do matter. Clearly, there are other production considerations, amenities, and environmental features that affect business investment in the regional economy. One interpretation of a great deal of research, up to and including Osborne's work, is that proponents of the exclusive "taxes matter" view may be reacting to the images in the funhouse mirror.

## CRITERIA FOR A "GOOD" TAX

Following a presentation of tax principles, current state-local fiscal practices, and peculiarities of taxation in a federal system, the next task in understanding state and local governments' tax systems is the development of a criteria that determines whether a tax is a *good tax*. That last statement is not meant to be an oxymoron. A good tax is not simply a low tax. The criteria for a good tax includes six dimensions of the tax; namely, economic efficiency, fairness, administration, revenue stability, the link between spending and taxing, and tax visibility (Musgrave and Musgrave, 1989; Break, 1970). By the very nature of the elements which make up the criteria, no tax can satisfy each element. So the tax-by-tax evaluation is designed to highlight the comparative strengths and weaknesses of a tax and the trade-offs that each tax possesses.

### Establishing the Criteria

*Economic Efficiency*. A tax should minimally affect an efficient economic decision. For example, if a small businessperson has decided where to locate his/her business based on transportation costs, location to input markets, location to the consumer market, and energy costs among other items in the absence of a tax, then the imposition of a tax should not alter that decision. (If the tax does alter the decision, then the tax creates economic inefficiencies which economists call *excess burdens*.) From an economic efficiency perspective, the smaller the excess burden of a tax, the better the tax is. The larger the excess burden associated with the tax, the worse the tax is. A good tax should not alter economic decisions which are efficient.

*Fairness*. A tax should be fair. Everyone should pay his/her fair share. No one can disagree with the notion of "paying one's fair share." What each one of us means by fair share is a controversial issue. The concepts of horizontal and vertical equity clarify how a tax burden is distributed (i.e., what each person pays). Recall horizontal equity measures how a tax treats people of similar economic circumstances and vertical equity measures how a tax distributes the tax burden among people of different economic circumstances.

*Administration*. This criterion involves the degree of difficulty associated with collecting tax revenues. The goal of any tax is administrative simplicity. Administrative simplicity means that the tax base and the rate are easy to calculate and that taxpayers understand and have confidence in the tax. A tax that is difficult to administer is not necessarily an undesirable tax. However, when administrative difficulties raise the cost of collecting taxes, erode public confidence in the tax, and make the tax incomprehensible to the citizens, the tax becomes unattractive. This fact does not mean that a good tax is one whose administrative costs are low. Low administrative costs may lead to an unsupervised tax and a highly inequitable one.

*Revenue Stability*. People expect state and local governments to provide basic public goods/services regardless of the condition of the private economy. To meet this expectation requires stable revenue sources; that is, the economic cycle of growth and recession should not produce dramatic government surpluses and deficits. A stable tax is one whose revenue elasticity is low, in the range of 1.0. The concept of revenue elasticity is defined by the percentage change in tax collections divided by the percentage change in personal income. Regardless of the percentage change (up or down) in personal income, tax collections are stable. They do not vary by all that much. Note this criterion stresses stability, not revenue adequacy.

*Link Between Spending and Taxing*. Voters can better evaluate public program options if they know how each program affects them (i.e., the distribution of benefits and costs for each program). The more local governments try to satisfy this rule of benefit taxation, the more explicit the benefits of a public service and its tax costs must be. Taxes that satisfy the benefit principle best fulfill this objective. If the link between taxes and spending is broken, then the tax collections go into a general fund to finance all types of public services. Voters cannot track their tax payments, what they finance, and what they receive back in program benefits. Without knowing the distribution of tax costs and service benefits, voters cannot be expected to make the most efficient fiscal decisions. This consequence could lead to a local government expanding beyond the wishes of the local electorate. One measure of a good tax is the degree to which it ties together the tax side with the spending side of the fiscal equation.

*Tax Visibility*. For the link between taxing and spending to have any meaning, people must be aware of the taxes that they pay. Recall the issue of public choice in Chapter 5. With the tax issue so much a part of everyday life, the question is not so much *are* people conscious of the taxes they pay as *how* conscious are they of the taxes they pay? The tax bite of some taxes make people wince much more than the tax bite of other taxes. For example, the few pennies consumers pay in general state sales taxes everyday on many, though not all, purchases have become such a part of daily transactions that people rarely notice the tax. Tax visibility depends on the form, size, and time of the tax (Bartlett, 1973).

The form of a tax refers to whether the tax is part of an economic transaction or separated from it. If the tax is part of the transaction, it is less visible. The size of the tax simply means how large is the tax payment. If the payment is relatively small, the tax is less visible. Last, the time of the tax refers to its frequency. If a tax is paid often, then it is less visible. In short, a low visibility tax is one which is part of an economic transaction, a small amount, and paid often. A highly visible tax is one which is separate from an economic transaction, a large amount, and paid infrequently.

The presentation of economic principles of taxation; features of taxation in a federal system; and finally a criteria to evaluate a given tax prepare the way for a detailed examination of the state-local revenue system in the United States.

## SUMMARY

1. Two economic principles of taxation should justify any specific tax. They are: the benefit principle which stresses tax payments linked to public good/service benefits received; and the ability to pay principle which stresses tax payments linked to economic well-being.

2. In a federal system, each jurisdiction may set its own independent tax policy. However, tax competition between and among jurisdictions tempers a jurisdiction's tax independence. The tax system becomes a bargaining chip as jurisdictions compete for people, jobs, and capital. So state-local revenue-raising systems become interdependent. The irony is that existing research evidence does not support the notion that tax breaks tempt people, jobs, or investment to move from one place to another.

3. Each tax—property, sales, personal income, and business income—creates different incentives for the movement of people, jobs, and capital. These incentives are greatest under the assumption of complete mobility and the ceteris paribus condition. Tax competition also introduces an incentive to engage in tax exportation.

4. Variations in own source revenue exist within geographic regions and across regions. High (or Low) revenue-raising states are often clustered together within a region for their own tax protection.

5. The criteria to evaluate a good tax involve: economic efficiency, fairness, administration, revenue stability, the link between spending and taxing, and tax visibility. No tax can satisfy each element. However, these elements highlight the strengths and weaknesses of any tax.

# CHAPTER 8

---

# Property Taxes

## PREVIEW

An understanding of property taxes begins with a profile of property tax usage in the United States. The chapter then considers whether either of the two principles of taxation justify the property tax. How the property tax system works is the next task. With theory and practice in place, issues surrounding the tax base, the tax rate, and tax incidence are set out. The chapter concludes with an assessment of the property tax built around the criteria for a good tax.

## INTRODUCTION

Polling information shows that the property tax is the one tax that every United States taxpayer loves to hate (ACIR, 1987). Despite all this hostility, the property tax performs yeoman service in the federal system. Not only is this tax the primary source of educational financing (generally at least 80.0 percent of school district revenues), but in 1986–87 it also raised approximately 21.2 percent of state and local own source revenues, and 45.9 percent of local own source revenues.

Unlike most other taxes in the United States, the property tax base is a *stock variable* (e.g., wealth) whose value is measured at one point in time. With most other taxes, the tax base is a *flow variable* (e.g., income, consumption) whose value is measured only over a period of time. In addition, the taxation of property wealth requires that the value of the property must be estimated. Often the appreciation in property wealth is unrealized; that is, the owner is paper rich, but wallet poor. This combination: first, a wealth base; then an estimated wealth base; and finally, an unrealized, estimated wealth base raises revenues along with the blood pressure of the taxpayers.

Although the property tax raises revenues from an unrealized, estimated wealth base, the connection between the property tax and a comprehensive wealth tax stops there. A comprehensive wealth tax has a base which includes all *real* property (land and improvement thereon), all *tangible personal* property (cars, furniture, clothing, jewelry, etc.), and all *intangible personal* property (stocks, bonds, cash, and other "paper" assets) (Musgrave and Musgrave, 1989). In addition, the tax rate for a comprehensive wealth tax would be uniform and the national government would most likely administer the wealth tax. The passage from this form of taxation to the property tax used in all the states is similar to comparing a principal clarinet in a professional symphony to a novice reed-squeaker in a young people's orchestra.

The local property tax base does not capture a household's wealth. In fact, taxable real estate probably accounts for no more than two-thirds of the value of the gross stock of fixed reproducible tangible wealth in the United States. Aside from the incomplete base, the wealth which is taxed—primarily real estate—is subject to numerous exemptions and deductions. Of course, the tax rate is not uniform across all jurisdictions and local governments administer the property tax, not the national government. The relationship between the wealth tax and the property tax is at best tenuous (Netzer, 1966). With this distinction between a wealth tax and a property tax made, a profile of property tax usage across the United States is in order.

## PROFILE OF PROPERTY TAXATION

Property taxes, more than other taxes, reflected people's ambivalent attitude toward government during the 1970s and 1980s: people supported the growth rate in property taxes, people rebelled against the growth rate, and now they are allowing the property tax growth rate to creep up again. Still government has not forgotten the taxpayers' rebellion. Table 8–1 puts figures on this on-again, off-again relationship. The table shows the trend in state and local government property taxation from 1970 to 1987. In addition, it measures the contribution of property tax revenue to total tax revenue and own source revenue (OSR); and compares the annual percentage change in the property tax levy with a measure of inflation. The measure is the *GNP deflator* which is a general measure of inflation that includes changes in the price of all final goods and services produced by the economy. The GNP deflator is a more inclusive measure of inflation than the often cited consumer price index (CPI).

The property tax levy (measured in billions of current dollars) has steadily grown over this period from $36.5 billion in 1970 to $121.2 billion in 1987. The slowest growth occurred in the late 1970s during the height of the property

**Table 8–1**
**Trends in State and Local Government Property Taxation, 1970–87 (levy in billions)**

| Year | Levy | Property Tax Levy As a Percent of | | Annual % Change | GNP Deflator |
|------|------|------------------------------------|--------------------|-----------------|--------------|
| | | Tax Revenues | Own Source Revenues | | |
| 1970 | $ 36.5 | 39.2% | 33.5% | | |
| 1971 | 40.3 | 39.8 | 33.9 | 10.4% | 5.7% |
| 1972 | 43.0 | 38.7 | 31.8 | 6.7 | 4.7 |
| 1973 | 46.0 | 37.4 | 30.5 | 7.0 | 6.5 |
| 1974 | 48.7 | 36.6 | 29.3 | 5.9 | 9.1 |
| 1975 | 52.3 | 36.5 | 28.9 | 7.4 | 9.8 |
| 1976 | 57.6 | 36.7 | 28.7 | 10.1 | 6.4 |
| 1977 | 62.8 | 35.7 | 28.2 | 9.0 | 6.7 |
| 1978 | 63.2 | 31.9 | 25.6 | .6 | 7.3 |
| 1979 | 63.9 | 30.2 | 25.8 | 1.1 | 8.9 |
| 1980 | 68.8 | 29.7 | 25.3 | 7.7 | 9.0 |
| 1981 | 77.1 | 29.8 | 25.3 | 12.1 | 9.7 |
| 1982 | 85.3 | 30.8 | 25.9 | 10.6 | 6.4 |
| 1983 | 91.9 | 30.1 | 24.5 | 7.7 | 3.9 |
| 1984 | 99.7 | 28.9 | 24.5 | 8.5 | 3.7 |
| 1985 | 107.1 | 28.9 | 24.5 | 7.4 | 3.2 |
| 1986 | 114.6 | 29.1 | 24.5 | 7.0 | 2.6 |
| 1987 | 121.2 | 29.9 | 21.2 | 5.8 | 3.3 |

*Source*: U.S. Bureau of Census, *Government Finances*, various years.

tax revolt. Since 1980, the annual percentage change has been at least 5.8 percent. Compared to the GNP deflator, the annual growth in the property tax levy has exceeded the GNP deflator since 1981. In fact, it exceeded this measure of inflation in twelve of the seventeen years displayed in Table 8–1. This result means that the property tax levy has been claiming an ever-increasing share of property taxpayers' income. This real growth can be attributed to new (perhaps, mandated) responsibilities assigned to local governments; and increases in public good/services costs (Baumol's disease) among other factors.

In spite of this real increase in the levy, property taxes have declined in relative contribution to state and local governments' revenues. Over the 1970 to 1987 period, property taxes have dropped from approximately 40 to 30 percent of tax revenues and from approximately 34 to 21 percent of OSR. Other sources of state and local revenues are increasing faster than the property tax levy.

Table 8–2 looks at the state-by-state breakdown of per capita property taxes, the relation of property taxes to personal income in $1,000 increments, and the local share of property tax collections. The nationwide per capita property tax level is $498 and the relation of property tax to $1,000 personal income is $34. (For every $1,000 in personal income, property taxes claim $34.) Even putting aside Alaska ($1,187 and $63) and Wyoming ($1,108 and $84), the range in per capita property taxes goes from Alabama ($124) to New Hampshire ($862). The range in the tax effort measure goes from Alabama ($11) to New Hampshire ($56). While the tax data are presented as state and local government figures, the "Local Share" column shows that property taxes are overwhelmingly (96.2

**Table 8–2**
**State-Local Per Capita Property Taxes (PTAX), the Relation of PTAX to $1,000 Personal Income (PY), and Local Share of Property Tax, 1986–87**

| Region & State | Per Capita PTAX | Relation of PTAX to $1000 PY | Local Share | Region & State | Per Capita PTAX | Relation of PTAX to $1000 PY | Local Share |
|---|---|---|---|---|---|---|---|
| USA | $ 498 | $34 | 96.2% | | | | |
| N.E. | | | | E.S.C. | | | |
| ME | 531 | 42 | 98.7 | KY | $ 205 | $18 | 67.1% |
| NH | 862 | 56 | 98.8 | TN | 249 | 21 | 100.0 |
| VT | 643 | 49 | 99.9 | AL | 124 | 11 | 86.4 |
| MA | 640 | 36 | 100.0* | MS | 235 | 24 | 100.0* |
| RI | 653 | 45 | 98.9 | | | | |
| CT | 842 | 43 | 100.0* | W.S.C. | | | |
| M.A. | | | | AR | 197 | 18 | 98.8 |
| | | | | LA | 198 | 18 | 99.5 |
| NY | 799 | 47 | 100.0 | OK | 245 | 20 | 100.0 |
| NJ | 845 | 46 | 99.5 | TX | 549 | 41 | 100.0 |
| PA | 412 | 29 | 97.2 | | | | |
| | | | | Mt. | | | |
| E.N.C. | | | | MT | 659 | 55 | 92.2 |
| OH | 414 | 30 | 99.6 | ID | 334 | 30 | 100.0* |
| IN | 417 | 32 | 98.3 | WY | 1108 | 84 | 81.7 |
| IL | 570 | 37 | 96.6 | CO | 572 | 38 | 99.6 |
| MI | 669 | 46 | 96.7 | NM | 153 | 14 | 98.6 |
| WI | 617 | 45 | 96.6 | AZ | 468 | 35 | 92.8 |
| | | | | UT | 393 | 36 | 100.0* |
| W.N.C. | | | | NV | 360 | 24 | 89.4 |
| MN | 572 | 38 | 99.7 | Pac. | | | |
| IA | 578 | 43 | 100.0 | | | | |
| MO | 271 | 20 | 99.3 | WA | 483 | 33 | 59.4 |
| ND | 404 | 32 | 99.2 | OR | 715 | 54 | 100.0* |
| SD | 495 | 42 | 100.0 | CA | 495 | 30 | 87.8 |
| NE | 636 | 46 | 99.6 | AK | 1187 | 66 | 83.6 |
| KS | 563 | 39 | 97.8 | HI | 320 | 22 | 100.0 |
| S.A. | | | | | | | |
| DE | 241 | 16 | 100.0 | | | | |
| MD | 464 | 28 | 93.9 | *rounded to 1 decimal place | | | |
| VA | 430 | 28 | 99.1 | | | | |
| WV | 213 | 20 | 99.5 | | | | |
| NC | 291 | 24 | 95.8 | | | | |
| SC | 288 | 26 | 99.1 | | | | |
| GA | 347 | 26 | 99.2 | | | | |
| FL | 453 | 32 | 95.9 | | | | |

*Source*: U.S. Bureau of Census, *Government Finances*, 1988.

percent) used by local governments. School districts alone collect approximately 42 percent of all property taxes levied in the United States.

Table 8–2 also shows traces of the tax competition model. Throughout the New England, South Atlantic, East South Central, and West South Central regions, the per capita property tax level and to some extent the relation of property taxes to personal income are very similar. Maine and Vermont differ from their neighbors in the New England region; Maryland and Florida in the South Atlantic region; and Texas in the West South Central region.

There are some differences in the other regions. Pennsylvania is the low property tax state in the Middle Atlantic region; Ohio, Illinois, and Indiana play that role in the East North Central region; Missouri, North Dakota, and South Dakota do the same in the West North Central region; and California and Washington use the property tax sparingly in the Pacific region. The United States also divides along regional lines. The South region (S.A., E.S.C., W.S.C.), in particular, relies less heavily on the property tax than states in the Northeast, Middle West, and West regions.

The place of the property tax in the state and local tax system will take on more meaning as the tax revolt and tax limit movement is explained, tax equity issues are developed, additional taxes are reviewed, and the local aid system is introduced. For now, this profile tells us that the property tax levy is increasing even after the tax revolt, although its relative contribution is declining; and there are regional differences in the usage of the tax that opens the way for tax competition and tax harmony policy questions.

## PROPERTY TAX: ITS RATIONALE AND HOW IT WORKS

The property tax is useful because it raises so much revenue. Humor an economist for a moment. Aside from the revenue capacity of the property tax, can economic tax principles justify its use? If so, the rationale must come from the benefit principle or the ability to pay principle.

### Benefit Rationale

If the rationale for the property tax comes from the benefit principle, then individuals choose where they will live based in part on the level of taxes and public goods/services of the jurisdiction (Hamilton, 1983). The individuals' choice of a relatively high tax/high service jurisdiction versus a relatively low tax/low service jurisdiction depends upon whether the level and the quality of locally provided public goods/services increase the market value of real property. Public goods/services must add to the value of private property if the benefit principle justifies the property tax (Edel and Sclar, 1974; Hamilton, 1976; Oates, 1969).

This "addition to value" argument (also called "capitalization") has its most merit when the local public goods/service yield "protection services," such as police and fire protection or when the property tax acts like a user charge which directly enhances the property value, for example, special assessments for the public installation of curbing and sewage pipes (Rybeck, 1983). When nonprotection services are involved, such as elementary and secondary education, public welfare, or recreation, the merit of this argument becomes less convincing. Since the bulk of property tax revenues finances services which generate benefits only casually associated with property ownership, the benefit principle is not the uncontestable rationale for the local property tax. There are enough weak points in the benefit principle rationale that it does not provide the most compelling case for the property tax.

## Ability to Pay Rationale

If real estate and tangible personal property measured an individual's wealth, then the property tax might be an appropriate method to tax wealth according to the ability-to-pay principle (Heilbrun, 1983; Gaffney, 1973). The ability to pay principle ties taxes to one's ability (as measured by wealth or income) to pay for the cost of public goods/services. However, the property tax is an imperfect wealth tax. Some of the characteristics that are necessary if wealth is to be taxed according to this principle have already been set out. They are: the unit of taxation should be the individual, not the property; the tax base should be net wealth, not gross wealth; the wealth tax should be a uniform rate structure across the country, not a locally determined rate structure; and the base should include all forms of assets, not only real estate and some personal property. The local property tax does not have these features. There is neither a uniform tax rate structure nor a comprehensive base.

Where does this discussion leave the property tax? The local property tax is a crude attempt at a wealth tax which cannot easily be justified by the benefit principle or the ability-to-pay principle. While the property tax does not fall into any of the tax classifications that economists have devised, it endures nonetheless. Why? The property tax is locally administered which means that it preserves some degree of local autonomy. It generates significant tax revenues. No local tax which is an important revenue source is going to be discarded simply because neither tax principle is satisfied. However, the fact that the property tax is such a flawed version of a comprehensive form of taxation may explain taxpayers continued hostility to it (Raimondo and Torto, 1987).

## How the Property Tax System Works

By now it should be clear that the local property tax is a significant component in the local government budget equation (Behrens, 1983). That equation must balance local expenditures with local revenues from all sources. The local expenditures include: executive department budgets, the school budget, payments for state-rendered services, and debt services and pension contributions. Local revenues from all sources consist of state aid, federal aid, local fees and charges, and property tax collections.

Like all taxes, the property tax conforms to a simple relationship; namely, (tax revenue) equals (tax rate) times (tax base). In the case of property taxes, the tax revenue, or the amount to be raised, is called the *levy*. The *tax rate* is the dollar amount a taxpayer owes the local government for every $1,000 of assessed property value. This amount is found by dividing the levy by the assessed value of property. For example, if Eastown raises $600 million on a tax base of $2.4 billion, then the tax rate equals $25 for every $1,000 of assessed value, or 2.5 percent of the tax base. The *tax base* consists of the full market value of real property (realty) and personal tangible property (personalty). Assessors must place a value on this base.

The property owner may reduce the liability by filing for an abatement, by receiving an exemption, or by applying for a personal deduction. An abatement is a partial refund of a property tax payment based on a reduction of the assessed value of the property. For example, an appeal of an overvaluation could reduce the assessed value of the property. An exemption is based on the nature of the property owned. Examples of exemptions are: government property; religious, charitable, and educational property; certain business property; pollution control devices; bomb shelters; and solar and wind-powered systems. Examples of people eligible for deductions are: elderly persons, veterans, blindness, surviving spouse and children, and the like.

Most taxpayers understand the simple relationship which states that (levy) equals (tax rate) times (tax base). Most taxpayers also know that no tax is that simple. This brief overview alerts taxpayers to the fact that the relationship spelled out above involves the full market assessment of real and personal property, the determination of the tax rate, and the review of abatement, exemptions, and deductions before local officials can collect the levy. There are several property tax issues that deserve more attention. These issues will be organized around the property tax base and the property tax rate.

## PROPERTY TAX BASE

### Composition and Growth of the Property Base

Tables 8–3 and 8–4 place a dollar value on the largest component of the property tax base; that is, locally assessed real property. (For a description, see: Raphaelson, 1987.) In 1986, this property was worth $4.1 trillion, an increase of 63.2 percent from the value of $2.5 trillion in 1981. Commercial property has grown even more rapidly during the period, 101.0 percent. By far, residential (nonfarm) property constituted the bulk of this value, 61.2 percent. Commercial (17.3 percent of the base), acreage and farms (7.5 percent of the base), and industrial (7.0 percent of the base) property ranked behind residential property in relative importance to the composition of the property tax base. This make-up of the property tax base means that when state and local governments impose a tax on property, this tax will fall most heavily on residential property values.

Table 8–4 tells the state-by-state story of per capita property tax values for 1986 and the growth in the state property tax base from 1981–86. The variations in per capita property tax base are substantial across the United States. Putting aside the high of Alaska ($52,820) and the low of Vermont ($370), the range of per capita values is still substantial. For example, if the top five and bottom five states are excluded, the range is still wide: Washington ($32,019) versus

**Table 8–3**
**Gross Assessed Values, Locally Assessed Realty, and Use Categories, 1981 and 1986 (in billions)**

| | 1981 | 1986 | Percentage Change 1981-86 |
|---|---|---|---|
| United States Total | $2514.9 | $4104.5 | 63.2% |
| | | | |
| Residential (nonfarm) | 1520.0 | 2511.6 | 65.2 |
| Commercial | 353.5 | 710.5 | 101.0 |
| Industrial | 195.8 | 286.9 | 46.5 |
| Acreage and farms | 247.8 | 309.3 | 24.8 |
| Vacant lots | 109.4 | 189.2 | 72.9 |
| Other and Unallocable | 88.3 | 97.0 | 9.9 |

| | Percentage Distribution | |
|---|---|---|
| | 1981 | 1986 |
| United States Total | 100.0% | 100.0% |
| Residential (nonfarm) | 60.4 | 61.2 |
| Commercial | 14.1 | 17.3 |
| Industrial | 7.8 | 7.0 |
| Acreage and farms | 9.9 | 7.5 |
| Vacant lots | 4.4 | 4.6 |
| Other and Unallocable | 3.5 | 2.4 |

*Source*: U.S. Census of Governments, *Taxable Property Values and Assessment-Sales Ratios*, 1982 and 1989.

Oklahoma ($2,208). These variations hold two lessons: First, the revenue capacity of the states vary as the per capita property tax base varies. Second, the relative values of the property tax base and the corresponding growth rates are associated with the performance of the regional economies (Ladd, 1975). Rapidly growing regional economies will increase the demand for property—residential, commercial, and industrial—so the values of these properties will increase. In the 1981–86 period, Alaska, Hawaii, Massachusetts, Rhode Island, Texas, and Vermont have appreciating property tax bases and growing regional economies. While Tables 8–3 and 8–4 sum up the value of the property tax base, the next aspect of the property tax takes us back a step; namely, how do assessors estimate the unrealized value of real estate? The assessment procedure may vary from state to state and can greatly influence the figures in Table 8–4.

## Assessing the Value of Real Property

Assessors face a complex task. They must develop a fair procedure for estimating the unrealized market value of real property. There is more than one approach to such a complicated task. In fact, assessors have their choice of three procedures: *cost, market,* and *income.* The type of real property, administrative costs, and availability of data among other factors dictate the choice of a procedure or what combination of procedures can be called upon (Corusy, 1983).

**Table 8–4**
**Locally Assessed Real Property Base Per Capita (1981), Growth (1976–81), and
Effective Property Tax Rate (1986)**

| Region & State | Per Capita | Growth | Tax Rate | | Region & State | Per Capita | Growth | Tax Rate |
|---|---|---|---|---|---|---|---|---|
| USA | $10967 | 153.4% | 1.16% | | | | | |
| | | | | | | | | |
| N.E. | | | | | E.S.C. | | | |
| | | | | | | | | |
| ME | 15109 | 124.0 | 1.21 | | KY | $11694 | 77.8% | 1.10% |
| NH | 15958 | 101.0 | 1.55 | | TN | 3113 | 63.6 | 1.04 |
| VT | 13440 | 186.3 | NA | | AL | 1430 | 87.8 | .39 |
| MA | 13725 | 144.3 | 1.08 | | MS | 1003 | 33.3 | .77 |
| RI | 7863 | 52.5 | 1.49 | | | | | |
| CT | 12747 | 87.1 | 1.46 | | W.S.C. | | | |
| | | | | | | | | |
| M.A. | | | | | AR | 1526 | 77.6 | 1.09 |
| | | | | | LA | 1231 | 51.8 | .25 |
| NY | 5791 | 28.3 | 2.22 | | OK | 1579 | 43.6 | .90 |
| NJ | 14755 | 41.9 | 2.33 | | TX | 18589 | 723.0 | 1.44 |
| PA | 2568 | 20.9 | 1.37 | | Mt. | | | |
| | | | | | | | | |
| E.N.C. | | | | | MT | 939 | 23.1 | 1.32 |
| OH | 5918 | 61.3 | 1.80 | | ID | 20270 | 1524.0 | .91 |
| IN | 3187 | 72.5 | 1.28 | | WY | 1890 | 55.5 | .57 |
| IL | 7224 | 67.7 | 1.59 | | CO | 3969 | 44.5 | 1.09 |
| MI | 8854 | 70.0 | 2.26 | | NM | 2633 | 48.9 | 1.01 |
| WI | 14319 | 102.2 | 2.27 | | AZ | 2226 | 66.6 | .68 |
| | | | | | UT | 2617 | 115.5 | .93 |
| W.N.C. | | | | | NV | 8143 | 167.1 | .61 |
| | | | | | | | | |
| MN | 5732 | 77.5 | 1.03 | | Pac. | | | |
| IA | 1231 | 41.9 | 1.96 | | | | | |
| MO | 2351 | 21.0 | .89 | | WA | 24413 | 153.2 | 1.10 |
| ND | 1313 | 28.6 | 1.37 | | OR | 23018 | 105.8 | 2.26 |
| SD | 7793 | 88.4 | 2.31 | | CA | 24141 | 664.8 | 1.06 |
| NE | 20099 | 550.7 | 2.21 | | AK | 29066 | 127.4 | .82 |
| KS | 2115 | 16.3 | 1.06 | | HI | 20679 | 74.3 | .51 |
| | | | | | | | | |
| S.A. | | | | | | | | |
| | | | | | | | | |
| DE | 6898 | 23.4 | .73 | | | | | |
| MD | 8193 | 49.8 | 1.30 | | | | | |
| VA | 19171 | 350.6 | 1.42 | | | | | |
| WV | 3245 | 61.2 | .88 | | | | | |
| NC | 11501 | 76.2 | NA | | | | | |
| SC | 506 | 33.1 | .70 | | | | | |
| GA | 5699 | 68.4 | .90 | | | | | |
| FL | 20805 | 123.2 | .89 | | | | | |

*Source*: U.S. Census of Governments, *Taxable Property Values and Assessment-Sales Ratios*, 1977, 1982; ACIR, 1986b.

A brief description of each procedure provides a glimpse of the challenge that faces local assessors (Franklin et al., 1983).

*Cost Procedure.* Using this approach, assessors separate the cost of buildings and improvements from the cost of land on which the structures are built. Local assessors estimate the reproduction costs of these buildings and improvements. To calculate these costs, assessors usually acquire construction costs per square foot or cubic foot for the specific structures from building contractors, architects, and engineers. Then they adjust them to costs in the local area. For many structures, this information is not difficult to obtain. However, this approach may miscalculate the value of old or unusually designed structures and structures used primarily for their income generating capability.

Since the buildings and improvements are not always new, assessors must account for depreciation (the difference between reproduction cost and value) of the structures using a combination of factors, such as the age of the structures, their condition, their design, and the surrounding neighborhood. For the old or unusually designed buildings, depreciation can be difficult to determine. Building materials and plans, for example, may no longer be in use. The reproduction cost less depreciation is then added back to the value of the land. It is this value that the local government taxes using the locally set property tax rate.

The cost approach is straightforward. It stresses uniformity in the assessment procedure through its use of carefully defined cost information. Moreover, computer assisted mass appraisal (CAMA) has in many circumstances reduced this approach to a mechanical exercise (Cook, 1983).

*Market Procedure*. This approach mimics the private market's determination of the value of real property. The local assessor compares the value of real property *on* the market with the value of comparable real property not on the market. In this comparison, the local assessor is searching for the value of real property in its highest and best use.

The market procedure requires the development and maintenance of a comprehensive data base on the physical description of buildings and land (Almy, 1973; Downing, 1970). This data base contains information on age of the building, its condition, lot size, number of bedrooms and bathrooms, garage, and location among other characteristics. For residential property, the local assessor estimates the value per square foot, the value per room, or the value per bedroom found in actual sales of residential property. These values serve as proxies for comparable residential property that has not changed hands. This process is similar to neighbors estimating the current market value of their homes based on the sale price of a home on the same street. For office property, the local assessor estimates the value per square foot or cubic foot found in actual sales of office property. Again, these values serve as proxies for comparable office property that has not changed hands. Because conventional wisdom tells us that no two properties are exactly alike, assessors must adjust the estimated values to the local circumstances. This phase is the art, more than the science, of assessing real property.

The training of assessors, the cost of the data base, and its constant updating make the market procedure expensive to implement. Of course, in return for these costs the taxpayers are receiving real property assessments that approximate market values based on actual transactions.

*Income Procedure*. The third approach is exclusively used to estimate the market value of income producing real property; for example, retail stores, apartments, office buildings, forest land, and small businesses. Often there is not a sufficient number of comparable sales in a jurisdiction to apply the market procedure to this type of real property. Like the market procedure, the income procedure also requires a comprehensive data base in order to estimate the income stream over time for the specific real property under consideration. In effect, the assessor is looking at the real property in the same fashion as an interested investor.

The income procedure makes the assessor work through several steps. The assessor estimates the actual (not potential) gross income stream for the real property. Next, the operating costs must be calculated. These costs include such items as heat and utilities, repair and maintenance, and insurance. These two elements produce net income (actual gross income minus operating costs).

To convert this stream of net income over time into present market value, a capitalization rate is necessary. (For a review of present value, see Musgrave and Musgrave, 1989). The capitalization rate translates future earnings into present income using the formula: (income) equals (market value) times (capitalization rate). So (value) equals (income) divided by (capitalization rate). Obviously, the selection of a capitalization rate is crucial to the income procedure: for similar income streams the lower the capitalization rate, the higher the market value; the higher the capitalization rate, the lower the market value. The capitalization rate can come from comparable sales information, if available, or an analysis of financial factors operating in the local area.

Each of these methods or some combination of them produced the data on market values presented in Tables 8–3 and 8–4. The confidence a taxpayer places in these methods depends on the quality of the assessor. While assessors are better trained and more experienced than ever before, taxpayers do have an appeals procedure to reconsider the assessor's decision.

### Exemptions: Property Value Excluded from the Base

If government at any level permits a special exclusion, exemption, or deduction from the tax base, then tax revenue is lost. That lost tax revenue is called a *tax expenditure* (Surrey, 1973; Surrey and McDaniel, 1985). Tax expenditures not only reduce tax revenues, but they also affect who pays the tax (if you qualify for a tax expenditure, then you don't pay as much and someone else who does not qualify pays more). Faced with revenue reduction and shifting tax burdens, there had better be a good reason for the public sector to enact tax expenditures. In fact, there had better be two good reasons.

There is an efficiency justification. Suppose that a private institution provides a good/service that possesses public good/service qualities. This privately produced public good/service may well substitute for (or complement) an equivalent publicly produced public good/service. The tax expenditure serves as (perhaps partial) compensation to the private institution for the public good/service; for example, nonprofit hospitals provide emergency room care for indigent patients, in exchange they receive a property tax exemption.

There is also a redistribution justification. The government may use the tax expenditure to support private institutions that engage in redistributive activities that substitute for (or complement) public sector redistributive functions; for example, religious institutions sponsor recreation programs for children from low income families, in exchange they receive a property tax exemption. As you might predict, there is an on-going debate concerning the value of the service benefits versus the value of the lost tax revenue associated with any tax expenditure regardless of the justification.

Tax expenditures are common in the federal tax revenue system. For the federal personal income tax system, tax expenditures represented $281 billion in lost tax revenue in 1988. That amount is approximately 40 percent of what is actually collected! Some pertinent examples of federal tax expenditures and their 1988 tax revenue loss are: deductibility of property taxes on owner-occupied homes ($7.2 billion), exclusion of interest on public purpose state and local debt ($8.0 billion), and deductibility of state and local taxes ($14.8 billion).

Each state and local tax system has a set of tax expenditures that reduce tax revenues for some purpose. In the case of the property tax, not all property is subject to property taxes. State and local governments have created a class of property that is exempt from local property taxes. This class is primarily made-up of property used by government, charitable organizations, and educational and religious institutions although other users are also considered for exemption (Quigley and Schmenner, 1975).

The U.S. Bureau of Census has collected the available data on tax exempt property for 1986. Only eighteen states reported assessed values for some tax exempt property, amounting to $322.2 billion. That amount represented approximately 7.8 percent of the value of locally assessed real property in the eighteen states. Of this amount, government owned property accounted for 50.7 percent of the value, educational institutions 7.6 percent, and religious and charitable organizations 11.4 percent each. The remaining 30.3 percent was in the "other or unallocable" class. Tax exempt government real property is consistent with the notion of dual federalism discussed in Chapter 3. Each level of government must respect the real estate holdings of other levels of government. The concern is that if one level of government taxes the real estate holdings of another level, this might restrict the taxed government's ability to discharge its functional responsibilities.

The fiscal impact of tax exempt property appears to fall hardest on urban areas. Greater numbers of the types of institutions which receive exemptions tend to be located in urban areas. Also, urban real estate generally commands high market values. This concentration of high priced real estate that is tax free means that if tax exempt property has an adverse fiscal impact, then urban areas are going to experience it more than other local jurisdictions.

The adverse fiscal impact that is traditionally associated with tax exempt property takes on two forms (Raimondo, 1980). The first form is the *foregone tax base*. Tax exempt property is removed from the tax base. The result is that the local governments are unable to raise revenue to the desired level or can only do so with extra tax effort. The tax burden is shifted to the other classes of tax-paying properties, especially residential, commercial, and industrial. The second form is *imposed public service costs*. Whether tax exempt properties pay taxes or not, they draw upon the locally provided public services; for example, police and fire protection, sanitation, and transportation facilities. These services may be in excess of what the tax-paying population would demand, yet this population must pay for them. Administrators of institutions that have received or seek tax exempt status point out that the adverse fiscal impact which these two forms identify can be overstated. Government, charitable organizations, and educational institutions also contribute to the economic vitality of the local economy.

Even with the contributions made by tax exempt organizations taken into account, local government officials have sought legislation to ameliorate the adverse fiscal impact of tax exempt property. The legislation has called upon the tax exempt organizations to make payments of one of two types: first, tax equivalency payments; and second, reimbursement for imposed public service costs. The tax equivalency payment is designed to approximate the tax payment on the property as if it were not exempt. Of course, the tax equivalency also establishes the principle that all property, regardless of its use, is subject to local property taxes. The reimbursement for imposed public service costs is designed to cover the costs of the public services which the tax exempt organization uses. This payment would at least neutralize the adverse public service impact associated with the tax exempt property.

There are two policy questions which elected officials, public administrators, and researchers have raised concerning the treatment of government owned tax exempt property. First, is the most equitable method of compensating local jurisdictions for the presence of tax exempt property through a local aid formula rather than tax equivalency or reimbursement methods? If the local aid formula successfully captures resource, cost, and tax effort differences across the state's local jurisdictions, then that formula might be a more equitable method to compensate local governments for any lost tax base or imposed public service costs associated with tax exempt property. This approach would emphasize the overall fiscal resources of a local jurisdiction rather than reimbursing jurisdictions for a specific condition. Second, if reimbursement for tax exempt property is preferred, then which approach reimburses local jurisdictions more equitably: tax equivalency or service cost reimbursement? A full tax equivalency payment, despite its administrative problems, corresponds to the tax treatment of private property. A payment for the cost of public services would give tax exempt property preferential treatment over taxed property since the tax liability on property has little formal relationship to the value of public services directed to the property. The public policy stance toward tax exempt property in general and government owned tax exempt property in particular is very much unsettled. It is a contentious point whenever state and local government officials discuss fiscal relations between these levels of government. Government owned tax exempt property is just one more example of the complications which a federal system creates.

### Deductions: Property Value Removed from the Base

Since the early 1880s, forty-one states have removed property value from the property tax base. In 1986, the property value removed amounted to $198.1 billion in the thirty states which responded to the U.S. Bureau of Census survey. These removals are designed to account for the impact of state and local fiscal policy on the overall state income distribution, as well as recognize outstanding public service on the part of specific groups of state residents. The reductions can take two forms: homestead relief and personal exemptions. The homestead relief program removes specified amounts of assessed property value from the tax base in order to lower property tax liabilities. Personal exemptions cover taxpayers in certain circumstances; for example, the elderly, veterans (in some cases their survivors), the blind, paraplegics, surviving spouse and children, surviving spouse and children of firefighters and police who died in the line of duty, and those faced with hardship based on age, infirmity, or income (ACIR, 1986b, 1988).

Often eligibility is for a year and must be renewed. State statutes restrict the eligibility by income, the value of the property (estate), ownership, and duration of occupancy. The form of the personal deduction is generally a choice between a reduction in the market value of the real property or a specified credit against the property tax liability, whichever is greater.

The removal of property value from the tax base reduces the property tax base of the local jurisdictions throughout a state much like the tax exemption for government, charitable organizations, and educational and religious institutions. For the forty-one states which have personal deduction programs, the revenue loss from the personal deductions has ranged from several hundred thousand dollars to several hundred million dollars. Local governments have requested that the state government replace the lost tax revenues. The state government has tried. Fifteen states with comparable programs reimburse the local governments. Of those fifteen, ten state governments completely reimburse the local jurisdictions for the lost tax revenue.

There are two policy issues surrounding the removal of property from the tax base. The first deals with the use of personal exemptions to carry out state income redistribution policy. The traditional assumption is that the property tax falls hardest on low income people. To reduce this financial stress, state and local governments subsidize the tax payments of these lower income people. To some extent, personal exemptions identify a ''needy'' group (e.g., elderly, low income, surviving spouse and children) and reduce their property tax liability. If the reduction of the local property tax burden for specific groups of taxpayers is part of the overall state income redistribution policy, then the implementation of this policy should be the responsibility of the state government, not local governments. Recall that the redistribution function in Chapter 4 is not delegated to decentralized or local governments. The implication is that the state government should provide full reimbursement for the tax revenue that local governments lose, not the partial reimbursement policy which currently exists.

The second policy question concerns the reward for outstanding service to the nation (e.g., veterans) or the local community (e.g., firefighters and police). The reasons for the recognition of this individual service are obvious. What is not apparent is who should bear the financial responsibility for this recognition? In the case of veterans who have served the nation, the financial responsibility for this portion of the personal exemption program should fall to the national or the state government, not the local government. Since these personal exemptions are part of the state's tribute to national veterans, the state government should reimburse local governments for the lost property tax revenue. The same analysis leads to the conclusion that the local governments must bear the cost of the personal exemption for survivors of police and firefighters who have died in the line of duty.

This section concludes the discussion of property tax base issues. It touched upon the composition and growth of the base, assessing the value of real property, and property value excluded or removed from the base. The other dimension of the property tax system is the property tax rate. Its profile and the public policy questions surrounding the rate are next.

## PROPERTY TAX RATE

### Trend and Level of the Property Tax Rate

The growth in the property tax base (recall how the property tax system works), the use of alternative revenue sources including state aid to local governments, and the imposition of limits on the use of property taxes have influenced the trend and the level of property tax rates. Since 1971, the nationwide average effective property tax rate on existing single family homes (with Federal Housing Assistance (FHA) insured mortgages) has been declining. The average in 1971 was 1.98 percent of the market value of the home. In 1986, that figure had dropped to 1.16 percent. The decline was especially dramatic from 1971 to 1981 (1.98 percent to 1.26 percent); and less dramatic, but still evident from 1981 to 1986 (1.26 percent to 1.16 percent). Even with this decline, property tax rates in larger cities tend to remain above smaller cities, suburban places, or rural areas (ACIR, 1986b, 1988; Raphaelson, 1987).

Table 8–4 shows that in 1986 the level of property tax rates varied by region and state. The South region was generally a low rate region, while the Northeast and Midwest regions were generally high rate regions. Michigan (2.26), Nebraska (2.21), New Jersey (2.33), New York (2.22), Oregon (2.26), South Dakota (2.31), and Wisconsin (2.27) have effective rates on single family homes in excess of two percent. On the other extreme, Alabama (.39), Arizona (.68), Hawaii (.51), Louisiana (.25), Nevada (.61), South Carolina (.70), and Wyoming (.57) are less than three-quarters of a percent. In line with the tax competition model (of Chapter 7), this range allows for the appearance of tax rate competition among the regions and the states. For example, compare Michigan (2.26) and Wisconsin (2.27) with Minnesota (1.03), Ohio (1.08), and Indiana (1.28); New Jersey (2.33) and New York (2.22) with Delaware (.73), Maryland (1.30), and Pennsylvania (1.37); and Oregon (2.26) with Washington (1.10) and California (1.06). If tax rates differentials alone influence the location of economic activity and residences, then tax competition thrives among these states.

Concern over the burden which these property tax rates generate, especially among the elderly and low income people has resulted in two public policy initiatives: circuit breakers and property tax limits. Both are designed to reduce the financial burden of property tax rates on taxpayers, although their approaches differ. Circuit breakers lead off the discussion on relief from high property tax rates.

### Circuit Breakers

Two conditions make the case for a circuit breaker program. First, property taxes place an undue burden on low income families. Second, this burden is measured using the cash flow test; namely, property taxes are considered as a percentage of annual family income (Gold, 1983a; Thomassen, 1978; Quindry and Cook, 1969). The conclusion is simple. The state government should step in to reduce property tax burdens when they exceed some limit. There you have it, a circuit breaker program. A formal description is that a circuit breaker program establishes a state financed property tax refund whenever property tax liabilities exceed a specified amount (or percentage) of household income.

Thirty-two states have state financed circuit breaker programs. These programs (twenty-four of them) tend to shield the elderly and low income people from the burdens of the property tax, although some (seven of them) focus on low income people regardless of age. Over 5.5 million people receive assistance from these circuit breaker programs at a cost of almost $1.6 billion in 1986. The bulk of these thirty-two state programs deliver an average payment in the $100 to $200 per household range (ACIR, 1986b, 1988).

While the vast majority of state and local government officials and researchers supported the circuit breaker program, some critics feared that the widespread use of the program encouraged greater reliance on local property taxes (Shannon, 1973; Aaron, 1973). The emergence of the property tax limit movement dramatically countered that fear. The limit movement was fueled by high property tax rates, but sought to address a more general discontent with government finances. Circuit breakers accepted the property tax and tried to make it more humane. The limit movement challenged local governments' right to tax property.

## Tax Limitation Movement

In June 1976, California voters approved Proposition 13 which limited local property taxes. Like so many other California trends of the 1970s, this one rippled across the country and reached the eastern shore with the passage of Proposition 2 1/2 in Massachusetts. At last count, twenty-eight states have imposed tax limits on local governments (ACIR, 1986b, 1988).

A state government may impose three types of limit on local government. *Rate limit* sets the maximum rate that may be applied against the assessed value of property without a vote of the local electorate. *Levy limit* establishes the maximum revenue that a jurisdiction can raise from the property tax. This limit is typically enacted as an allowed annual percentage increase in the property tax levy. *Expenditure limit* is the maximum amount that a jurisdiction can either appropriate or spend during a fiscal year. This limit is usually legislated as an allowed annual percentage increase in operating expense (ACIR, 1977b).

During the latter part of the 1970s, voters felt that their economic security was threatened by the uncertainties of the macroeconomy; by the expansion of the government; and by the inequities of the tax system, particularly the local property tax system. Voters rebelled against the traditional enemy, namely, the government. A simple, blunt instrument is often used to finish off the enemy in a rebellion. In the tax rebellion, the local tax limit is that instrument.

Its simplicity and blunt edge is appealing. Not only does it purport to limit property tax burdens at once, but it rebukes the politicians who let the problem get out-of-hand in the first place by taking the power to tax out of their hands. So a local tax limit came. Its coming significantly changed federalism in the United States, as described in Chapter 3. Few seemed to notice. Local governments may have howled, but enough apparent fat and waste were exposed to make their howls sound like squeals.

Time passes. Passions cool. Pocketbooks swell. Economic and political pressures are brought to bear on state governments to relax the fiscal squeeze on local governments. Of course, the symbol of the tax rebellion—the local tax limit—cannot be dismantled. So state governments let their revenues grow and, in turn, the revenues are converted into state aid to local governments.

Whether the limits were appropriate has already been debated, if not resolved. (For example, Ladd, 1978; Lowery and Sigelman, 1981; Raimondo, 1983b.) The next section takes up the issue of state aid to support local governments faced with state imposed tax limits. It presents a comparative assessment of local government revenue sources within states which have imposed limits (limit states) versus those which have not (non-limit states). Between these two groups, differences in the state's relative aid levels to local governments are especially noticeable.

## FISCAL IMPACT OF TAX LIMITS

A review of the revenue data for local governments indicates that the imposition of a tax limit produces certain observable consequences. Following the imposition of the tax limit, there does appear to be a greater degree of centralization in state-local fiscal matters; a surge in state aid to local governments which eventually abates; and a change in the composition of local revenue sources (Raimondo, 1988). U.S. Bureau of Census fiscal data for local governments—counties, municipalities, and townships—were collected for all states. These data include state aid, own source revenue, property taxes, and miscellaneous revenues (i.e., current charges, interest earnings, special assessments, etc.). In addition, these data were converted into real 1972 dollars to allow comparisons through time.

The time period over which these data were collected is 1968 to 1984. While there are limits in the state statute books prior to the 1970s, it is not until that decade that the tax revolt gave the local limit its fiscal bite. The first "modern" limit makes its appearance in the year 1972. In order to describe the state's fiscal behavior prior to the limit, four years' fiscal data were collected. Therefore, the earliest year is 1968.

The states were divided into limit states versus non-limit states. The number of states in each of these groups changes over time. For example, by 1980 eighteen states imposed local tax limits. The next year twenty-one states made up the limit state group. The first look at these data is a comparison of limit states versus non-limit states over time regardless of the year when the limit was imposed. These data show the trends in the two groups of states at different times in the life of the limit law. Recall that from 1968 to 1972, no state falls into the limit group. Thereafter, that group increases steadily until there are twenty-eight states in it by 1984 (and twenty-two states in the non-limit group).

Figure 8–1 shows the ratio of state aid to local governments' own source revenue for the two groups of states. The non-limit states show an increase in this ratio until 1975. Thereafter, it drops. The ratio in non-limit states declines from .482 to .344 during the 1975 to 1984 period. The limit states show an initial surge in relative state grants to local governments, but this surge is followed by a steady ratcheting downward in the relative grant to .396 in 1984. Still, in relative terms state aid plays a slightly larger role in local governments' fiscal plans in limit states (.396) than in non-limit states (.344).

Figure 8–2 compares miscellaneous revenue as a share of local own source revenue. The non-limit states show an increase (in some cases at an increasing rate) in the proportion of local own source revenue which comes from this revenue source (e.g., in 1972: .257 and in 1984: .330). The above general observation

**Figure 8–1**
**State Aid Contribution to Local Governments: Limit Versus Non-Limit States**

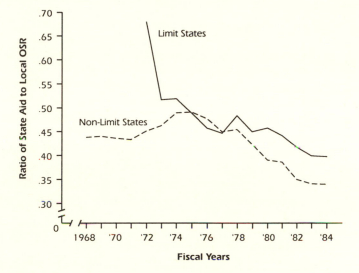

**Figure 8–2**
**Miscellaneous Revenues as a Share of Local Own Source Revenue (OSR): Limit Versus Non-Limit States**

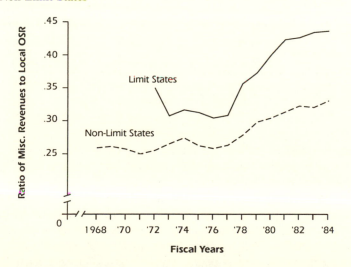

also holds for limit states. With the exception of the period 1976–77, miscellaneous revenues have accounted for an increasing share of local governments' own source revenues (e.g., in 1972: .356 and in 1984: .436). While the trends across the groups are similar, Figure 8–2 shows that limit states rely more heavily upon miscellaneous revenues than do non-limit states.

**Figure 8–3**
**Property Taxes as a Share of Local Own Source Revenue (OSR): Limit Versus Non-Limit States**

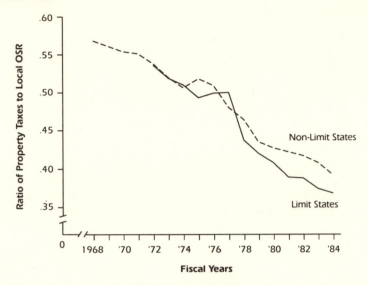

**Table 8–5**
**Summary Data from Figures 8–1, 8–2, and 8–3 for 1984**

| State Groupings | -----Ratio of .... to Local Own Source Revenues------ | | |
| | State Aid | Property Taxes | Miscellaneous Revenues |
|---|---|---|---|
| Limit States | .396 | .368 | .436 |
| Non-Limit States | .344 | .392 | .330 |

Figures 8–1 and 8–2 allow the reader to anticipate the results of the next figure. Figure 8–3 shows the proportion of local own source revenue raised by the property tax. In the non-limit states, there is a steady decline in the relative importance of property taxes from .540 in 1972 to .392 in 1984. After some erratic behavior in the early years of limit legislation, the trend settles down after 1977 to reveal a steady fall in the relative contribution of property taxes from .493 in 1977 to .368 in 1984. Increases in state aid and miscellaneous revenues make this decline possible. Property taxes are still relatively more important in non-limit states than limit states.

What do the data say about whether non-limit states exhibit a pattern of fiscal behavior different than the limit states? Using the three figures, Table 8–5 provides the answer. Limit states rely upon state financial assistance and miscellaneous revenues to replace lost property taxes more than non-limit states; and

**Figure 8–4**
**Pattern of Revenue for Local Governments in Limit States**

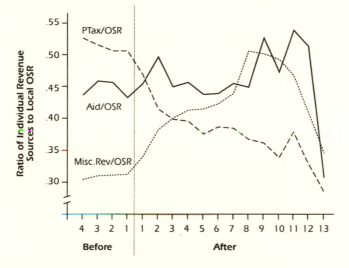

Years Before & After Limit Enacted

both groups have reduced their reliance upon property taxes, although limit states rely even less upon them.

The second look at these fiscal data focuses on limit states exclusively. It arranges the data set to reveal the fiscal life of the local limit, some sense of how the limit law ages. Figure 8–4 sets out the data. There are three cautions: (1) the first four years represent pre-limit trends and the next thirteen years post-limit trends; (2) the three ratios do not add to 100.0 percent; and (3) while the early years (one through seven) represent all twenty-eight states, there is a drop-off after year seven. The later years in particular (twelve and thirteen) represent only two states. The reader should beware of drawing general conclusions from the out year data.

The interpretation of Figure 8–4 begins with local aid. An initial (years five and six) surge in local aid accompanies the imposition of a local limit. One hand of the state takes property taxes away and the other replaces some or all of it with state aid. That surge seems to level off over the later years (at least from years seven through thirteen) of the limit. Miscellaneous revenues steadily (years five through thirteen) fill the void left as a result of the local limit. Of course, property taxes fall; at first (years five and six) by ever increasing amounts then by lesser amounts (years seven through thirteen). The property tax decline appears to be tied more to increases in miscellaneous revenues than to increases in state aid.

Figures 8–1 through 8–4 give a warning to local government officials in limit states. Initially, the state government will swap local aid for property tax relief to make the limit palatable. Property taxes are reduced without dramatic cuts in local public services. The political outcry is muted. However, the local aid will fade over the life of the limit, not intensify. So alternative revenue sources must be found to avert service cuts. Past fiscal practice indicates that those alternative sources will likely come from miscellaneous revenues.

## INCIDENCE OF THE PROPERTY TAX

The incidence of a tax is concerned with who pays the tax (Musgrave and Musgrave, 1989). While it may appear obvious who pays a tax, individuals may alter their behavior to avoid a tax and in the process shift the tax liability to some other individuals or economic activities. For this reason, a distinction is made between *legislated* incidence and *economic* incidence. Legislated incidence indicates who or what activity must pay the tax under the law. Economic incidence indicates who or what activity actually does pay the tax after behavior changes are accounted for.

Who pays the property tax is not a trick question, but the answer is not as straightforward as one might imagine. Economists, who never have a shortage of answers, have two for this question. The answers depend upon whether the property tax is considered an excise tax, or a capital tax (Heilbrun, 1983). This division over excise tax or capital tax does not affect the analysis of the property tax on land. Let's begin there. (The detailed discussion of property tax incidence is summarized in Table 8–6.)

### Property Tax on Land

The analysis of the portion of the property tax that falls on land begins with an assumption. If the property tax is levied regardless of land use, then the owners of the land must pay the tax. The owners cannot alter their behavior to avoid the tax. There are no uses which go untaxed. Even if owners keep the land vacant and undeveloped, they will be taxed as if the land were in its "highest and best use." Legislated incidence is the same as economic incidence. (If use affects property taxes, this conclusion is weakened. Differential property tax rates based on agricultural, conservation, or residential uses and personal deductions will also affect this conclusion.)

Figure 8–5 illustrates the principle argument. The analysis begins in the land market. Initially, there is no property tax. Rent, or the price of land, is plotted on the y-axis. The amount of land is plotted on the x-axis. In the short run, we assume that the supply of land is fixed at amount L. Regardless of what the rent is, only a fixed amount of land, L, is available. This situation is depicted using a vertical supply schedule, SL. The demand for land follows the law of demand. As price increases, the quantity demanded decreases; and as price decreases, the quantity demanded increases. This situation gives us the downward sloping demand schedule, DD. DD represents the maximum rent that land buyers are

**Figure 8–5**
**Incidence of the Property Tax on Land**

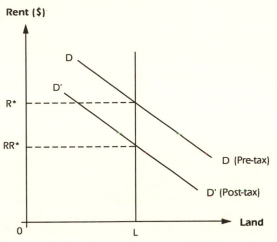

willing and able to pay. They are simply unable and/or unwilling to pay more than the amounts shown along DD. The equilibrium rent for land is found at the intersection of SL and DD, or R*. Land buyers are willing and able to pay land sellers a maximum of R* for their landholdings.

Now the bad news! A property tax is levied on all land. What does not change? The supply of land, L, does not change. That is fixed. The demand schedule, DD, does not change. That shows the maximum amount that land buyers are willing and able to pay for different amounts of land, tax or no tax. The equilibrium price, R*, does not change. That is the maximum amount that land buyers will pay for the fixed quantity supplied of land. What does change? The amount that land sellers receive for their land changes. It decreases from R* to R**.

Since R* is the maximum land price, land buyers will not offer a higher rent for the fixed supply of land, L. If land buyers are unable and/or unwilling to pay the property tax, then land sellers must. So the tax comes out of the rent, R*. When you subtract the property tax from R*, you arrive at the amount that land sellers receive after taxes, or R**. The vertical distance from R* to R** is the tax on (a "unit" of) land. Landholders pay the property tax because they cannot change their behavior in an attempt to avoid the tax.

The burden of the property tax follows the distribution of income generated by the ownership of land. Since the share of income from land ownership tends to increase as personal income increases, this portion of the property tax is considered progressive. The percent of personal income claimed by the property tax on land increases as income increases.

The qualification to this conclusion is that the property tax falls on the landowners who own the land at the time that the tax is imposed or increased.

Subsequent owners will adjust their bid price for the land taking the tax burden into account. Ceteris paribus, higher taxes will result in lower bid prices for the land (again, the notion of capitalization).

### Property Tax on Improvements

The other portion of the property tax falls on improvements. Analysis of the incidence of this portion of the property tax divides the economics profession into two camps. The division rests on whether economists believe that this portion of the tax is an excise tax on improvements (traditional view) or a tax on capital (new view).

*Traditional View—An Excise Tax.* The analysis of the portion of the property tax that falls on improvements also begins with an assumption. Capital for improvements commands a nationally determined rate of return. If the property tax were to lower the rate of return, then owners of capital would not use their capital for improvements. To avoid this reduction in the rate of return, the owners of capital must be able to shift this portion of the property tax. Under these circumstances, the owners of capital do not pay the property tax. In the case of residential property, the occupants—owners or renters—do. In the case of non-residential property, the consumers of goods and services pay the property tax in the form of higher prices. Higher property taxes lead to higher rents, and higher costs of doing business. The economic incidence of the property tax differs with the legislated incidence. The incidence of the property tax begins to resemble that of a consumption tax; that is, it is considered *regressive* (Netzer, 1966). The percent of personal income claimed by the property tax on improvements decreases as income increases.

This result, especially in the case of residential improvements, rests heavily on whether the proportion of income dedicated to improvements increases or decreases as income increases. Surprisingly, the economic evidence on this question is mixed. If annual income is used as the basis for analysis, the proportion of income spent on improvements falls as annual income increases. However, a measure of normal or permanent income (income averaged over some number of years), instead of annual income shows that the proportion of permanent income spent on improvements remains constant as income increases. The permanent income measure argues that the portion of the property tax which falls on improvements is proportional or progressive (Musgrave, 1974; Aaron, 1975; Gaffney, 1973).

In public debates about the incidence of the property tax on improvements, the results of the annual income studies are cited. The use of these studies leads to the popular acceptance of the traditional view that the property tax is regressive. The tax's regressive nature comes from the regressive tax on improvements outweighing the progressive tax on land. It is this view which supports extensive personal exemptions and circuit breaker programs described earlier in the base and rate sections of this chapter.

*New View—Capital Tax.* The new view of the incidence of the property tax differs with the traditional view on that portion of the property tax which falls on improvements (McClure, 1977; Aaron, 1974, 1975; Netzer, 1973; Mieszkowski, 1972; Harberger, 1962). The analysis begins with the same assumption that the traditional view used. Capital for improvements commands a nationally determined rate of return. Further, the analysis assumes that all jurisdictions levy the property tax at a uniform rate. This assumption means that no change in the behavior of the owners of capital can avoid the national, uniform property tax. Again, the legislated incidence is the same as the economic incidence. The result is a reduction in the real rate of return in capital. For example, if the rate of return on capital is 7 percent and the property tax claims 1.5 percent, then the rate of return falls nationwide to 5.5 percent. No alternative use of capital avoids this tax or this reduction in the rate of return. Owners of capital do not, for instance, switch their resources to saving.

If the share of personal income from capital sources increases as income increases and if the property tax reduces the rate of return on capital, then it reduces the capital income to these higher income brackets. The distribution of the property tax liabilities increases as income increases. Therefore, this portion of the property tax is progressive. When the progressive portion of the property tax on land is combined with the progressive portion of the property tax on capital, the property tax turns out to be a *progressive tax*. The exact opposite conclusion of the traditional view.

The conclusion does not change if the property tax rate is not uniform. It may vary across types of property and among jurisdictions. Different tax rates will have different impacts on rates of return on capital. High property tax rates in Eastown will lead to low rates of return there, while low property tax rates in Westown will lead to high rates of return there. This conclusion is in line with the simple tax competition model of Chapter 7. The result you already know. Capital that is mobile will move away from the high rate in Eastown to the low rate in Westown. A disequilibrium is created in the national capital market.

Supply and demand now comes into effect. The increase in the supply of capital in the low rate Westown will drive down the before tax rate of return (holding demand fixed, in other words ceteris paribus). The opposite happens in the high rate Eastown. The decrease in the supply of capital will drive up the before tax rate of return in the high rate Eastown (holding demand fixed, in other words ceteris paribus). The process of changing rates of return in the high and low rate jurisdictions will continue until the after tax rates of return are equal in low tax rate Westown and the high tax rate Eastown. All owners of capital, regardless of the local property tax rate, experience a decline in the rate of return on capital. The economic incidence differs with the legislated incidence of the property tax.

**Figure 8–6**
**New View of the Incidence of the Property Tax**

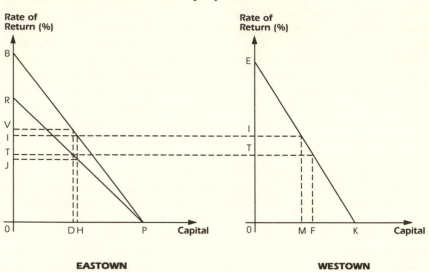

EASTOWN                              WESTOWN

Figure 8–6 gives us a picture of the argument for the new view of the incidence of the property tax. It shows the rate of return on capital on the y-axis and the amount of capital on the x-axis. For Eastown, the initial rate of return schedule is BP. For Westown, the rate of return schedule is EK.

We begin in a no property tax world. (Calm down; it's only theory.) Neither Eastown nor Westown levy a property tax. In equilibrium, the rate of return on capital (not necessarily the amount of capital) is the same in both communities. For Eastown, that means a rate of return of OI. For Westown? OI is also the rate of return. This identical rate of return divides the total capital stock (OH + OM) between Eastown (OH) and Westown (OM).

Eastown now introduces a property tax. The owners of capital in Eastown are shocked. The owners of capital in Westown are amused, but not for long. Following the new view, the owners of capital pay for the property tax out of the returns to capital. So the after-tax rate of return on capital in Eastown will fall. In fact, there is now a before and an after tax rate of return schedule. The before tax schedule is still BP. The after tax schedule is RP. Since the after tax rate of return has fallen in Eastown from OI to OJ, capital which is mobile in a Tiebout world will move from Eastown to Westown.

The flow of capital into Westown also reduces the rate of return on capital. There is a movement along the schedule EK away from the origin. With capital leaving Eastown and entering Westown, at what level will rates of return on capital in Eastown and Westown stabilize? The answer is that rates of return will stabilize at the point when the after tax rate of return in Eastown is equal to the tax-free rate of return in Westown.

For example, suppose the flight of capital from Eastown to Westown reduces the amount of capital in Eastown from OH to OD. At the same time, the influx of capital to Westown increases capital from OM to OF. An equilibrium has been reached because the rate of return to the owners of capital is identical in both towns; namely, OT. In Eastown, the before tax rate of return is higher; that is, OV. However, when the capital movement comes to a halt, the property tax burden that the owners of capital in Eastown initially paid (shown as drop in the rate from OI to OT) is eventually shared by the owners of capital in Westown as well (shown as a drop in the rate from OI to OT). In a Tiebout world with mobile capital, property tax rate differentials mask the fact that the property tax burden is shared by the high taxed and low taxed (or untaxed) owners of capital.

You have seen the conclusion before. If the share of personal income from capital sources increases as income increases and if the property tax reduces the rate of return on capital, then it reduces the capital income to these higher income brackets. The distribution of the property tax liabilities increases as income increases. Therefore, this portion of the property tax is progressive. When the progressive portion of the property tax on land is combined with the progressive portion of the property tax on capital, the property tax turns out to be a *progressive* tax. The exact opposite conclusion of the traditional view. Table 8–6 summarizes the views on the incidence of the property tax.

### Empirical Evidence

There have been numerous studies of the economic incidence of the property tax (Pechman, 1985; Phares, 1980; Aaron, 1975; Pechman and Okner, 1974). Most of the studies have accepted the traditional view of the incidence of the property tax. More recent studies have estimated the new view of the incidence of the property tax. A sample of the empirical studies which illustrates both views is presented in Table 8–7. Under the traditional view, the share of income claimed by the property tax decreases from 7.9 percent from the less than $5,000 income class to 2.3 percent in the $1,000,000 and over income class. Under the new view, the share of income claimed by the property tax increases from 1.0 percent to 5.8 percent for the corresponding income brackets.

The selection of a view—traditional or new—is significant. Circuit breaker programs, personal deductions, and tax limit programs take on different meanings depending on the view of incidence. The traditional view justifies these programs on fairness grounds. The new view undermines the rationale for these programs.

What do these views on the incidence of the property tax mean for public policy? From a national perspective, the new view argues that the property tax is a progressive tax. From a local perspective, the property tax is still unattractive because this tax increases the cost of doing business in a high tax jurisdiction. According to the tax competition model, this end result puts the high tax jurisdiction at a competitive disadvantage.

**Table 8–6**
**Summary of the Views on the Incidence of the Property Tax**

| Tax on | Incidence | Rationale |
|--------|-----------|-----------|
| Land | PROGRESSIVE | If the tax on land is independent of use, then it cannot be shifted and falls on landowners. Property tax liability follows the distribution of income generated by land ownership. |
| Improvements | | |
| a) Traditional View | REGRESSIVE | The property tax is shifted forward .... <br> o  Owner Occupied, Residential:  owner occupant pays the property tax. <br> o  Renter, Residential:  property tax passed to renter. <br> o  Commercial & Industrial:  property tax passed to consumers of goods and services. |
| b) New View | PROGRESSIVE | If a uniform, nationwide property tax rate is assumed, then it reduces the real rate of return on capital.  Property tax liability follows the distribution of income generated by ownership of capital. <br><br> If a varied, local property tax rate is assumed, then capital mobility will result in a reduction in the rate of return on capital.  Again, property tax liability follows the distribution of income generated by ownership of capital. |
| Land and Improvements | | (See Caution #1 below.) |
| a) Traditional View | REGRESSIVE | Regressive tax on improvements outweighs progressive tax on land. |
| b) New View | PROGRESSIVE | Progressive tax on land is complemented by the progressive tax on improvements. (See Caution #2 below.) |

Caution #1:  The use of annual income, instead of permanent income,  to measure the incidence of the property tax tends to make the property tax appear regressive.  A permanent income measure tends to make the property tax appear progressive, regardless of the view of the tax on improvements.

Caution #2:  From a national perspective, property taxes are progressive; however, from a local perspective, property taxes may still be unattractive because of their impact on the local economy.

Public opinion on the property tax firmly embraces the traditional view. Voters, government practitioners, and politicians simply do not believe that the property tax is progressive. This public perception coupled with the competition argument makes the property tax unpopular—extremely unpopular.

## EVALUATION OF THE PROPERTY TAX

After a discussion of the theory, operation, and incidence of the property tax, there should be an assessment which determines whether the property tax is a

**Table 8–7**
**Effective Rates of Property Taxes by Family Income Class, 1980**

| Family Income | -----Pechman's Estimates----- Traditional View | New View | Phares's Estimate Traditional View |
|---|---|---|---|
| Less than $ 5,000 | 7.9% | 1.0% | 5.2 - 10.3% |
| 5,000 - 10,000 | 3.0 | .6 | 3.4 - 4.7 |
| 10,000 - 15,000 | 2.4 | .9 | 2.7 - 3.1 |
| 15,000 - 20,000 | 2.1 | .9 | 2.4 |
| 20,000 - 25,000 | 2.1 | 1.0 | 2.2 |
| 25,000 - 30,000 | 2.1 | 1.2 | 2.1 |
| 30,000 - 50,000 | 2.2 | 1.4 | 2.1 - 2.8 |
| 50,000 - 100,000 | 2.3 | 2.2 | |
| 100,000 - 500,000 | 2.2 | 3.9 | |
| 500,000 - 1,000,000 | 2.2 | 5.2 | |
| Over 1,000,000 | 2.3 | 5.8 | |

*Source*: Pechman, 1985; Phares, 1980.

"good" tax. As described in Chapter 7, the criteria for a good tax include six dimensions of the tax: economic efficiency, fairness, administration, revenue stability, link between spending and taxing, and tax visibility.

## Applying the Criteria to the Property Tax

By the very nature of the elements which make up the criteria, no tax can satisfy each element. So this evaluation is designed to highlight the comparative strengths and weaknesses of the property tax. In this way, all interested parties—homeowners, renters, businesspeople, and government officials—will know the consequences when they support/deplore the local property tax. The assessment begins where all economic analysis should start, with economic efficiency.

*Economic Efficiency*. The effect of the property tax on economic efficiency comes in two forms. The property tax could act as a disincentive to spend on land and improvements. The strength of the disincentive is uncertain. It will depend upon the alternatives open to the investor and the relative tax on these alternatives. For example, the property tax raises the cost of home-ownership and rental units. Before we conclude that the property tax has an adverse effect on these activities, recall that the price elasticity for these items may be inelastic (there are few substitutes for shelter). Also, personal income taxes have established provisions which are very favorable toward home ownership. So the effect of the property tax in isolation may be adverse, but in concert with other taxes the net effect is less obvious.

The same argument holds for business use of land and capital as productive inputs. The property tax would encourage the substitution of other factors for these two. The effect in isolation could be adverse; that is, a production process has the efficient combination of these inputs then changes the mix as a result of the imposition of the property tax. However, the personal income tax and the payroll tax on labor and the favorable tax treatment of capital gains and the deduction for capital depreciation may offset the adverse effects of the property tax on real property and capital. Again, the net result is not clear.

Another effect is that the property tax affects the location of investment. If resources for business investment and home construction are mobile (a Tiebout world), then businesspeople and homeowners will move to the low property tax jurisdiction. If that jurisdiction is different from a site which businesspeople or homeowners would have selected if there were no property tax, then the property tax has introduced an economic inefficiency. Despite some shortcomings in the empirical evidence, the conclusion is that property taxes may influence locational decisions (Wasylenko, 1980; Charney, 1983). Ceteris paribus, property taxes may discourage firm location and expansion, as the tax competition model of Chapter 7 predicted. This effect may be offset by the benefits associated with public services which the tax revenues finance, state aid to local governments, and the federal income tax treatment referred to above.

Does the property tax create economic inefficiencies in the market for structures and the market for factor inputs for production? A qualified yes! Does the property tax influence the location of house and business investment decisions so that inefficient locations may be substituted for efficient ones? A qualified yes! Within the complex U.S. federal system, the degree of the inefficiency is tempered by the availability of substitutes (i.e., shelter, productive inputs, and locations) and the tax treatment of those alternatives. Some of the inefficiency which is traditionally associated with the property tax may be offset by the operation of other federal and state taxes.

*Fairness.* The discussion begins with horizontal equity. If two people who receive the same income and who own equally valued real estate have the same tax burden (i.e., taxes as percent of income), then the property tax satisfies the horizontal equity rule. Since the property tax is a local tax, the likelihood of horizontal equity being confirmed for two people who live in different jurisdictions is quite small. Different tax rates and different assessment outcomes make horizontal equity unlikely across jurisdictions. The lack of horizontal equity can increase the possibility of inefficient housing and business location decisions which were mentioned above. Within a jurisdiction, horizontal equity is very sensitive to the local assessment practices. If the assessor is accurate and all property is valued at full market value, then horizontal equity is possible. The greater the spread in assessments within a property class, the less likely that economic equals will be treated the same.

The incidence section of this text presented the analysis on the vertical equity of the property tax. Briefly, the traditional view holds that the property tax is regressive. The new view holds that it is progressive. While there is some evidence for the progressivity of the property tax, public policy debates have always assumed that it is regressive.

*Administration.* The administrative problems associated with the property tax have a long history. The problems start with assessing the property base, determining the property tax levy parcel by parcel, collecting the tax, and conducting appeals hearings. Add these considerations to a major reevaluation effort, part-time assessing staff, and small tax districts and the administrative costs of the property tax will climb. Previous studies have shown that under the optimum conditions (e.g., full-time professional staff and population of 40,000 to 50,000 within the tax district) the administrative cost of the property tax can be as low as 1.0 to 1.5 percent of the tax collection (Break, 1970).

*Revenue Stability.* People expect local governments to provide basic public services—education, police and fire protection, recreation, and sanitation—regardless of the condition of the private economy. This expectation means that local governments require stable revenue sources. Stability means that the economic cycles of growth and recession should not produce dramatic local government surpluses and deficits. A stable tax is one whose revenue elasticity is close to 1.0. The concept of revenue elasticity relates the percentage change in tax collections to the percentage change in personal income. Regardless of the percentage change (up or down) in personal income, tax collections do not change radically. This element of the criteria stresses stability, not revenue adequacy. The property tax is not especially sensitive to changes in the private economy. Past studies of the stability of the property tax have shown that it fluctuates less with changes in personal income than any other major state-local tax (Phares, 1980).

*Link Between Spending and Taxing.* While there are some who argue that the property tax satisfies the benefit principle of taxation and is nothing more than a user charge, most disagree. At the most general level, property taxes do form a link between spending and taxing insofar as public services financed by the property tax increase the value of real property. This outcome does not hold for all public services and for all classes of real property.

How would public welfare, recreation, even education fit into this analysis? Not very neatly! There is no convincing evidence which supports the fact that all real property benefits equally from local public services. The link between property taxes paid and the benefits of local public services cannot be dismissed as out-of-hand, but there is no obvious support for such linkage in the case of the property tax. With this link weakened, if not broken, the local public sector may be subject to pressures which cause it to expand beyond the preferences of the local voters. The tax limit movement is an attempt to prevent this outcome.

*Tax Visibility.* Tax visibility determines how conscious people are about the taxes that they pay. The more aware taxpayers are about their tax burdens, the more the local public sector will conform to their preferences. Visibility is related to the form, size, and timing of a tax. The form of the property tax separates it from an economic transaction. So taxpayers are very much aware that they are

**Table 8–8**
**Summary of the Evaluation of the Property Tax**

--------------------------------------------------------------------------

| Criteria | Comments |
|----------|----------|
| Efficiency | o Adversely affects spending on structures, and land;<br>o Distorts the use of capital;<br>o Distorts the location of homeownership and business investment;<br>o Within context of available substitutes, other taxes, and the benefits of local public services, these distortions are reduced. |
| Fairness | o Equity influenced by assessment practices, tax rates, and local property classification scheme;<br>o Horizontal equity across jurisdictions unlikely;<br>o Horizontal equity within a jurisdiction likely, but dependent upon assessment procedures;<br>o Vertical equity depends upon view of property tax incidence: traditional view -- regressive, and new view -- progressive. |
| Administration | o Relatively difficult to administer;<br>o Improvements dependent upon assessment district size, quality of staff, use of new technologies (CAMA), and appeals procedure;<br>o Under optimum conditons, the adminsitrative cost of the property tax is 1.0 - 1.5 % of the revenue. |
| Revenue Stability | o Property tax is relatively stable;<br>o Estimate of revenue elasticity between .4 and 1.2. |
| Link Between Spending and Taxing | o Property tax is not a user charge except in the most general sense.<br>o No link may lead to overexpansion of the local public sector. |
| Tax Visibility | o Form - separate from economic transaction<br>o Size - substantial amount from unrealized gains<br>o Timing - Infrequent<br>o Highly visible tax, target of taxpayer frustration |

paying this tax. The size of the property tax is usually substantial, although for residents of some rural communities this may not be the case. Another point on the size is that the tax is on unrealized economic gains. People must pay taxes as if they are wealthier, but they do not see that wealth in their income. Last, the timing of the tax also calls attention to it. The property tax is collected infrequently; at most four times a year.

The separation from a transaction, its large amount on unrealized gains, and its infrequent collection make the property tax a highly visible tax. In many cases, the single most visible tax in U.S. federal system. This visibility makes people very aware of it, but it also makes the property tax the target of taxpayer hostility and frustration. Not surprisingly, the property tax is not a politically popular tax.

Table 8–8 summarizes the evaluation of the property tax. An individual's position on the tax may depend upon his/her assessment of the unsettled issues in economic theory concerning economic efficiency and tax fairness.

## SUMMARY

1. The property tax cannot be justified using the benefit principle or the ability to pay principle. As if to underscore this point, the criteria for a good tax to the property tax reveal that the tax may induce inefficient behavior, is inequitable, and is difficult to administer. Still the real value of the property tax levy continues to increase even though its relative contribution to the local government has declined. Property tax usage also varies by region. Local governments in the Northeast, the Midwest, and the West levy the property tax more than their counterparts in the South.

2. Assessors have placed a value on the property tax base using three methods—cost, market, or income. The resulting assessments have shown that the property base has grown over the years. Residential property makes up the bulk of the tax base. Not all property is taxed. Some is exempt by use; and some is removed from the base because of the characteristics of the owner. When all is said and done, the property tax base accounts for no more than two-thirds of the wealth in the United States.

3. Property tax rates have also declined, especially on owner residential property. State governments have implemented other public policies to lower the effective rate: circuit breakers and tax limits. Tax limits have helped make local governments less dependent on the property tax and more dependent on state aid and user charges.

4. The incidence of the property tax is an unsettled issue in tax theory. The traditional view which has widespread support, especially outside the economics profession, is that the tax is regressive. The new view is that the tax is progressive.

# CHAPTER 9

---

# Sales Taxes

## PREVIEW

If any tax has popular support, then it is the sales tax. It is the second most important source of tax revenue for state and local governments. The discussion of sales taxes proceeds along similar lines as that of the property tax: a profile of sales tax use, a search for the economic justification of the tax, an examination of base and rate issues, and an explanation of tax incidence questions. The chapter concludes with an evaluation of the sales tax using the ''good'' tax criteria.

## INTRODUCTION

The voting public has very different views about state and local governments' two principle sources of tax revenue. In contrast to the property tax, the voting public is almost enthusiastic about sales taxes. A sales tax is simply an add-on to the economic cost of a good or service. The Advisory Commission on Intergovernmental Relations (ACIR) polling results consistently find the highest level of public support for the sales tax in answer to the question, ''Suppose your state (local) government must raise taxes substantially, which would be a better way to do it?'' (ACIR, 1987). Sales taxes may win out simply because the other options are so unpalatable. Still sales taxes win!

State and local sales taxes come in two versions: general and selective (or specific). We begin with a simple distinction. *General sales taxes* are levied on sales of goods and services (the transfer of title) at the retail level. All but five states impose a general sales tax at the state government level (i.e., Alaska, Delaware, Montana, New Hampshire, and Oregon). *Selective sales taxes* are imposed on specific items, usually gasoline, alcohol, and tobacco (Musgrave and Musgrave, 1989). Selective sales taxes on these last two items are frequently referred to as "sin taxes." All fifty states levy selective sales taxes. Whether general or selective, sales taxes are an example of a *flow variable* (unlike property taxes). Sales taxes place a tax on the value of consumption expenditures or the quantity purchased over a specified period of time. Whether general or selective, sales taxes are designed to modify consumption behavior. The general sales tax is meant to discourage "high" consumption and, as a result, encourage increased savings. The selective sales tax is meant to temper the consumption of alcohol and tobacco (but not too much or there would be no tax revenue) and to conserve gasoline (Due, 1963; Morgan, 1963). Exactly how important are sales taxes to the state and local governments' general fund? A profile provides the answer.

**PROFILE OF SALES TAXES**

Sales tax collections reflect the general public support that the tax enjoys. Table 9–1 shows the trend in state and local government sales taxation from 1970 to 1987. In addition, it measures the contribution of sales tax revenue to total tax revenue and own source revenue (OSR); and compares the annual percentage change in sales taxes with the GNP deflator, the comprehensive measure of inflation introduced in Chapter 8.

Sales tax revenue (measured in billions of current dollars) has steadily grown over this period from $31.5 billion in 1970 to $144.3 billion in 1987. The slowest growth occurred from 1979 through 1982 and more recently from 1985 to 1986. Compared to the GNP deflator, the annual growth in sales taxes has exceeded the GNP deflator since 1983. In fact, it exceeded this measure of inflation in eleven of the seventeen years displayed in Table 9–1.

Even with this real increase in sales tax revenues, it has remained a steady component of state and local governments' revenues. Over the 1970 to 1987 period, sales taxes have represented approximately 34 to 36 percent of tax revenues (most recently 35 percent) and approximately 28 to 31 percent of OSR (most recently 25 percent) (Rodgers, 1987).

Table 9–2 looks at the state-by-state breakdown of per capita sales taxes and the relation of sales taxes to personal income in $1,000 increments. This relation is a measure of sales tax effort. (We will discuss the column labeled State Share later.) The nationwide per capita sales tax level is $593 and the effort measure is $41. (For every $1,000 in personal income, sales taxes claim $41.) Even putting aside Nevada (per capita: $1,042 and effort: $71), Washington ($1,067 and $72), and Hawaii ($999 and $68), the range in per capita sales taxes goes

**Table 9–1**
**Trend in State and Local Government Sales Taxes, 1970–87 (revenue in billions)**

| Year | Sales Taxes | Sales Taxes As a Percent of | | Annual % Change | GNP Deflator |
|------|-------------|---------------|--------------------|-------------|---------|
|      |             | Tax Revenues | Own Source Revenues |             |         |
| 1970 | $ 31.5 | 33.8% | 28.9% |        |       |
| 1971 | 35.3   | 34.9  | 29.7  | 12.1%  | 5.7%  |
| 1972 | 39.6   | 35.6  | 29.3  | 12.2   | 4.7   |
| 1973 | 44.0   | 35.8  | 29.2  | 11.1   | 6.5   |
| 1974 | 48.0   | 36.1  | 28.9  | 9.1    | 9.1   |
| 1975 | 51.5   | 35.9  | 28.5  | 7.3    | 9.8   |
| 1976 | 57.8   | 36.8  | 28.8  | 12.2   | 6.4   |
| 1977 | 63.9   | 36.3  | 28.7  | 10.6   | 6.7   |
| 1978 | 71.3   | 36.0  | 28.9  | 11.6   | 7.3   |
| 1979 | 77.3   | 36.5  | 31.2  | 8.4    | 8.9   |
| 1980 | 82.9   | 35.8  | 30.5  | 7.2    | 9.0   |
| 1981 | 90.7   | 35.1  | 29.8  | 9.4    | 9.7   |
| 1982 | 96.2   | 34.7  | 29.2  | 6.1    | 6.4   |
| 1983 | 106.6  | 34.9  | 28.4  | 10.8   | 3.9   |
| 1984 | 120.8  | 35.0  | 29.7  | 13.3   | 3.7   |
| 1985 | 130.9  | 35.3  | 30.0  | 8.4    | 3.2   |
| 1986 | 139.8  | 35.5  | 29.9  | 6.8    | 2.6   |
| 1987 | 144.3  | 35.6  | 25.3  | 3.2    | 3.0   |

*Source*: U.S. Bureau of Census, *Government Finances*, various years.

from Oregon ($143) to Connecticut ($840). The range in the tax effort measure goes from Oregon ($10) to New Mexico ($63).

Table 9–2 also shows signs of the tax competition model at work. Whether it is effective or not, states compete for the consumer's dollar by keeping their sales taxes lower than their neighboring states. Chapter 7 referred to this aspect of tax competition as the border problem. Some of the extremes by region are: Connecticut ($840) and Maine ($563) versus New Hampshire ($230) in New England; Illinois ($632) versus the rest of the East North Central region; Missouri ($566), Minnesota ($579), and South Dakota ($546) versus the rest of the West North Central region; Florida ($721) and West Virginia ($600) versus Delaware ($216) in the South Atlantic region; Tennessee ($720) and Louisiana ($679) versus the rest of the South Central region; Nevada ($1,042), Arizona ($745), New Mexico ($712), and Washington ($1,067) versus Montana ($184) and Oregon ($143) in the West.

The sales tax is a cornerstone of the state-local revenue system in virtually every state and region. Even with that, there are regional differences in the usage of the tax that opens the way for tax competition and tax harmony policy questions (Aronson and Hilley, 1986).

## SALES TAX: ITS RATIONALE AND HOW IT WORKS

The search for the theoretical justification of the sales tax starts with the two principles of taxation: the benefit principle and the ability to pay principle. Recall that neither of these two principles justified the use of the property tax, but were

Table 9–2
State-Local Per Capita Sales Taxes (SALE), the Relation of SALE to $1,000
Personal Income (PY), and State Share of SALE, 1986–87

| Region & State | Per Capita SALE | Relation of SALE to $1000 PY | State Share | Region & State | Per Capita SALE | Relation of SALE to $1000 PY | State Share |
|---|---|---|---|---|---|---|---|
| USA | $ 593 | $41 | 84.3% | | | | |
| N.E. | | | | E.S.C. | | | |
| ME | 563 | 45 | 100.0 | KY | $ 450 | $40 | 100.0% |
| NH | 230 | 15 | 100.0 | TN | 720 | 61 | 81.4 |
| VT | 506 | 38 | 100.0 | AL | 567 | 50 | 70.0 |
| MA | 478 | 27 | 100.0 | MS | 505 | 52 | 99.6 |
| RI | 539 | 37 | 100.0 | | | | |
| CT | 840 | 43 | 100.0 | W.S.C. | | | |
| M.A. | | | | AR | 498 | 45 | 93.8 |
| | | | | LA | 679 | 60 | 61.3 |
| NY | 746 | 44 | 56.1 | OK | 509 | 41 | 65.2 |
| NJ | 641 | 35 | 100.0 | TX | 580 | 43 | 83.9 |
| PA | 485 | 34 | 100.0 | | | | |
| | | | | Mt. | | | |
| E.N.C. | | | | MT | 184 | 15 | 100.0 |
| OH | 518 | 37 | 90.6 | ID | 444 | 39 | 100.0 |
| IN | 520 | 40 | 100.0 | WY | 521 | 39 | 82.1 |
| IL | 632 | 41 | 76.2 | CO | 598 | 40 | 59.4 |
| MI | 450 | 31 | 100.0 | NM | 712 | 63 | 87.2 |
| WI | 518 | 37 | 100.0 | AZ | 745 | 56 | 84.9 |
| | | | | UT | 546 | 50 | 84.8 |
| W.N.C. | | | | NV | 1042 | 71 | 96.1 |
| MN | 579 | 39 | 99.4 | Pac. | | | |
| IA | 445 | 33 | 99.9 | | | | |
| MO | 566 | 41 | 78.0 | WA | 1067 | 72 | 90.0 |
| ND | 459 | 36 | 97.5 | OR | 143 | 11 | 93.9 |
| SD | 546 | 46 | 81.4 | CA | 642 | 39 | 81.5 |
| NE | 467 | 34 | 89.1 | AK | 275 | 15 | 36.7 |
| KS | 529 | 36 | 82.2 | HI | 999 | 68 | 97.2 |
| S.A. | | | | | | | |
| DE | 216 | 15 | 100.0 | | | | |
| MD | 533 | 32 | 100.0 | | | | |
| VA | 503 | 33 | 80.3 | | | | |
| WV | 600 | 57 | 100.0 | | | | |
| NC | 495 | 40 | 76.2 | | | | |
| SC | 514 | 46 | 100.0 | | | | |
| GA | 551 | 42 | 76.6 | | | | |
| FL | 721 | 51 | 95.5 | | | | |

*Source*: U.S. Bureau of Census, *Government Finances*, 1988.

nevertheless useful in understanding that tax. With this caution in mind, the question is does either tax principle justify the sales tax?

### Benefit Rationale

The benefit principle requires an equivalency between taxes paid to the public sector and benefits received from the public sector. Consumers pay general sales taxes into the general fund which, in turn, finances the full range of public goods/services. There is no expectation that the general sales taxes that a consumer pays will equal the benefits that he/she receives from the public sector. The amount of general sales taxes paid is related to consumption levels. Demand for public goods/services is related to an individual's circumstances. For example, a high income individual may spend a substantial amount. That translates into high general sales taxes. This individual may then receive little in public goods/services (measured in dollars). The benefit principle is not satisfied in this case.

A possible exception is selective sales taxes. These taxes are often earmarked or dedicated to a specific public function; for example, gasoline taxes finance highway maintenance and cigarette taxes might finance health care and hospitals. Earmarking a tax is in the spirit of the benefit principle, but that does not mean that the selective sales tax satisfies the benefit principle. The gasoline taxes that a driver pays are not necessarily linked to the benefit that he/she derives from cruising along the highway. So earmarking moves the selective sales tax in the direction of the benefit principle, but does not guarantee that the benefit principle justifies the selective sales tax.

### Ability to Pay Rationale

The ability to pay principle has two components. Horizontal equity requires that tax payments as a percent of income (a proxy for economic well-being) should be the same for individuals with the same level of income. Vertical equity requires that tax payments as a percent of income vary directly with an individual's level of income. How do sales taxes fare under these guidelines?

In dollar terms, the level of consumption dictates the level of sales tax payments. If two individuals with the same income spend different amounts on consumption expenditures, then the sales tax payment as a percent of their income will differ. The individual who spends less will pay a smaller percentage of his/her income in sales tax payments. That outcome contradicts the notion of horizontal equity. There is no certainty that people with comparable income levels will spend the same amount on consumption. There is a counterargument that some economists make. If economic capacity, or the basic potential to earn income, is used instead of actual annual income and if tax burdens are measured over a lifetime rather than over a year, then the consumption tax can satisfy horizontal equity (Kaldor, 1955).

Now look at the case where income increases. (The logic holds if income decreases.) As income increases, consumption expenditures increase in dollar terms. We assume that consumption expenditures decrease as a percent of income. (For high income people, saving increases faster than income increases.) Again, the level of consumption dictates the level of sales tax payments. So sales tax payments increase as income increases in dollar terms and sales tax payments decrease as income increases in percentage terms. That outcome contradicts the notion of vertical equity. It is doubtful that the ability to pay principle

justifies the general or selective sales tax. The discussion of sales tax incidence
will elaborate on these conclusions.

Just as with the property tax, these two tax principles offer no clear justification
for the sales tax. That fact does not dampen the appeal the sales tax has among
politicians, practitioners, or even the voting public. The sales tax is a proven
revenue raiser that purports to restrain people's spending habits and encourage
savings (Galbraith, 1958). Small wonder the federal government looks fondly
at the state and local government sales tax base and wishes it had a consumption-
based tax of its own.

## Administering the Sales Taxes

The general sales tax is ordinarily a tax on the value of consumption, an *ad
valorem* tax. The selective sales tax can either be an ad valorem tax or a tax on
quantity purchased (e.g., per gallon of gasoline or per pack of cigarettes), an
*ad rem* tax. The successful operation of the sales tax depends on three administrative areas: registration of vendors, tax collection, and auditing and compliance (Mieszkowski, 1978; Due and Mikesell, 1983).

The sales tax requires that all vendors register with the state government. For
the purposes of registration, a vendor is any business or individual who sells
tangible property. In thirty-eight states, a vendor's registration lasts as long as
the ownership of a business does not change hands. Since a list of vendors is
essential to sales tax collection, the state government seeks to keep the list as
comprehensive and up-to-date as possible. Sales tax evasion at the retail outlet
begins with a failure to register a retail business. For example, the street vendors
who crowd the sidewalks in major cities could and often do wreak havoc with
sales tax compliance.

Vendors serve as tax collectors. Businesses collect taxes on each sale and, in
turn, make regular payments to the state and the local governments. The state
and the local governments structure the payment schedule with an eye to min-
imizing the time that the tax revenues stay in the vendor's hands. Do the vendors
receive any compensation for this civic duty? Despite the fact that the vendor
is doing public bidding, twenty states offer no compensation. State and local
government officials argue that no taxpayer receives compensation for complying
with any other tax law. So the vendors generally collect the sales tax revenue
without compensation—much to their dismay.

The last component, auditing and compliance, holds the sales tax system together (Conn, Williams, and Young, 1984). With private retail businesses collecting public tax revenues, evasion can be more than a hypothetical issue. Tax
evasion can be minimized when the state implements computer-assisted auditing
techniques; keeps the sales tax base as comprehensive as possible (i.e., minimizes
sales tax exemptions); employs trained auditing staff; and imposes stiff penalties for
evasion. The effective implementation of these activities increases the chance for successful administration of a sales tax system (Fisher, 1985).

## SALES TAX BASE

Whatever appeal the state and local government sales tax possesses is rooted in the case for a national consumption tax. A consumption tax excludes taxes on savings and income-producing assets (e.g., land, business inventories, stocks, bonds, etc.). For a given amount of tax revenues, a switch from an income tax to a consumption tax would reduce taxes on capital income and increase taxes on labor income. The exclusion of capital income from taxation would increase savings and capital formation. The increase in tax payments on labor income would decrease work hours. The trade-off between an increase in capital formation and a decrease in labor hours would result in a net gain to the macroeconomy (Boskin, 1978). As a result, an expenditure tax is judged to be superior to an income tax on efficiency grounds. Couple this efficiency claim with the position that people should be taxed on what they take out of the economy (consumption), not on what they generate in the economy (income), a consumption tax would win widespread popular support (Bradford, 1980).

While this efficiency claim for a consumption tax is the stuff of economists' debates (see the counterclaims presented in Goode, 1980), one fact is certain: A retail sales tax bears little resemblance to the consumption tax just described. So much consumption spending escapes from the general and selective sales tax base that these taxes are a mere shadow of the consumption tax. How much consumption spending escapes general and selective sales taxes? Tax expenditures claim as much as 50 percent or $1.3 trillion out of $2.6 trillion in consumption expenditures! Fifty cents out of every one dollar spent could go untaxed. That is not exactly your comprehensive consumption tax.

The primary tax expenditures incorporated into the general state and local government sales taxes in 1988 are shown in Table 9–3. They usually include necessities: food (twenty-eight states), prescription drugs (forty-four states), and consumer electric utilities (twenty-nine states). States in the South Central region tend not to exempt spending on food; states in the North Central and South Atlantic regions are less likely to exempt spending on consumer electric utilities. Many other significant components of spending not listed in Table 9–3 are also exempt from the general sales tax.

All fifty states exempt some or all of a host of services: housing, health and medical, personal, legal, and business. For example, in 1990 three states taxed accounting services; four states barber and beauty services; three states engineering and architectural services; three states legal services; and four states management consulting services. In the 1987 legislative session, Florida enacted the most notorious attempt to tax services (Klott, 1987). The tax covered spending on advertising, legal services, accounting, and construction services. Another twist was that Florida would tax these services if they were purchased in Florida regardless of whether they were produced in Florida or elsewhere. So the Florida services tax extended the sales tax base and exported the tax beyond Florida's border. Not a bad idea for Florida. The uproar from service providers both in

**Table 9–3**

**Tax Exemptions from State Governments' General Sales Tax Base, 1988**

| Region & State | Food | Prescription Drugs | Consumer Utilities | Region & State | Food | Prescription Drugs | Consumer Utilities |
|---|---|---|---|---|---|---|---|
| USA | 28 | 44 | 29 | | | | |
| **N.E.** | | | | **E.S.C.** | | | |
| ME | X | X | X | KY | X | X | X |
| NH | No State General Sales Tax | | | TN | | X | X |
| VT | X | X | X | AL | | X | X |
| MA | X | X | X | MS | | X | |
| RI | X | X | X | | | | |
| CT | X | X | X | **W.S.C.** | | | |
| | | | | AR | | X | X |
| **M.A.** | | | | LA | X | X | X |
| NY | X | X | X | OK | | X | X |
| NJ | X | X | X | TX | X | X | X |
| PA | X | X | | | | | |
| | | | | **Mt.** | | | |
| **E.N.C.** | | | | MT | No State General Sales Tax | | |
| OH | X | X | X | ID | | X | X |
| IN | X | X | | WY | | X | |
| IL | X | X | | CO | X | X | X |
| MI | X | X | | NM | | | |
| WI | X | X | X | AZ | X | X | |
| | | | | UT | | X | X |
| **W.N.C.** | | | | NV | X | X | X |
| MN | X | X | X | | | | |
| IA | X | X | | **Pac.** | | | |
| MO | | X | X | WA | X | X | |
| ND | X | X | X | OR | No State General Sales Tax | | |
| SD | | X | | CA | X | X | X |
| NE | X | X | | AK | No State General Sales Tax | | |
| KS | | X | X | HI | | X | |
| **S.A.** | | | | | | | |
| DE | No State General Sales Tax | | | | | | |
| MD | X | X | | | | | |
| VA | | X | X | Source:  ACIR, 1988 | | | |
| WV | X | X | X | | | | |
| NC | | X | X | | | | |
| SC | | X | X | | | | |
| GA | | X | | | | | |
| FL | X | X | | | | | |

*Source*: ACIR, 1988.

and especially outside Florida forced the governor to withdraw the services tax (Hellerstein, 1988). In 1990, New York flirted with sales taxes on magazines, calls to "900" telephone numbers, and such services as detective, management, and public relations. The governor and the legislature soon looked elsewhere for tax revenues (Kolbert, 1990a, 1990c). The consequences of the reduced sales tax base is a loss in revenue potential, a revenue base sensitive to macroeconomic cycles, an increase in administrative problems, and distortions in consumption choices between taxed and untaxed goods and services and in the geographical location of consumer spending. Why suffer these consequences?

The conventional wisdom is that the sales tax fails to satisfy the ability to pay principle. It is regressive (i.e., claims a smaller percentage of income as income grows). To offset this regressive structure and restore some degree of vertical equity, tax reformers pushed for the exemption of such necessities as food, prescription drugs, clothing, utilities, and personal services. Since spending on these items as a share of income increases as income declines, the exemption of these items significantly reduces the sales tax burden on lower income individuals (Davies, 1971; Davies and Black, 1975; Schaefer, 1969).

Business services were also exempt to minimize the border problem. If the state government included business services in the general sales tax base, then businesses would pass on as much of the tax as they could. Such a pass-on would trigger a chain reaction: raising consumer prices, adversely affecting competition on a state-by-state basis, and driving consumer spending out of the high sales tax states. Whenever possible, large businesses would internalize the provision of business services (e.g., advertising, data processing, guard services, commercial art, etc.) to avoid the tax. Individual equity and perceived border problems for businesses form the case for exemptions from the sales tax base (Fox and Murray, 1988).

For the ad rem selective sales taxes, the base is retail gas sales (per gallon) for the gasoline tax; retail cigarette sales (per pack) for the cigarette tax; and retail sales of beer, wine, and spirits (per gallon) for the alcohol tax. No exceptions please.

## SALES TAX RATES

The rate at which state and local governments tax the consumption base determines not only sales tax revenues, but also the degree of actual or perceived sales tax competition which exists between/among states. Table 9–4 summarizes the state, local, and combined general sales tax rates. Forty-five states have selected rates between 3.0 percent (four states) and 7.5 percent (one state). The median rate nationwide is 5.0 percent. (Five states have no state general sales tax.) The threat of tax competition has often resulted in a clustering of sales tax rates within a region. For example, look at the East North Central region (dominated by 5.0 percent), the West North Central (dominated by 4.0 percent), and the West South Central (dominated by 4.0 percent). In regions where rates vary, for example, New England, South Atlantic, and the Pacific, the opportunity for tax competition exists.

Local governments—6,955 of them or less than 10 percent of all local governments—also levy a sales tax. Few local governments in the New England or Middle Atlantic regions have the power to do so. In the South Central, West North Central, and Mountain regions, the local governments that collect sales taxes are often highly urbanized counties or some of the nation's larger cities. Local sales tax rates vary from .5 percent to 5 percent. New York City levies a 4 percent rate while Juneau, Alaska and New Orleans Parish, Louisiana levy a 5 percent rate. In terms of revenue dependency, several cities collect at least

**Table 9–4**
**State, Local, and Combined General Sales Tax Rates, 1988**

| Region & State | --Sales Tax Rate--<br>State | Combined<br>State-Local | Units with<br>Local<br>Sales Tax | Region & State | --Sales Tax Rate--<br>State | Combined<br>State-Local | Units with<br>Local<br>Sales Tax |
|---|---|---|---|---|---|---|---|
| USA<br>(median) | 5.0 | | 6,955 | | | | |
| **N.E.** | | | | **E.S.C.** | | | |
| ME | 5.0 | 5.0 | | KY | 5.0 | 5.0 | |
| NH | 0.0 | 0.0 | | TN | 5.5 | 7.0 –7.75 | 106 |
| VT | 4.0 | 4.0 | | AL | 4.0 | 7.0 –8.0 | 389 |
| MA | 5.0 | 5.0 | | MS | 6.0 | 6.0 | |
| RI | 6.0 | 6.0 | | | | | |
| CT | 7.5 | 7.5 | | **W.S.C.** | | | |
| **M.A.** | | | | AR | 4.0 | 5.0 –6.0 | 142 |
| | | | | LA | 4.0 | 7.0 –9.0 | 302 |
| NY | 4.0 | 7.0 –8.25 | 83 | OK | 4.0 | 6.0 –8.5 | 479 |
| NJ | 6.0 | 6.0 | | TX | 6.0 | 7.0 –8.0 | 1,107 |
| PA | 6.0 | 6.0 | | | | | |
| **E.N.C.** | | | | **Mt.** | | | |
| | | | | MT | 0.0 | 0.0 | |
| OH | 5.0 | 5.5 –7.0 | 88 | ID | 5.0 | 5.0 | |
| IN | 5.0 | 5.0 | | WY | 3.0 | 4.0 –5.0 | 16 |
| IL | 5.0 | 7.25–9.0 | 1,383 | CO | 3.0 | 6.1 –7.1 | 235 |
| MI | 4.0 | 4.0 | | NM | 4.75 | 5.0 –5.375 | 132 |
| WI | 5.0 | 5.0 –5.5 | 18 | AZ | 5.0 | 6.7 –7.0 | 81 |
| | | | | UT | 5.0938 | 6.253 | 258 |
| **W.N.C.** | | | | NV | 5.75 | 6.0 –6.25 | 7 |
| MN | 6.0 | 6.5 –7.0 | 3 | **Pac.** | | | |
| IA | 4.0 | 5.0 | 38 | | | | |
| MO | 4.225 | 5.725–6.225 | 674 | WA | 6.5 | 7.8 –8.1 | 317 |
| ND | 5.5 | 6.0 | 4 | OR | 0.0 | 0.0 | |
| SD | 4.0 | 5.0 –6.0 | 120 | CA | 4.75 | 6.0 –6.5 | 446 |
| NE | 4.0 | 5.5 | 25 | AK | 0.0 | 0.0 –4.0 | 101 |
| KS | 4.0 | 5.0 6.0 | 175 | HI | 4.0 | 4.0 | |
| **S.A.** | | | | | | | |
| DE | 0.0 | 0.0 | | | | | |
| MD | 5.0 | 5.0 | | | | | |
| VA | 3.5 | 4.5 | 136 | | | | |
| WV | 6.0 | 6.0 | | | | | |
| NC | 3.0 | 5.0 | 100 | | | | |
| SC | 5.0 | 5.0 | | | | | |
| GA | 3.0 | 4.0 –5.0 | 155 | | | | |
| FL | 6.0 | 5.0 | 10 | | | | |

*Source*: ACIR, 1988.

20 percent of their tax revenues from the sales tax: Tucson, Arizona; Denver, Colorado; Omaha, Nebraska; and Tulsa, Oklahoma, for example. Even with these examples of local governments' use of the sales tax, the State Share column in Table 9–2 shows that state governments raise the vast bulk of sales tax revenue (84.3 percent of the tax revenue in 1986–87). While in the Northeast region generally the sales tax is a state tax, other regions show more variation. As Table 9–4 revealed, the South (State Share of 61.3 percent to 100.0 percent) and the West region (36.7 percent to 100.0 percent) are likely to permit local governments to levy sales taxes.

Table 9–4 also reintroduces the border problem. The border problem appears when neighboring jurisdictions have different sales tax rates (Hamovitch, 1966; McAllister, 1961; Mikesell, 1970, and 1971). For example, Table 9–4 hints at tax competition between Vermont (4.0 percent)-New Hampshire (no state general sales tax) versus Massachusetts (5.0 percent); East North Central versus West North Central regions; and Oregon (no state general sales tax) versus California (4.75 percent)-Washington (6.5 percent)-Nevada (5.75 percent).

These general state-by-state differences affect many people's livelihoods. For example, Connecticut recently (1989) expanded its sales tax base and raised its general sales tax rate from 7.5 percent to 8.0 percent. Connecticut's neighbor, Massachusetts, pegs its general sales tax rate at 5.0 percent. The "spread" between states is 3.0 percent. Merchants in Enfield, Connecticut, a retail center on the Connecticut-Massachusetts border, believe that the growing spread means lost business activity as Connecticut consumers drive by Enfield to Springfield-Holyoke, Massachusetts to shop. Accurate or not, the Enfield merchants believe that it is. That is the border problem at work (Johnson, 1989). In 1991 Connecticut reduced its general sales tax rate.

While this section has concentrated on the general sales tax, a summary of the selective sales tax rates by region provides some information about this form of consumption tax (Bowman and Mikesell, 1983). For the gasoline tax, the average rate per gallon is as follows (from low region to high region): Middle Atlantic (10.2 cents), Pacific (12 cents), South Atlantic (13 cents), New England (14.8 cents), East South Central (15 cents), West South Central (15.1 cents), East North Central (15.7 cents), and West North Central and Mountain (tied at 16.2 cents). On the state level, the low gas tax states are: Florida (4 cents), and Alaska, Georgia, New York, and Wyoming (all at 8 cents). The high gas tax states are: Connecticut, Minnesota, Montana, and Wisconsin (all at 20 cents).

Many of us probably do not realize the per gallon alcohol tax that we pay on beer, wine, and spirits (Wales, 1968). To get a sense of the alcohol tax on beer, the average rate per gallon is as follows (from low region to high region): Middle Atlantic (4.25 cents), New England (9 cents), East South Central (10.25 cents), East North Central (12.25 cents), Mountain (12.75 cents), West North Central (16.2 cents), West South Central (28.75 cents), South Atlantic (34.4 cents), and Pacific (40 cents). On the state level, the low alcohol tax states are: New Jersey (3 cents), California (4 cents), and Wisconsin (6 cents). The high alcohol tax states are Georgia and Louisiana (32 cents), Alaska (35 cents), Oklahoma (40 cents), and South Carolina (77 cents).

Cigarette taxes are the last major selective sales tax. Again, the average per pack state tax by region (from low region to high region) is: South Atlantic (11.4 cents), East South Central (12.6 cents), Mountain (16.9 cents), West South Central (21.5 cents), Middle Atlantic (22 cents), East North Central (22.1 cents), Pacific (22.6 cents), West North Central (26.6 cents), and New England (28.2 cents). The selective sales tax on cigarettes offers a dramatic illustration of how difficult it can be to design a state-local tax policy in a federal system which avoids the border problem.

### Buttlegging: The Case of Cigarette Tax Evasion

Chapter 7 looked at the impact of tax differentials on mobile factors between two towns: Eastown and Westown. When the people of Eastown introduced a sales tax while their neighbors in Westown did not, tax rate differentials became an issue for consumers. As a consequence, high spenders in Eastown could be predicted to move to Westown or at least shop in Westown. A variation of this outcome is found in the case of cigarettes where tax differentials create opportunities for illegal cigarette smuggling and cigarette tax evasion. If people do not come to the market, then the market will come to the people.

Several studies have argued that the motivation behind buttlegging consists of accessibility of retail outlets in low tax states to population centers in high tax states, length of the border, population near the border, risk of arrest and seizure of contraband, and most importantly, the tax differential (ACIR, 1985; Manchester, 1976). The high cigarette tax state will lose sales to the low tax state (in or out of the same region) via cigarette smuggling. The other side of the coin is that the low cigarette tax state will gain from the smuggling.

The ACIR study estimates the tax revenue gain/loss attributed to cigarette smuggling. Table 9–5 presents an extract from that study which illustrates the border problem specifically and the problem of designing taxes in a federal system in general. In illustration 1, New Hampshire and Vermont play the role of low tax states in New England with a cigarette tax rate of 17 cents. They gain tax revenue from the tax differential (NH: $14.8 million and VT: $1.9 million). Connecticut ( − $16.4 million), Massachusetts ( − $17.0 million), New Jersey ( − $15.4 million), and New York ( − $22.3 million) not only lose out to New Hampshire and Vermont, but more importantly, they lose out to North Carolina ( + $10.6 million) whose cigarette tax rate is 2 cents! North Carolina's tax "advantage" is not only felt in the Northeast, but also in the South where Georgia ( − $2.2 million), Florida ( − $23.9 million), and Tennessee ( − $9.1 million) lose tax revenues.

Not to confine the analysis to the East Coast, Illustration 2 shows the tax revenue winners and losers in the competition between the low tax states (Indiana and Kentucky) and the high tax states (Illinois, Michigan, and Wisconsin). The evidence states that buttlegging as a form of the border problem certainly exists. The general moral of this case study is that the federal system of decentralized fiscal decision making creates a unique environment where tax competition between/among jurisdictions with all of its economic dislocations can flourish unless state and local governments rise above self-interest to follow a policy of tax harmony.

## INCIDENCE OF THE SALES TAX

The legislated incidence of the general and the selective sales tax is that the taxes should fall on the consumer of the good or service. The degree to which

**Table 9–5**
**Tax Revenue Gains/Losses Associated with Buttlegging, 1983**

| Tax Competition State-by-State | | Cigarette Tax Rate | Revenue Gain/Loss (millions) |
|---|---|---|---|
| | | *Illustration #1* | |
| New Hampshire | \|__ | $.17 | +$14.8 |
| Vermont | \|  \| | | +  1.9 |
| | \|  \| | .17 | |
| | \|  \| | | |
| Connecticut | \|  \| | .26 | −  16.4 |
| Massachusetts | \|  \| | .26 | −  17.0 |
| New Jersey | \|<−\| | .25 | −  15.4 |
| New York | \|  \| | .21 | −  22.3 |
| | \|  \| | | |
| North Carolina | \|−−\| | .02 | +  10.6 |
| | \|  \| | | |
| Georgia | \|  \| | .12 | −   2.2 |
| Florida | \|<−\| | .21 | −  23.9 |
| Tennessee | \|  \| | .13 | −   9.1 |
| | \|  \| | | |
| | | *Illustration #2* | |
| Illinois | \|  \| | .12 | −  19.6 |
| Michigan | \|<−\| | .21 | −  20.3 |
| Wisconsin | \|  \| | .25 | −  16.8 |
| | \|  \| | | |
| Indiana | \|  \| | .105 | +   5.1 |
| Kentucky | \|−−\| | .03 | +  17.5 |

*Source*: ACIR, 1985.

this legal intent is satisfied depends upon how sensitive consumers are to price increases (*price elasticity of demand*). For example, if consumers are extremely sensitive to price increases (*price elastic*), then producers could be forced to absorb some of the per unit tax in order to sell their goods and services. Raising the sale price by the full amount of the tax would drive away potential customers. On the other hand, if consumers are extremely insensitive to price increases (*price inelastic*), then consumers would absorb most, if not all, of the per unit tax. Recall that this division of the tax between consumers and producers is called *tax shifting*. In contrast to legislative incidence, economic incidence defines who actually pays the tax after tax shifting takes place.

The analysis of the incidence of the sales tax assumes a comprehensive general sales tax and a national, single (fixed) tax rate. The assumption concerning the base of comparison is more complicated because it affects the structure of the sales tax. Should the base of comparison for a tax on consumption be income? Or should it be consumption spending? The choice has a bearing on the ability to pay justification of the sales tax. Practitioners tend to line up with the income base. Economists, of course, see advantages in both bases. Since public support for the sales tax may well hinge on the selection of a base, we will look at the argument for each base.

### Sales Tax Incidence with an Income Base

Sales tax incidence with income as the base results in a violation of horizontal equity (unequal treatment of equals) and a regressive tax structure. Taxes paid are traditionally compared to income since income is considered a rough measure of economic well-being. Sales tax incidence revolves around the estimation of the ratio of sales taxes paid (t times C, where t is the single tax rate and C is consumption spending) to income (Y), or (t times C) divided by Y. The analysis is first concerned with the taxes paid-income ratio for individuals with the same income. That is horizontal equity.

Horizontal equity would assume that each individual has identical income. Taxes paid would be a fixed percentage of consumption spending. If each individual spent the same proportion of his/her income, then taxes paid would be the same and the ratio of taxes paid to income would be the same. You and I earn $18,000. Both of us spend $10,000. The national, single tax rate is 5.0 percent. So the taxes paid-income ratio is (.05 times $10,000) divided by $18,000, or $500 divided by $18,000, or 2.8 percent.

However, there is no reason to believe that individuals with the same income will spend at the same rate. Some of us are spenders; and others are savers. Different levels of spending will result in different levels of taxes paid. Now although you and I earn $18,000, you still spend $10,000 and I spend $12,000. The taxes paid-income ratio remains 2.8 percent for you, but it becomes 3.3 percent for me (i.e., .05 times $12,000 divided by $18,000, or $600 divided by $18,000). For individuals with the same income, different levels of taxes paid means different ratios of taxes paid to income. In this situation, the sales tax fails the horizontal equity standard.

Vertical equity looks at the ratio of taxes paid to income as income changes. It classifies the tax as progressive, proportional, or regressive tax. The analysis assumes that individuals' income is increasing. Studies of consumption habits reveal that as income increases, the level of consumption spending increases, but the proportion of income spent decreases (the proportion saved increases). Sales taxes paid increase as consumption spending increases, but the proportion of income paid in sales taxes decrease (the taxes paid-income ratio is decreasing).

For example, the national, single sales tax rate is again 5.0 percent. You receive $18,000 and spend $10,000 for a taxes paid-income ratio of 2.8 percent. I receive $15,000 and spend $9,600 for a taxes paid-income ratio of 3.2 percent. Thus, the comprehensive sales tax is a classic regressive tax; that is, the proportion of income paid in sales taxes decrease as income increases.

### Sales Tax Incidence with a Consumption Base

Under this calculation of sales tax incidence, the sales taxes paid-income ratio is discarded. This view holds that the appropriate measure of tax incidence would be the ratio of sales taxes paid to consumption spending. Horizontal equity would be defined in terms of identical levels of consumption spending across individuals. In turn, vertical equity would be defined in terms of different levels of consumption spending across individuals. Sales tax incidence with consumption as the base results in horizontal equity and a proportional tax structure.

Horizontal equity singles out individuals with equal levels of consumption spending. The sales taxes paid would be a fixed proportion of consumption spending (t times C, where t is the national, single tax rate and C is consumption spending). When the taxes paid-consumption spending ratio is estimated, it would be the same for all individuals with identical consumption levels; namely, (t times C) divided by C, or t. For example, you and I spend $10,000 regardless of our income levels. Taxes paid are .05 times $10,000, or $500. The ratio of taxes paid to consumption spending is $500 divided by $10,000, or 5 percent for both of us. That results meets the horizontal equity rule.

Vertical equity looks at individuals with different levels of consumption spending. The taxes paid-consumption spending ratio determines the structure of the sales tax. For example, you spend $10,000 and pay $500 in taxes. I spend $12,000 and pay $600 in taxes. Both of us have a ratio of taxes paid to consumption spending of 5.0 percent. That ratio would be constant across all levels of consumption. Under this measure, the comprehensive sales tax would be proportional; that is, the proportion of consumption spending paid in sales taxes remains the same as income increases.

In addition to exemptions from the tax base and the choice of a base, one other element influences sales tax incidence, federal income tax deductibility. Prior to the Tax Reform Act of 1986, taxpayers who itemized their deductions (did not claim the standard deduction) could subtract their sales tax payments from their taxable income. This subtraction had the effect of having the federal government pay some portion of the sales tax bill. It reduced the taxpayer's sales taxes.

The Tax Reform Act of 1986 ended this deduction. Now all taxpayers pay the full amount of the sales tax (no behind-the-scenes help from Uncle Sam). Eliminating this deduction has consequences which have yet to materialize fully in the state and local tax system. Deductibility reduced the price effects associated with the sales tax. So choices between present and future consumption and between taxed and untaxed goods and services were not so stark. They are now. Deductibility blunted tax differentials and therefore, interstate tax competition. Now that competition can flourish. Last, deductibility placed all state and local taxes—property, sales, and income—on equal footing. All were deductible. After 1986, the sales tax was not. Whether this change pushes state and local governments away from sales taxes and to property and/or income tax use remains

Table 9–6
Estimates of the Incidence of the General and the Selective Sales Tax

| Family Income | Sales & Excise Taxes (1) | Sales (2) | Selective Sales (2) |
|---|---|---|---|
| Less than $ 5,000 | 17.9 | 3.75 – 6.09 | 2.57 – 4.81 |
| 5,000 – 10,000 | 7.7 | 3.17 – 3.70 | 1.80 – 2.28 |
| 10,000 – 15,000 | 6.2 | 2.63 – 2.80 | 1.59 – 1.64 |
| 15,000 – 20,000 | 5.6 | 2.46 | 1.36 |
| 20,000 – 25,000 | 5.2 | 2.35 | 1.26 |
| 25,000 – 30,000 | 4.9 | 2.27 | 1.19 |
| 30,000 – 50,000 | 4.5 | 1.93 – 2.18 | 1.01 – 1.14 |
| 50,000 – 100,000 | 3.3 | ‖ | ‖ |
| 100,000 – 500,000 | 1.6 | ‖ | ‖ |
| 500,000 – 1,000,000 | .7 | ‖ | ‖ |
| Over 1,000,000 | .6 | ∨ | ∨ |

*Sources*: (1) Pechman, 1985; (2) Phares, 1980.

to be seen. The obvious attraction to a deductible tax is that the federal government shares the state and local government tax payments with the taxpayer. The
taxpayer does not face the taxman alone. Uncle Sam is at hand. In the case of
sales taxes, the taxpayer is now on his/her own.

### Empirical Evidence

Numerous studies over the years have estimated the horizontal and the vertical
equity of general and selective sales taxes. (For examples, see Davies, 1963;
Due and Mikesell, 1980; Morgan, 1963.) These studies use income as the base
and they account for the exemptions granted to reduce the regressive nature of
the sales tax. The estimates in Table 9–6 display the results of the economic
incidence of the general and the selective sales taxes with base exemptions and
various state and local tax rates.

While the actual numbers vary slightly from the Pechman to the Phares es-
timations, both researchers show that the sales tax is regressive at the low end
of the income distribution (certainly below $10,000) and mildly regressive in
the Pechman study (almost proportional in the Phares study) through most of
the income distribution (from $10,000 to $50,000). State and local exemptions
form the base and the declining share of consumption as income increases are
behind these results. Perhaps these incidence results help explain the popular
support for the sales tax. Society is willing to tolerate some degree of regressivity
in order to temper consumption spending.

**Table 9–7**
**Summary of the Evaluation of the Sales Tax**

| Criteria | Comments |
|---|---|
| Efficiency | o Sales taxes introduce price effects into the private market. The price effects influence the choice on consumption versus savings; taxed versus untaxed goods and services; and the geographical location of consumer spending (the border problem).<br>o Cigarette smuggling is a single dramatic example of the border problem. |
| Fairness | o Choice of a base for determining tax burden influences the equity of the sales tax.<br>o An income base generates a sales tax which does not satisfy horizontal equity and one which is regressive from a vertical equity perspective.<br>o A consumption base generates a sales tax which satisfies horizontal equity and is proportional from a vertical equity perspective.<br>o Actual state and local sales taxes are only modestly regressive because of numerous tax base exemptions. |
| Administration | o Private vendors are primarily responsible for sales tax administration.<br>o State and local governments should maintain a registration list of vendors, a system for rapid tax collection, and thorough auditing of vendors.<br>o Under optimum conditions, the administrative cost of the sales tax is 1.5 - 2.5 % of the revenue. |
| Revenue Stability | o Sales taxes are relatively stable.<br>o Estimates of revenue elasticity fall between .63 and 1.33 with an average of .94. |
| Link Between Taxing and Spending | o Benefit principle does not justify general sales taxes; therefore, there is no link between spending and taxing.<br>o Selective sales taxes which are earmarked may establish this linkage; the gasoline tax is the closest example, but the link is very loose. |
| Tax Visibility | o Form - integrated with almost every economic transaction<br>o Size - relatively modest amounts except in the case of consumer durables and luxuries |

## EVALUATION OF THE SALES TAX

The criteria for a good tax includes six dimensions of the tax: economic efficiency, fairness, administration, revenue stability, link between spending and taxing, and tax visibility. This evaluation highlights the comparative strengths and weaknesses of the sales tax. Table 9–7 summarizes the evaluation of the property tax.

### Applying the Criteria to the Sales Tax

*Efficiency.* Sales taxes introduce changes, some could be considered ineffi-ciencies, into the private market through price effects. Price increases traced to the imposition of a sales tax, distort consumption behavior in several ways. First, a sales tax may tip the consumption-savings choice in favor of savings. By raising the price on goods and services, a sales tax discourages consumption. Consumers are gently pushed to postpone current consumption and save instead. Second, by raising the price on *some* goods and services, a sales tax will alter the consumer's choice between taxed and untaxed goods and services. The degree of the shift will depend on how sensitive consumers are to price increases ("price elasticity of demand"). Third, by raising the price on goods and services by different amounts in different states, a sales tax introduces a border problem. if the cost of time and travel is lower than the cost of the sales tax, then consumers will travel to the place with the lower/lowest sales tax rate. Cigarette smuggling, for example, offered a single dramatic example of the border problem.

*Fairness.* The choice of a base for calculating tax burden determines how fair the sales tax is. An income base is the choice of most analysts, practitioners, and the voting public. If the sales tax had a comprehensive base and a national, single tax rate, then the income base conjures up a picture of the sales tax that violates the notion of horizontal equity and produces a regressive tax from the perspective of vertical equity. In fact, the sales tax is only modestly regressive because of numerous tax base exemptions for food, electric utilities, prescription drugs, and business, medical, and personal services.

If the sales tax is evaluated using a consumption base, then the conclusions change. A consumption base will show the sales tax satisfies horizontal equity. What about vertical equity? A consumption base produces a proportional tax structure.

*Administration.* Private vendors carry the burden of sales tax administration. For this reason, state and local government sales tax administration requires the registration of vendors and the maintenance of that registration list, frequent tax collection to minimize the delay between payment of the tax and the receipt of the tax revenue, and a comprehensive tax auditing system. The administrative cost of the sales tax varies between 1.5 and 2.5 percent of the tax collected.

*Revenue Stability.* State and local governments require stable revenue sources. Stability means that the economic cycles of growth and recession should not produce dramatic government surpluses or deficits. Recall that the concept of revenue elasticity relates the percentage change in tax collections to the percentage change in personal income. Studies have shown revenue elasticity for the sales tax ranges from .63 to 1.33 with an average of .94. For every 1 percent change in personal income, there is a .94 percent change in sales tax revenues (ACIR, 1977c; Legler and Shapiro, 1968; Friedlaender, Swanson, and Due, 1973; Fox and Campbell, 1984). Again this element of the criteria stresses stability, *not* revenue adequacy. The sales tax is not especially sensitive to changes in the private economy. A look at Table 9–1 shows that sales taxes have been a steady source of revenue for state and local governments over the years.

*Link Between Spending and Taxing.* Any tax which satisfies the benefit principle links public spending and taxing. That linkage brings private marketlike forces to bear in the provision of public goods/services. However, the benefit principle does not justify the general sales tax. Sales tax revenues pour into the general fund and finance the full variety of state and local public goods/services. There is no benefit principle at work in that arrangement!

If the link between spending and taxing is secured, then it would likely occur when state and local governments earmark sales tax revenues. Selective sales taxes, especially on gasoline, come the closest to meeting the benefit principle test. However, before efficiency-minded people get too exited, the link is very loose indeed. Even selective sales taxes on gasoline which are dedicated to highway maintenance and construction do not firmly satisfy the benefit principle.

*Tax Visibility.* Tax visibility determines how conscious people are about the taxes which they pay. Visibility is related to the form, size, and timing of a tax. The form of the sales tax integrates it with an economic transaction. So taxpayers are less aware of this tax. The size of the sales tax is usually modest except in the case of consumer durables or luxuries. Last, the timing of the tax also works to keep it out of sight. The sales tax is collected frequently; with virtually every transaction.

Its integration with a transaction, its relatively small amount, and its frequent collection make the sales tax a less visible tax. This lack of visibility may explain why the sales tax enjoys substantial public support. We are not aware of it so we do not oppose it!

## SUMMARY

1. The sales tax does not satisfy the benefit principle or the ability to pay principle. The criteria for a good tax reveal that the sales tax may create market inefficiencies and is inequitable. The sales tax remains popular with practitioners and the public given its ease of administration, reliable revenue production, and its relative invisibility. Sales taxes are a stable among state government revenue sources across all geographic regions.

2. Exemptions such as spending on food, utilities, prescription drugs, and services reduce the sales tax base by as much as 50 percent. The consequences are a loss in revenue potential, increases in administrative costs, and improved equity.

3. Sales tax rate differentials invite jurisdiction competition known as the border problem. This fact encourages a clustering of sales tax rates across the states. Competition still exists. A popular example is cigarette smuggling which is much in evidence along the East Coast.

4. The incidence of the sales tax rests on the selection of a base. An income base results in a violation of horizontal equity and a modestly regressive tax structure. The loss of sales tax deductibility within the federal personal income tax will only magnify this outcome.

# CHAPTER 10

---

# Personal Income Taxes

## PREVIEW

The personal income tax comes next in the state and local revenue-raising pecking order. Although it ranks third, personal income tax revenues have increased more rapidly in the 1980s than revenues from the property or the sales tax. The analysis of this highly productive tax proceeds in a way with which you are now familiar: a profile of personal income tax use, an economic justification of the tax, an examination of base and rate issues, and an explanation of tax incidence. The chapter concludes with an evaluation of the personal income tax using the "good" tax criteria.

## INTRODUCTION

The need for tax revenue always keeps the taxman's imagination churning. In order to finance the Civil War, the federal government levied the first albeit temporary personal income tax. While the U.S. Supreme Court upheld the federal government's right to levy such a tax then, it was not long before it reversed itself. When the Court was asked to rule on the personal income tax provision in the Wilson-Gorham Tariff in 1894, the Court decided that the personal income tax violated Article 1, Section 3 of the Constitution. (The requirement to apportion a "direct" tax among the states according to population.) The Sixteenth Amendment (1913) changed all of that at the federal level (Peltason, 1979). Personal income taxation came to the states two years earlier. In 1911 Wisconsin

**Table 10–1**
**Trend in State and Local Government Personal Income Tax (PIT), 1970–87**
**(revenue in billions)**

| Year | PIT Taxes | ------Personal Income Tax------- As a Percent of | | Annual % Change | GNP Deflator |
|------|-----------|------------------|----------------------|----------|----------|
| | | Tax Revenues | Own Source Revenues | | |
| 1970 | $10.8 | 11.6% | 8.5% | | |
| 1971 | 11.8 | 11.7 | 9.9 | 9.3% | 5.7% |
| 1972 | 15.2 | 13.7 | 11.3 | 28.8 | 4.7 |
| 1973 | 18.0 | 14.6 | 11.9 | 18.4 | 6.5 |
| 1974 | 19.5 | 14.7 | 11.8 | 8.3 | 9.1 |
| 1975 | 21.4 | 14.9 | 11.8 | 9.7 | 9.8 |
| 1976 | 24.5 | 15.6 | 12.2 | 14.5 | 6.4 |
| 1977 | 29.3 | 16.7 | 13.1 | 19.6 | 6.7 |
| 1978 | 33.2 | 16.8 | 13.5 | 13.3 | 7.3 |
| 1979 | 36.9 | 17.4 | 13.8 | 11.1 | 8.9 |
| 1980 | 42.1 | 18.2 | 14.1 | 14.1 | 9.0 |
| 1981 | 46.4 | 17.9 | 13.9 | 10.2 | 9.7 |
| 1982 | 50.8 | 18.3 | 13.8 | 9.5 | 6.4 |
| 1983 | 55.1 | 18.0 | 13.9 | 9.3 | 3.9 |
| 1984 | 64.6 | 18.7 | 14.5 | 17.2 | 3.7 |
| 1985 | 70.1 | 18.9 | 14.3 | 8.5 | 3.2 |
| 1986 | 74.4 | 18.9 | 14.1 | 6.1 | 2.6 |
| 1987 | 83.7 | 20.6 | 14.7 | 12.5 | 3.0 |

*Source*: U.S. Bureau of Census, *Government Finances*, various years.

taxed personal incomes. In 1939 Philadelphia, Pennsylvania levied the first local personal income tax. A willingness to raise tax rates and expand the tax base coupled with improved tax administration has dramatically increased the attractiveness of the state and local personal income tax. Our lives have never been the same come the springtime.

## PROFILE OF PERSONAL INCOME TAX

Table 10–1 shows the trend in state and local government personal income taxation from 1970 to 1987. In addition, it measures the contribution of personal income tax revenue to total tax revenue and own source revenue (OSR); and compares the annual percentage change in personal income taxes with the GNP deflator, the comprehensive measure of inflation. Personal income tax revenue (measured in billions of current dollars) has steadily grown over this period from $10.8 billion in 1970 to $83.7 billion in 1987. The growth has been in double digits for ten of the seventeen years. Compared to the GNP deflator, the annual growth in personal income taxes has exceeded the GNP deflator since 1976. In fact, it exceeded this measure of inflation in fifteen of the seventeen years displayed in Table 10–1. This tax produces almost 21 percent of total state-local tax revenue and almost 15 percent of total state-local own source revenue. While it is third in revenue production, the personal income tax is a fast growing, attractive revenue source.

Table 10–2 reports the per capita personal income tax (PIT), the relation of PIT to $1,000 of personal income (an effort measure), and the state government

**Table 10–2**
**State-Local Per Capita Personal Income Taxes (PIT), the Relation of PIT to**
**$1,000 Personal Income (PY), and the State Government Share of PIT, 1986–87**

| Region & State | Per Capita PIT | Relation of PIT to $1000 PY | State Share | Region & State | Per Capita PIT | Relation of PIT to $1000 PY | State Share |
|---|---|---|---|---|---|---|---|
| USA | $342 | $24 | 91.6% | | | | |
| N.E. | | | | E.S.C. | | | |
| ME | 357 | 28 | 100.0 | KY | $277 | $25 | 89.0% |
| NH* | 8 | 1 | 100.0 | TN* | 14 | 1 | 100.0 |
| VT | 296 | 22 | 100.0 | AL | 225 | 20 | 96.7 |
| MA | 680 | 39 | 100.0 | MS | 120 | 12 | 100.0 |
| RI | 364 | 25 | 100.0 | | | | |
| CT* | 145 | 7 | 100.0 | W.S.C. | | | |
| M.A. | | | | AR | 224 | 20 | 100.0 |
| | | | | LA | 98 | 9 | 100.0 |
| NY | 923 | 54 | 75.9 | OK | 207 | 17 | 100.0 |
| NJ | 339 | 18 | 100.0 | TX | ------- | No PIT | ------- |
| PA | 307 | 22 | 75.1 | | | | |
| | | | | Mt. | | | |
| E.N.C. | | | | MT | 59 | 20 | 100.0 |
| OH | 369 | 27 | 80.8 | ID | 266 | 24 | 100.0 |
| IN | 266 | 20 | 98.8 | WY | ------- | No PIT | ------- |
| IL | 267 | 17 | 100.0 | CO | 314 | 21 | 100.0 |
| MI | 384 | 26 | .90.8 | NM | 162 | 14 | 100.0 |
| WI | 463 | 33 | 100.0 | AZ | 225 | 17 | 100.0 |
| | | | | UT | 316 | 29 | 100.0 |
| W.N.C. | | | | NV | ------- | No PIT | ------- |
| MN | 545 | 37 | 100.0 | Pac. | | | |
| IA | 337 | 25 | 100.0 | | | | |
| MO | 278 | 20 | 87.8 | WA | ------- | No PIT | ------- |
| ND | 119 | 9 | 100.0 | OR | 537 | 41 | 100.0 |
| SD | ------- | No PIT | ------- | CA | 502 | 30 | 100.0 |
| NE | 226 | 16 | 100.0 | AK | ------- | No PIT | ------- |
| KS | 256 | 18 | 100.0 | HI | 501 | 34 | 100.0 |
| S.A. | | | | | | | |
| DE | 588 | 40 | 94.7 | * limited personal income tax | | | |
| MD | 627 | 38 | 76.7 | | | | |
| VA | 414 | 27 | 100.0 | | | | |
| WV | 254 | 24 | 100.0 | | | | |
| NC | 400 | 7 | 100.0 | | | | |
| SC | 295 | 7 | 100.0 | | | | |
| GA | 345 | 26 | 100.0 | | | | |
| FL | ------- | No PIT | ------- | | | | |

*Source*: U.S. Bureau of Census, *Government Finances*, 1988.

share of the PIT revenues. Forty-three states impose a PIT; three states (Connecticut, New Hampshire, and Tennessee) in a limited way; and seven states (Alaska, Florida, Nevada, South Dakota, Texas, Washington, and Wyoming) have no PIT. The average values for these measures across the forty-three states with a PIT are: $342 per capita, $24 per $1,000 of personal income, and a state share of PIT revenues at 91.6 percent.

Of course, there is variation around these average values. Eight states collect more than $500 per capita from the personal income tax; for example, New York ($923), Massachusetts ($680), and Maryland ($627), while six states collect under $200 per capita: for example, Connecticut ($145), Mississippi ($120), and New Mexico ($162). This amount will change in Connecticut. In most states the personal income tax is exclusively a state government tax. However, nine states permit a total of 4,200 local jurisdictions to levy a personal income tax. These local governments are most often large counties or cities including Birmingham, Alabama; Louisville, Kentucky; Detroit, Michigan; St. Louis, Missouri; New York, New York; Cleveland, Ohio; and Philadelphia, Pennsylvania. In some states school districts have the authority to levy a personal income tax.

New York state allows New York City and Yonkers to collect income taxes which amount to almost 25 percent of the total personal income tax revenues; Maryland allows its counties which collect almost 25 percent of these revenues; and Pennsylvania allows virtually all local governments which raise almost 25 percent of these revenues (ACIR, 1989). As fiscal pressure builds on local governments, they will seriously consider imposing a personal income tax.

## PERSONAL INCOME TAX: ITS RATIONALE AND HOW IT WORKS

### Benefit Rationale

The benefit principle does not justify the personal income tax. The personal income tax that an individual pays has little or, more often than not, no connection to benefits that an individual receives from public goods/services. With a personal income tax, an individual's income determines his/her tax liability, while the individual's personal circumstances determines his/her demand for public goods/services. For example, a low income person may pay a small amount in personal income taxes, but this same person may demand a high level of public goods/services. This lack of a connection between taxes paid and benefits received violates the benefit principle straight out and implies some degree of redistribution in state and local fiscal policies.

### Ability to Pay Rationale

The ability to pay principle goes right to questions of horizontal and vertical equity. Horizontal equity requires equal tax treatment for people of equal income levels regardless of the source of the income. Within any given state, there are many sources of income which receive preferential treatment under state personal income taxes; for example, income from the sales of an asset which has appreciated since its purchase, or capital gains income; dividend income; and social security benefits. Preferential treatment of income by source violates the notion of horizontal equity. Since most, if not all, state personal income tax systems have provisions which allow for preferential tax treatment, horizontal equity is violated. Across the states, horizontal equity would be a fortunate coincidence; no, make that a miracle!

Local personal income tax systems that tax only wage income make no pretense of satisfying horizontal equity. Even though there may be sound administrative reasons for taxing only wage income and leaving other sources of income (e.g., dividends, rent, interest) tax free, these local systems show no concern for the horizontal equity standard. A disregard for horizontal equity is not just unfair. It can distort people's choice of a source of income (if they have a choice) and at the subnational level may even have locational implications for economic activities.

With such lukewarm concern for horizontal equity, should we ask how state-local personal income taxes stack up on vertical equity grounds? On one level, vertical equity in a personal income system requires that the greater an individual's income, the more (amount) that individual must pay in taxes. Even a personal income tax which is primarily a wage tax and uses a single tax rate can usually meet this standard. On another level, vertical equity requires a progressive tax structure (not just the amount, but the percent of an individual's income needed to pay personal income taxes increases as income increases). State-local personal income taxes often show a very modest degree of progressivity throughout the entire income distribution. In fact, these systems are usually proportional except at the lowest income levels. Forced to choose a rationale for state-local personal income taxes, we conclude that the ability to pay principle weakly supports this form of taxation.

## How the Personal Income Tax Works

The administration of any state-local personal income tax centers around a calculation of the income tax liability, a procedure for withholding tax payments from the taxpayers' incomes, a means of auditing tax returns, and a system of enforcing taxpayer compliance (Penniman, 1980; Rodgers, 1987). Before any of this administrative apparatus can be brought to bear, the taxman and the taxpayers must be clear about the definition of the tax base and the structure of the tax rates.

*Personal Income Tax Base.* Not long after the personal income tax joined death as a certainty in American lives, two economists defined a comprehensive income tax base suitable for any level of government to use. In its simplest form, the *Haig-Simons* definition of comprehensive annual income is the sum of consumption and increases in net worth over the year (Rosen, 1988; Goode, 1977). Tax practitioners shake their heads at two aspects of the Haig-Simons definition of income. Although the income tax base would include actual income received from the sale of an asset (''realized'' capital gains), it would also tax ''paper'' gains tallied from the appreciation of unsold assets (''unrealized'' capital gains) on such diverse assets as stocks, bonds, real estate, antiques, jewelry, etc. Further, with its emphasis on net worth, the Haig-Simons criterion permits the subtraction of the "costs of earning income." There is no disagreement with the intention, but measuring these costs would simultaneously be a tax accountant's livelihood and nightmare.

If Haig-Simons is theory, what is practice? Any taxable personal income base departs substantially from the Haig-Simons definition. It counts only cash transactions (it excludes most noncash transactions); and allows equity and incentive based adjustments. The taxable personal income base equals a cash measure of income minus personal exemptions and deductions. *Personal exemptions* are equity adjustments. They reduce taxable income to account for living expenses incurred by the taxpayer for him/herself, child dependents, and elderly dependents. This device removes low income people from the taxroll and differentiates tax payments by the number of dependents. *Deductions* are equity and incentive adjustments. They include expenditures on specific activities which the government wishes to subsidize; for example, medical care (35 states), charitable enterprises (33 states), and home buying/mortgage interest (33 states) (ACIR, 1989). State personal income taxes also permit the deduction of property and sales taxes. By way of illustration, if the federal personal income tax base is compared with the gross national product (which itself is less than the Haig-Simons income definition), all the excluded income and income adjustments reduce the actual federal personal income tax base to anywhere from one-third to one-half of the gross national product.

If we push the issue of tax practice further, then we find that thirty of the forty-three states which levy a state personal income tax have some elements of the federal system of exemptions and deductions: twelve states follow the federal system very closely; thirteen states use their own system of exemptions and deductions; seven states start with the federal definition of income then incorporate their own exemptions and deductions. Table 10–3 displays the personal exemptions and standard deductions for a married couple who file a joint return. As a reference point, the parallel federal personal income tax data are given: $3,900 for personal exemptions and $5,000 for the standard deduction. The value of a personal exemption clusters between $2,000-$3,000 and goes as high as $9,500 in Mississippi. The value of the standard deduction ranges from $650 (Kentucky) to the high value of $8,500 (New York). Of the eleven states that permit local income taxes, six states limit the tax base to wage income. The remaining three states authorize local governments to tie their personal income tax systems to the state's by using the state income base (two states) or by having them tax the state income tax liability (one state).

Any departure from the Haig-Simons income definition is a form of tax expenditure. The exclusion of noncash transactions and unrealized capital gains is a tax expenditure, as are the legislated personal exemptions and deductions. All these tax expenditures shrink the state-local personal income tax base.

*Personal Income Tax Rates.* Changes in tax rates determine the structure of a tax. If the tax rate increases as income increases, the tax structure is progressive. If the tax rate decreases as income increases, the tax structure is regressive. Last,

**Table 10-3**
**Personal Exemptions and Standard Deductions for a Married Couple Who File a Joint Return, 1988**

| Region & State | Personal Exemption | Standard Deduction | Region & State | Personal Exemption | Standard Deduction |
|---|---|---|---|---|---|
| USA | $3900 | $5000 | | | |
| **N.E.** | | | **E.S.C.** | | |
| ME | 80 credit | 100 credit | KY | $40 credit | $650 |
| NH | - limited income tax - | | TN | - limited income tax - | |
| VT | - 23% of federal tax - | | AL | 3000 | 4000 |
| MA | 4400 | none | MS | 9500 | 3400 |
| RI | 22.96% of federal tax | | **W.S.C.** | | |
| CT | - limited income tax - | | | | |
| **M.A.** | | | AR | 40 credit | 1000 |
| | | | LA | 9000 | none |
| NY | none | 8500 | OK | 2000 | 2000 |
| NJ | 2000 | none | TX | --- no income tax --- | |
| PA | none | none | **Mt.** | | |
| **E.N.C.** | | | MT | 2280 | 4280 |
| OH | 1300 | none | ID | 3800 | federal |
| IN | 2000 | none | WY | --- no income tax --- | |
| IL | 2000 | none | CO | - 5% of federal tax - | |
| MI | 3600 | none | NM | 4000 | federal |
| WI | none | 8900 | AZ | 4250 | 2125 |
| | | | UT | 75% federal | federal |
| **W.N.C.** | | | NV | --- no income tax --- | |
| MN | -- same as federal -- | | **Pac.** | | |
| IA | 40 credit | 3030 | | | |
| MO | 2400 | federal | WA | --- no income tax --- | |
| ND | -- same as federal -- | | OR | 180 credit | 3000 |
| SD | --- no income tax --- | | CA | 104 credit | 3932 |
| NE | 2260 | 3780 | AK | --- no income tax --- | |
| KS | 3900 | 5000 | HI | 2080 | 1700 |
| **S.A.** | | | | | |
| DE | 2500 | 1600 | | | |
| MD | 2000 | 4000 | | | |
| VA | 1600 | 2700 | | | |
| WV | 4000 | none | | | |
| NC | 2200 | none | | | |
| SC | -- same as federal -- | | | | |
| GA | 3000 | 3000 | | | |
| FL | --- no income tax --- | | | | |

*Source*: ACIR, 1989.

if the tax rate remains constant as income increases, the tax structure is proportional. The tax rate which is referred to is called the *marginal tax rate*. It measures how the tax payment changes as income changes. Income changes are measured in increments, or *tax brackets*. For example, the New Jersey state personal income tax uses three tax brackets to measure income changes: the first $20,000; $20,001 to $50,000; and over $50,000. The tax rates which are associated with these three brackets are: 2.0 percent; 2.5 percent; and 3.5 percent, respectively. Any taxable income changes which occur within the range of

$20,000 would have a marginal tax rate of 2.0 percent. (My taxable income increases from $10,000 to $15,000. My tax liability increases from $200 to $300. Notice that the marginal tax rate is the change in tax liability, or $100, divided by the change in taxable income, or $5,000, which equals 2.0 percent.) Any taxable income changes which cross brackets will have an increasing marginal tax rate. (My taxable income increases from $20,000 to $40,000. My tax liability increases from $400 to $900. Notice that the marginal tax rate is the change in tax liability, or $500, divided by the change in taxable income, or $20,000, which equals 2.5 percent.) The increasing marginal tax rate is essential for a progressive tax.

The federal personal income tax rate structure will serve as a benchmark for a discussion of state personal income tax rates. Prior to 1986, the federal personal income tax had fourteen brackets each with an increasing marginal tax rate. The highest marginal tax rate was 50.0 percent. The Tax Reform Act of 1986 reduced the number of brackets to three (later two). The highest marginal tax rate is 33.0 percent. Table 10–4 summarizes the tax rates and brackets for state personal income taxes. Many states have a rate structure with six brackets, although the number of brackets goes as low as one bracket and as high as eighteen brackets. Usually the highest state-local personal income tax rate falls in the 6.0–8.0 percent range with the highest marginal tax rate at 12.0 percent (compared with the federal rate of 33.0 percent). Local governments tend to levy single rate, proportional personal income taxes in the 1.0 to 3.0 percent range. The most noteable exception is New York City with a fourteen-bracket local income tax. With all these brackets, it still climbs only to a marginal rate of 3.5 percent.

## PERSONAL INCOME TAX BASE ISSUES

You are already familiar with the theory (e.g., Haig-Simons criterion) and the practices (e.g., tax expenditures in the form of deductions and exemptions) that lead to the determination of the personal income tax base. There are two other public policy issues associated with the base that will be introduced below: taxation at the origin versus the residence (integrating the personal income tax into a federal system) and indexation (adjusting the personal income tax for inflation).

### Origin versus Residence

In a federal system which consists of numerous decentralized governments, and in a market economy which stresses the need for mobile labor and capital, policymakers run up against the problem of how should an individual who is employed in one jurisdiction and resides in another jurisdiction be taxed under a state-local personal income tax system? Should the tax be paid to the state in which the individual works and income originates ("origin") or the state in

**Table 10–4**

**Range of Income Tax Rates and Taxable Income Brackets for State Personal
Income Taxes, 1988**

| Region & State | Income Tax Rate (percent) | Taxable Income Brackets ----Income---- Under | Over | Region & State | Income Tax Rate (percent) | Taxable Income Brackets ----Income---- Under | Over |
|---|---|---|---|---|---|---|---|
| **N.E.** | | | | **E.S.C.** | | | |
| ME | 2.0 - 8.0 | $ 6000 | $30000 | KY | 2.0 - 6.0 | $ 3000 | $ 8000 |
| NH | - limited income tax - | | | TN | - limited income tax - | | |
| VT | - 23% of federal tax - | | | AL | 2.0 - 5.0 | 500 | 3000 |
| MA | 5.0 -10.0 | flat rate | | MS | 3.0 - 5.0 | 5000 | 10000 |
| RI | 22.96% of federal tax | | | | | | |
| CT | - limited income tax - | | | **W.S.C.** | | | |
| **M.A.** | | | | AR | 1.0 - 7.0 | 3000 | 25000 |
| | | | | LA | 2.0 - 6.0 | 10000 | 50000 |
| NY | 3.0 - 8.0 | 3000 | 12400 | OK | .5 - 6.0 | 1000 | 7500 |
| NJ | 2.0 - 3.5 | 20000 | 50000 | TX | --- no income tax --- | | |
| PA | 2.1 | flat rate | | | | | |
| **E.N.C.** | | | | **Mt.** | | | |
| | | | | MT | 2.0 -11.0 | 1400 | 50000 |
| OH | .743-6.9 | 5000 | 100000 | ID | 2.0 - 8.2 | 1000 | 20000 |
| IN | 3.4 | flat rate | | WY | --- no income tax --- | | |
| IL | 2.5 | flat rate | | CO | - 5% of federal tax - | | |
| MI | 4.6 | flat rate | | NM | 1.8 - 8.5 | 5200 | 41600 |
| WI | 4.9 - 6.93 | 7500 | 15000 | AZ | 2.0 - 8.0 | 1229 | 7375 |
| | | | | UT | 2.6 - 7.35 | 750 | 3750 |
| **W.N.C.** | | | | NV | --- no income tax --- | | |
| MN | 6.0 - 8.0 | 3000 | 16000 | **Pac.** | | | |
| IA | .4 - 9.98 | 1000 | 45000 | | | | |
| MO | 1.5 - 6.0 | 1000 | 9000 | WA | --- no income tax --- | | |
| ND | 2.67-12.0 | 3000 | 50000 | OR | 5.0 - 9.0 | 2000 | 5000 |
| SD | --- no income tax --- | | | CA | 1.0 - 9.3 | 3818 | 25052 |
| NE | 2.0 - 5.9 | 1800 | 27000 | AK | --- no income tax --- | | |
| KS | 4.8 - 6.1 | 27500 | 27500 | HI | 2.25-10.0 | 1200 | 20200 |
| **S.A.** | | | | | | | |
| DE | 3.2 - 7.7 | 1000 | 40000 | | | | |
| MD | 2.0 - 5.0 | 1000 | 3000 | | | | |
| VA | 2.0 - 5.75 | 3000 | 15000 | | | | |
| WV | 3.0 - 6.5 | 10000 | 60000 | | | | |
| NC | 3.0 - 7.0 | 2000 | 10000 | | | | |
| SC | 3.0 - 7.0 | 4000 | 10000 | | | | |
| GA | 1.0 - 6.0 | 750 | 7000 | | | | |
| FL | --- no income tax --- | | | | | | |

*Source*: ACIR, 1989.

which the individual resides ("residence")? (ACIR, 1974d). After all, we want
to avoid the case of double taxation.

Even though the benefit principle does not justify a personal income tax,
economists (ever logical) have used this tax principle to formulate an answer.
The benefit principle argues that taxes should be paid to the state in which the
individual works. Ideally, information about the time spent in the state and the
mix of public services provided in the state would refine the calculation of public
good/service benefits received. For example, the longer the workday and the

more public services are geared toward workers' needs (i.e., transportation, public safety, parking), the greater the benefit received. As a result, the greater the personal income tax bill should be.

Of course, the dilemma is that the benefit principle can also be used to make a case for the state in which the worker resides. If time spent in the state and the mix of public services is important, then the state in which the worker resides also deserves tax consideration. The worker spends much of his/her day at home and derives benefits from public safety, trash pickup, a sewerage system, recreation programs, and public education.

A legitimate case, in fact, can be made for origin and for residence. What to do? Split the difference. The accepted tax policy in a circumstance where two jurisdictions tax an individual's income gives priority to the state in which the individual resides. The state taxes the income of its residents regardless of where it was earned (Aronson and Hilley, 1986; Ernst and Whinney, 1989; Pechman, 1983). In turn, state residents are permitted a tax credit (a deduction against the tax bill) for the personal income taxes paid elsewhere.

One form of this arrangement, called a *commuter tax*, is a common solution to the origin versus residence problem. For example, a commuter tax is in place between Northern New Jersey and New York City and Southern New Jersey and Philadelphia. The commuter tax is an example of a policy of tax harmony. It attempts to minimize tax competition and to preserve some horizontal tax equity across political jurisdictions. A successful commuter tax also requires a sensitive political touch. Recently, Maine and New Hampshire became embroiled in a commuter tax dispute when New Hampshire sought to levy a personal income tax on Maine residents who worked in New Hampshire. Why the dispute? Remember New Hampshire does not have a state personal income tax.

### Indexation

The components of state and local personal income taxes—income brackets, personal exemptions, and deductions—are usually set in fixed dollar amounts, or current dollars. They do not adjust from year to year to any measure of inflation. Suppose that when inflation hits the national or regional economy, it triggers cost of living adjustments (COLA) in an individual's income. These increases in income are not increases in real purchasing power. Rather they increase only current income to maintain real (inflation adjusted) income levels. But there is another, perhaps unanticipated, consequence of the COLA (Aaron, 1976).

The COLA adjustment decreases the dollar value of exemptions and deductions and, even more important, pushes the individual into higher tax brackets with higher marginal tax rates. The result is a greater tax bill for the individual although his/her real income has not changed. This tax increase has been called an *inflation tax*. The more progressive the personal income tax is, the more the inflation tax becomes (ACIR, 1976, 1980b).

**Table 10–5**
**Illustration of Tax Indexation Using the California Personal Income Tax (Inflation = 5.0%)**

------------------------------------------------------------------

Part (a)

| Brackets | Rate | Taxable Income $19,000 Tax Liability | Inflation Adjusted Taxable Income $19,950 Tax Liability |
|---|---|---|---|
| 0 – 3818 | 1.0 | $ 38.18 | $ 38.18 |
| 3819 – 9048 | 2.0 | 104.60 | 104.60 |
| 9049 – 14278 | 4.0 | 209.20 | 209.20 |
| 14279 – 19822 | 6.0 | 283.32 | 332.64 |
| 19823 – 25052 | 8.0 |  | 10.24 |
| Total ........................ |  | $635.30 | $694.86 |
| Taxes as a % of Taxable Income |  | 3.34% | 3.48 |

Part (b)

| Brackets | Rate | Inflation Adjusted Taxable Income $19,950 Tax Liability |
|---|---|---|
| 0 – 4009 | 1.0 | $ 40.09 |
| 4010 – 9500 | 2.0 | 109.82 |
| 9501 – 14992 | 4.0 | 219.69 |
| 14993 – 20813 | 6.0 | 297.48 |
| Total ........................ |  | $667.07 |
| Taxes as a % of Taxable Income |  | 3.34% |

*Source*: Calculation from California state personal income tax table.

Using the California tax table, Table 10–5, Part a illustrates the point. The example greatly simplifies what a California taxpayer would face. Assume that a single taxpayer had a taxable income of $19,000. Her tax liability is $635.30, or 3.34 percent of taxable income. Now suppose that the California economy experiences an annual rate of inflation of 5.0 percent. A COLA protects our taxpayer's income. To keep the illustration simple, assume that her taxable income increases by 5.0 percent to $19,950. If the California personal income tax brackets were not adjusted for inflation, then the individual's tax bill would increase to $694.86, or 3.48 percent of her taxable income. The change in the bill is $59.56, or a 9.38 percent increase. The progressive tax structure means that a 5.0 percent increase in taxable income increases the tax liability by 9.38 percent. The inflation tax takes its toll.

To avoid the inflation tax, some tax policymakers have argued for the *indexation* of personal exemptions, claimed deductions, and income brackets. Indexation means that some measure of inflation would adjust these components of the personal income tax. Table 10–5, Part b shows in very simple terms how indexation works. The tax brackets are adjusted by 5.0 percent. The lowest bracket goes from ($0-$3818) to ($0-$4009), and so on. The result is that the tax bill goes up by 5.0 percent from $635.30 to $667.07. In inflation adjusted terms, there is no real increase in tax liability.

Supporters of tax indexation argue that indexation eliminates the inflation tax. Its elimination has several attractive features; tax equity is maintained; inflation cannot fuel the real growth of the public sector; and political accountability is enhanced since state and local government officials must make their case for a revenue increase to the voters rather than receive an inflation tax bonus. Sounds too good to resist.

A review of states' experiences with indexation shows that they manage to resist (Feenberg and Rosen, 1988). We begin with the fact that only ten states have passed some form of indexation legislation. Some of that legislation "overindexed" the personal income tax so that the states actually lost tax revenues as a result of inflation. As states were forced to reconcile fluctuations in their regional economy with the demands for public services, seven of the ten states reneged on their indexation promises. Of some interest is the fact that states with high levels of per capita debt were less likely to index in the first place and more likely to renege after the fact, if they did index. While the logic of indexation is appealing, the limited state experience with indexation indicates that it may be one of those tax practices that is discussed in public with great enthusiasm and is rejected in private in short order.

## PERSONAL INCOME TAX RATE ISSUES

Following up on the earlier description of the structure of state personal income tax rates, there are two tax rate issues which deserve attention: work disincentives and tax compliance.

### Work Disincentives

The discussion of work disincentives and personal income tax rates begins with an unlikely situation. Suppose the personal income tax rate was 100.0 percent. (Calm down. It's only as assumption.) The state government takes every dollar earned. Under these unpleasant circumstances, output and earned income in the state economy would probably be zero. The tax disincentive would be so strong that no one would want to work in that state. The state government, as a result, collects nothing. At the other extreme, suppose that the personal income tax rate was zero percent. That's right, zero! People keep all that they earn. Much would probably be produced in the state economy, but the state government again collects nothing. At both extreme rates—100.0 percent and zero percent—state government personal income tax revenues are zero. In between these extremes there must be some tax rate at which state government tax revenues are maximized. For our discussion, let's say 50 percent.

As tax rates move between zero and 50 percent, state government tax revenues increase and reach a maximum. As tax rates move between 50 percent and 100 percent, state government tax revenues decrease and reach zero. This relationship is popularly known as the *Laffer Curve* (Laffer, 1979). While the Laffer Curve is usually applied to the federal tax system, it has also been used to analyze state tax systems (for example, Laffer Associates, 1981).

Do state personal income tax systems create such significant disincentives to work that they crash on the dreaded Laffer Curve? While Laffer often answers affirmatively, not all economists agree. The dispute centers on how responsive an individual's willingness to work is to changes in the net wage. For every change in the tax rate, there is a change in the net wage and a subsequent change in willingness to work. Research plays down the notion that personal income tax rates create a disincentive to work particularly among married men. Women appear to be more sensitive to this disincentive to work (Hansson and Stuart, 1985). (For an alternative view see Hausman, 1981.) The research evidence also does not support the notion that tax rates have passed the maximum tax revenue point and have settled into the relatively high rate and decreasing tax revenue range of the Laffer Curve (Fullerton, 1982).

An exchange between New York Governor Mario M. Cuomo and an audience at a Brooklyn community forum which was grumbling about high taxes illustrates the research results. The governor asked his audience if it knew the New York state personal income tax rates. No one shouted out the correct answer (Kolbert, 1989). The inference the governor drew was that tax rates are not uppermost in people's minds. They do not, therefore, significantly influence work decisions.

### Tax Compliance

Any personal income tax system requires taxpayer compliance. Taxpayer compliance means that an individual taxpayer correctly calculates his/her tax payment, files the appropriate tax forms, and pays his/her tax bill. The confidence a taxpayer has in this process (or put another way, the fear that the taxpayer has that he/she will be discovered if the rules are violated) spells the difference between an effective or a failed personal income tax system.

Tax compliance is a tax rate issue because tax evasion is tied to the level of the rate and the progressivity of the rate structure. A progressive tax structure increases the gains associated with cheating on one's taxes (Spicer, 1986; Clotfelter, 1983). So cheating becomes more prevalent. Dishonesty among taxpayers is a clear explanation of noncompliance, but inattention to detail, ignorance of the tax law, and laxity also play a role. If not dealt with, these problems can severely undermine the entire personal income tax system (Penniman, 1980).

In states where tax compliance has been a problem, tax administrators have turned to a *tax amnesty* program. A tax amnesty is a specified period of time when tax evaders (noncompliers) can come forward and pay their back taxes without fear of legal prosecution or financial penalties (Mikesell, 1986). Since 1982, twenty-six states have launched tax amnesty programs. The tax amnesty creates an environment where tax evaders are encouraged to come forward. Tax evaders know that they avoid financial and legal penalties and put the guilt associated with being a tax cheat behind them. While redemption is always nice, a contrite tax evader is in the interest of the state government: he/she generates state tax revenues.

Before this source of tax revenue grows too big in our imaginations, fragmentary evidence suggests that the revenue gains may be relatively small (Fisher, Goddeeris, and Young, 1989). However, advocates of a tax amnesty program argue that there is more than additional short term tax revenues involved in any successful amnesty program. A successful tax amnesty program identifies tax evaders; makes taxpayers even more thorough in filing their returns; and serves as the transition step to a tougher tax law enforcement posture.

## LINK BETWEEN FEDERAL AND STATE-LOCAL PERSONAL INCOME TAXES

With so many governmental units collecting taxes in the U.S. federal system, administration and equity concerns have forced policymakers at each level of government to recognize the intergovernmental dimension of their tax system. Tax policy can no longer be formulated, implemented, or evaluated from a single level's perspective. In the case of the federal and the state-local personal income tax, there are two provisions that connect the tax system: the calculation of the personal income tax base and the deductibility of state-local taxes from federal personal income taxes.

### Calculation of the Tax Base

An earlier section recounted the fact that thirty of the forty-three states which levy a state personal income tax have some elements of the federal system's calculation of the tax base (twelve states follow the federal personal income tax very closely). The Tax Reform Act of 1986 did more than broaden the federal personal income tax base. Without any legislative action on the part of these states, this act also broadened the personal income tax base of state-local systems coupled to the federal base. If these states did not lower their rates and accepted the broadened base (which are unrealistic political assumptions), then they would have received a personal income tax revenue "bonus." To understand the magnitude of this bonus, twenty-two states would have collected 7.0 percent or more revenue than they did prior to the reform (with Louisiana collecting 28.0 percent more); eleven would have collected between 1.0 and 6.0 percent; seven would have experienced no change; ten would have lost between 1.0 and 11.0 percent (with Rhode Island losing 11.0 percent) (Lynch, 1987).

### Deductibility of State-Local Personal Income Taxes

Since its inception, the federal personal income tax has permitted taxpayers to deduct taxes paid (i.e., property, sales, and income) to state and local governments. In recent times, this deduction cost the federal treasury upwards of $30 billion annually. While many Congresses and presidents have "reformed" the federal personal income tax several times over the years, it was not until the Tax Reform Act of 1986 that a serious proposal ("Treasury I") called for the elimination of the deductibility of state and local taxes. The tax reform that Congress passed eliminated the deduction for state and local sales taxes only. Taxpayers can still deduct local property and state-local personal income taxes. But for how long? The Bush administration has reportedly raised the issue of eliminating the deductibility of state personal income tax payments from the federal personal income tax in order to assist in deficit reduction efforts (Smothers, 1990).

Those who favor the abolition of the deductibility provision in exchange for lower federal marginal tax rates argue that the swap would lower taxes for most Americans; and remove a tax break which the richest 20 percent of Americans enjoy (Scheiner, 1985). A simulation of the effects of discontinuing the deduction for state and local taxes (under the assumption that the behavior of state and local governments and households does not change) shows that the removal of the deduction coupled with a reduced federal tax rate leads to an overall decrease in federal taxes across all income groups in virtually all states (Feenberg and Rosen, 1986).

Those who favor the deductibility provision stress its value to state and local governments. That value takes on three forms. It lowers the relative price of state-local public goods/services. It moderates any tax competition which exists between/among governmental units. It also encourages the use of progressive state-local taxes (as the next section explains) (Miller, 1985).

### Exploiting the Deductibility Provision

This section describes a strategy for increasing state personal income taxes which exploits the federal deduction for state personal income taxes paid (Raimondo and Gray, 1986). The end result is that the federal treasury would lose more through federal deductibility than the state treasury gains through a state personal income tax increase. For the average state taxpayer, an increase in the state personal income tax decreases combined federal-state personal income taxes.

By increasing the progressivity of its personal income tax, a state can not only improve tax equity, but also generate additional tax revenues. This strategy requires the state to lower the marginal tax rate for the lower income brackets and raise the marginal tax rate for the higher income brackets (compared to the state's present rate structure). The combined tax cut for one portion of the income

**Figure 10–1**
**Illustration of Federal Deductibility of State-Local Personal Income Taxes**

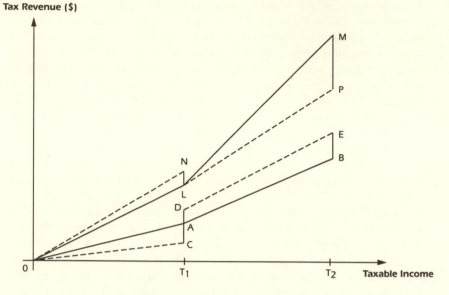

distribution and tax increase for the other portion must be set so that there is a net increase in state personal income tax collections. Therefore, the increased marginal tax rate for the upper income taxpayers must generate more than enough new revenue to offset the revenue lost because of the decrease in the marginal tax rate for the lower income taxpayers.

Figure 10–1 illustrates the relationship between federal personal income tax revenue and state personal income tax revenue under this strategy. Tax revenue in dollars is plotted on the y-axis and taxable income brackets on the x-axis. To keep the diagram simple, two income brackets are shown. The first bracket includes income from 0 to T1 and the second bracket includes income from T1 to T2. The solid line segment OAB is the initial state personal income tax revenue. The slope of the segment OA is the marginal tax rate for the first bracket. The slope of the segment AB is the marginal tax rate for the second bracket. The solid line segment OLM is the federal tax revenues associated with the initial state personal income revenues. The slope of the line segment OL is the federal marginal tax rate for the first bracket adjusted for the rate of federal deductibility of state personal income tax liability. The slope of the line segment LM is the comparable measure for the second bracket.

If the state government increases its personal income tax by decreasing the marginal tax rate for lower income levels and increasing the marginal tax rate for higher income levels, then Figure 10–1 changes in the following manner. The state tax liability is reduced for the first bracket (0 to T1). This change is shown by a rotation of the OA segment to the broken segment OC. The state tax loss in the first bracket is the area of OAC. A shift of the solid line segment from AB to the broken segment DE shows the state tax gain in the second bracket. The gain in state tax revenue is the area of BADE. The net revenue gain is the area of BADE minus the area of OAC. The new state tax revenue schedule is OCDE.

Federal tax liabilities also change because of the deductibility of state personal income taxes. Since the state tax bill in the first bracket decreased, the federal tax bill increases, a shift from the solid segment OL to the broken segment ON. The gain in federal tax revenue is the area of OLN. (If no low income taxpayer deducted state personal income taxes from his/her federal return, the federal tax gain is zero and ON and OL merge). With an increase in the state personal income tax bill in the second bracket, the federal personal income tax bill decreases, a shift from the solid segment LM to the broken segment LP. The federal tax revenue loss is the area of MLP. The net federal loss is MLP minus OLN. The new federal revenue schedule after the state tax increase is ONLP.

An increase in state personal income taxes according to this strategy means that the federal tax loss is greater than the state tax gain, or (MLP − OLN) > (BADE − OAC). Of course, Figure 10–1 has been constructed to illustrate this outcome. The income level that divides the income distribution between those that pay less state tax and those that pay more state tax will be dependent upon the state's income distribution and the level of the state's marginal tax rates. If the state income distribution gathers at the high end, then the switch from state tax cut to state tax increase will occur at a relatively high level of income. If the state income distribution gathers at the low end, then the switch will occur at a relatively low level of income. In either case, under this strategy the federal treasury actually loses more through the federal deductibility provision than the state treasury gains. For the state taxpayer, this outcome means that even with a state personal income tax increase, the average taxpayer's combined federal and state personal income tax bill will decline.

## INCIDENCE OF THE PERSONAL INCOME TAX

Legislators expect that the individual worker, owner of capital, and landlord pay the personal income tax. The economic incidence of the personal income tax depends upon how the tax bite affects these individuals' decision to work, invest in capital, or own land. In the case of labor, the more workers are sensitive to the imposition of the personal income tax, the more likely that the tax is shifted away from the worker to the employer. Legislated and economic incidence diverge. Conversely, the less sensitive workers are to the imposition of the personal income tax, the less likely that the tax is shifted away from the worker. Legislated incidence and economic incidence converge. Individuals' response to the personal income tax determines their overall tax burden. How is the tax burden distributed within and across income classes?

The earlier discussion of horizontal equity within a state stated that horizontal equity is legislated away if a state personal income tax system permits deductions for such items as home mortgage interest, charitable contributions, and medical expenses (i.e., tax expenditures) and if it varies tax rates by source of income— wage versus capital gains. Generally, horizontal equity across states is not the concern of policymakers, and is rarely achieved. For example, a look at effective rates across states for individuals with incomes between $12,000-$14,999 ranges from .03 percent (Tennessee) to 2.8 percent (Massachusetts); and for individuals with incomes over $35,000 from .13 percent (Tennessee again) to 3.64 percent (Delaware) (Phares, 1980).

The distribution of personal income tax burdens across income classes is the stuff of vertical equity. A progressive tax structure easily answers the vertical equity concern. The dollar payment, as well as the rate itself, increases as income increases. While most state personal income tax systems are progressive, the degree of progressivity is modest. A fear of flight, flight of higher income individuals from one state to another, tempers any progressive tax leanings that state tax planners might harbor. It is no surprise that the degree of progressivity varies widely across state personal income tax systems. The evidence please?

### Empirical Evidence

The estimates in Table 10–6 display the economic incidence of the state personal income tax with various state tax rates, deductions, and exemptions. The Phares estimate shows that the state personal income tax is modestly progressive until the over $35,000 income level. The effective rate (the percent of income actually paid in taxes) climbs steadily from .01 percent for the under $3,000 class to 1.96 percent for the $30,000-$34,999 class. Only at the $35,000 and above class does the effective rate slip back to 1.72 percent. With all this talk about progressivity, remember the effective rates in question are less than 2.0 percent!

## EVALUATION OF THE PERSONAL INCOME TAX

By now you are familiar with the six criteria for a good tax: economic efficiency, fairness, administration, revenue stability, link between spending and taxing, and tax visibility. This evaluation highlights the comparative strengths and weaknesses of the personal income tax. Table 10–7 summarizes the evaluation of the personal income tax.

### Applying the Criteria to the Personal Income Tax

*Efficiency.* The list of alleged inefficiencies associated with any personal income tax—federal, state, or local—begins with disincentives to work and save. There are more allegations against the tax than evidence to support them. The discussion on work disincentives showed that the empirical results generally find

**Table 10–6**
**An Estimate of the Incidence of the State Personal Income Tax**

| Family Income | State Personal Income Taxes |
|---|---|
| Less than $ 5,000 | .01 – .26 |
| 5,000 – 10,000 | .43 – .89 |
| 10,000 – 15,000 | 1.11 – 1.32 |
| 15,000 – 20,000 | 1.60 |
| 20,000 – 25,000 | 1.82 |
| 25,000 – 30,000 | 1.92 |
| 30,000 – 50,000 | 1.72 |
| 50,000 – 100,000 | \| \| |
| 100,000 – 500,000 | \| \| |
| 500,000 – 1,000,000 | \| \| |
| Over 1,000,000 | V |

*Source*: Phares, 1980.

small changes in hours of work associated with the imposition of a personal income tax. In a federal system characterized by factor mobility (people and capital can move), the imposition of a personal income tax can lead to a border problem where high income individuals move to low income tax states. Again, there is no strong evidence on this contention. On efficiency grounds, the bulk of the existing evidence fails to uncover significant levels of inefficiency associated with the personal income tax.

*Fairness*. When it comes to the income base for most state personal income systems, Haig and Simons would have little to cheer. Personal exemptions and deductions exclude income from the tax base. The horizontal equity test shows that individuals' tax treatment varies depending on family size, source of income, and deductions. Vertical equity shows state personal income systems leaning toward a very modest progressive tax structure. Because of the fear of a border problem, states shy away from progressivity. However, when individual taxpayers itemize their deductions on the federal personal income tax, they can reduce the degree of progressivity of any state personal income tax. To sum up, there is no strong commitment to horizontal equity and only a modest commitment to progressivity.

*Administration*. Effective administration of the personal income tax requires a definition of the income tax base, the determination of a tax rate structure; withholding of tax payments at the source where income is generated; taxpayer

**Table 10–7**
**Summary of the Evaluation of the Personal Income Tax**

| Criteria | Comments |
|---|---|
| Efficiency | o At the federal level, personal income taxes allegedly discourage work, and savings. The economic evidence is, however, ambiguous. At the state level, any effects of this type would certainly be of a far smaller magnitude.<br>o The Laffer curve is a dramatic illustration of these effects.<br>o In addition, given the level of mobility of high income persons, a state personal income tax might influence residential location decisions. |
| Fairness | o Without exception, state personal income tax systems fail to satisfy the Haig-Simons criterion. Personal exemptions and deductions adversely affect horizontal equity.<br>o Concerns about vertical equity show that most state personal income tax systems are modestly progressive.<br>o Federal deductibility actually reduces the progressivity of a state personal income tax. |
| Administration | o States can piggyback their personal income tax systems on the federal system and most do in some way. Local governments can, in turn, do the same with the state system.<br>o Withholding is the centerpiece of the personal income tax system. A withholding system collects taxes, but enforcement of the tax laws is equally important.<br>o Administrative costs could run as high as 5.0 % of the income tax revenue. |
| Revenue Stability | o Personal income taxes are relatively stable.<br>o Estimates of revenue elasticity for most states fall between .50 and 1.50 with an average for all states of 1.64. |
| Link Between Taxing and Spending | o Benefit principle does not justify personal income taxes; therefore, there is no link between and taxing. |
| Tax Visibility | o Form - integrated with every labor market transaction; however, separate day of accounting once a year<br>o Size - relatively modest amounts<br>o Timing - frequent<br>o Modest degree of visibility |

compliance; and enforcement of tax regulations. Some state and local governments administer their tax systems through a piggyback (or coupling) arrangement with the next higher level of government (states with the federal and locals with the state). What does this administrative system cost? Estimates for the personal income tax range as high as 5.0 percent of the revenue raised (Penniman, 1980).

*Revenue Stability.* A stable revenue source is the goal of every state and local government. Revenue elasticity gives us some indication of the revenue stability of a specific tax. Revenue elasticity relates the percentage change in tax collections to the percentage change in personal income. Studies have shown that for most states the revenue elasticity for the personal income tax ranges from .50 to 1.50 with an average of 1.64. For every 1 percent change in personal income, there is a 1.64 percent change in personal income tax revenues (Phares, 1980). Again this element of the criteria stresses stability, not revenue adequacy.

*Link Between Spending and Taxing.* Any tax that satisfies the benefit principle links public spending and taxing. However, the personal income tax does not satisfy the benefit principle. Personal income tax revenues go into the general fund to finance numerous public services. Many of these public services have a redistributive component. That arrangement describes an ability to pay tax much more than a benefit tax. Therefore, there is no link between spending and taxes.

*Tax Visibility.* Tax visibility is related to the form, size, and timing of a tax. Since the bulk of the revenue from the personal income tax comes from labor income, we concentrate on it. The personal income tax is paid through a system of withholding. Therefore, the form of the tax is integrated with every labor market transaction. So taxpayers routinely get used to paying it; they become less aware of the tax. Of course, we have a national day of reconciliation with the taxman every April fifteenth. The size of the personal income tax is relatively modest. Last, the timing of the tax is frequent, with every paycheck. This fact works to keep it out of sight. Its integration with a transaction, its relatively small amount, and its frequent collection make the personal income tax a less visible tax. However, the tradition of calling attention to April fifteenth raises the visibility of the tax above the sales tax, but probably below the property tax.

## SUMMARY

1. The ability to pay principle offers modest justification for state-local personal income taxes so the link between taxing and spending is broken. While the rationale of the tax in theory may be lukewarm, the use of the tax in practice is growing. A state government initially levied the tax; the federal government soon claimed it; and now state and local governments are reclaiming the personal income tax. Forty-three states and 4,200 local jurisdictions either have the authority to collect this tax or do collect revenue from this tax source. It accounts for one-fifth of state-local tax revenues.

2. There are variations in the value of personal exemptions and deductions across the states. These tax expenditures leave the personal income tax base far from the comprehensive base which the Haig-Simons criterion envisioned. Horizontal equity especially across states is rarely aspired to, let alone achieved. Complicating the estimates of the personal income tax base are issues of taxation at the origin versus at the residence which often involves commuter taxes and indexation of the tax which involves adjustments to account for inflation. Few states have followed through on their indexation rhetoric.

3. For most state-local tax systems, the tax rate structure is either flat or slightly progressive. Vertical equity rules are generally ignored. At most the states endorse modest progressivity in the tax structure because they fear the border problem, work disin-

centives which the Laffer Curve demonstrates in their most dramatic form, and problems with tax compliance which has led to tax amnesty programs. Where tried, these have been moderately successful.

4. Federal deductibility of state and local personal income taxes offers headaches and opportunities for state tax practitioners. The headaches take the form of changes in the state personal income tax base which the federal government can unilaterally cause. Any federal actions leave the state revenue authorities playing catch-up. The opportunities take the form of increases in the state personal income tax bill which state taxpayers can pass on to Uncle Sam.

5. The criteria for a good tax show that the state personal income tax creates few inefficiencies, is not overly concerned with progressivity, exhibits administrative difficulties somewhere between the property tax and the sales tax, is a stable revenue source, and like the flowers becomes very visible each springtime, but otherwise is out of sight.

# CHAPTER 11

## Nontax Revenues: User Charges and Gambling Revenues

**PREVIEW**

In the political environment that the antitax movement has defined, state and local government officials are always on the lookout for alternatives to tax revenues. Two forms of nontax revenues are currently quite popular: user charges and state-sponsored gambling activities. Both are voluntary; both are tied to a good/service; and both leave state and local finance experts uneasy.

If public goods/services can be produced and distributed using a private market mechanism rather than the political budget process, then user charges play the role of private market prices, congestion charges, or impact fees. All of these forms of a user charge lead to efficiency in good/service provision. Equity, however, may suffer. Equity may also be pushed aside in the case of gambling activities. Gambling has a long and fascinating history in state and local finance. Of recent concern is the growth of state-sponsored lotteries around the United States, as well as notable experiments with legalized casino gambling. There is an on-going debate regarding gambling as the elixir for state fiscal ills.

**USER/CURRENT CHARGES**

Events sometimes dust-off the routine and give it a new look. The apparent success of the tax limitation movement, especially with respect to the use of the property tax, and the decade-long reduction in real, per capita federal aid to local governments have forced state and local government officials to try user charges "again for the first time." A user charge is a payment to government for a specific good, service, or privilege. Ideally, the payment equals the cost of the good or service, but often it does not. The laundry list of user charges includes fees for: police protection (parking fees, police services at special events); transportation (bus, subway, tolls); health and hospitals (public hospital charges, ambulance charges); public education (tuition); recreation (admission fees, permit charges); sanitation (trash collection); public utility operation (water and electric charges); and licenses (dog tags, various permits, taxi operating licenses, and landfill) (Downing and DiLorenzo, 1987).

The federal system has adapted itself to the growing attraction of user charges. Instead of providing a good/service to the entire political jurisdiction, local government officials often take a different approach. If the local officials can identify the households that make use of the public good/service; if they can measure the degree to which the households benefit from the provision of the good/service; and if they are not especially concerned about universal access to the public good/service, then the public good/service can be separated from the local budget and financed with a user charge. An administrative district that collects the user charge and provides the public good/service only to those that pay can be established. That administrative district is a *special district*. Not all special districts rely solely on user charges. Many also use the property tax.

This process of "peeling off" specific public goods/services from the municipal or township budget has resulted in 29,532 special districts (in 1987) that cut across local jurisdictions to provide water, sewer, refuse, transit, parks and recreation, and development. Some have argued that if a public good/service can be peeled off the local budget, financed through a user charge, and delivered through a special district, then local government officials should take the next daring step. The next step is to provide the good/service through private vendors, or "privatize" the delivery of the good/service. (Recall the discussion of privatization in Chapter 3.)

## PROFILE OF CURRENT CHARGES

Revenue collections from current charges generally confirm their new found appeal. Table 11–1 shows the trend in state and local government current charges from 1970 to 1987. In addition, it measures the contribution of user charge revenues to own source revenue (OSR); and compares the annual percentage change in current charges with the GNP deflator.

Revenues from user charges (measured in billions of current dollars) have steadily grown over this period from $14.9 billion in 1970 to $86.2 billion in 1987. The slowest growth occurred from 1984 through 1987. Compared to the GNP deflator, the annual growth in user charge revenues has exceeded the GNP deflator for every year shown in Table 11–1. With this real increase in user charge revenues, user charges have slowly increased their share of state and local governments' revenues.

Over the 1970s, user charges represented approximately 14 percent of OSR.

**Table 11–1**
**Trend in State and Local Government Current Charges, 1970–87 (revenue in billions)**

| Year | Current Charges | Current Charges As a Percent of Own Source Revenues | Annual % Change | GNP Deflator |
|------|-----------------|-----------------------------------------------------|-----------------|--------------|
| 1970 | $14.9 | 13.7% |       |      |
| 1971 | 16.9  | 14.2  | 13.4% | 5.7% |
| 1972 | 18.7  | 13.8  | 10.7  | 4.7  |
| 1973 | 20.9  | 13.9  | 11.8  | 6.5  |
| 1974 | 23.2  | 14.0  | 11.0  | 9.1  |
| 1975 | 25.6  | 14.1  | 10.3  | 9.8  |
| 1976 | 29.3  | 14.6  | 14.5  | 6.4  |
| 1977 | 31.7  | 14.2  | 8.2   | 6.7  |
| 1978 | 34.7  | 14.1  | 9.5   | 7.3  |
| 1979 | 39.5  | 15.9  | 13.8  | 8.9  |
| 1980 | 44.4  | 16.3  | 12.4  | 9.0  |
| 1981 | 50.2  | 16.5  | 13.1  | 9.7  |
| 1982 | 56.9  | 17.3  | 13.3  | 6.4  |
| 1983 | 62.6  | 16.7  | 10.0  | 3.9  |
| 1984 | 69.0  | 17.0  | 10.2  | 3.7  |
| 1985 | 74.3  | 17.0  | 7.7   | 3.2  |
| 1986 | 80.4  | 17.2  | 8.2   | 2.6  |
| 1987 | 86.2  | 15.1  | 6.7   | 3.0  |

*Source*: U.S. Bureau of Census, *Government Finances*, various years.

Over the 1980s, they grew to approximately 17 percent (with the exception of 15 percent in 1987). This modest, but increasing use of current charges is completely consistent with the search for alternative revenue sources upon which local government officials have embarked following the imposition of tax limitation laws. Current charges are generally exempt from tax limit laws. Local officials use this loophole to finance public goods/services without initiating a vote to override the tax limitation law.

Table 11–2 looks at the state-by-state breakdown of per capita current charges; the relation of current charges to personal income in $1,000 increments; and the state share of current charge revenues. The nationwide per capita current charge level is $354. For every $1,000 in personal income, current charges claim $24. Generally, state governments collect 37.0 percent of current charge revenues. Putting aside Alaska (per capita: $970), Delaware ($542), Wyoming ($538), and North Dakota ($522), the range in per capita current charges goes from Connecticut ($214) to Georgia ($418). The range in user charges per $1,000 of personal income goes from Illinois ($16) to Mississippi ($43). At this time, there are few, if any, unambiguous geographic patterns that emerge from Table 11–2 in the per capita level of current charges or the state share of user charge revenues.

## THREE JUSTIFICATIONS FOR IMPLEMENTING USER CHARGES

### Quasi-Private Market Prices

User charges have escaped the wrath of the advocates of tax limitation. Because they act as private market prices, user charges have the aura of efficiency about

**Table 11-2**
**State-Local Per Capita Current Charges (CHARGE), the Relation of CHARGE to $1,000 Personal Income (PY), and State Share of CHARGE, 1986–87**

| Region & State | Per Capita CHARGE | Relation of CHARGE to $1000 PY | State Share | Region & State | Per Capita CHARGE | Relation of CHARGE to $1000 PY | State Share |
|---|---|---|---|---|---|---|---|
| USA | $ 354 | $24 | 37.0% | | | | |
| N.E. | | | | E.S.C. | | | |
| ME | 226 | 18 | 53.0 | KY | $ 259 | $23 | 54.5% |
| NH | 249 | 16 | 62.2 | TN | 364 | 31 | 30.9 |
| VT | 314 | 24 | 78.0 | AL | 432 | 38 | 42.5 |
| MA | 313 | 18 | 49.0 | MS | 413 | 43 | 29.8 |
| RI | 260 | 18 | 78.1 | | | | |
| CT | 214 | 11 | 51.6 | W.S.C. | | | |
| M.A. | | | | AR | 266 | 24 | 38.6 |
| | | | | LA | 390 | 35 | 41.1 |
| NY | 389 | 23 | 24.4 | OK | 368 | 30 | 43.4 |
| NJ | 315 | 17 | 51.7 | TX | 317 | 24 | 28.8 |
| PA | 236 | 17 | 43.2 | Mt. | | | |
| E.N.C. | | | | MT | 263 | 22 | 43.1 |
| OH | 323 | 23 | 46.0 | ID | 344 | 31 | 30.6 |
| IN | 387 | 30 | 50.3 | WY | 538 | 41 | 17.4 |
| IL | 250 | 16 | 34.3 | CO | 420 | 28 | 43.6 |
| MI | 409 | 28 | 41.9 | NM | 322 | 29 | 53.6 |
| WI | 387 | 28 | 43.3 | AZ | 293 | 22 | 36.0 |
| | | | | UT | 348 | 32 | 62.5 |
| W.N.C. | | | | NV | 449 | 30 | 18.6 |
| MN | 479 | 32 | 38.9 | Pac. | | | |
| IA | 449 | 33 | 45.2 | | | | |
| MO | 288 | 21 | 34.0 | WA | 396 | 27 | 30.8 |
| ND | 522 | 41 | 75.4 | OR | 379 | 29 | 39.5 |
| SD | 287 | 24 | 58.8 | CA | 419 | 25 | 28.7 |
| NE | 477 | 35 | 35.7 | AK | 970 | 54 | 43.7 |
| KS | 356 | 24 | 43.4 | HI | 367 | 25 | 84.2 |
| S.A. | | | | | | | |
| DE | 542 | 37 | 66.0 | | | | |
| MD | 290 | 17 | 50.1 | | | | |
| VA | 329 | 22 | 54.0 | | | | |
| WV | 253 | 24 | 47.1 | | | | |
| NC | 267 | 22 | 50.5 | | | | |
| SC | 375 | 34 | 42.2 | | | | |
| GA | 488 | 37 | 20.1 | | | | |
| FL | 384 | 27 | 16.9 | | | | |

*Source*: U.S. Bureau of Census, *Government Finances*, 1988.

them (Brownlee, 1961; Mushkin, 1972; Downing, 1977; Krashinsky, 1981). Moreover, they appeal to politicians because you pay the charge only if you are a user! (That doesn't sound quite right in today's drug climate.) In other words, no payment, no access to the public good/service. If a user charge were a tax (and it is not), then the user charge would satisfy the benefit principle of taxation.

Like a private market price, a user charge seeks to capture demand and supply considerations in order to determine how much of a public good/service will be produced and who will receive it. On the demand side, the user charge requires that consumers reveal their preferences for the public good. Let's go back to Eastown. Do enough people in Eastown want emergency ambulance service at Eastown General to pay for it? How about paying for the upkeep of the Eastown ball fields? Or picnic grills in the Eastown park? Just as in the private market, if the revenues from the user charge do not cover the cost of the service, then the Eastown government will not provide the public good/service. So people must be willing and able to pay for Eastown General's ambulance service, Eastown's ball fields, and Eastown park grills. Otherwise, they will not be available through the agencies of the Eastown government.

On the supply side, the user charge reflects production and cost considerations. The cost of a public good/service will account for density of development, transportation costs, and administration costs. Density affects cost in the following way: the fewer the households, the higher the costs and vice versa. There is an inverse relationship between density of development and the cost of the public good/service. For example, a few households may be unable to finance a public golf course because the fees would be too high. If the number of golf-playing households increases, then the fees for the golf course will decline. You have seen this argument earlier in discussion of the Tiebout model and the theory of clubs.

Transportation costs incorporate the distance from the site of production to the point of usage. Generally, the longer that distance is, the higher the costs and vice versa. There is a direct relationship between distance and the cost of the public good/service. For example, one study found that the cost per mile of providing police services was $438, fire protection $216, and sanitation $3,360 (Downing and Gustely, 1977).

Administration costs include the calculation of individual consumption of public goods/services and the preparation of individual bills which reflect use levels. The greater the complexity of calculating individual consumption of public goods/services is, the higher the cost and vice versa. There is a direct relationship between the number of bill-paying consumers who draw upon the public good/service and administrative costs. This relationship, in turn, influences the cost of providing the public good/service. For example, in the case of a water fee, a billing system must be set up to identify users and prepare a water bill for each household. That can be expensive.

There are also differences between a user charge and a market pricing device. Unlike the private market price, a user charge may not be equal to the additional (marginal) cost of producing another unit of the good/service; may not cover total costs; and may not be set using profit maximization as the government agency's objective.

### Congestion Charge

Congestion costs occur in the situation when an additional consumer of a public good/service imposes an extra cost on other consumers of that good/

service. A congestion charge is designed to discourage that additional consumer from using the public good/service and, thereby, avoiding the extra cost. For example, the Garden State Parkway (GSP) in New Jersey has plenty of room to accommodate passenger cars at midday (or after midnight) at the legal speed. No congestion costs are present. However, all vehicles which are heading to the Jersey shore on a summer's weekend or traveling at weekday "rush" hours can only dream about the legal speed limit on the GSP. Congestion costs are now present.

In the first instance, there are no congestion costs because an additional vehicle on the GSP does not slow down any other vehicles already on the roadway. In the second, there are congestion costs because an additional vehicle on the GSP slows down every other vehicle. (This situation has also been called the *peakload problem*.)

Whenever the capacity of the public good/service has been exceeded (e.g., the jammed highway, the crowded public pool, the overscheduled tennis court, street parking downtown, urban gridlock, etc.), user charges can reduce (or eliminate) the peakload problem. The excess demand should dissipate when the government increases the charge during peak use time and at peak use locations. The supply of the public good/service remains unchanged, but the law of demand indicates that the quantity demanded will decrease. Congestion and its associated costs will decrease.

Think for a moment what local officials have done when they impose a congestion charge. They have followed the economists' advice that whenever people are waiting in line for a good/service, then the price for that good/service is too low. Sound economic reasoning, but potentially foolish political action. Consumers of public goods/services do not want charges raised at the very moment that they "must" use the public good/service. We believe that we have a "right" to sit on a crowded highway, a crowded beach, or stand on a crowded subway or bus. The imposition of user charges to solve a peakload problem is efficient, but often not popular.

## Impact Fee

The most recent reincarnation of the user charge is as an impact fee. An impact fee is a one-time charge that private entrepreneurs, often developers, must pay to the local government in order to undertake their projects. In turn, the revenue from the impact fee finances public goods/services associated with the private project, but which the private entrepreneur would not provide voluntarily.

For example, the local government could request an impact fee from a private developer to extend water and sewer lines, build streets and recreational facilities, and even construct affordable housing as part of the project (Berglas, 1982; Downing and Frank, 1983; Rubin and Seneca, 1989). California has explored the possibilities of the impact fee more than most other states, especially to finance recreational facilities which complement private residential construction projects (Mercer and Morgan, 1983).

## THE EQUITY OF USER CHARGES

User charges make some equity-minded people uncomfortable. If a high income person and a low income person value the Eastown campgrounds equally, then (assuming income is not an impediment) each will pay the same camping fee to the Eastown government. Efficiency has been served, but the charge is regressive; that is, it claims a greater percentage of income from the low income person than the high income person. There is some evidence that a user charge system is more regressive than a property tax (judged from the traditional view of property tax incidence).

Should the residents of Eastown or the Eastown government officials care? The answer requires weighing efficiency versus equity objectives. If efficiency is paramount, then the answer to the above question may be no! If equity is paramount, then the answer to the above question is yes! The residents of Eastown could reduce the regressive nature of the user charge through a program that adjusts the user charge by level of income; that is, the higher one's income, the higher the fee and vice versa. A subsidized user charge promises efficiency and equity, an attractive combination.

User charges may do the job of allocating public goods/services, but have little glamour. A nontax revenue source that quickens the blood and makes the palms sweat comes up next.

## STATE-SPONSORED GAMBLING REVENUES

The news is filled with the "business of risk" (Abt, Amith, and Christiansen, 1985). Some noteworthy samples are: the Mohawk Indians are operating gambling casinos on their St. Regis Indian Reservation, New York; the people of Deadwood, South Dakota hope to revive their moribund local economy with legal casinos; the voters in two Iowa counties have agreed to go back in time and permit gambling on a Mississippi Riverboat; and even the people of Oregon have broken new ground in legal gambling activities when they have approved a weekly lottery on National Football League games. They hope that the NFL lottery will raise anywhere from $4 to $9 million (Litsky, 1989).

Whether it's legal or not, in 1988 Americans bet as much as $241 billion, almost $1,000 per person to prove wrong what we all know is right; namely, that you can't beat the house. In a national CBS/*New York Times* poll published in 1989, 63 percent of Americans polled approved of legalized gambling in some form (Barron, 1989a, 1989b). The approval levels were the highest along the east and west coasts. (For a discussion of the broad consequences of gambling in the United States, see Frey and Eadington, 1984.) The above examples and statistics may leave the impression that gambling in the United States is a recent chance flirtation. That's not the case. In colonial times, Americans used legal gambling to raise revenues to build roads, bridges, defenses, schools, and churches (Blakely, 1979).

Modern state-sponsored gambling activities include parimutuel taxes, amusement taxes, and lotteries. Lotteries raise the vast bulk of legal gambling revenues, almost 92 cents out of every one dollar bet. While lottery history in America also goes back to the colonies (and you thought the Puritans were dull!), we are more concerned with recent lottery activity. New Hampshire could change the motto on its license plates to Live to Bet—the Granite State instituted a state lottery in 1964. New York began its own game of chance in 1967.

Remarkably, these two lotteries were not very successful. State lotteries looked as if they would fade from the entertainment/fiscal scene. That is until New Jersey started its lottery in 1971. Learning from the mistakes of New Hampshire and New York, New Jersey officials structured the lottery games to increase the number of "winners" and marketed the entire venture so that the state lottery raised more revenue than predicted. In short order, voters in eleven states followed New Jersey and initiated state-sponsored lotteries during the 1970s. Nine more states joined the business during the 1980s. At this time, a total of twenty-two states have their own lottery.

There is another form of gambling that has tempted state governments, but attracted few, or rather two. Two states have authorized casino gambling: Nevada and New Jersey. While casino gambling is a statewide enterprise in Nevada, voters in New Jersey approved a 1976 referendum that limited the casino industry to Atlantic City, an experiment-of-sorts isolated in one place. With years of experience on record, analysts have begun to evaluate the seashore crapshoot (Sternlieb and Hughes, 1983; Lehne, 1986).

The evaluation is mixed. The casino industry has created 30,000 new casino-hotel jobs in one five-year period, but the employment gains for the residents of Atlantic City have been modest. Atlantic City's revenue-raising capacity has grown enormously thanks to the coming of the casino industry. However, Atlantic City's public service–dependent population has forced an equally dramatic growth in public expenditures. In addition, the costs of new public infrastructure investment (e.g., roads, sewers, etc.) to meet the needs of the casino industry has raised doubts about the real fiscal gains for Atlantic City. The casino industry was also introduced into Atlantic City with the promise that it would contribute to re-building the area's housing stock. For many reasons, it has not. The casino industry did, however, contribute to the city's crime rate which is the highest in the state. As the financial health of the casino industry falters and revives throughout the 1990s, state governments will watch Nevada and, especially Atlantic City, to decide whether they wish to test their luck with casino gambling.

## PROFILE OF GAMBLING REVENUES

Gambling revenues, especially lottery revenues, contribute a modest, but growing amount to state own source revenues. Table 11–3 shows the trend in

**Table 11–3**
**Trend in State Gambling Revenues, 1975–87 (revenue in billions)**

| | | ------Gambling Revenues------ | | |
|---|---|---|---|---|
| Year | Gambling Revenues | As a Percent of Own Source Revenues | Annual % Change | GNP Deflator |
| 1975 | $ 1.6 | .9% | | |
| 1976 | 1.7 | .8 | 6.3 | 6.4 |
| 1977 | 1.9 | .9 | 11.8 | 6.7 |
| 1978 | 2.3 | .9 | 21.1 | 7.3 |
| 1979 | 2.5 | 1.0 | 8.7 | 8.9 |
| 1980 | 3.2 | 1.2 | 28.0 | 9.0 |
| 1981 | 3.7 | 1.2 | 15.6 | 9.7 |
| 1982 | 4.6 | 1.4 | 28.1 | 6.4 |
| 1983 | 5.9 | 1.6 | 28.3 | 3.9 |
| 1984 | 7.4 | 1.8 | 25.4 | 3.7 |
| 1985 | 9.2 | 2.1 | 24.3 | 3.2 |
| 1986 | 12.2 | 2.6 | 32.6 | 2.6 |
| 1987 | 12.6 | 2.2 | 3.3 | 3.0 |

*Source*: U.S. Bureau of Census, *Government Finances*, various years.

state government gambling revenues from 1975 to 1987. In addition, it measures the contribution of gambling revenues to own source revenue (OSR); and compares the annual percentage change in gambling revenues with the GNP deflator.

Gambling revenues (measured in billions of current dollars) have steadily grown over this period from $1.6 billion in 1975 to $12.6 billion in 1987, with revenues doubling from 1983 to 1987. This amount is a small percentage of the amount actually wagered in the United States. The annual growth in gambling revenues has significantly exceeded the GNP deflator with the exception of the annual growth rates in 1976 and 1979. With this real increase in gambling revenues, it has gradually increased as a share of state governments' revenues. Over the 1975 to 1987 period, gambling revenues have moved from approximately 1.0 percent of OSR to approximately 2.0 percent. An increase in the number of states that authorize legal games of chance and people's participation in those games have resulted in the steady increase in gambling revenues.

Table 11–4 looks at the state-by-state breakdown of per capita gambling revenues (think of it as a "bet per person"), the relation of gambling revenues to personal income in $1,000 increments, and the share of gambling revenues that state-run lotteries generate. The nationwide per capita (legal) gambling level is $52 (much lower than the combined legal and illegal wager per person) and the dollar amount per $1,000 of personal income is $4. (For every $1,000 in personal income, gambling attracts $4.) In states where gambling is legal, the range in per capita gambling goes from less than $1 per person (Oklahoma), $2 per person (Kentucky and New Mexico), to over $160 per person (Maryland, New Jersey, Connecticut, Massachusetts, and Nevada).

## TWO PERSPECTIVES ON STATE-SPONSORED LOTTERIES

Praise for state-sponsored lotteries always includes the voluntary nature of the lottery and the lottery as a ready-source of previously untapped revenue. Com-

**Table 11–4**
**State Per Capita Gambling Revenues (GAMBLE), the Relation of GAMBLE to $1,000 Personal Income (PY), and Lottery Share of GAMBLE, 1986–87**

| Region & State | Per Capita GAMBLE | Relation of GAMBLE to $1000 PY | Lottery Share | Region & State | Per Capita GAMBLE | Relation of GAMBLE to $1000 PY | Lottery Share |
|---|---|---|---|---|---|---|---|
| USA | $ 52 | $ 4 | 92.0% | | | | |
| | | | | | | | |
| N.E. | | | | E.S.C. | | | |
| | | | | | | | |
| ME | 47 | 4 | 97.1 | KY | $ 2 | * | 0.0% |
| NH | 65 | 4 | 84.8 | TN | ----------None---------- | | |
| VT | 44 | 3 | 99.2 | AL | ----------None---------- | | |
| MA | 190 | 11 | 96.1 | MS | ----------None---------- | | |
| RI | 59 | 4 | 88.5 | | | | |
| CT | 169 | 9 | 85.2 | W.S.C. | | | |
| | | | | | | | |
| M.A. | | | | AR | 9 | 4 | 0.0 |
| | | | | LA | 5 | * | 0.0 |
| NY | 79 | 5 | 94.0 | OK | * | * | 0.0 |
| NJ | 165 | 9 | 83.6 | TX | ----------None---------- | | |
| PA | 105 | 7 | 99.2 | | | | |
| | | | | Mt. | | | |
| E.N.C. | | | | | | | |
| | | | | MT | ----------None---------- | | |
| OH | 95 | 7 | 98.8 | ID | ----------None---------- | | |
| IN | ----------None---------- | | | WY | ----------None---------- | | |
| IL | 111 | 7 | 95.3 | CO | 35 | 2 | 92.0 |
| MI | 105 | 7 | 97.4 | NM | 2 | * | ** |
| WI | ----------None---------- | | | AZ | 43 | 3 | 92.0 |
| | | | | UT | ----------None---------- | | |
| W.N.C. | | | | NV | 222 | 15 | 0.0 |
| | | | | | | | |
| MN | ----------None---------- | | | Pac. | | | |
| IA | 5 | * | 0.0 | | | | |
| MO | 32 | 2 | 100.0 | WA | 45 | 3 | 95.4 |
| ND | ----------None---------- | | | OR | 37 | 3 | 95.2 |
| SD | 5 | * | 0.0 | CA | 52 | 3 | 92.2 |
| NE | 7 | * | 0.0 | AK | ----------None---------- | | |
| KS | ----------None---------- | | | HI | ----------None---------- | | |
| | | | | | | | |
| S.A. | | | | | *less than $1 | | |
| | | | | | **less than 1.0% | | |
| DE | 66 | 4 | 99.8 | | | | |
| MD | 160 | 10 | 99.4 | | | | |
| VA | ----------None---------- | | | | | | |
| WV | 35 | 3 | 100.0 | | | | |
| NC | ----------None---------- | | | | | | |
| SC | 3 | * | 0.0 | | | | |
| GA | ----------None---------- | | | | | | |
| FL | 10 | 10 | 0.0 | | | | |

*Source*: U.S. Bureau of Census, *Government Finances*, 1988.

plaints against state-sponsored lotteries warn of their less-than-spectacular revenue yield, their high administrative costs, and their adverse impact on low income people (Stocker, 1972; Blakey, 1979; Mikesell and Zorn, 1986). Let's start with the praise.

Proponents of state-sponsored lotteries are always quick to point out that buying lottery tickets is voluntary. The state does not make an individual participate in the lottery. It might tempt us; it might make it easy for us to play; but buying a lottery ticket is by choice. Public support for the lottery is put to the market test. The more people the lottery entertains, the more revenue it brings into the state treasury. Those who play also pay a tax to the state. The tax, however, is a "painless tax," willingly paid by a gambler, unlike any other tax paid by a citizen. Those who detest the lottery don't play. If enough people oppose a lottery, then it will simply fail the market test and fade away.

The lottery is also a ready source of revenue. Tables 11–3 and 11–4 documented this claim. Not only does state-sponsored gambling generate in excess of $12 billion, most of which comes from the lottery, but that money is used for education, transportation, economic development, senior citizens, aid to local governments, and general purpose activities. Some state officials view gambling revenues as the answer to cash-squeezed state treasuries. The tax limitation movement has made the search for a painless tax a high priority.

Complaints about the lottery start with this claim of its being a ready source of revenue. Opponents assert that gambling, and especially the lottery, generate less-than-spectacular revenues. Prize money and administrative costs reduce the net contribution to the state government. Based on 1987 data, on average 58 cents out of every dollar spent on the lottery went for prizes and administration. Only 42 cents out of every one dollar spent on the lottery found its way into the state treasury. Instead of receiving $11.5 billion in lottery revenues (1987), states actually receive $4.8 billion. In addition, individuals' preferences for gambling, their income, and the game format may well define a "ceiling" on lottery revenues (Suits, 1979).

Some evidence argues that the increase in the number of states and the participation in each state's lottery may have peaked. One study took a chance and predicted that 1995 will be the year of maximum gambling revenues (DeBoer, 1986). In any case, the long-term outlook for unlimited lottery revenue growth has recently been challenged (Peppard, 1987). Ceiling or no ceiling, let's put the lottery revenue in perspective. On average, it contributes approximately 2.0 percent of own source revenue to the state-local sector. For some individual states, it can contribute as much as 4.0 percent. It is a minor source of state own source revenues.

The second complaint against the lottery has already been mentioned; namely, high administrative costs. The administrative costs associated with a lottery are higher than those associated with any other state-local taxes. In 1987, lotteries generated average administrative costs of approximately 13 percent of *net* lottery revenues with several states far in excess of that level; for example, Oregon and Vermont (both at 66 percent), and Colorado and New Hampshire (both at approximately 45 percent).

The third complaint is perhaps the most serious. A disproportionately large share of revenues from state-sponsored gambling comes from low income people. Table 11–5 displays the estimates of the incidence of state-sponsored gambling. These estimates used 1973 and 1974 data for family income. The first panel shows the incidence for all types of gambling. The percent of family income spent on wagering varies from approximately 1.0 percent (.98 percent) for fam-

**Table 11–5**
**Estimates of the Incidence of State-Sponsored Gambling**

| Family Income | All Types of Gambling 1974 Family Income(1) | Sample of Lotteries (2) CT | MA | PA |
|---|---|---|---|---|
| Less than $ 5,000 | .98% | .55% | .70% | .53% |
| 5,000 – 10,000 | .50 | .41 | .44 | .44 |
| 10,000 – 15,000 | .19 | .37 | .33 | .30 |
| 15,000 – 20,000 | .21 | .17 | .14 | .15 |
| 20,000 – 25,000 | .25 | ↓ | ↓ | ↓ |
| 25,000 – 30,000 | ↓ | .06 | .05 | .04 |
| 30,000 – 50,000 | .18 | ↓ | ↓ | ↓ |
| 50,000 – 100,000 | ↓ | ↓ | ↓ | ↓ |
| 100,000 – 500,000 | ↓ | ↓ | ↓ | ↓ |
| 500,000 – 1,000,000 | ↓ | ↓ | ↓ | ↓ |
| Over 1,000,000 | ↓ | ↓ | ↓ | ↓ |

*Sources*: (1) Suits, 1977; (2) Brinner and Clotfelter, 1975.

ilies whose income is $5,000 or less to .18 percent for families whose income is $30,000 or more. The second panel shows the incidence for three state lotteries: Connecticut, Massachusetts, and Pennsylvania. The effective "tax rate" on this painless tax varies from .53–.70 percent for families whose income is $5,000 or less to .04–.06 percent for families whose income is $30,000 or more. While the actual percentages seem small (e.g., .98 percent versus .18 percent), the regressive structure of state-sponsored gambling enterprises makes them more regressive than a sales tax. The painless tax falls disproportionately on the lowest income people. (More recent studies confirm Suits' findings. See: Heavey, 1978; Clotfelter, 1979; Clotfelter and Cook, 1987.) While some state and local public finance experts are uncomfortable with this peculiar method of financing public goods/services, gambling revenues are now an accepted part of the state and local financial mosaic.

## SUMMARY

1. User charges are a source of nontax revenues that may be employed when public goods/services can be produced and distributed using a private market mechanism. The implementation of a user charge system may be justified as a quasi-private market price, a congestion charge, or an impact fee.
2. The financial contribution of user charges to state and local governments has grown in recent times. Generally, revenues from user charges finance water, sewer, refuse, transit, parks and recreation, and development activities. These services, in turn, are often provided through special districts.

3. Gambling is another popular source of nontax revenues. Games of chance, horse-racing, lotteries, and the like contribute a growing, but still relatively modest amount to state governments' treasuries. These revenues fund education, transportation, economic development, senior citizens, aid to local governments, and general purpose activities.

4. Some see state-sponsored gambling enterprises as a "painless tax" that is a ready source of revenues. Others see the claim of abundant gambling revenues as overblown especially in light of the administrative costs associated with lotteries.

5. Whether it is user charges or state-sponsored gambling, equity takes a blow. Both forms of nontax revenue are regressive.

# CHAPTER 12

---

## Spending, Taxes, and the Distribution of Personal Income

### PREVIEW

While the bulk of the preceding chapters has divided state-local fiscal policy into its tax and expenditure components, this chapter looks at the redistribution of personal income that results from the assembled tax and spending package. That look proceeds along the following lines: a review of state-local tax incidence, the distribution of tax burdens, expenditure benefits, and net benefits by income class across the United States, a ranking of states by their redistribution efforts, and finally some characteristics associated with differences in state-local redistribution efforts.

### PUTTING TOGETHER THE TAX INCIDENCE PUZZLE

Chapters 8 through 10 spread out the major pieces of the state-local tax incidence puzzle. The first piece was property taxes (Table 8–7), the second piece sales taxes (Table 9–6), and the third piece personal income taxes (Table 10–6). Unlike many other toys, puzzles require assembly. It's time to put the pieces of the state-local tax incidence together. While there is no picture on the cover of the box to guide us, there are two excellent tax incidence studies upon which previous discussions have relied.

Pechman (1985) and Phares (1980) have assembled the evidence on state-local tax incidence. The authors have estimated the most progressive and least progressive distribution of tax liabilities. The difference between the degree of

**Table 12-1**
**Estimates of the Incidence of State-Local Taxes**

| Family Income | Pechman (1985) Progressivity | | Phares (1980) Progressivity | |
|---|---|---|---|---|
| | Most | Least | -- Most -- | -- Least -- |
| Less than $ 5,000 | 18.3 | 27.9 | 13.8 - 22.6 | 15.5 - 26.8 |
| 5,000 - 10,000 | 8.1 | 10.9 | 10.6 - 12.5 | 12.0 - 14.2 |
| 10,000 - 15,000 | 7.2 | 9.0 | 9.0 - 9.8 | 10.8 - 11.4 |
| 15,000 - 20,000 | 7.0 | 8.3 | 8.9 | 10.3 |
| 20,000 - 25,000 | 6.9 | 8.2 | 9.0 | 10.0 |
| 25,000 - 30,000 | 7.0 | 8.1 | 9.1 | 9.8 |
| 30,000 - 50,000 | 7.2 | 8.0 | 10.0 - 18.9 | 9.8 - 10.6 |
| 50,000 - 100,000 | 7.4 | 7.5 | ‖ | ‖ |
| 100,000 - 500,000 | 8.1 | 6.1 | ‖ | ‖ |
| 500,000 - 1,000,000 | 8.9 | 5.2 | ‖ | ‖ |
| Over 1,000,000 | 9.7 | 5.1 | ∨ | ∨ |

*Sources*: Pechman, 1985; Phares, 1980.

progressivity usually depends upon the incidence assumptions regarding property taxes and corporation net income taxes. State-local sales taxes are generally thought to be regressive and state-local personal income taxes modestly progressive.

Chapter 8 set out the arguments for progressive versus regressive property taxes. A regressive property tax assumes that the tax on improvements is shifted forward to owner-occupants of residential housing, renters of residential housing, and consumers of goods and services. A progressive property tax assumes that the tax on improvements lowers the rate of return on capital and, in turn, capital income (Table 8-6). In the case of state-local corporation net income taxes, whether the taxes are shifted to consumers through the price mechanism or paid by corporate stockholders is central to the distribution of corporation net income liabilities. If the researcher assumes that some portion of this business tax is passed on to the consumer in the form of higher prices, then the tax structure tends to be less progressive. If the researcher assumes that some portion of this business tax is passed on to the owners of corporate stocks in the form of reduced dividend income, then the tax structure tends to be more progressive. It goes without saying that economic evidence on the question of the relationship between corporation net income taxes and higher prices or lower dividend income has not resolved the issue (Harberger, 1962; Krzyzaniak and Musgrave, 1963; Gregg, Harberger, and Mieszkowski, 1967). So two estimates are offered to satisfy all parties.

Table 12-1 neatly puts the tax incidence puzzle together. It displays the tax incidence, or taxes paid as a percentage of income, by income class under the assumptions that result in the most and the least progressive tax structure. For example, according to the Pechman estimates, families whose income is less than $5,000 paid from 18.3 to 27.9 percent of their income in state-local taxes. That percentage drops to approximately 7.0 percent throughout the $10,000 to $100,000 range. Beyond the $100,000 figure, state-local taxes claim 8.0 to 10.0 percent of family income.

Economists and practitioners alike generally accept the conclusion that state-local tax systems are regressive at the low end of the personal income distribution, almost proportional (fixed percentage) across the middle, and regressive at the high end of the personal income distribution. This is so because they accept the notion that the property tax and the net corporation income tax are regressive. A description that fits Pechman's and Phares's "least" progressive estimates is shown in Table 12–1.

## EXPENDITURES, TAXES, AND NET BENEFITS

A broader perspective on incidence is the comparison of the distribution of state-local tax burdens with the distribution of state-local expenditure benefits across income classes. The net benefit of state-local fiscal policy by income class, or the *fiscal residuum*, can then be calculated (Buchanan, 1950).

Research of this type was popular in the 1960s and 1970s. Constant disagreements over the assumptions used to allocate expenditure benefits have made economists reluctant to replicate these studies using more recent data. Table 12–2 shows the results of two worthwhile studies regarding the distribution of the state-local tax burdens and expenditure benefits even though the studies reach back to 1960 and 1970. The top portion of Table 12–2 reports on the findings of Reynolds and Smolensky (1974 and 1977) and the bottom portion the results of Gillespie (1965).

Reynolds and Smolensky defined income in terms of net national product, the sum of wages, rent, interest, and profits. State-local taxes are generally regressive. For example, in the less than $2,000 income category, state-local taxes account for 24.0 percent of income, while in the $10,000 to $15,000 category they account for 11.4 percent. State-local expenditures are found to be strongly "pro-poor," expenditures received as a percentage of income increases as income decreases. Again, in the less than $2,000 income category, state-local expenditure benefits are equal to 79.9 percent of the income in the category (for every $1 in income, state-local government expenditures add another 79.9 cents), while in the $10,000 to $15,000 category, state-local expenditures are equal to 13.2 percent. The calculation of the net impact is straightforward. In the less than $2,000 income category, the net benefit of state-local fiscal policy is 55.9 percent. After taxes, the expenditure benefits are equal to 55.9 percent of the income in the category (for every $1 of income, state-local after-tax expenditure benefits equal 55.9 cents). In the $10,000 to $15,000 category, the net benefit of state-local fiscal policy is 1.8 percent. After taxes, the expenditure benefits are equal

**Table 12–2**
**Estimates of the Incidence of State-Local Taxes and Expenditures (as a percent of income)**

| Net National Income, 1970 | Reynolds & Smolensky (1977) State-Local | | |
|---|---|---|---|
| | Taxes (−) | Expenditures (+) | Net (+/−) |
| Less than $ 2,000 | 24.0 | 79.9 | +55.9 |
| 2,000 − 3,000 | 18.5 | 50.3 | +31.8 |
| 3,000 − 4,000 | 16.8 | 36.3 | +19.5 |
| 4,000 − 5,000 | 15.6 | 29.6 | +14.0 |
| 5,000 − 6,000 | 14.6 | 22.0 | + 7.4 |
| 6,000 − 7,000 | 13.6 | 18.7 | + 5.1 |
| 7,000 − 8,000 | 12.9 | 17.0 | + 4.1 |
| 8,000 − 10,000 | 12.6 | 15.6 | + 3.0 |
| 10,000 − 15,000 | 11.4 | 13.2 | + 1.8 |
| 15,000 − 25,000 | 10.9 | 10.0 | − .9 |
| Over $25,000 | 13.6 | 8.1 | − 5.5 |

| Family Income, 1960 | Gillespie (1965) State-Local | | |
|---|---|---|---|
| | Taxes (−) | Expenditures (+) | Net (+/−) |
| Less than $ 2,000 | 12.3 | 43.4 | +31.1 |
| 2,000 − 3,000 | 14.4 | 39.1 | +24.7 |
| 3,000 − 4,000 | 14.9 | 24.0 | 9.1 |
| 4,000 − 5,000 | 17.8 | 19.2 | 1.4 |
| 5,000 − 7,500 | 12.9 | 12.6 | − .3 |
| 7,500 − 10,000 | 7.0 | 8.3 | + 1.3 |
| Over $10,000 | 6.1 | 6.2 | + .1 |

*Sources*: Gillespie, 1965; Reynolds and Smolensky, 1977.

to 1.8 percent of the income in the category (for every $1 of income, state-local after-tax expenditure benefits equal 1.8 cents). In economics jargon, the highest two income categories ($15,000 and over) receive *negative* benefits, a great economics term. To everyone else, the people in these categories receive less than they pay in taxes; they lose money in the state-local tax/spend game.

Gillespie defines family income as the sum of wages, rent, interest, transfer payments, realized capital gains, distributed retained earnings of corporations, and certain nonmoney income (e.g., rent of owner-occupied dwellings, food and fuel grown and consumed on farms, etc.). While the years and income categories are different from one study to the next, Gillespie's earlier findings are consistent with Reynold's and Smolensky's subsequent findings that the end result of state-local fiscal policy actions is to redistribute income to the low income families— at least in 1960 and 1970! A strong pro-poor tilt in state-local government expenditure decisions more than compensates for the regressive tax structure which most, if not all, state-local governments employ.

## STATE PERSPECTIVE ON THE REDISTRIBUTION FUNCTION

Of course, there is yet another approach to this question of how fair is state-local fiscal policy? Instead of looking at the redistribution outcome of state-local taxes and expenditures across income classes from a national perspective, concentrate on the impact state by state. This vantage point allows for across state comparisons. Again, this area of applied public policy research has not received all the research attention that it deserves.

Two studies—Fry and Winters (1970) and Booms and Halldorson (1973)— have tackled the redistribution issue in a fashion that permits across state comparisons. Our discussion takes us through the more recent study. Booms and Halldorson allocate state-local tax burdens and expenditures benefits across income classes within a state. They have formed an index that is the *ratio of redistribution* for those people who earn less than $4,000. (An income of $4,000 should strike you as awfully low, but remember the study year is 1960.) The ratio of redistribution is nothing more than the quotient of the expenditure benefits received by those people whose incomes were less than $4,000 divided by the tax liabilities incurred by those people.

Table 12–3 displays the ratio of redistribution for the forty-eight contiguous United States. In 1960, Massachusetts ranked first with an index of 6.004 while South Dakota ranked forty-eighth with an index of 1.537. The interpretation is that for every $1 that the Massachusetts state-local tax system collected from people whose income was less than $4,000, the state's expenditure decisions gave back $6.00. The comparable numbers for South Dakota would be that for every $1 that the South Dakota state-local tax system collected from people whose income was less than $4,000, the state's expenditure decisions gave back $1.54.

Table 12–3 also reveals potential interstate competition around the redistribution function. Recall from the discussion in Chapter 4 leading up to Table 4–2 that the redistribution function should be the primary concern of the central government. States that become overly preoccupied with the redistribution of income invite interstate competition for people, jobs, income, and construction. In a Tiebout world, households and businesses opposed to state-level redistri-

**Table 12–3**

**The Distribution of State-Local Tax Burdens and Expenditure Benefits by State (1960) ("ratio of redistribution")**

| Region & State | Rank | Ratio | Region & State | Rank | Ratio |
|---|---|---|---|---|---|
| N.E. | | | E.S.C. | | |
| ME | 31 | 2.211 | KY | 28 | 2.398 |
| NH | 43 | 1.845 | TN | 30 | 2.216 |
| VT | 42 | 1.908 | AL | 29 | 2.304 |
| MA | 1 | 6.004 | MS | 32 | 2.198 |
| RI | 14 | 3.375 | | | |
| CT | 5 | 4.700 | W.S.C. | | |
| M.A. | | | AR | 39 | 2.036 |
| | | | LA | 38 | 2.123 |
| NY | 7 | 4.348 | OK | 21 | 2.653 |
| NJ | 9 | 3.900 | TX | 47 | 1.574 |
| PA | 17 | 2.995 | | | |
| | | | Mt. | | |
| E.N.C. | | | | | |
| | | | MT | 41 | 1.910 |
| OH | 8 | 4.343 | ID | 11 | 3.679 |
| IN | 16 | 3.348 | WY | 33 | 2.184 |
| IL | 2 | 5.904 | CO | 4 | 5.385 |
| MI | 12 | 3.549 | NM | 40 | 1.971 |
| WI | 24 | 2.522 | AZ | 27 | 2.435 |
| | | | UT | 23 | 2.559 |
| W.N.C. | | | NV | 20 | 2.774 |
| MN | 19 | 2.785 | Pac. | | |
| IA | 26 | 2.482 | | | |
| MO | 10 | 3.694 | WA | 6 | 4.680 |
| ND | 45 | 1.728 | OR | 18 | 2.958 |
| SD | 48 | 1.537 | CA | 3 | 5.804 |
| NE | 35 | 2.128 | AK | NA | NA |
| KS | 13 | 3.501 | HI | NA | NA |
| S.A. | | | | | |
| DE | 34 | 2.166 | | | |
| MD | 15 | 3.372 | | | |
| VA | 46 | 1.661 | | | |
| WV | 22 | 2.590 | | | |
| NC | 45 | 1.728 | | | |
| SC | 44 | 1.740 | | | |
| GA | 25 | 2.522 | | | |
| FL | 37 | 2.126 | | | |

*Source*: Booms and Halldorson, 1973.

bution activities will move from one state to another in order to avoid losing their income to finance redistribution programs. For example, in the New England region, Massachusetts finds itself in that predicament; in the East North Central region, Illinois; in the South Atlantic region, Maryland; and in the Mountain region, Colorado.

There is another twist to this line of inquiry. A group of sociologists used the data in Table 12–3 to assert that labor union presence within a state and Democrat party strength in the state-local governments are associated with higher values of the ratio of redistribution, a higher per dollar level of redistribution; corporate presence within a state is associated with lower values of the ratio of redistribution, a lower per dollar level of redistribution. A pro-poor state-local fiscal structure is likely to be in place in states with labor unions and Democrat political strength. Labor unions are an organization base used to further the economic interests of workers and the poor. The Democrat party also protects the interests of workers and lower income people who, in turn, support Democrat candidates for elective offices. The degree of redistribution will be less in states with corporate power present. Corporations provide a parallel organizational base to advance the interests of business and high income people (Hicks, Friedland, and Johnson, 1978).

Of course, all these findings are for 1960 data. Much has changed which will make the state-by-state perspective even more interesting in the 1990s. The drive for decentralization under the New Federalism banner, the stepped up interstate competition to attract economic development, the fall-off of federal aid to state and local governments in the 1980s, and the tax limitation movement stacked up against the calls for affordable housing, AIDS clinics, more prisons, and improved education have pushed and pulled at the collective will behind state-local redistribution policies. In fact, one recent study argues that progressivity in the state-local tax system tends to reduce income inequality (Hayes and Slottje, 1989). This result implies a fiscal residuum consistent with the findings in Table 12–2.

## SUMMARY

1. Estimates of the incidence of state-local taxes across income classes are generally regressive; specifically, state-local taxes are regressive on the low end of the income distribution, proportional in the middle, and regressive again on the high end of the income distribution.

2. Early studies of the distribution of tax burdens, expenditure benefits, and net benefit of state-local governments reveal a strong pro-poor tilt to state-local fiscal activities.

3. From a state perspective, the ratio of redistribution associated with each state's tax and spend policies differs across the United States. The variation opens the way for interstate competition that could well pit economic development concerns against social welfare programs.

4. The presence of labor union and Democrat party strength within a state is associated with a greater degree of redistribution, while the presence of corporations within a state is associated with a lesser degree of redistribution.

# CHAPTER 13

---

# Grants-in-Aid System

## PREVIEW

Federalism requires the transfer of resources among the levels of government. A *grant-in-aid* system carries out these intergovernmental transfers. The transfer usually cuts across levels of government; that is, federal to state or local, and state to local. The rationale for a grants-in-aid system brings together economics and politics. After knowing why there is a grants-in-aid system, a fiscal history of federal and state grants-in-aid programs is in order. The presentation then moves on to the classification of grants-in-aid. Finally, the effects of grants-in-aid on public spending is reviewed.

## RATIONALE FOR A GRANTS-IN-AID SYSTEM

The justification for a grants-in-aid system can be teased out of several topics already covered. Efficiency concerns initiate most, if not all, economic analysis. So it is with grants-in-aid. The principle of fiscal equivalency (Chapter 4) set out the condition for the efficient provision of a public good/service in a federal system; namely, that the boundaries of the benefit area associated with that public good/service must coincide with the boundaries of the political jurisdiction that provides the public good/service.

If the benefit area exceeds the political boundary (externalities are present), then too much or too little of the public good/service will be produced. In any case, the delegation of functional responsibilities results in the inefficient provision of the public good/service. The Tiebout model and the adaptability of the organization of subnational governments made the point that people who act on their own or through their governments can meet the principle of fiscal equivalency. A grants-in-aid system can also achieve the desired outcome.

Suppose there is an externalities problem between Eastown and Westown regarding the operation of a local airport for which the people of Eastown currently pay. The airport, however, is used as much by the people in Westown as the people in Eastown. Fiscal equivalency has not been achieved. The boundaries of the benefit area exceed the boundaries of the political jurisdiction. Among the fiscal solutions would be the regionalization of the airport, the imposition of a user charge system to be collected from all air passengers, the establishment of a grant-in-aid system to finance airport operations, or some combination of all three.

A grant-in-aid for the airport would require that some portion of those tax dollars that residents of Eastown and Westown pay to the state government finance a grant, or intergovernmental transfer, to Eastown in order to operate the airport. Ideally, the individuals who benefit from the airport would pay taxes equal to the value of the benefits received. In this way, the people of Westown pay for the benefits that they receive from the operation of the airport by Eastown. Fiscal equivalency is, therefore, achieved without the Tiebout model or a change in the organization of the Eastown and Westown local governments. The case of education financing is another example when the state government sees fit to redistribute resources among the local jurisdictions to account for positive externalities of education. Efficiency considerations, specifically, satisfying the principle of fiscal equivalency, become the first justification for a grants-in-aid system within federalism.

Equity follows efficiency. The review of the determinants of public expenditures (Chapter 5) made clear that the level of economic activity, measured in personal income or gross state product, has a positive association with the level of per capita public spending. Differences in the levels of economic activity exist across regions. The federal government will redistribute national resources among the states to redress fiscal imbalances. State governments will also compensate local governments for unequal fiscal resources so that each jurisdiction may provide an appropriate level of a public good/service.

Suppose Eastown is less well-off than Westown. In fact, Eastown's economy is declining. (With the tax policy experiments in Chapter 7 and the operation of the airport, it's no small wonder that Eastown is not doing so well!) Eastown can afford neither a full array of public goods/services nor an adequate level of specific public goods/services (e.g., police and fire protection, sanitation, etc.). With a declining regional economy, the demand for public goods/services can exceed the town's ability to finance those public goods/services.

Elected officials in the state legislature could endorse a plan that redistributes some portion of state tax revenues to local jurisdictions based on their fiscal "need." Fiscal need measures often involve some mix of population, tax effort, urbanization, or the value of the property base. (For example, see Bradbury et al., 1984.) This intergovernmental transfer falls within the redistribution function of the public sector. The recipient of redistributed dollars through the tax and expenditure system in this case is a government rather than an individual. With equity-based grants, Eastown has the resources to finance the public goods/services that its residents choose. Without equity-based grants, Eastown may be unable to finance even a minimum level of public goods/services. Equity considerations, specifically redistributing fiscal resources away from well-off jurisdictions to less well-off jurisdictions, become the second justification for a grants-in-aid system within federalism.

There is another dimension to equity-based grants. Equity-based grants may well be necessary for the successful workings of federalism. The promise of autonomous decision making for state and local governments can be as empty or as full as the public till. Equity-based grants-in-aid bring sense to a federal system that features decentralized decision making and fiscal imbalances across levels of government and geographic regions. This dimension of equity-based grants is sometimes referred to as the institutional rationale for grants-in-aid. It becomes the third justification for a grants-in-aid system within federalism.

For many economists, efficiency and equity arguments would sum up the case for a grants-in-aid system. The earlier discussion of public choice theory (Chapter 5) hints that there is one more element to the grants-in-aid rationale: politics. (Act surprised!) Politicians who are always on the lookout to maximize their vote totals can use the distribution of grants across states and localities to reward supporters and win over the reluctant.

Incumbent legislators and executives can spread grant money to reward voters. Jurisdictions that have supported the incumbent in the past expect their grant levels to rise in accordance with the incumbent's victory margin. This payoff contributes to the candidate's victory in the future. Constituents see it as their representative's, governor's, president's, or party's bringing home the bacon. Elected public officials can also use grant money to woo voters whose support is "soft." Jurisdictions that the incumbent views as political battlegrounds can see their grants levels rise as the politician uses the power of incumbency to win swing voters. There is empirical evidence that presidents and governors are well aware of the political gains to be had through the grants-in-aid system (Wright, 1974; Tufte, 1978; Raimondo, 1983a). Political considerations, specifically spreading fiscal resources to secure voter support for the incumbent, become the fourth justification for a grants-in-aid system within federalism.

## FISCAL HISTORY OF FEDERAL GRANTS-IN-AID

This brief fiscal history of the federal grants-in-aid system chronicles many significant changes in intergovernmental fiscal relations in recent times. No brief description can provide a sense of how important and fascinating these developments were and continue to be. In some instances, they haunt U.S. federalism

**Table 13–1**
**Trends in Federal Aid to State and Local Governments, 1970–87 (aid in billions)**

```
--------------------------------------------------------------------------
                        -------------Federal Aid------------
            Federal   As a Percent of State & Local          Annual      GNP
   Year       Aid    Tax Revenues    Own Source Revenues    % Change   Deflator
--------------------------------------------------------------------------
   1970    $  24.4       26.2%              22.4%
   1971       29.0       28.6               24.4            18.9%        5.7%
   1972       37.5       33.8               27.7            29.3         4.7
   1973       40.6       33.0               26.9             8.3         6.5
   1974       43.9       33.0               26.4             8.1         9.1
   1975       54.6       38.1               30.2            24.4         9.8
   1976       61.0       38.9               30.4            11.7         6.4
   1977       67.6       38.4               30.4            10.8         6.7
   1978       77.3       39.0               31.3            14.3         7.3
   1979       80.4       38.0               32.5             4.0         8.9
   1980       88.7       38.3               32.6            10.3         9.0
   1981       87.9       34.0               28.8           - .8         9.7
   1982       83.9       30.3               25.5           - 4.6         6.4
   1983       86.2       28.2               23.0             2.7         3.9
   1984       93.6       27.1               23.0             8.6         3.7
   1985       99.7       26.9               22.8             6.5         3.2
   1986      106.9       27.1               22.9             7.2         2.6
   1987      115.0       28.4               20.1             7.6         3.3
--------------------------------------------------------------------------
```

*Source*: U.S. Bureau of Census, *Government Finances*, various years.

to this day. (Follow-up reading includes: Brown et al., 1984; Gramlich, 1985; Nathan and Dolittle, 1987.)

The grants-in-aid system in the United States came to life during the presidency of Lyndon B. Johnson. Chapter 3 mentioned that President Johnson was an advocate of creative federalism which emphasized a direct federal-local government association and agreements between government and nongovernmental organizations to solve public problems, especially poverty and urban problems. LBJ and the Congress expanded the number of available grants and the dollars allocated to intergovernmental grants. From 1965 to 1969, grant dollars rose form $10.9 billion to $20.3 billion.

The direct link between the federal government and local governments came with the introduction of a *block grant*. A block grant permitted federal funds to be given to local governments (in some cases, state governments) for broad functional responsibilities (e.g., housing, public safety, health, and education), while the specific uses of the grant money (e.g., low income housing, police training, subsidized hospital clinics, and compensatory education programs in mathematics) would be at the discretion of the grant-receiving governments.

The focus of the grant system on poverty and urban problems resulted in grants-in-aid for health care to the indigent (Medicaid 1965); direct, broad-based federal support of elementary and secondary education (Elementary and Secondary Education Act of 1965); and urban renewal (Demonstration Cities and Metropolitan Development Act 1966, more popularly known as model cities) to name three of the many grants that President Johnson and the Congress put in place.

Table 13–1 picks up the trend in the grants-in-aid system with the Nixon administration in 1970. The data in Table 13–1 include direct grants to state and local governments, as well as grants for income support and Medicaid programs. The Nixon-Ford administrations include the years 1970 to 1977. As in the Great Society years, expansion marks this period. In 1970, federal aid stood at $24.4 billion which represented 26.2 percent of state and local tax revenues and 22.4 percent of state and local own source revenues. In 1976, the comparable figures were $61.0 billion, 38.9 percent of tax revenues, and 30.4 percent of own source revenues. With the exception of 1974, annual growth in grants-in-aid always exceeded (often substantially so) the inflation rate, as measured by the GNP deflator. The most significant increases in funding occurred in the areas of natural resources and the environment, transportation, community and regional development, job training, and general government assistance.

It is not just the funding level that changed during the Nixon-Ford years. Reacting to the proliferation of grants and the expansion of federal government involvement in what some practitioners viewed as local government affairs during the Great Society era, President Nixon advanced his own brand of "new federalism." It concentrated federal grant funding on education, health, and welfare. Also, new federalism meant a decentralization of responsibilities away from Washington, DC to the statehouse, the county courthouse, and city and town halls, though there was no clear tilt to the urban areas (Raimondo, 1984).

The elements of Nixon's new federalism were the centralization of welfare under the Family Assistance Program (FAP) which was never enacted; job training under the Comprehensive Training and Employment Act (CETA 1973); housing and community development which encompassed urban renewal, model cities, water and sewer facilities, open spaces, and neighborhood facilities under the Housing and Community Development Act (1974), the largest block grant during the Nixon-Ford period; and unconditional cash grants to state and local governments under the State and Local Fiscal Assistance Act (1972), more commonly known as general revenue sharing (GRS). The block grant concept coupled with general revenue sharing was designed to transfer power to state and local governments and give them the resources to implement their decisions. Some thought this novel, or even radical, in the 1970s, but it is a notion of federalism that dates back to the founding of the United States.

Bouts of recession and inflation limited President Jimmy Carter's influence over the intergovernmental grants system during the years 1977 to 1981. There is a slowdown in the expansion of the system. In 1977, federal aid stood at $67.6 billion which represented 38.4 percent of state and local tax revenues and 30.4 percent of state and local own source revenues. In 1980, the comparable figures were $88.7 billion, 38.3 percent of tax revenues, and 32.6 percent of own source revenues. With the exception of 1979, annual growth in grants-in-aid always exceeded the inflation rate, as measured by the GNP deflator. Most notably, funding increased for transportation, job training, and community and regional development.

If a theory of federalism guided grants policy at this time, then President

Carter returned to a notion of creative federalism. He was concerned with federal-local relations, poverty, and the fiscal impact of the recession on local governments. The centerpiece of his grants policy was a stimulus package that he especially intended for urban areas. The stimulus package included a counter-cyclical aid component, funding for public works, and portions of the Comprehensive Training and Employment Act (CETA). While there was nothing in that package that was innovative or dramatic, the emphasis on urban areas was reminiscent of the Great Society days.

Unlike many of his immediate predecessors, President Ronald Reagan brought some passion to the issue of intergovernmental relations in the United States. No small feat! From his experiences as governor of California, President Reagan believed that the grants-in-aid system had lost its focus. The growth in the number of grants and the dollars involved convinced the president that the federal government was intruding in local government affairs. (Do you hear an echo from the Nixon White House?) Reagan's vision of intergovernmental relations included: a reduction in the dollars committed to grants-in-aid; the delineation of the functional responsibilities by level of government; and the decentralization of the public sector in line with the Leviathan hypothesis introduced in Chapter 7.

Federalism "junkies" from economics, political science, and public management have concluded that the rhetoric of the president exceeded his ability to change intergovernmental relations and the grants-in-aid system. As evidence, they point to the "New Federalism" proposal that the Reagan administration advanced in early 1982. The plan had three parts: the SWAP, the TURNBACK, and the TRUSTFUND (Donnelly, 1982; Gramlich and Laren, 1982; Inman, 1985).

The SWAP involved the federal government trading AFDC (Aid to Families with Dependent Children) and food stamps to the states' governments for Medicaid. At the fiscal year 1984 levels, AFDC and food stamps cost $16.5 billion and Medicaid $19.1 billion. (Using the administration's figures, the states would be winners. Using the National Governors Association's figures, the states would be losers.) The TURNBACK called for the federal government to relinquish to the states a variety of programs in such areas as income assistance; social, health, and nutrition services; transportation; community development and facilities; and education and training. If they "accepted" these programs, then the states would need $30.2 billion (fiscal year 1984) to pay for these programs. This is the place where the TRUSTFUND enters the picture. The TRUSTFUND would initially hold states harmless; they would be given the funds to administer the TURN-BACK programs. The TRUSTFUND which federal excise taxes, oil windfall profits taxes, and taxes on alcohol, tobacco, and gasoline would finance would phase out by 1991. Each state would then decide whether or not it wished to continue the program. (Remember that the Leviathan hypothesis predicts that they generally won't continue the programs!) After some negotiations between the Reagan administration and the governors, the proposal for a new federalism went gently into the night.

In contrast to the official withdrawal of his proposal, President Reagan was not ready to head into the sunset. He continued changing the intergovernmental grant system with two Tiebout-like principles in mind: unless there is a clear national interest (a national benefit area), local voters should decide which programs they supported and at what funding levels; and local voters should have control over the implementation of federal programs in their jurisdictions (Peterson, 1984).

Table 13–1 shows the results of the Reagan push on grants-in-aid. In 1981, federal aid stood at $87.9 billion which represented 34.0 percent of state and local tax revenues and 28.8 percent of state and local own source revenues. In 1987, the comparable figures were $115.0 billion, 28.4 percent of tax revenues, and 20.1 percent of own source revenues. These figures mask two trends in the intergovernmental grants area. From 1981 through 1983, grants dollar levels actually declined, first in real and nominal terms (1981 and 1982) and then in real terms (1983). This reduction set off an interstate scramble for federal aid in which the South and West regions fared very well. Thereafter, annual growth in grants-in-aid always exceeded the inflation rate, as measured by the GNP deflator.

In addition, Reagan administration grants-in-aid policy elevated the states to the preeminent recipients of federal grants. This emphasis contrasts with the Johnson and Carter preferences for local governments as the preeminent recipients of federal grants. The block grant, so prominent during the Nixon-Ford days, also reemerged as the federal grant of choice as the federal government combined seventy-six *categorical*, or specific use, grants in nine block grants.

Although the formal New Federalism proposal was never enacted, the Reagan administration, especially during its first term, did cut federal grant assistance level to individuals and governments and decentralize program management. The states' (and in some cases the local jurisdictions') response to these changes provides some insights into the workings of contemporary federalism. Of particular interest is whether states ratified the changes (went along with them), or replaced lost federal funding with state funding; and whether states reordered federal priorities after the federal government turned program management over to them.

The states complied with changes in two federal programs. The federal government tightened eligibility requirements to qualify for AFDC payments and the states generally let the change stand. The federal government reduced funding levels for Medicaid if the states permitted health care costs to exceed a predetermined growth limit and the states generally stayed within the limit. Based on fiscal year 1982 data, there is also some evidence that the withdrawal of federal funding from certain functional areas led to a reordering of state spending priorities.

With federal funding cut, states usually did not replace the federal dollars. Expenditure growth in functional areas in which the federal government significantly reduced grants-in-aid (e.g., highways, natural resources, education, and health and hospitals) grew at a slower pace then in functional areas in which the state governments funded out of own source revenues (e.g., retirement, corrections, general control, and financial administration). Still some states did replace lost federal funding with state funding. Most notably, Oklahoma, New York, and Massachusetts replaced between 10 and 25 percent of the lost federal funding, while Arizona, Florida, New Jersey, California, and South Dakota replaced less than 10 percent. Generally, economically well-to-do states with some liberal political leanings replaced lost federal grant money (as the material in Chapters 2, 5, and 11 would have predicted) (Peterson, 1984; Nathan, Dolittle and Associates, 1983 and 1987; Van Horn and Raimondo, 1983).

This brief fiscal history takes us to the current levels of federal grants-in-aid to state and local governments. Almost three-quarters of the federal grants-in-aid subsidizes transportation, education and employment training, health (Medicaid), and income security (AFDC). Table 13–2 displays per capita federal aid FAID) to state-local governments, the relation of FAID to personal income, and the state government share of FAID for 1986–87. The average FAID is $472 with a high of $1,067 (Alaska) and a low of $305 (Florida), for a ratio of high to low of 3.50. For every $1 that Florida receives, Alaska receives $3.50. If the highest five and the lowest five states in terms of FAID levels are discarded, then the ratio closes to 1.72. For every $1 that New Hampshire receives $367 per capita), North Dakota receives $1.72 ($630 per capita).

Another measure of federal aid levels and differences is amount of federal aid that state and local governments receive for every $1,000 of personal income in the state. The national average for this measure is $33 (for every $1,000 of personal income, federal aid is $33). The high for this figure is Wyoming ($71) and the low is Arizona ($27). The differences in per capita federal aid and the federal aid per $1,000 of personal income across the states should be traced back to the rationale for these grants: externalities, fiscal imbalances, institutional requirements, and politics. In light of the Reagan administration's emphasis on the states, the column marked State Share tells the percentage of federal aid that goes directly to the state government. On average this figure is 83.0 percent. It varies from over 90.0 percent in Vermont, West Virginia, and Wyoming to under 80.0 percent in Massachusetts and Nevada.

The data in Table 13–2 fuel another regional conflict similar to the interstate tax competition that simmers just below the surface in any federal system. Regardless of the reasons, as long as some states receive relatively high levels of per capita federal aid (e.g., Alaska, Wyoming, New York, Montana, and Vermont) and some states relatively low levels of federal aid (e.g., Florida, Texas, Kansas, Missouri, and New Hampshire), the grants-in-aid system will be at the center of regional disputes among the nation's governors and the subject of much political crossfire in Washington, DC. (A discussion of the fairness of

**Table 13–2**
**State-Local Per Capita Federal Aid (FAID), the Relation of FAID to $1,000**
**Personal Income (PY), and the State Share of Federal Aid, 1986–87**

| Region & State | Per Capita FAID | Relation of FAID to $1000 PY | State Share | Region & State | Per Capita FAID | Relation of FAID to $1000 PY | State Share |
|---|---|---|---|---|---|---|---|
| USA | $ 472 | $33 | 83.0% | | | | |
| **N.E.** | | | | **E.S.C.** | | | |
| ME | 576 | 46 | 89.0 | KY | $ 426 | $38 | 88.9% |
| NH | 367 | 24 | 84.3 | TN | 439 | 37 | 86.9 |
| VT | 661 | 50 | 92.0 | AL | 427 | 38 | 85.0 |
| MA | 532 | 30 | 74.6 | MS | 500 | 52 | 87.5 |
| RI | 559 | 39 | 88.9 | | | | |
| CT | 428 | 22 | 88.1 | **W.S.C.** | | | |
| **M.A.** | | | | AR | 426 | 39 | 89.4 |
| | | | | LA | 613 | 54 | 89.6 |
| NY | 700 | 41 | 86.3 | OK | 390 | 31 | 86.7 |
| NJ | 446 | 24 | 84.0 | TX | 334 | 25 | 80.5 |
| PA | 473 | 33 | 82.2 | | | | |
| **E.N.C.** | | | | **Mt.** | | | |
| | | | | MT | 698 | 58 | 86.0 |
| OH | 421 | 30 | 82.3 | ID | 424 | 38 | 88.9 |
| IN | 400 | 31 | 84.8 | WY | 937 | 71 | 91.5 |
| IL | 444 | 29 | 78.2 | CO | 434 | 29 | 85.3 |
| MI | 513 | 35 | 85.1 | NM | 464 | 41 | 81.2 |
| WI | 503 | 36 | 87.8 | AZ | 347 | 26 | 77.6 |
| | | | | UT | 532 | 49 | 87.1 |
| **W.N.C.** | | | | NV | 394 | 27 | 75.5 |
| MN | 536 | 36 | 83.7 | **Pac.** | | | |
| IA | 433 | 32 | 85.1 | | | | |
| MO | 363 | 27 | 84.2 | WA | 539 | 36 | 78.4 |
| ND | 630 | 50 | 86.5 | OR | 544 | 41 | 79.2 |
| SD | 571 | 48 | 84.7 | CA | 520 | 32 | 86.3 |
| NE | 424 | 31 | 86.6 | AK | 1067 | 59 | 86.6 |
| KS | 363 | 25 | 89.4 | HI | 488 | 33 | 80.7 |
| **S.A.** | | | | | | | |
| DE | 493 | 33 | 87.4 | | | | |
| MD | 487 | 29 | 77.9 | | | | |
| VA | 383 | 25 | 86.1 | | | | |
| WV | 515 | 49 | 92.6 | | | | |
| NC | 372 | 30 | 85.2 | | | | |
| SC | 395 | 35 | 88.5 | | | | |
| GA | 443 | 34 | 83.0 | | | | |
| FL | 305 | 21 | 76.3 | | | | |

*Source*: U.S. Bureau of Census, *Government Finances*, 1988.

federal aid distributions is found in ACIR, 1980a.) In the 1970s, differences in the federal aid levels led to charges that the Northeast and North Central regions were subsidizing the South and West regions at a time when the Northeast and North Central regions were declining and the South and West regions were prospering. This debate was part of the so-called conflict between the Frostbelt and the Sunbelt (Pack, 1982).

**Table 13-3**
**Trends in State Aid to Local Governments, 1970-87 (aid in billions)**

| Year | State Aid | As a Percent of Local Tax Revenues | As a Percent of Local Own Source Revenues | Annual % Change | GNP Deflator |
|------|-----------|-----------|-----------|-----------|-----------|
| 1970 | $ 28.9 | 74.5% | 56.2% | | |
| 1971 | 32.6 | 75.1 | 57.3 | 11.3% | 5.7% |
| 1972 | 36.7 | 73.8 | 57.0 | 12.6 | 4.7 |
| 1973 | 40.8 | 77.0 | 57.9 | 11.2 | 6.5 |
| 1974 | 45.6 | 80.7 | 59.4 | 11.8 | 9.1 |
| 1975 | 51.0 | 83.2 | 60.5 | 11.8 | 9.8 |
| 1976 | 56.7 | 83.9 | 60.8 | 11.2 | 6.4 |
| 1977 | 61.1 | 81.6 | 59.9 | 7.8 | 6.7 |
| 1978 | 65.8 | 81.8 | 59.4 | 7.7 | 7.3 |
| 1979 | 74.5 | 92.4 | 63.5 | 13.2 | 8.9 |
| 1980 | 82.8 | 95.8 | 63.6 | 11.1 | 9.0 |
| 1981 | 91.3 | 96.3 | 62.7 | 10.3 | 9.7 |
| 1982 | 97.0 | 106.8 | 59.4 | 6.2 | 6.4 |
| 1983 | 100.0 | 88.4 | 55.6 | 3.1 | 3.9 |
| 1984 | 106.7 | 86.5 | 54.3 | 6.7 | 3.7 |
| 1985 | 119.6 | 88.9 | 55.3 | 12.1 | 3.2 |
| 1986 | 126.8 | 87.4 | 54.3 | 6.0 | 2.6 |
| 1987 | 136.8 | 86.4 | 53.8 | 7.9 | 3.3 |

*Source*: U.S. Bureau of Census, *Government Finances*, various years.

## STATE GRANTS-IN-AID PROGRAMS

State governments also engage in intergovernmental transfers with their local governments. The reasons behind these transfers are identical to those presented for the federal grants-in-aid system: efficiency, equity, institutional needs of federalism, and politics. More than sixty cents out of every state aid dollar subsidizes education; more than ten cents subsidizes public welfare; and another ten cents subsidizes general local government support. School districts, counties, and municipalities (in descending order of support level) are the recipients of state aid disbursements (ACIR 1977d and 1980c; Gold, 1983b).

Table 13-3 shows the trends in state aid (in billions of dollars) to local governments from 1970 to 1987. Several obvious patterns appear in the table. State aid has grown continuously during this period from $28.9 billion in 1970 to $136.8 billion in 1987. Ten of the seventeen annual percentage changes have been double digit growth. Only from 1982 to 1983 and from 1983 to 1984 did the annual percentage change fall in real terms (it was less than the GNP deflator). State aid as a percentage of local government tax revenues has shown a long-term increase over the period. It rose from a figure of 74.5 percent in 1970 (for every $1 raised through the local tax system, state aid contributed 75 cents) to a high of 106.8 percent in 1982 and then settled at 86.4 percent in 1987. A similar pattern exists for state aid as a percentage of local own source revenue. It rose from a figure of 56.2 percent in 1970 (for every $1 raised through the local revenue tax system, state aid contributed 56 cents) to a high of 63.6 percent in 1980 and then settled at 53.8 percent in 1987.

These surges in state support for local government functional responsibilities can be traced to five events that will be part of the dynamics of state-local intergovernmental grant policy for years to come: the performance of the national and the regional economy; the changes in federal aid to state and local governments; the legal challenges to education financing; the imposition of local tax limits; and the expansion of state mandated services.

A boom in the national and the regional economy often drives the upswing in state aid. Chapter 2 stressed the importance of the regional economy in state-local finances. States with prosperous economies are able to fund grants-in-aid more generously than states with slow growing or declining economies. The growth in state aid in the early 1970s occurred at a time when the national economy was expanding. The slow growth in state aid in the late 1970s and early 1980s coincides with a national recession. For example, the economic slowdown from 1981 to 1983 translates into a decline ($-4.6$ percent) followed by a modest increase in federal aid ($+2.7$ percent) coupled with a relatively low growth rate in state aid ($+6.2$ percent and $+3.1$ percent). If the U.S. economy stalls in the 1990s, the question to state and local government practitioners is how will that fact affect federal and state aid levels and growth rates?

The unilateral changes in federal aid throughout the decade of the 1980s put pressure on state grants-in-aid systems to react to lower growth, or an outright reduction, in federal aid. Generally, federal and state aid moved in tandem in the recent past. Double digit growth in federal aid and double digit growth in state aid were common. (Federal aid dollars funded some portion of state aid dollars.) However, the annual percentage change figures in Tables 13–1 and 13–3 reveal some of the twists and turns the intergovernmental grants-in-aid system has taken in the 1980s. Since 1981, federal aid has grown at a lower rate than it did throughout the 1970s, as did state aid. The long-term concern for financial officers at the subnational level is how will state and local governments respond to the new reality of reduced intergovernmental support. Externalities, fiscal imbalances, and the institutional need for intergovernmental grants have not declined (they may have worsened), but the growth rate of grants has declined. To what degree will this development hamper the delivery of public goods/services?

Go back to the issues involved in education finances. The combination of legal challenges to the state-local school finance schemes, resource disparities across school districts, and the on-going drive to improve local public schools has contributed to the growth in state aid throughout the 1970s and again in the latter part of the 1980s. Calls for more state aid support for local public schools will get louder in the 1990s. If state officials try to turn a deaf ear to these calls for increased school aid, then they may well find the courts shouting in their other ear that state aid for schools must be increased—or else!

The imposition of limits on local government revenue-raising prompted state governments to increase their level of financial support to local governments. This was the argument advanced in Figures 8–1 through 8–4 in Chapter 8. That increase is also reflected in the double digit growth rates for state aid during the

1970s and into the 1980s. As local dependency on state aid increases, how will state governments balance the fiscal needs of local governments against other equally pressing claims on state financial resources?

In listing the several issues that influence state-local expenditure decisions, Chapter 5 mentioned state mandated public goods/services. In many states (especially if they have local tax limits), whenever the state legislature requires that local governments provide a specific public good/service, the grants-in-aid system is supposed to increase to finance that specific public good/service. Whether that arrangement exists in a state or not, as mandated public goods/ services becomes more appealing, the demands for increased state aid will intensify. State and local government officials will be looking at more mandates-more state aid, fewer mandates-less state aid, or the worst combination, more mandates-less state aid. Again, the issue is more than the politics of a fiscal suicide squeeze on local governments. It is the same issue that the previous four points have raised; namely, how have the changes in the intergovernmental grants-in-aid system affected the efficacy of the federal system?

The last look at the state grants-in-aid system comes in the form of a state-by-state comparison. Table 13–4 displays per capita state aid (SAID) to local governments, the relation of SAID to personal income, and the share of SAID that funds education for 1986–87. The average SAID is $562 with a high of $1,532 (Alaska) and a low of $60 (Hawaii). Right off, let's admit that state grants-in-aid systems in these two states are not typical. If the highest five and the lowest five states in terms of SAID levels are discarded, then the ratio closes to 2.34. For every $1 that Missouri distributes in state grants ($311 per capita), New Mexico distributes $2.34 ($727 per capita).

Another measure of state aid levels and differences is amount of state aid which local governments receive for every $1,000 of personal income in the state. The national average for this measure is $39 (for every $1,000 of personal income, state aid is $39). The high for this figure is Alaska ($81) and the low is Hawaii ($4). Again, if the highest five and the lowest five states in terms of SAID levels are discarded, then the high for this figure is Wisconsin ($52) and the low is Kansas ($25). The differences in per capita state aid and the state aid per $1,000 of personal income across the states should be traced back to the rationale for these grants: externalities, fiscal imbalances, institutional requirements, and politics. The column marked Education Share tells the percentage of state aid that goes to finance local public schools. On average this figure is 64.3 percent. It varies from over 90.0 percent in Delaware, West Virginia, and Texas to under 55.0 percent in California, Michigan, and Hawaii.

Aside from this litany of state aid variations, the data in Table 12–4 illustrate in a simple way a relationship mentioned earlier. It ties together the performance of the regional economy, the state government spending level, and the state aid level to local governments. For example, of the eleven states with above an average per capita state aid level ($562)—Alaska, Wyoming, New York, Minnesota, New Mexico, Wisconsin, Nevada, Washington, Arizona, Massachusetts,

**Table 13–4**
**Local Per Capita State Aid (SAID), the Relation of SAID to $1,000 Personal Income (PY), and Education Share of State Aid, 1986–87**

| Region & State | Per Capita SAID | Relation of SAID to $1000 PY | Education Share | Region & State | Per Capita SAID | Relation of SAID to $1000 PY | Education Share |
|---|---|---|---|---|---|---|---|
| USA | $ 562 | $39 | 64.3% | | | | |
| **N.E.** | | | | **E.S.C.** | | | |
| ME | 350 | 28 | 80.7 | KY | $ 401 | $35 | 83.4% |
| NH | 154 | 9 | 32.5 | TN | 325 | 28 | 66.9 |
| VT | 320 | 22 | 84.4 | AL | 364 | 33 | 83.7 |
| MA | 623 | 36 | 48.1 | MS | 495 | 50 | 74.0 |
| RI | 302 | 21 | 80.1 | | | | |
| CT | 357 | 18 | 67.9 | **W.S.C.** | | | |
| **M.A.** | | | | AR | 369 | 34 | 80.6 |
| | | | | LA | 381 | 34 | 83.1 |
| NY | 940 | 55 | 47.0 | OK | 386 | 31 | 86.2 |
| NJ | 589 | 32 | 55.2 | TX | 387 | 29 | 91.5 |
| PA | 457 | 32 | 67.1 | | | | |
| **E.N.C.** | | | | **Mt.** | | | |
| | | | | MT | 364 | 30 | 84.9 |
| OH | 498 | 36 | 62.6 | ID | 434 | 38 | 79.0 |
| IN | 516 | 39 | 69.4 | WY | 940 | 72 | 67.5 |
| IL | 415 | 27 | 69.9 | CO | 458 | 30 | 65.0 |
| MI | 538 | 37 | 50.7 | NM | 727 | 65 | 77.3 |
| WI | 721 | 52 | 47.9 | AZ | 625 | 48 | 56.2 |
| | | | | UT | 448 | 42 | 89.4 |
| **W.N.C.** | | | | NV | 679 | 46 | 58.6 |
| MN | 877 | 58 | 56.5 | **Pac.** | | | |
| IA | 535 | 39 | 71.1 | | | | |
| MO | 311 | 23 | 85.1 | WA | 662 | 44 | 79.6 |
| ND | 474 | 39 | 72.3 | OR | 407 | 31 | 63.0 |
| SD | 257 | 21 | 76.1 | CA | 947 | 58 | 54.9 |
| NE | 291 | 21 | 60.7 | AK | 1532 | 81 | 64.0 |
| KS | 356 | 25 | 83.8 | HI | 60 | 4 | 0.0 |
| **S.A.** | | | | | | | |
| DE | 538 | 34 | 96.9 | | | | |
| MD | 440 | 26 | 56.2 | | | | |
| VA | 444 | 29 | 71.3 | | | | |
| WV | 466 | 44 | 95.3 | | | | |
| NC | 542 | 44 | 81.0 | | | | |
| SC | 371 | 33 | 84.8 | | | | |
| GA | 504 | 30 | 80.6 | | | | |
| FL | 477 | 33 | 77.3 | | | | |

*Source*: U.S. Bureau of Census, *Government Finances*, 1988.

and New Jersey, eight have an above average per capita gross state product (see Table 2–7). Of these eight states, seven have an above average per capita state spending level (see Table 5–4). It's the prosperous state whose state government is a relatively high spending one that will commit itself to an above average state grants-in-aid system.

The review of the grants-in-aid figures is useful, but these numbers change, sometimes dramatically, from year to year. When they change, they define a new fiscal reality to which federalism must try to adapt. So it is not so much the figures that should be remembered, but the insights that the figures reveal. One important insight is the linkage of economic performance-spending on state aid. This linkage is essential to any speculation concerning the trends in intergovernmental transfers in the 1990s. The direction that intergovernmental grants takes will say much about the provision of specific public good/service areas, as well as the effectiveness of federalism in the United States.

## CLASSIFYING INTERGOVERNMENTAL TRANSFERS

Behind the fiscal profiles shown in Table 13-1 through 13-4 are several hundred individual grant programs. Four features of a grant help organize these several hundred individual grants. In addition, these features often reveal what the rationale of the grant is. The four features are: restrictions, disbursements, matching, and amount (Break, 1980; Oates, 1972).

### Restrictions

The question, "Are there any strings attached?", is a significant one for any intergovernmental grant. Grants can either be conditional or unconditional. A conditional grant is called a *categorical grant*. A categorical grant is given by one level of government to another for a specific purpose; hence, there are conditions on the use of the grant money. A state grant to assist in the operation of Eastown's airport would be a categorical grant. An unconditional grant is called a *general grant*. A general grant is given by one level of government to another without a specific use in mind; hence, there are no conditions on the use of the grant money. General Revenue Sharing (GRS) was an unconditional grant. Municipalities spent the GRS money on whatever they wished: tax relief, capital outlays, and/or general operations. Incidentally, a block grant is a combination categorical and general grant: categorical because it specifies a functional use and general because within the functional use it permits the grant-receiving government to determine how the grant will be spent.

The choice of a categorical versus a general grant reflects the intent of the grant-giving level of government. A government will institute a categorical grant program if the intergovernmental grant addresses an identifiable externalities problem. If, for example, the benefit area exceeds the political jurisdiction (a "Case I" situation, as defined by the principle of fiscal equivalency), then the categorical grant is given to the political jurisdiction to restore efficiency in the provision of the public good/service. Categorical grants also can achieve *specific equity*. Specific equity involves transferring grant money from one government to another in order to offset a fiscal imbalance so that a specific public good/ service can be provided. Suppose fiscal disparities among political jurisdictions prevents the less well-off jurisdictions from providing summer recreation programs for elementary schoolchildren. For equity reasons alone, the state government may transfer funds to these localities so that they have the means to provide these programs.

A general grant can also deal with an externalities problem, especially if the externalities are more difficult to quantify. More often than not, a general grant has an equity-based objective. Any intergovernmental transfer that attempts to reduce fiscal differences among political jurisdictions without any conditions on the use of the grant is a general grant. At the federal government level, General Revenue Sharing under the Nixon administration and antirecession aid (so-called *countercyclical* aid) under the Carter administration would qualify as general grants. At the state government level, local aid programs that involve the state sharing some portion of its revenue with local governments would be a general grant (Thurow, 1966).

Categorical grants are restricted use grants that are designed to deal with specific externalities or specific equity problems. In contrast, general grants are unrestricted grants that are designed primarily to lessen fiscal imbalances among political jurisdictions.

### Disbursement

This dimension of a grant explains how the funds are transferred from one level of government to another. There are two broad methods: project and formula. The *project* method of disbursement evaluates each application for grant money from a potential grant-receiving government on a case-by-case basis. For example, project grants would look at school building asbestos levels across school districts to determine which district would receive aid; or government officials would rank toxic waste sites to establish a priority list for clean-up. If identifiable externalities exist in the provision of a public good/service or if specific equity is the issue, then the project method of disbursement is appropriate.

Often the legislative branch (either the U.S. Congress or a state legislature) establishes the project guidelines and the bureaucracy applies them. Consequently, there can be a great deal of discretion in the awarding of the project grant. By its nature, the project disbursement method is open to charges of government intrusion (federal into state or local affairs and state into local affairs) and political favoritism. (Recall the political rationale for a grant system, as well as the role of the politician and the bureaucracy in the public choice model presented in Chapter 5.) The Reagan administration was so convinced that these charges were true that it worked long, hard, and successfully to reduce the number of project grants.

If the grant-giving government does not use a project disbursement method, then it will employ a formula. A *formula* disbursement method awards grant money on the basis of the presence of certain characteristics within the political jurisdiction. A transportation grant to bus students from home to school may be based on passenger-miles traveled; and a law enforcement grant may be based on a jurisdiction's crime rate statistics. The formula disbursement method is automatic. There is little room for discretionary decision making. Either a jurisdiction has the prerequisite characteristics or it does not. If it does, the jurisdiction gets the money; otherwise, it does not. In this sense, the formula disbursement method has an apolitical appearance. Of course, every formula can serve a political purpose!

This discussion closes on a generalization. (Doesn't every discussion?) The most likely combinations are: categorical grants with a project disbursement method and general grants with a formula disbursement. Of course, there are always exceptions.

### Matching

When the grant-giving government requires that the grant-receiving government shares the cost of providing a public good/service, the intergovernmental transfer has a *matching requirement*. Cost sharing is a necessary component of a matching grant. For example, if the federal government is willing to pay 60 percent of the costs of a waste treatment facility while the local government pays 40 percent, then the grant has a matching requirement. The alternative to a matching grant is a lump sum grant. A *lump sum* grant is a fixed amount of dollars transferred from one government to another without any cost sharing. Go back to the waste treatment facility. If the federal government completely financed the local waste treatment facility, then there is no matching requirement. There is only a lump sum transfer.

The use and the relative size (e.g., 10 percent of the costs, 35 percent of the costs, etc.) of a matching requirement have multiple purposes. To begin with, the use of a matching requirement implies that the public good/service possesses a benefit area that involves more than one level of government. The size of the match could reflect the proportion of local versus external (spillover) benefits found in a Case I situation, defined by the principle of fiscal equivalency. For example, suppose the state government wished to help fund Eastown's airport. Assume that one-third of Eastown's airport benefits goes to people who reside in Eastown and two-thirds goes to people who reside in the state, but outside Eastown. The cost sharing might be one-third from Eastown and two-thirds from a state airport/transportation grant. That cost division, one-third/two thirds, is also the matching requirement for the state grant. So in its simplest form, the match reflects the proportion of local versus spillover benefits found in a Case I situation.

The size of the match could also relate to economic conditions. Suppose economic conditions in Eastown prevent the locality from paying the share of their costs (one-third). If Eastown was unable to pay its share, then the operation of the Eastown airport could be jeopardized. The state could change the matching requirement of its airport/transportation grant. The state could subsidize the *tax price* (i.e., what Eastown actually pays from its own source revenues) of the airport to Eastown. Instead of demanding one-third the costs, the state could ask for one-quarter of the costs. A lower matching requirement permits a locality, especially a financially squeezed locality, to provide a specific public good/ service.

There is another reason why a grant-giving government would lower the matching requirement to a grant-receiving government for a specific public good/ service. A lower matching requirement could stimulate greater spending on a specific public good/service by the grant-receiving government. The reasoning goes as follows. A matching grant lowers the cost of a public good/service. Reducing the cost has the same effect as lowering the price of that public good/ service to the grant-receiving government. Lowering prices increases demand for that public good/service and may ultimately increase the amount spent on the subsidized public good/service (Wilde, 1971).

Suppose spending on local recreational programs is relatively price elastic; that is, governments are very responsive to price changes. If the tax-price of recreational services decreases by 1 percent, then the quantity demanded for these recreational services will increase by more than 1 percent. Spending on recreational services will increase as a result of the tax-price decrease. To illustrate this point, suppose a local government pays the full cost of a summer swimming program. The cost is $25,000. Tax revenues fully fund the cost of the service. A new state government grant lowers the tax-price so that for every $1 of recreational services the local government pays 95 cents from local own source revenues. The result of the lower price of the service (a 5 percent reduction) is that the local government now spends a total of $26,000 on the swimming program. A price reduction leads to a spending increase. The amount of the spending increase will depend on the price elasticity of the public good/ service. For a given matching requirement, the greater the price elasticity of demand (i.e., the more responsive the grant-receiving government), the greater the increase in spending.

The matching requirement can, therefore, stimulate increased spending on a specific public good/service by the grant-receiving government. To fund the increased spending, the grant-receiving government may divert its own source revenues away from other public goods/services. The preferences imposed by the grant-giving government push aside the consumer-voters' preferences that the grant-receiving government represents. This substitution of the preferences of the grant-giving government for the preferences of the grant-receiving government is called the *distortion hypothesis* (Smith, 1968). For example, if the grant-receiving government took funds away from a community music program that its people supported in order to qualify for a grant subsidized summer swimming program, then the distortion hypothesis may be at work. This situation has also been called the greedy politician model. The assertion is that local politicians spend as much as they can on grant subsidized public goods/services (McGuire, 1973). The degree to which this distortion occurs depends upon the price elasticity of demand for the subsidized public good/service. Again, the greater the price elasticity of a specific public good/service, the more likely that the distortion hypothesis will hold.

Pulling together the features of a grant that we have mentioned up to this point gives us the following likely combinations. Categorical grants employ the project disbursement method regardless of the matching requirement. General grants use a formula disbursement method with no matching requirement; in other words, a lump sum grant.

### Amount

Funding for a given grant-in-aid is either limited or unlimited. A limited funding level for a grant is called a *closed-ended grant*. An unlimited funding level for a grant is called an *open-ended grant*. For all practical purposes, both categorical and general grants tend to be closed-ended.

## EFFECT OF GRANTS ON STATE-LOCAL SPENDING

Regardless of the rationale for grants—efficiency, equity, institutional needs, or politics—intergovernmental transfers stimulate state and local government spending. If they did not, then any grant-in-aid program would be nothing more than a tax relief package. There are certainly better ways to achieve tax relief than through an intergovernmental transfer. Proponents of a grants-in-aid system view the increased spending as a necessary means to accomplish a public policy objective: compensate for positive externalities, redress fiscal imbalances, or maintain a vibrant federal system. Critics of a grant-in-aid system view the increased spending as sign of unnecessary growth in government and government waste and inefficiency induced by the grant-giving government. Whatever the viewpoint, the fact remains unchanged: grants increase public spending (Gramlich, 1977).

The type of grant affects the magnitude of the increase in state-local spending. The four features of any grant offered us enough possible grant forms. Two forms are most common in the federal system: categorical grants with a matching requirement that are closed-ended *and* general, lump sum grants that are closed-ended. As an aside, two major grants-in-aid programs are a third type. AFDC (Aid to Families with Dependent Children) and Medicaid are categorical grants with a matching requirement that are open-ended. Our analysis will concentrate, however, on the two most commonly used grants. The appendix to this chapter provides a graphical explanation using indifference curve analysis of the effect of grants on state-local spending.

### Categorical Grants, Matching Requirement, Closed-Ended

This form of a grant-in-aid often funds public goods/services that state and local governments might not provide in the absence of the grant (e.g., child nutrition programs, community action programs such as vocational counseling and low income energy assistance, and preventive health care programs). This grant reduces the tax-price of a public good/service. By reducing the tax-price, the purchasing power of the grant-receiving government is increased. (With a fixed income, if prices fall, then purchasing power increases.) The combination of a reduced tax-price and increased purchasing power results in the grant-receiving government spending more on the subsidized public good/service. The price elasticity of demand (the responsiveness of government demand to a reduction in tax price) is not very large (inelastic) for most public goods/services. As a consequence, this form of a grant-in-aid will increase spending, but usually by less than the amount of the grant. The grant-receiving government can divert fiscal resources to other public goods/services or tax relief. This diversion of local own source revenues can occur even in cases where the grant-giving government requires a maintenance of effort on the part of the grant-receiving government. *Fungibility* is the label that is used to describe this diversion of funds. Empirical studies of public good/service spending associated with this form of grant show an increase in spending which ranges from no change to $1.00 for each grant dollar received.

To illustrate this argument in very simple terms, we go back in the water. Suppose a local government planned to spend $25,000 on its summer swimming program. The state government gets into the swim and offers a grant-in-aid of $1,500. As a result, spending on the summer swimming program jumps to $26,000. The grant was stimulative. Spending increased, but by less than the amount of the grant ($1,500 grant versus $1,000 spending increase). While all $1,500 of the grant went to the summer swimming program, $500 of local own source revenues was reallocated to other public goods/services or tax relief. Put another way, $500 was fungible.

### General Grants, Lump Sum, Closed-Ended

This form of grant-in-aid simply increases the financial resources available to the grant-receiving government. It is nothing more than a lump sum cash grant from the grant-giving government to the grant-receiving government, often to be used as the grant-receiving government sees fit. There is no price subsidy for a specified public good/service. This form of grant-in-aid will also increase spending, but usually by less than the amount of the grant. Again, the grant-receiving government will divert fiscal resources to tax relief. Fungibility strikes again! Empirical studies of public good/service spending associated with this form of grant show an increase in spending which ranges from 20 cents to $1.00 for each grant dollar received. Most of the empirical findings cluster between 25 cents and 50 cents for each grant dollar received.

Suppose that Eastown receives a general, lump sum, closed-ended grant in the amount of $270,000. The empirical evidence would lead us to believe that Eastown's spending will increase anywhere from $67,500 (.25 times $270,000) to $135,000 (.50 times $270,000) as a result of the grant. The difference between the amount of the grant and the actual increase in spending (either $135,000 or $202,500) has been used for tax relief.

Analysts have also been interested in whether a lump sum grant to a jurisdiction or an increase in the personal income of the residents of the jurisdiction has a greater impact on public spending. The empirical findings show that for every $1 increase in the personal income of the residents of a jurisdiction, public spending increases by 5 to 10 cents. This size of increase is less than the 25 to 50 cents increase for the lump sum grant. The fact that grant dollars tend to stay with the grant-receiving government and increases in personal income tend to stay in the pockets of the people who have earned that money leads to the general notion that money sticks where it lands. In the case of a grant-in-aid, this observation has come to be known as the *flypaper effect*.

Both types of grants-in-aid increase spending, but by less than the amount of the grant. Repeated investigations of the two types of grants have concluded that the categorical, matching requirement, closed-ended grant increases spending more than the general, lump sum, closed-ended grant. Recall that categorical, matching requirement, closed-ended grants often fund public good/services that the grant-receiving government might not otherwise provide. Couple that fact with the imposition of a maintenance of effort requirement for the grant-receiving government and categorical, matching requirement, closed-ended grants stimulate greater spending increases than the general, lump sum, closed-ended grant. The choice of the appropriate grant instrument depends upon the public objective in mind. If the grant-giving government is concerned with something more than fiscal imbalances than the categorical, matching requirement, closed-ended grant is appropriate. If fiscal imbalances are at issue, then general, lump sum, closed-ended grants should be used.

## SUMMARY

1. Intergovernmental grants are a necessary component of federalism. They are justified on efficiency, equity, institutional, and political grounds.

2. The history of federal government grant-in-aid programs varies with the occupant of the White House. Expansion marked the LBJ and Nixon-Ford administrations. LBJ stressed a brand of creative federalism that linked federal and local governments in an effort to deal with poverty and urban problems. The Nixon-Ford years were characterized by decentralization, block grants, and general revenue sharing. Carter focused on antirecession aid. During the Carter administration, the federal intergovernmental transfers reached their financial zenith. President Reagan launched a new federalism that featured decentralization and a contraction in the grants-in-aid system.

3. The history of state government grant-in-aid programs is written by fluctuating economic conditions, changes in federal aid levels, reforms in education financing, the imposition of tax limits, and state mandated public goods/services.

4. Four features classify any intergovernmental grant: restrictions, disbursement, match-

ing requirements, and amount. These features are geared toward meeting different public policy objectives; for example, increasing the spending on a specific public good/service (an efficiency or specific equity concern) versus reducing the fiscal imbalances among jurisdictions (a general equity concern).

5. Grants stimulate the spending levels of the grant-receiving governments. Categorical grants with a matching requirement that are closed-ended increase public spending more than general grants that are lump sum and closed-ended. In both cases, the spending increase is less than the amount of the grant. Grants also raise exotic issues such as spending distortions, fungibility, and flypaper effects!

## APPENDIX TO CHAPTER 13:
## EFFECT OF GRANTS ON STATE-LOCAL GOVERNMENT
## SPENDING: A GRAPHICAL ANALYSIS

Standard indifference curve analysis can illustrate the impact of intergovernmental grants on state-local government spending. (This appendix presumes some familiarity with indifference curve analysis. To review this analytical technique, see: Apgar and Brown, 1987, and Nicholson, 1990.) The analysis assumes that the decision-making body of government has a set of preferences for private and public goods/services; that the indifference map displays these preferences; and that government seeks to maximize community welfare subject to the prices of public and private goods/services and available community resources. Available community resources include the personal income of the community's residents minus taxes paid to other levels of government plus external assistance. (Two readings that develop this approach are: Wilde, 1971, and Gramlich, 1977.) We will apply the graphical analysis using indifference curves to categorical, matching grants and general, lump sum grants.

Figure 13–1 looks at how a categorical, matching grant influences a grant-receiving government's spending decisions. The analysis starts with the pre-grant community welfare equilibrium. The original budget line is BR; the original indifference curve is I; and the corresponding equilibrium is point A. At this equilibrium, government purchases the amount OG of public goods/services, while consumers purchase the amount OH of private goods/services.

A grant-giving government now establishes a categorical, matching grant. Since it is a categorical grant, the financial assistance must be spent on a specific public good/service. The categorical grant has the effect of lowering the price of public goods/services. In Figure 13–1, a lower price for the specific public good/service is shown by a rotation of the budget line in a counter clockwise fashion. The pre-grant budget line, BR, moves to the post-grant budget line, BK. A new equilibrium is reached at point M on indifference curve II. This equilibrium is a higher level of community welfare than was available at the pre-grant equilibrium. At point M, the grant-receiving government's purchase of the specific public good/service moves from OG to OL. The consumer's purchases of private goods equal OD, an increase from OH.

**Figure 13–1**
**Effect of a Categorical, Matching Grant on State-Local Government Spending**

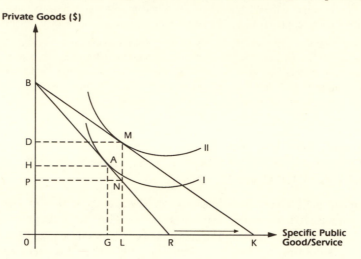

The match required for the categorical grant pictured in Figure 13–1 can be calculated by dividing RK by OK. For every one dollar spent by the grant-receiving government, the grant-giving government will contribute RK/OK cents. Total spending on the specific public good/service can also be divided between grant-giving and the grant-receiving government. The total amount spent on the specific public good/service at equilibrium point M is equal to BP dollars. The grant-receiving government spends BD dollars and the grant-giving government contributes DP dollars.

Although the categorical grant was designed to be spent on the specific public good/service (public spending increased from OG to OL), spending on private goods has also increased (private spending increased from OH to OD). Fungibility is present. The categorical, matching grant freed resources that were formerly claimed by the grant-receiving government. These freed-up resources were then reclaimed by the community's tax-paying residents.

The degree that spending on private goods will increase under a categorical grant depends on the price elasticity of demand for the subsidized public good/service. If this price elasticity is equal to 1.0 (unitary), then there will be no change in the spending on private goods even though the government has received a categorical grant. If this price elasticity is greater than 1.0, then there will be a decrease in the spending on private goods associated with the categorical grant. Last, if this price elasticity is less than 1.0, then there will be an increase in the spending on private goods associated with the categorical grant.

The second major type of grant is the general, lump sum grant. Figure 13–2 shows how a grant-receiving government behaves when it obtains such a grant. The analysis begins with the pre-grant budget line of BR, an indifference curve

**Figure 13–2**
**Effect of a General, Lump Sum Grant on State-Local Government Spending**

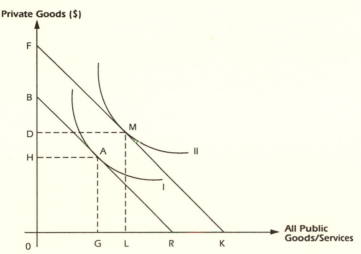

of I, and an equilibrium achieved at point A. The pre-grant equilibrium point A indicates that the community consumes private goods at the level of OH and public goods/services at the level of OG.

Suppose the grant-giving government offers a general, lump sum grant that has a dollar value equal to BF. The budget line shifts from BR to FK. A new equilibrium is established at point M with indifference curve II. A general, lump sum grant increases community income and welfare. It does not change the relative prices of private or public goods/services. The post-grant equilibrium point M tells us that the community now consumes private goods at the level OD (up from OH) and public goods/services at the level OL (up from OG). Since the grant is general in nature (there are no restrictions on grant use), the grant-receiving government can use it any way the government chooses. This fact is important. The grant need not be used exclusively to increase spending on public goods/services. Tax relief, for example, is another possible use. This is an example of fungibility.

In Figure 13–2, not only did the grant-receiving government spend more on public goods/services, but the grant allowed the community's residents to spend more on private goods. In this case, a fraction of the general, lump sum grant [I minus (HD/BF)] has been spent on public goods/services. This conclusion confirms the earlier statement in Chapter 13; that is, a general grant will increase government spending, but usually by less than the amount of the grant. This result requires that the income elasticity for private and public goods/services be greater than zero.

# References

Aaron, Henry J. "What Do Circuit Breaker Laws Accomplish?" In *Property Tax Reform*, ed. George E. Peterson. Washington, DC: The Urban Institute, 1973.

———. "A New View of Property Tax Incidence." *American Economic Review* 64 (May 1974): 212–21.

———. *Who Pays the Property Tax*. Washington, DC: The Brookings Institution, 1975.

———. "Inflation and the Income Tax: An Introduction." In *Inflation and the Income Tax*, ed. Henry J. Aaron. Washington, DC: Brookings Institution, 1976.

Abt, Vicki, James F. Smith, and Eugene Martin Christiansen. *The Business of Risk*. Lawrence, KS: University Press of Kansas, 1985.

Advisory Commission on Intergovernmental Relations (ACIR). *Regional Decision Making: New Strategies for Substate*. Washington, DC: Government Printing Office, 1973.

———. *Governmental Functions and Processes: Local and Areawide*. Washington, DC: Government Printing Office, 1974a.

———. *The Challenge of Local Governmental Reorganization*. Washington, DC: Government Printing Office, 1974b.

———. *Governmental Functions and Processes: Local Areawide*. Washington, DC: Government Printing Office, 1974c.

———. *Local Revenue Diversification: Income, Sales Taxes, and User Charges*. Washington, DC: Government Printing Office, 1974d.

———. *Inflation and Federal and State Income Taxes*. Washington, DC: Government Printing Office, 1976.

———. *Measuring the Fiscal 'Blood Pressure' of the States—1964–1975*. Washington, DC: Government Printing Office, 1977a.

————. *State Limitations on Local Taxes and Expenditures*. Washington, DC: Government Printing Office, 1977b.

————. *Cigarette Bootlegging: A State and Federal Responsibility*. Washington, DC: Government Printing Office, 1977c.

————. *The State and Intergovernmental Aids*. Washington, DC: Government Printing Office, 1977d.

————. *State Mandating of Local Expenditures*. Washington, DC: Government Printing Office, 1978.

————. *Regional Growth: Historic Perspective*. Washington, DC: Government Printing Office, 1980a.

————. *The Inflation Tax: The Case for Indexing Federal and State Income Taxes*. Washington, DC: Government Printing Office, 1980b.

————. *The State of State-Local Revenue Sharing*. Washington, DC: Government Printing Office, 1980c.

————. *Studies in Comparative Federalism: Canada*. Washington, DC: Government Printing Office, 1981a.

————. *Studies in Comparative Federalism: West Germany*. Washington, DC: Government Printing Office, 1981b.

————. *Studies in Comparative Federalism: Australia*. Washington, DC: Government Printing Office, 1981c.

————. *The Condition of Contemporary Federalism: Conflicting Theories and Collapsing Constraints*. Washington, DC: Government Printing Office, 1981d.

————. *Intergovernmentalizing the Classroom: Federal Involvement in Elementary and Secondary Education*. Washington, DC: Government Printing Office, 1981e.

————. *Cigarette Tax Evasion: A Second Look*. Washington, DC: Government Printing Office, 1985.

————. *Measuring State Fiscal Capacity: Alternative Methods and Their Uses*. Washington, DC: Government Printing Office, 1986a.

————. *Significant Features of Fiscal Federalism*. Washington, DC: Government Printing Office, 1986b.

————. *Changing Public Attitudes on Governments and Taxes*. Washington, DC: Government Printing Office, 1987.

————. *Significant Features of Fiscal Federalism*. Washington, DC: Government Printing Office, 1988.

————. *Significant Features of Fiscal Federalism*. Washington, DC: Government Printing Office, 1989.

Allvin, Paul G. "Dukakis Raps Gregg for Wooing Mass. Firms." *Boston Globe*. August 3, 1990, p. 28.

Almy, Richard R. "Rationalizing the Assessment Process." In *Property Tax Reform*, ed. George E. Peterson. Washington, DC: The Urban Institute, 1973.

Apgar, William C., and H. James Brown. *Microeconomics and Public Policy*. Glenview, IL: Scott, Foresman and Company, 1987.

Aronson, J. Richard, and John L. Hilley. *Financing State and Local Governments*. Washington, DC: The Brookings Institution, 1986.

Arrow, Kenneth J. "A Utilitarian Approach to the Concept of Equality in Public Expenditures." *Quarterly Journal of Economics* 85 (August 1971): pp. 409–15.

Atkinson, Scott E., and Robert Halvorsen. "The Relative Efficiency of Public and Private

Firms in a Regulated Environment: The Case of U.S. Electric Utilities.'' *Journal of Public Economics* 29 (April 1986): pp. 281–94.

Bahl, Roy. "Studies on Determinants of Public Expenditures: A Review." In *Sharing Federal Funds for State and Local Needs*, ed. Selma J. Mushkin and John F. Cotton. New York: Praeger, 1969.

Bahl, Roy, and Robert Saunders. "Determinants of Changes in State and Local Government Expenditures." *National Tax Journal* 18 (March 1965): pp. 50–57.

Barlow, Robin. "Efficiency Aspects of Local School Finance." *Journal of Political Economy* 78 (September/October 1970): pp. 1,028–40.

Barr, J. L., and O. A. Davis,. "An Elementary Political and Economic Theory of the Expenditures of Local Governments." *Southern Economic Journal* 33 (October 1966): pp. 149–65.

Barron, James. "States Sell Chances for Gold as a Rush Turns to Stampede." *New York Times*. May 28, 1989a, pp. 1 and 24.

———. "Has the Growth of Legal Gambling Made Society the Loser in the Long Run?" *New York Times*. May 31, 1989b, p. A18.

Bartlett, Randall. *Economic Foundations of Political Power*. New York: Free Press, 1973.

Baumol, William J. "Macroeconomics of Unbalanced Growth: The Anatomy of Urban Crisis." *American Economic Review* 57 (June 1967): pp. 415–26.

Behrens, John O. "The General Nature of 'the' Property Tax Today." In *The Property Tax and Local Finance*, ed. C. Lowell Harriss. Montpelier, VT: Capital City Press, 1983.

Bennett, James T., and Manuel H. Johnson. "Public versus Private Provision of Collective Goods and Services: Garbage Collection Revisited." *Public Choice* 34 (1979): pp. 61–2.

Berglas, Eitan. "User Charges, Local Services, and Taxation of Land Rents." *Public Finance* 37 (1982): pp. 178–88.

Bergstrom, T. C., and R. P. Goodman. "Private Demands for Public Goods." *American Economic Review* 63 (June 1973): pp. 280–96.

Bewley, Truman F. "A Critique of Tiebout's Theory of Local Public Expenditures." *Econometrica* 49 (May 1981): pp. 713–39.

Bish, Robert L. *The Public Economy of Metropolitan Areas*. Chicago: Markham Publishing Company, 1971.

Blakey, G. Robert. "State Conducted Lotteries: History, Problems, and Promises." *Journal of Social Issues* 35 (1979): pp. 62–86.

Blum, Walter, and Harry Kalven. *The Uneasy Case for Progressive Taxation*. Chicago: University of Chicago Press, 1953.

Booms, Bernard H., and James R. Halldorson. "The Politics of Redistribution: A Reformulation." *American Political Science Review* 77 (September 1973): pp. 920–33.

"Boost for School Financing Parity." *New York Times*. September 5, 1988, p. 20.

Borcherding, Thomas E., and R. T. Deacon. "The Demand for the Services of Non-Federal Governments." *American Economic Review* 62 (December 1972): pp. 891–901.

Borcherding, Thomas E., Werner W. Pommerehne, and Friedrich Schneider. "Comparing the Efficiency of Private and Public Production: The Evidence from Five Countries." *Z. Nationalökon* Supplement 2 (1982): pp. 127–56.

Boskin, Michael J. "Taxation, Saving, and Rate of Interest." *Journal of Political Economy* 80 (April 1978): pp. 13–28.

Bowman, John H., and John L. Mikesell. "Recent Changes in State Gasoline Taxation: An Analysis of Structure and Rates." *National Tax Journal* 36 (June 1983): pp. 163–82.

Bradbury, Katherine L., Helen F. Ladd, Mark Perrault, Andrew Reschovsky, and John Yinger. "State Aid to Offset Fiscal Disparities Across Communities." *National Tax Journal* 37 (June 1984): pp. 151–70.

Bradbury, Katherine L., and Lynn E. Browne. "New England Approaches the 1990s." *The New England Economic Review* (January/February 1988): pp. 31–45.

Bradford, David F. "The Case for a Personal Income Tax." In *What Should Be Taxed: Income or Expenditure?*, ed. Joseph A. Pechman. Washington, DC: The Brookings Institution, 1980.

Brazer, Harvey. "The Case for Local Control and Financing of Elementary and Secondary Education." Presented at the Annual Conference of the National Tax Association, Kansas City, MO. September 1971.

Break, George F. *Agenda for Local Tax Reform*. Berkeley, CA: Institute of Governmental Studies, University of California, 1970.

———. *Financing Government in a Federal System*. Washington, DC: The Brookings Institution, 1980.

Brennan, Gregory, and James M. Buchanan. *The Power to Tax*. New York: Cambridge University Press, 1980.

Breton, Albert, and Anthony Scott. *The Economic Constitution of Federal States*. Toronto: University of Toronto Press, 1978.

Bridges, Benjamin. "Deductibility of State and Local Nonbusiness Taxes Under the Federal Individual Income Tax." *National Tax Journal* 19 (March 1966): pp. 1–17.

Brinner, Roger E., and Charles T. Clotfelter. "An Economic Appraisal of State Lotteries." *National Tax Journal* 28 (December 1975): pp. 395–404.

Brown, Lawrence D., James W. Fossett, and Kenneth T. Palmer. *The Changing Politics of Federal Grants*. Washington, DC: The Brookings Institution, 1984.

Brownlee, Oswald H. "User Prices vs. Taxes." In *Public Finances: Needs, Sources, and Utilization*. National Bureau of Economic Research. Princeton: Princeton University Press, 1961.

Buchanan, James M. "Federalism and Fiscal Equity." *American Economic Review* 40 (September 1950): pp. 583–99.

———. "The Economics of Earmarked Taxes." *Journal of Political Economy* 71 (October 1963): pp. 457–69.

———. "An Economic Theory of Clubs." *Economica* 32 (February 1965): pp. 1–14.

———. "Public Finance and Public Choice." *National Tax Journal* 28 (December 1975): pp. 383–95.

Buchanan, James M., and Charles J. Goetz. "Efficiency Limits of Fiscal Mobility: An Assessment of the Tiebout Model." *Journal of Public Economics* 1 (April 1972): pp. 25–43.

Butterfield, Fox. "In New England, Worst Recession in U.S. Takes Hold." *New York Times*. July 23, 1990, pp. A1, A12.

Byrners, Patricia, Shawna Grosskopf, and Kathy Hayes. "Efficiency and Ownership: Further Evidence." *Review of Economics and Statistics* 68 (May 1986): pp. 337–41.

Carlson, Eugene. "Rating Business Climates Becomes a Confusing—and Nasty—Game." *Wall Street Journal*. May 3, 1988, p. 33.

Carnevale, John. "Recent Trends in the Finances of the State and Local Sector." *Public Budgeting & Finance*. 8 (Summer 1988): pp. 33–49.

Celis, William, 3d. "Impasse on Money Stalls Mississippi School Plan." *New York Times*. August 8, 1990a, p. B6.

———. "Oregon Considers Tax Credits to Aid Private Schooling." *New York Times*. August 22, 1990b, pp. A1, B6.

Charney, Alberta, H. "Intraurban Manufacturing Location Decisions and Local Tax Differentials." *Journal of Urban Economics* 14 (September 1983): pp. 184–205.

Clotfelter, Charles T. "On the Regressivity of State-Operated 'Numbers' Games." *National Tax Journal* 32 (December 1979): pp. 543–48.

———. "Tax Evasion and Tax Rates: An Analysis of Individual Returns." *Review of Economics and Statistics* 65 (August 1983), pp. 363–73.

Clotfelter, Charles T., and Philip J. Cook. "Implicit Taxation in Lottery Finance." *National Tax Journal* 40 (December 1987): pp. 533–46.

Cohen, Stephen S., and John Zysman. *Manufacturing Matters*. New York: Basic Books, 1987.

Coleman, James S. "Equal Schools or Equal Students." *The Public Interest* (Summer 1966): pp. 70–75.

Coleman, James S., and Sara D. Kelly. "Education." In *The Urban Predicament*, ed. William Gorham and Nathan Glazer. Washington, DC: The Urban Institute, 1976.

Conn, Robert L., Paul F. Williams, and William E. Young. "Sales Tax Audit Performance Among the States." *Public Finance Quarterly* 12 (October 1984): pp. 487–99.

Cook, Charles C. "Computers in Local Property Tax Administration." In *The Property Tax and Local Finance*, ed. C. Lowell Harriss. Montpelier, VT: Capital City Press, 1983.

Coons, John, William H. Clune III, and Stephen D. Sugarman. *Private Wealth and Public Education*. Cambridge, MA: Harvard University Press, 1970.

Cooper, Paul. "State Takeover of Education Financing." *National Tax Journal* 24 (September 1971): pp. 337–56.

Corporation for Enterprise Development (CED). *Making the Grade: The Development Report Card for the States*. Washington, DC: CED, 1987.

Corusy, Paul V. "Improving the Administration of the Property Tax." In *The Property Tax and Local Finance*, ed. C. Lowell Harriss. Montpelier, VT: Capital City Press, 1983.

Cushman, John H., Jr. "U.S. Plans to Shift Responsibility For Many Road Projects to States." *New York Times*. March 7, 1990, pp. A1, A21.

Davies, Daniel G. "A Further Reappraisal of Sales Taxation." *National Tax Journal* 16 (December 1963): pp. 410–15.

———. "Clothing Exemption and Sales Tax Regressivity." *American Economic Review* 61 (March 1971): pp. 187–89.

———. *United States Taxes and Tax Policy*. Cambridge, UK: Cambridge University Press, 1986.

Davies, Daniel G., and D. E. Black. "Equity Effects of Including Housing Services in a Sales Tax Base." *National Tax Journal* 28 (March, 1975), pp. 135–37.

Davis, Otto A., and G. H., Haines. "A Political Approach to a Theory of Public Expenditures: The Case of Municipalities." *National Tax Journal* 19 (September 1966): pp. 259–75.

DeBoer, Larry. "When Will State Lottery Sales Growth Slow?" *Growth and Change* 17 (January 1986): pp. 28–36.

deCourcy Hinds, Michael. "Half of States Strive to Avert Perilous Deficits." *New York Times*. March 4, 1990, pp. A1, 27.

Denzau, Arthur T. "An Empirical Survey of Studies of Public School Spending." *National Tax Journal* 28 (June 1975): pp. 241–49.

Doeringer, Peter B., and David G. Terkla, and Gregory Topakian. *Invisible Factors in Local Economic Development*. New York: Oxford University Press, 1987.

Doeringer, Peter B., and David G. Terkla. "How Intangible Factors Contribute to Economic Development: Lessons from a Mature Local Economy." *World Development* 18 (1990): pp. 1295–1308.

Donahue, John D. *The Privatization Decision*. New York: Basic Books, 1989.

Donnelly, Harrison. "Reagan Changes the Focus with Federalism Plan." *Congressional Quarterly* 40 (January 30, 1982): pp. 147–54.

Downing, Paul B. "Estimating Residential Land Value by Multivariate Analysis." In *The Assessment of Land Value*, ed. Daniel Holland. Madison, WI: University of Wisconsin Press, 1970.

———. "Policy Perspectives on User Charges and Urban Spacial Structure." In *Local Service Pricing Policies and Their Effect on Urban Spacial Structure*, ed. Paul B. Downing. Vancouver: University of British Columbia Press, 1977.

Downing, Paul B., and Richard D. Gustely. "The Public Service Costs of Alternative Development Patterns: A Review of the Evidence." In *Local Service Pricing Policies and Their Effect on Urban Spacial Structure*, ed. Paul B. Downing. Vancouver: University of British Columbia Press, 1977.

Downing, Paul B., and James E. Frank. "Recreational Impact Fees: Characteristics and Current Usage." *National Tax Journal* 36 (December 1983): pp. 477–90.

Downing, Paul B., and Thomas J. DiLorenzo. "User Charges and Special Districts." In *Management Policies in Local Government Finance*, ed. J. Richard Aronson and Eli Schwartz. Washington, DC: ICMA, 1987.

Due, John F. "Studies of State-Local Tax Influences on Location of Industry." *National Tax Journal* 14 (June 1961): pp. 163–73.

———. "Sales Taxation and the Consumer." *American Economic Review* 53 (December 1963): pp. 1,078–83.

Due, John F., and John L. Mikesell. "State Sales Tax Structure and Operation in the Last Decade: A Sample Study." *National Tax Journal* 33 (March 1980): pp. 21–43.

———. *Sales Taxation: State and Local Structure and Administration*. Baltimore, MD: Johns Hopkins University Press, 1983.

Durenberger, David. U.S. Senator. Speech to the National Conference of State Legislatures. July 28, 1982.

Edel, Matthew, and Elliott Sclar. "Taxes, Spending, and Property Values: Supply Adjustment in the Tiebout-Oates Model." *Journal of Political Economy* 82 (September/October 1974): pp. 941–54.

Elazar, Daniel. *The American Partnership*. Chicago: University of Chicago Press, 1962.

Ernst and Whinney. *1989 Guide to State Corporate and Individual Taxes in the United States*. Washington, DC: Ernst and Whinney, 1989.

Fabricant, Solomon. *The Trend of Government Activity in the United States Since 1900*. Washington, DC: National Bureau of Economic Research, 1952.

"Federalism's Funeral?" *Wall Street Journal*. April 27, 1988, p. 26.

*Federalist Papers*. New York: Washington Square Press, 1964.

Feenberg, Daniel R., and Harvey S. Rosen. "The Deductibility of State and Local Taxes: Impact Effects by State and Income Class." *Growth and Change* 17 (April 1986): pp. 11–31.

————. "Promises, Promises: The States' Experience with Income Tax Indexing." *National Tax Journal* 41 (December 1988): pp. 525–42.

Feldstein, Martin S. "Wealth Neutrality and Local Choice in Public Education." *American Economic Review* 65 (March 1975): pp. 75–89.

Fisher, Glenn. "Determinants of State and Local Government Expenditures." *National Tax Journal* 14 (December 1961), pp. 349–55.

Fisher, Ronald C., John H. Goddeeris, and James C. Young. "Participation in Tax Amnesties: The Individual Income Tax." *National Tax Journal* 42 (March 1989): pp. 15–27.

Fisher, Vickie L. "Recent Innovation in State Tax Compliance Programs," *National Tax Journal* 38 (September 1985): pp. 365–72.

Fiske, Edward. "Historic Shift Seen in School Finance." *New York Times*. October 4, 1989, p. B9.

————. "In Kentucky, Schools Face Broad Change." *New York Times*. March 30, 1990, p. A1 and 12.

Fox, William, and Charles Campbell. "Stability of the State Sales Tax Income Elasticities." *National Tax Journal* 37 (June 1984): pp. 201–12.

Fox, William, and Matthew Murray. "Economic Aspects of Taxing Services." *National Tax Journal* 61 (March 1988): pp. 19–36.

Franklin, Douglas, Thaddeus J. Jankowski, and Raymond Torto. *Massachusetts Property Revaluation*. Boston: Butterworth Legal Publishers, 1983.

Frey, James H., and William R. Eadington, eds. "Gambling: Views from the Social Sciences." In *Annals of the American Academy of Politics and Social Science* 474 (July 1984).

Friedlaender, A, G. J. Swanson, and John F. Due. "Estimating Sales Tax Changes in Response to Changes in Personal Income and Sales Tax Rates." *National Tax Journal* 26 (March 1973): pp. 103–10.

Friedman, Milton. *Capitalism and Freedom*. Chicago: University of Chicago Press, 1962.

Fry, Brian R., and Richard F. Winters. "The Politics of Redistribution." *American Political Science Review* 49 (June 1970), pp. 508–22.

Fullerton, Don. "On the Possibility of an Inverse Relationship between Tax Rates and Government Revenues." *Journal of Public Economics* 19 (October 1982), pp. 3–22.

Gaffney, Mason. "An Agenda for Strengthening the Property Tax." In *Property Tax Reform*, ed. George E. Peterson. Washington, DC: The Urban Institute, 1973.

Galbraith, John K. *The Affluent Society*. Boston: Houghton-Mifflin, 1958.

Garreau, Joel. *The Nine Nations of North America*. New York: Avon, 1981.

Gillespie, W. Irwin. "Effect of Public Expenditures on the Distribution of Income." In *Essays in Fiscal Federalism*, ed. Richard A. Musgrave. Washington, DC: The Brookings Institution, 1965.

Gold, Allan R. "New Shots in New England's Border War." *New York Times*. July 17, 1989, p. A12.

Gold, Steven D. "Circuit Breakers and Other Relief Measures." In *The Property Tax and Local Finance*, ed. C. Lowell Harriss. Montpelier, VT: Capital City Press, 1983a.

———. *State and Local Fiscal Relations in the Early 1980s*. Washington, DC: The Urban Institute Press, 1983b.

Goldman, Sheldon. *Constitutional Law*. New York: Harper and Row, 1987.

Gonzalez, R., and S. Mehay. "Consumption and Production Economies of Local Government Services." In *Perspectives in Local Public Finance and Public Policy*, ed. J., Quigley. Greenwich, CT: JAI, 1985.

Goode, Richard. "The Economic Definition of Income." In *Comprehensive Income Taxation*, ed. Joseph A. Pechman. Washington, DC: Brookings Institution, 1977.

———. "The Superiority of the Income Tax." In *What Should Be Taxed: Income or Expenditure?*, ed. Joseph A. Pechman. Washington, DC: The Brookings Institution, 1980.

Gramlich, Edward M. "Intergovernmental Grants: A Review of the Empirical Literature." In *The Political Economy of Fiscal Federalism*, ed. Wallace Oates. Lexington, MA: Lexington, 1977.

———. "Reforming U.S. Federal Fiscal Arrangements." In *American Domestic Priorities*, ed. John M. Quigley and Daniel L. Rubinfeld. Berkeley, CA: University of California Press, 1985.

Gramlich, Edward M., and Deborah S. Laren. "The New Federalism." In *Setting National Priorities, The 1983 Budget*, ed. Joseph A. Pechman. The Brookings Institution, Washington, DC: 1982.

Grant Thornton. *The Seventh Annual Study of General Manufacturing Climates of the Forty-Eight Contiguous States of America*. Chicago: Grant Thornton, 1986.

Greenhouse, Linda. "Court Says Judge May Order Taxes to Alleviate Bias." *New York Times*. April 19, 1990, pp. A1, A22.

Gregg, John G., Arnold C. Harberger, and Peter Mieszkowski. "Empirical Evidence on the Incidence of the Corporation Income Tax." *Journal of Policy Economy* 75 (December 1967): pp. 811–21.

Greytak, David, Richard Gustely, and Robert J. Dinkelmeyer. "The Effects of Inflation on Local Government Expenditures." *National Tax Journal* (December 1974): pp. 583–93.

Grodzins, Mortin. "The Federal System." In *Goals for Americans: The Report of the President's Commission on National Goals*. Englewood Cliffs, NJ: Prentice Hall, 1965.

Guskind, Robert. "The Giveaway Game Continues." *Planning* 56 (February 1990): pp. 4–8.

Gwartney, James, and Richard E. Wagner. "The Public Choice Revolution." *The Intercollegiate Review* 23 (Spring 1988): pp. 17–26.

Hallman, Howard W. *Government by Neighborhoods*. Washington, DC: Center for Governmental Studies, 1973.

———. *Small and Large Together: Governing the Metropolis*. Beverly Hills, CA: Sage Publications, 1977.

Hamilton, Bruce. "Property Taxes and the Tiebout Hypothesis: Some Empirical Evidence." In *Fiscal Zoning and Land Use Controls: The Economic Issues*, ed. Edwin S. Mills and Wallace E. Oates. Lexington, MA: Lexington Books, 1975a.

———. "Zoning and Property Taxation in a System of Local Governments." *Urban Studies* 12 (June 1975b): pp. 205–11.

————. "The Effect of Property Taxes and Local Public Spending on Property Values: A Theoretical Comment." *Journal of Political Economy* 84 (June 1976): 647–50.

————. "A Review: Is the Property Tax a Benefit Tax?" In *Local Provision of Public Services: The Tiebout Model after Twenty-Five Years*, ed. George R. Zodrow. New York: Academic Press, 1983.

Hamovitch, William. "Sales Taxation: Analysis of the Effects of Rate Increases in Two Contrasting Cases." *National Tax Journal* 24 (December 1966): pp. 411–20.

Hansson, Ingemar, and Charles Stuart. "Tax Revenue and Marginal Cost of Public Funds in Sweden." *Journal of Public Economics* 27 (August 1985); pp. 331–54.

Harberger, Arnold C. "The Incidence of the Corporation Income Tax." *Journal of Political Economy* 70 (June 1962): pp. 215–40.

Hausman, Jerry A. "Labor Supply." In *How Taxes Affect Economic Behavior*, ed. Henry J. Aaron and Joseph A. Pechman. Washington, DC: Brookings Institution, 1981.

Havemann, Joel, and Rochelle L. Stanfield. "A Year Later, the Frostbelt Strikes Back." *National Journal* 9 (July 2, 1977): pp. 1,028–37.

Hayes, Kathy, and Daniel J. Slottje. "The Efficacy of State and Local Governments' Redistributional Policies." *Public Finance Quarterly* 17 (July 1989): pp. 304–22.

Heavey, Jerome F. "The Incidence of State Lottery Taxes." *Public Finance Quarterly* 6 (October 1978): pp. 415–26.

Heibrun, James. "Who Bears the Burden of the Property Tax?" In *The Property Tax and Local Finance*, ed. C. Lowell Harriss. Montpelier, VT: Capital City Press, 1983.

Hellerstein, Walter. "Florida's Sales Tax on Services." *National Tax Journal* 61 (March 1988): pp. 1–18.

Hicks, Alexander, Roger Friedland, and Edwin Johnson. "Class Power and State Policy: The Case of Large Business Corporations, Labor Unions, and Governmental Redistribution in the American States." *American Sociological Review* 43 (June 1978): pp. 302–15.

Hirsch, Werner Z. "Determinants of Public Education Expenditures." *National Tax Journal* 13 (March 1960): pp. 29–40.

————. "Local versus Areawide Urban Government Services." *National Tax Journal* 17 (December 1965: pp. 331–39.

Hogan, T. D., and R. B. Shelton. "Interstate Tax Exportation and States Fiscal Structure." *National Tax Journal* 26 (December 1973): pp. 553–64.

Holcombe, Randall G. "An Empirical Test of the Median Voter Model." *Economic Inquiry* 18 (April 1980); pp. 260–74.

Hyman, David N. *Public Finance*. New York: The Dryden Press, 1983.

INC. "INC.'s Annual Report on the States." INC. (October 1989): pp. 76–77.

Inman, Robert P. "Testing Political Economy's 'As If' Assumption: Is the Median Income Voter Really Decisive?" *Public Choice* 33 (1978): pp. 45–65.

————. "The Fiscal Performance of Local Governments: An Interpretative Review." In *Current Issues in Urban Economics*, ed. Peter Mieszkowski and Mahlon Straszheim, pp. 270–321. Baltimore: Johns Hopkins University Press, 1979.

————. "Fiscal Allocations in a Federalist System: Understanding the 'New Federalism'." In *American Domestic Priorities*, ed. John M. Quigley and Daniel L. Rubinfeld. Berkeley, CA: University of California Press, 1985.

Johnson, Kenneth P., John R. Kort, and Howard L. Friedenberg. "Regional and State Projections of Income, Employment, and Population to the Year 2000." *Survey of Current Business* (May 1990): pp. 33–54.

Johnson, Kirk. "Nervously Border Town Awaits Taxes." *New York Times*. June 15, 1989, p. B1.

Johnson, Lyndon B. *My Hope for America*. New York: Random House, 1964.

Kaldor, Nicholas. *An Expenditure Tax*. London, U.K.: Allen, 1955.

Kettl, Donald F. *The Regulation of American Federalism*. Baltimore: The Johns Hopkins University Press, 1983.

Kiesling, Herbert J. "Measuring a Local Government Service: A Study of School Districts in New York State." *Review of Economics and Statistics* 49 (August 1967): pp. 356–67.

King, David. *Fiscal Tiers*. London, UK: George Allen & Unwin, 1984.

Klott, Gary. "Florida Widening Sales Tax's Reach." *New York Times*. April 25, 1987, pp. 1, 40.

Knight, Prentice, L., and Richard A. Barff. "Employment Growth and the Turnaround in the New England Economy." *The Northeast Journal of Business & Economics* 14 (Fall/Winter 1987/88): pp. 1–15.

Kolbert, Elizabeth. "The Fine Art of Delaying the Tax Cut." *New York Times*. September 3, 1989, p. B1.

———. "Albany Leaders, in Budget Push, Agree on Sales Taxes for Services." *New York Times*. May 1, 1990a, pp. A1, B2.

———. "Groups in Northeast Protest Plan to Cap Deductions for Taxes." *New York Times*. July 28, 1990b, p. 8.

———. "7 Weeks Late, New York State Has a Budget Pact." *New York Times*. May 19, 1990c, pp. 1, 28.

Krashinsky, Michael. *User Charges in the Social Services: An Economic Theory of Need and Inability*. Ontario Economic Council. Toronto: University of Toronto Press, 1981.

Krzyzaniak, Marion, and Richard Musgrave. *The Shifting of the Corporate Income Tax*. Baltimore: Johns Hopkins Press, 1963.

Kurnow, Ernest. "Determinants of State and Local Expenditures Reexamined." *National Tax Journal* 16 (September 1963): pp. 337–53.

Ladd, Helen. "Local Education Expenditures, Fiscal Capacity, and the Composition of the Property Tax Base." *National Tax Journal* 28 (June 1975): pp. 145–58.

———. "An Economic Evaluation of State Limitations on Local Taxing and Spending Powers." *National Tax Journal* 31 (March 1978): pp. 1–18.

Laffer, Arthur B. "Statement Prepared for the Joint Economic Committee, May 20." Reprinted in *The Economics of the Tax Revolt*, ed. Arthur B. Laffer and Jan P. Seymour. New York: Harcourt Brace Jovanovich, 1979.

Laffer Associates. "An Analysis of Fiscal Policy and Economic Growth in Massachusetts." Rolling Hills Estates, CA: A. B. Laffer Associates, 1981.

Leach, Richard H. *American Federalism*. New York: W. W. Norton, 1970.

Legler, John B., and P. Shapiro. "The Responsiveness of State Revenue to Economic Growth." *National Tax Journal* 21 (March 1968): pp. 46–57.

Lehne, Richard. *Casino Policy*. New Brunswick, NJ: Rutgers University Press, 1986.

Levine, Richard. "Job Growth in New York Region Shifts to Losses as Economy Lags." *New York Times*. July 31, 1990, pp. A1, B4.

Lewis, Neil A. "The Limits of Power." *New York Times*. April 20, 1990, p. A12.

Linowes, David F. *Privatization: Toward More Effective Government*. Report of the President's Commission on Privatization. Chicago, IL: University of Illinois Press, 1988.

Lipsey, Richard G., Peter O. Steiner, and Douglas D. Purvis. *Economics*. New York: Harper & Row, 1987.

Litsky, Frank. "Oregon Lottery Creates Weekly NFL Betting Plan." *New York Times*. July 18, 1989, pp. A1, B10.

"Living on a Coast Pays Off, U.S. Says." *New York Times*. August 21, 1988, p. A32.

Loth, Renee. "Bulger Proposes Allowing Students to Go to Any School Parents Choose." *Boston Globe*. May 25, 1988, pp. 21, 69.

Lowery, David, and Lee Sigelman. "Understanding the Tax Revolt: Eight Explanations." *American Political Science Review* 75 (December 1981): pp. 963–74.

Lynch, Carolyn D. "The Impact of Federal Tax Reform on State Personal Income Taxes." *Intergovernmental Perspective* 13 (Winter 1987): pp. 37–38.

Manchester, Paul. "Interstate Cigarette Smuggling." *Public Finance Quarterly* 4 (April 1976): pp. 225–38.

McAllister, Harry E. "The Border Problem in Washington." *National Tax Journal* 14 (December 1961): p. 374.

McClure, Charles E. "Interstate Exporting of State and Local Taxes: Estimates for 1962." *National Tax Journal* 20 (March 1967): pp. 49–77.

———. "The 'New View' of the Property Tax: A Caveat." *National Tax Journal* 30 (March 1977): pp. 69–75.

McEachern, William A. "Collective Decision Rules and Local Debt Choice: A Test of the Median-Voter Hypothesis." *National Tax Journal* 31 (June 1978): pp. 129–36.

McGuire, Martin C. "Notes on Grants-in-Aid and Economic Interactions among Governments." *Canadian Journal of Economics* 6 (May 1973): pp. 207–21.

Meadows, George R. "Taxes, Spending, and Property Values: A Comment and Further Results." *Journal of Political Economy* 84 (August 1976): pp. 869–80.

Mercer, Lloyd, and W. Morgan. "The Relative Efficiency and Revenue Potential of Local User Charges: The California Case." *The National Tax Journal* 36 (June 1983): pp. 203–12.

Mieszkowski, Peter. "The Property Tax: An Excise Tax or A Profits Tax?" *Journal of Public Economics* 1 (April 1972): pp. 73–96.

———. "The Choice of Tax Base: Consumption versus Income Taxation." In *Federal Tax Reform: Myths and Realities*, ed. Michael J. Boskin. San Francisco: Institute for Contemporary Studies, 1978.

Mikesell, John L. "Central Cities and Sales Tax Rate Differentials: The Border Problem." *National Tax Journal* 23 (June 1970): pp. 206–13.

———. "Sales Taxation and the Border County Problem." *Quarterly Review of Economics and Business* 11 (Spring 1971): pp. 23–30.

———. "Amnesties for State Tax Evaders: The Nature of and Response to Recent Programs." *National Tax Journal* 39 (December 1986): pp. 507–25.

Mikesell, John L., and C. Kurt Zorn. "State Lotteries as Fiscal Savior or Fiscal Fraud: A Look at the Evidence." *Public Administration Review* 46 (July/August, 1986): pp. 311–20.

Miller, Gerald H. "Repeal of Tax Deductibility: Bad Rx for Federalism." *Intergovernmental Perspective* 11 (Fall 1985): pp. 18–20.

Miner, Jerry. *Social and Economic Factors in Spending for Public Education*. Syracuse: Syracuse University Press, 1963.

Minge, David. "Law As a Determinant of Resource Allocation by Local Government." *National Tax Journal* 30 (December 1977: pp. 399–410.

Mitchell, Broadus, and Louise Mitchell. *A Biography of the Constitution of the United States*. New York: Oxford University Press, 1975.

Morgan, Daniel C. "Reappraisal of Sales Taxation: Some Recent Arguments." *National Tax Journal* 16 (March 1963): pp. 89–101.

Morris, Charles R. *The Cost of Good Intentions: New York City and the Liberal Experiment*. New York: W. W. Norton, 1980.

Morrison, Henry. *School Revenue*. Chicago: University of Chicago Press, 1930.

Moscovitch, Edward. "The Massachusetts Miracle." *Wall Street Journal*. July 8, 1986, p. 28.

Mueller, Dennis C. *Public Choice*. Cambridge: Cambridge University Press, 1979.

Munley, Vincent G. "Has the Median Voter Found a Ballot Box He Can Control?" *Economic Inquiry* 22 (July 1984): pp. 323–36.

Murname, Richard J. "An Economist's Look at Federal and State Education Policies." In *American Domestic Priorities*, ed. John M. Quigley and Daniel L. Rubinfeld. Berkeley, CA: University of California Press, 1985.

Musgrave, Richard A. "Is a Property Tax on Housing Regressive?" *American Economic Review* 64 (May 1974): pp. 222–29.

Musgrave, Richard A., and Peggy B. Musgrave. *Public Finance in Theory and Practice*. New York: McGraw-Hill Book Company, 1989.

Mushkin, Selma, ed. *Public Prices for Public Products*. Washington, DC: Urban Institute, 1972.

Nathan, Richard P., Fred C. Dolittle, and Associates. *The Consequences of Cuts*. Princeton, NJ: Princeton Urban and Regional Research Center, 1983.

———. *Reagan and the States*. Princeton, NJ: Princeton University Press, 1987.

Netzer, Dick. *Economics of the Property Tax*. Washington, DC: The Brookings Institution, 1966.

———. "The Incidence of the Property Tax Revisited." *National Tax Journal* 26 (December 1973): pp. 515–36.

———. "State-Local Finance and Intergovernmental Fiscal Relations." In *The Economics of Public Finance*. Washington, DC: The Brookings Institution, 1974.

Newman, Robert J., and Dennis Sullivan. "Econometric Analysis of Business Tax Impacts on Industrial Location: What Do We Know, and How Do We Know It?" *Journal of Urban Economics* 23 (March 1988): pp. 215–34.

Nice, David C. *Federalism: The Politics of Intergovernmental Relations*. New York: St. Martin's Press, 1987.

Nicholson, Walter. *Intermediate Microeconomics*. Philadelphia: The Dryden Press, 1990.

Niskanen, William A., Jr. "Bureaucrats and Politicians." *Journal of Law and Economics* 18 (December 1975): pp. 617–43.

Nourse, Hugh. O. *Regional Economics: A Study in the Economic Structure, Stability, and Growth of Regions*. New York: McGraw Hill, 1968.

Oakland, William H. "Local Taxes and Intraurban Industrial Location: A Survey." In *Metropolitan Financing and Growth Management Policies*, ed. George F. Break. Madison, WI: University of Wisconsin Press, 1978.

———. "Alternative Models for Assessing Regional Public Policy Impacts." In *In-*

*terregional Movements and Regional Growth*, ed. William C. Wheaton. Washington, DC: The Urban Institute, 1979.

————. Testimony to the Joint Economic Committee, U.S. Congress, "The Effect of the President's Tax Plan on State and Local Taxpayers," May 29, 1985.

Oates, Wallace. "The Effects of Property Taxes and Local Public Spending on Property Values: An Empirical Study of Tax Capitalization and the Tiebout Hypothesis." *Journal of Political Economy* 77 (November/December 1969): pp. 957–71.

————. *Fiscal Federalism*. New York: Harcourt Brace Jovanovich, 1972.

————. "Searching for Leviathan: An Empirical Study." *American Economic Review* 75 (September 1985): pp. 748–57.

Ohls, James C., and Terence J. Wales. "Supply and Demand for State and Local Services." *Review of Economics and Statistics* 54 (November 1972): pp. 424–30.

Olson, Mancur. "The Principle of 'Fiscal Equivalence': The Division of Responsibilities Among Different Levels of Government." *American Economic Review* 59 (May 1969): pp. 479–87.

Osborne, David. *Economic Competitiveness: The States Take the Lead*. Washington, DC: Economic Policy Institute, 1987.

————. *The Next Agenda: Lessons from the Laboratories of Democracy*. Cambridge, MA: Harvard Business School Press, 1988.

Osman, Jack. "The Dual Impact of Federal Aid on State and Local Government Expenditures." *National Tax Journal* 19 (March 1966): pp. 362–72.

Pack, Hans, and Janet Pack. "Metropolitan Fragmentation and Local Public Expenditures." *National Tax Journal* 31 (December 1978): pp. 349–62.

Pack, Janet. "The States' Scramble for Federal Funds." *Journal of Policy Analysis and Management* 1 (Winter 1982): pp. 175–95.

Papke, James A., and Leslie Papke. "State Tax Incentives and Investment Location Decisions." In *Indiana's Revenue Structure: Major Components and Issues, Part II*, ed. James Papke. West Lafayette, IN: Purdue University Press, 1984.

Pauly, Mark V. "Income Redistribution as a Local Public Good." *Journal of Public Economics* 2 (February 1973): pp. 35–58.

Pechman, Joseph A. *Federal Tax Policy*. Washington, DC: The Brookings Institution, 1983.

————. *Who Paid the Taxes, 1966–85?* Washington, DC: The Brookings Institution, 1985.

Pechman, Joseph A., and Benjamin Okner. *Who Bears the Tax Burden?* Washington, DC: The Brookings Institution, 1974.

Peirce, Neal R. *The Megastates of America*. New York: Norton, 1972.

Peltason, J. W. *Understanding the Constitution*. New York: Holt, Rinehart, and Winston, 1979.

Penniman, Clara. *State Income Taxation*. Baltimore: The Johns Hopkins University Press, 1980.

Peppard, Donald M. "Government As Bookie: Explaining the Rise of Lotteries for Revenue." *Review of Radical Political Economy* 19 (Fall 1987): pp. 56–68.

Peterson, George E. "Federalism and the States." In *The Reagan Record*, ed. John L. Palmer and Isabel V. Sawhill. Cambridge, MA: Ballinger Publishing Company, 1984.

Phares, Donald. *Who Pays State and Local Taxes?* Cambridge, MA: Oelgeschlager, Gunn, and Hain, 1980.

Pommerehne, Werner W. "Institutional Approaches to Public Expenditures: Empirical Evidence From Swiss Municipalities." *Journal of Public Economics* 9 (April 1978): pp. 163–201.

"President's Tax Proposals to Congress for Fairness, Growth, and Simplicity." Washington, DC: Government Printing Office, 1985.

Putka, Gary. "Parents in Minnesota Are Getting to Send Kids Where They Like." *Wall Street Journal*. May 13, 1988, pp. 1, 9.

Quigley, John M., and Roger W. Schmenner. "Property Tax Exemption and Public Policy." *Public Policy* 23 (Summer 1975): pp. 259–97.

Quindry, Kenneth E., and Billy D. Cook. "Humanization of the Property Tax for the Low Income Households." *National Tax Journal* 22 (September 1969): pp. 357–67.

Raimondo, Henry J. "Compensation Policy for Tax Exempt Property in Theory and Practice." *Land Economics* 56 (February 1980): pp. 33–42.

———. "The Political Economy of State Intergovernmental Grants." *Growth and Change* 14 (April 1983a): pp. 17–23.

———. "State Limitations on Local Taxing and Spending: Theory and Practice." *Journal of Public Budgeting and Finance* 3 (August 1983b): pp. 33–42.

———. "Central City Isolation and Grant Distribution." *Growth and Change* 13 (June 1984): pp. 26–36.

———. Testimony to the Joint Economic Committee, U.S. Congress, "The Effect of the President's Tax Plan on State and Local Taxpayers," May 29, 1985.

———. "The State Aid Formula: Corporations, Democrats, and Tax Limits." Mimeographed. 1988.

———. "Leviathan and Federalism in the United States." *Public Finance Quarterly* 17 (April 1989): pp. 204–15.

Raimondo, Henry J., and H. Peter Gray. "A Suggested Method to Increase State Personal Income Taxes." Mimeographed. 1986.

Raimondo, Henry J. and Raymondo G. Torto. *Property Taxation in Massachusetts*. The Fourteenth Interim Report of the Special Commission. Boston, MA: House Bill No. 5317, 1987.

Ramstad, Evan. "Conn., Wyoming Schools Given Top Marks By Parents Group." *Boston Globe*. August 29, 1990, p. 8.

Raphaelson, Arnold. "The Property Tax." In *Management Policies in Local Government Finance*, ed. J. Richard Aronson and Eli Schwartz. Washington, DC: ICMA, 1987.

Reagan, Michael D., and John G. Sanzone. *The New Federalism*. New York: Oxford University Press, 1981.

Reischauer, Robert D., and Robert W. Hartman. *Reforming School Finance*. Washington, DC: The Brookings Institution, 1973.

Reschovsky, Andrew. "Residential Choice and the Local Public Sector: An Alternative Test of the 'Tiebout Hypothesis'." *Journal of Urban Economics* 6 (October 1979): pp. 501–20.

Reschovsky, Andrew, Gregory Topakian, Francoise Carre, Randall Crane, Peter Miller, and Paul Smoke. *State Tax Policy*. Cambridge, MA: Joint Center for Urban Studies of MIT and Harvard University, 1983.

Reynolds, Morgan, and Eugene Smolensky. "The Post Fisc Distribution: 1961 and 1970 Compared." *National Tax Journal* 27 (December 1974): pp. 515–30.

————. *Public Expenditures, Taxes, and the Distribution of Income*. New York: Academic Press, 1977.

Richardson, Harry A. *Urban Economics*. Hinsdale, IL: The Dryden Press, 1978.

Riew, John. "Economies of Scale in High School Operation." *Review of Economics and Statistics* 47 (August 1966: pp. 280–87.

Robbins, William. "Rise in Exports Spurs Job Boom in Midwest." *New York Times*. May 2, 1988, p. 1.

Rockefeller, Nelson A. *The Future of Federalism*. Cambridge, MA: Harvard University Press, 1962.

Rodgers, James D. "Sales Taxes, Income Taxes, and Other Non-Property Tax Revenues." In *Management Policies in Local Government Finance*, ed. J. Richard Aronson and Eli Schwartz. Washington, DC: International City Management Association, 1987.

Rosen, Harvey S. *Public Finance*. Homewood, IL: Irwin, 1988.

Rosenbaum, David E. "A Tax Debt Revived." *New York Times*. July 29, 1990, pp. 1, 22.

Rossmiller, Richard. *Full State Funding*. Report to the National Association of State Boards of Education. Washington, DC, 1972.

Rubin, Jeffrey I., and Joseph J. Seneca. "Density Bonuses, Exactions, and the Supply of Affordable Housing." Mimeographed. 1989.

Ruffin, Roy J., and Paul R. Gregory. *Principles of Economics*. Glenview, IL: Scott, Foresman and Company, 1986.

Rybeck, Walter. "The Property Tax as a Super User Charge." In *The Property Tax and Local Finance*, ed. C. Lowell Harriss. Montpelier, VT: Capital City Press, 1983.

Sacks, Seymour, and Robert Harris. "The Determinants of State and Local Government Expenditures and Intergovernmental Flows of Funds." *National Tax Journal* 17 (March 1965): pp. 75–85.

Sale, Kirkpatrick. *Power Shift*. New York: Vintage Books. 1975.

Samuelson, Paul A. "The Pure Theory of Public Expenditure." *Review of Economics and Statistics* 36 (November 1954: pp. 387–89.

————. "Diagrammatic Exposition of a Theory of Public Expenditure." *Review of Economics and Statistics* 37 (November 1955): pp. 350–56.

Sandler, Todd, and John T. Tschirhart. "The Economic Theory of Clubs: An Evaluative Survey." *Journal of Economic Literature* 18 (December 1980): pp. 1,481–521.

Savas, E.S. "Policy Analysis for Local Government: Public vs. Private Refuse Collection." *Policy Analysis* 3 (Winter 1977): pp. 54–55.

————. *Privatizing the Public Sector*. Chatham, NJ: Chatham House Publishers, 1982.

Schaefer, J. M. "Clothing Exemptions and Sales Tax Regressivity." *American Economic Review* 59 (September 1969): pp. 596–99.

Scheiner, James I. "Federal Deductibility of State and Local Taxes: Fact and Fiction." *Intergovernmental Perspective* 11 (Fall 1985): pp. 13–17.

Schmandt, Henry J., and Stephens G. Ross. "Measuring Municipal Output." *National Tax Journal* 13 (December 1960): pp. 369–75.

Schoettle, Ferdinand. "Judicial Requirements for School Financing and Property Tax Redesign: The Rapidly Evolving Case Law." *National Tax Journal* 25 (September 1972): pp. 455–72.

Schwab, David. "More Jersey Firms Pull Up Stakes to Seek 'Better Climate' in Pennsy." *The Star Ledger*. July 16, 1990, pp. 1, 6.

Schwaneberg, Robert. "Jersey Exodus—Florio Places Blame for Flight of Firms." *The Star Ledger*. July 17, 1990, pp. 1, 22.

Shannon, John. "The Property Tax: Reform or Relief?" In *Property Tax Reform*, ed. George E. Peterson. Washington, DC: The Urban Institute, 1973.

Shelton, R. B., and D. P. Vogt. "The Incidence of Coal Severance Taxes: Political Perceptions and Economic Realities." *Natural Resources Journal* 22 (July 1982): pp. 539–58.

Siegel, Barry. "On the Positive Theory of State and Local Expenditures." In *Public Finance and Welfare*, ed. Paul Kleinsorge. Eugene: University of Oregon Books, 1966.

Smith, David L. "The Response of State and Local Governments to Federal Grants." *National Tax Journal* 21 (September 1968): pp. 349–57.

Smothers, Ronald. "Governors Assail Proposal for Lid on Tax Deductions." *New York Times*. July 30, 1990, pp. A1, A11.

Spicer, Michael W. "Civilization at a Discount: The Problem of Tax Evasion." *National Tax Journal* 39 (March 1986): pp. 13–20.

Sternlieb, George, and James W. Hughes. "The New Economic Geography of America." Mimeographed. New Brunswick, NJ: Center for Urban Policy Research, Rutgers University, 1977a.

———. *Post-Industrial America: Metropolitan Decline & Inter-Regional Job Shifts*. New Brunswick, NJ: Center for Urban Policy Research, Rutgers University, 1977b.

———. *The Atlantic City Gamble*. Cambridge, MA: Harvard University Press, 1983.

Stevens, Barbara J., ed. *Delivering Municipal Services Efficiently*. (Washington, DC: HUD Office of Policy Development and Research, June 1984).

Stiglitz, Joseph E. *Economics of the Public Sector*. New York: W. W. Norton, 1988.

Stocker, Frederick D. "State Sponsored Gambling as a Source of Public Revenue." *National Tax Journal* 25 (September 1972): pp. 437–41.

Suits, Daniel B. "Gambling Taxes: Regressivity and Revenue Potential." *National Tax Journal* 30 (March 1977): pp. 19–35.

———. "The Elasticity of Demand for Gambling." *Quarterly Journal of Economics* 93 (February 1979): pp. 155–62.

Sullivan, Joseph F. "New Jersey Ruling to Lift School Aid for Poor Districts." *New York Times*. June 6, 1990, pp. A1, B4.

Suro, Roberto. "High Court in Texas Rules Schools in the State are Illegally Financed." *New York Times*. October 3, 1989, pp. A1, A15.

Surrey, Stanley. *Pathways to Tax Reform*. Cambridge, MA: Harvard University Press, 1973.

Surrey, Stanley, and Paul McDaniel. *Tax Expenditures*. Cambridge, MA: Harvard University Press, 1985.

Terkla, David G. and Peter B. Doeringer. "Explaining Variations in Employment Growth: Structural and Cyclical Change Among States and Local Areas." *Journal of Urban Economics* 26 (March 1991): pp. 1–20.

Testa, William, and David Allardice. "Bidding for Business." *Chicago Fed Letter*, number 16 (December 1988).

Thomassen, Henry. "Circuit Breaking and Life-Cycle Lock-In." *National Tax Journal* 31 (March 1978): pp. 59–65.

Thurow, Lester. "The Theory of Grants-in-Aid." *National Tax Journal* 19 (December 1966): pp. 373–77.

Tiebout, Charles M. "A Pure Theory of Local Expenditures." *Journal of Political Economy* 64 (October 1956), pp. 416–24.

Tolchin, Martin. "States Take Up New Burdens to Pay for 'New Federalism'." *New York Times*. May 21, 1990a: pp. A1, B14.

———. "15 States Rally Behind Calls for Constitutional Amendment to Give Them More Power." *New York Times*. June 26, 1990b: p. A17.

Treacy, John L., and Lloyd W. French II. "Power Equalization and the Reform of Public School Finance." *National Tax Journal* 27 (June 1974): pp. 416–24.

Tufte, Edward. *Political Control of the Economy*. Princeton, NJ: Princeton University Press, 1978.

Valente, Carl, and Lydia Manchester. *Rethinking Local Services: Examining Alternative Delivery*. Washington, DC: International City Management Association, 1984.

Van Horn, Carl E., and Henry J. Raimondo. "Living with Less: New Jersey Copes with Federal Aid Cutbacks." *Journal of Public Budgeting & Finance* 3 (Spring 1983): pp. 41–56.

Vernon, Raymond. "International Investment and International Trade in the Product Cycle." *Quarterly Journal of Economics* 46 (May 1966): pp. 113–19.

Wales, T. J. "Distilled Spirits and Interstate Consumption Effects." *American Economic Review* 58 (September 1968): pp. 853–63.

Wasylenko, Michael J. "Evidence of Fiscal Differentials and Intrametropolitan Firm Relocation." *Land Economics* 56 (August 1980): pp. 339–49.

Weinstein, Bernard L., Harold T. Gross, and John Rees. *Regional Growth and Decline in the United States*. New York: Praeger, 1985.

Wells, Amy Stuart. "School-Choice Program is Upheld in Wisconsin." *New York Times*. August 9, 1990a, p. B6.

———. "Experiment Pioneered the School Choice Concept." *New York Times*. August 22, 1990b, p. B6.

Wheaton, William C. "Interstate Differences in the Level of Business Taxation." *National Tax Journal* 36 (March 1983): pp. 83–94.

Wilde, James A. "The Expenditure Effects of Grant-in-Aid Programs." *National Tax Journal* 21 (September 1968): pp. 340–48.

Wills, Garry. *Explaining America: The Federalist*. Garden City, NY: Doubleday, 1981.

Wise, Arthur. *Rich Schools, Poor Schools*. Chicago: University of Chicago Press, 1972.

Wright, Gavin. "The Political Economy of New Deal Spending: An Econometric Analysis." *Review of Economics and Statistics* 56 (February 1974): pp. 30–38.

Zodrow, George, ed. *Local Provision of Public Services: The Tiebout Model after Twenty-Five Years*. New York: Academic Press, 1983.

# Index

## About the Author

HENRY J. RAIMONDO is Associate Professor in the Eagleton Institute of Politics and the Department of Urban Planning and Policy Development at Rutgers University. He has served on the faculty of the Department of Economics at the University of Massachusetts at Boston. Professor Raimondo has written in the areas of state-local public finance, economics of sports, and economic education. His research has appeared in *Growth and Change, Journal of Economic Education, Journal of Labor Research, Land Economics, Public Budgeting and Finance*, and *Public Finance Quarterly*.